Pentecostal Hermeneutics

Pentecostal Hermeneutics

A Reader

Edited by

Lee Roy Martin

BRILL

LEIDEN • BOSTON
2013

Library of Congress Cataloging-in-Publication Data

Pentecostal hermeneutics : a reader / edited by Lee Roy Martin.
　　pages cm
　Includes bibliographical references and index.
　ISBN 978-90-04-25729-0 (pbk. : alk. paper) — ISBN 978-90-04-25825-9 (e-book) 1. Pentecostal churches—Doctrines. 2. Bible—Hermeneutics. 3. Bible—Criticism, interpretation, etc. 4. Pentecostalism. I. Martin, Lee Roy.

BX8762.Z5P46 2013
220.601—dc23

2013028015

This publication has been typeset in the multilingual "Brill" typeface. With over 5,100 characters covering Latin, IPA, Greek, and Cyrillic, this typeface is especially suitable for use in the humanities. For more information, please see www.brill.com/brill-typeface.

ISBN 978-90-04-25729-0 (paperback)
ISBN 978-90-04-25825-9 (e-book)

Copyright 2013 by Koninklijke Brill NV, Leiden, The Netherlands.
Koninklijke Brill NV incorporates the imprints Brill, Global Oriental, Hotei Publishing, IDC Publishers and Martinus Nijhoff Publishers.

All rights reserved. No part of this publication may be reproduced, translated, stored in a retrieval system, or transmitted in any form or by any means, electronic, mechanical, photocopying, recording or otherwise, without prior written permission from the publisher.

Authorization to photocopy items for internal or personal use is granted by Koninklijke Brill NV provided that the appropriate fees are paid directly to The Copyright Clearance Center, 222 Rosewood Drive, Suite 910, Danvers, MA 01923, USA.
Fees are subject to change.

This book is printed on acid-free paper.

MIX
Paper from
responsible sources
FSC   FSC® C109576
www.fsc.org

Printed by Printforce, the Netherlands

CONTENTS

Preface vii

1. Introduction to Pentecostal Hermeneutics 1
   Lee Roy Martin

2. A Pentecostal Approach to Scripture 11
   Rickie D. Moore

3. Canon and Charisma in the Book of Deuteronomy 15
   Rickie D. Moore

4. Yielding to the Spirit: A Pentecostal Approach to Group
   Bible Study 33
   Jackie David Johns and Cheryl Bridges Johns

5. When the Veil is Taken Away: The Impact of Prophetic
   Experience on Biblical Interpretation 57
   John W. McKay

6. Women, Pentecostalism, and the Bible: An Experiment in
   Pentecostal Hermeneutics 81
   John Christopher Thomas

7. Pentecostal Bible Reading: Toward a Model of Reading for
   the Formation of the Affections 95
   Robert O. Baker

8. Deuteronomy and the Fire of God: A Critical Charismatic
   Interpretation 109
   Rickie D. Moore

9. Pentecostal Hermeneutics: Retrospect and Prospect 131
   Kenneth J. Archer

10. Pentecostalism and the Authority of Scripture 149
    Scott A. Ellington

11. Hearing What the Spirit Says to the Churches: Profile of a
    Pentecostal Reader of the Apocalypse 171
    Robby Waddell

12. Hearing the Voice of God: Pentecostal Hermeneutics and
    The Book of Judges 205
    Lee Roy Martin

13. The Work of the Spirit in the Interpretation of Holy Scripture
    from the Perspective of a Charismatic Biblical Theologian 233
    Clark H. Pinnock

14. What Does It Mean to Read the Bible as a Pentecostal? 249
    Andrew Davies

15. Psalm 63 and Pentecostal Spirituality: An Exercise in Affective
    Hermeneutics 263
    Lee Roy Martin

Bibliography of Works on Pentecostal Hermeneutics 285
Index of Biblical References 291
Index of Authors 298

PREFACE

This collection of essays brings together many of the most important contributions to the recent discussion of Pentecostal biblical hermeneutics. This volume provides easy access for the classroom and for researchers who are investigating Pentecostal hermeneutics. Those researchers may be established scholars seeking to bring themselves up-to-date or young scholars who had not yet begun their academic journeys when many of the essays were originally written.

Most of the chapters of this reader are reprinted from the *Journal of Pentecostal Theology*. From its first issue until now, *JPT* has been in the forefront of publishing constructive scholarship on the topic of Pentecostal hermeneutics. The first issue of *JPT*, in the Fall of 1992, included two significant articles on hermeneutics: Rickie D. Moore, 'Canon and Charisma in the Book of Deuteronomy', and Jackie Johns and Cheryl Bridges Johns, 'Yielding to the Spirit: A Pentecostal Approach to Group Bible Study'. The publication of Scott A. Ellington's 'Locating Pentecostals at the Hermeneutical Round Table' in the Fall 2013 issue means that, in its short history, *JPT* has published more than 30 pieces that contribute to the development of Pentecostal biblical hermeneutics.

As beneficial as it would have been to republish all of the *JPT* articles on hermeneutics (as well as those from other academic journals), considerations of cost and space would not allow it. Therefore, the following criteria guided the composition of this volume. First, each essay must have made a significant contribution to the discussion of Pentecostal hermeneutics. Second, each piece must fit into the volume's overall design in demonstrating the chronological development of the discipline. Third, an attempt was made to represent the variety of components that may constitute a Pentecostal hermeneutic. Fourth, it was important to include as many different writers as possible. Fifth, there was an attempt explore both the theory and the practice of Pentecostal hermeneutics. Therefore, while a number of the chapters are purely theoretical, other chapters engage in the interpretation of specific biblical texts.

Each writer in this compilation argues that a distinctively Pentecostal hermeneutic is needed. It is acknowledged, however, that not all Pentecostal scholars are convinced that a Pentecostal hermeneutic is necessary or legitimate. Some scholars are content to utilize either historical-critical or Evangelical approaches, both of which are founded upon the modernist notion of rational objective criteria for truth.

It is also acknowledged that the *Journal of Pentecostal Theology* is not the only significant source for researching Pentecostal hermeneutics. Many important contributions to the discussion have been published in other journals and in monographs. Therefore, an extensive bibliography is included here.

I would like to offer my thanks to the authors who have agreed to have their writings republished in this collection. I would also express my deep appreciation to the all of those Pentecostal readers of the Bible whose love for the Word of God has stimulated the recent quest for a Pentecostal hermeneutic. The developments represented in this volume did not occur in a vacuum. We are particularly indebted to the Pentecostal communities in which we participate: the local churches, the faculties and students of Pentecostal colleges and seminaries, and the Society for Pentecostal Studies. I have been privileged to serve for 21 years at the Pentecostal Theological Seminary, the home to many who have published seminal works in the field of Pentecostal hermeneutics. I give thanks daily for my context, which affords me the opportunity to study the Bible alongside dedicated Pentecostal colleagues and to teach the Bible to enthusiastic Pentecostal students.

The 'word of God is living and powerful' (Heb. 4.12), and its interpretation requires a hermeneutic that takes seriously its dynamic and transforming capacity. It is my hope, therefore, that this volume will provide fuel for continued development and refining of Pentecostal biblical hermeneutics.

Lee Roy Martin
Cleveland, TN
May 2013

CHAPTER ONE

INTRODUCTION TO PENTECOSTAL BIBLICAL HERMENEUTICS

Lee Roy Martin[*]

Only recently have Pentecostal scholars begun to reflect critically upon their practices of biblical interpretation, but distinctive hermeneutical approaches were present from the beginning of the movement. The dynamic Pentecostal revival created a unique interpretive matrix from which emerged fresh interpretive strategies. The old hermeneutical wine skins were incapable of containing the new wine of the Holy Spirit that God was pouring out on all people.

Early Pentecostals found themselves in a position similar to that of the early Church in the book of Acts. Before the Day of Pentecost, the disciples had operated under the assumption that Jesus the Messiah would restore Israel to its proper position in the world (Acts 1.6). The outpouring of the Spirit, however, gave them an alternative vision of God's plan, which was supported by a new understanding of Scripture. In the early church, we find 'a perplexing tension between a breaking into this world of the kingdom of God, in which Christian believers act as servants in God's redemption of the world, and the need to wait for God to fulfil the promises of the Old Testament according to God's own timing'.[1]

Pentecost produced a radical transformation of the epistemology, worldview, and hermeneutics of the early believers. Before Pentecost, the disciples would have subscribed to the common worldview and interpretive assumptions of first-century Judaism (though Judaism itself was not monolithic). They also would have been influenced by the spread of Greek philosophy, which was not only ubiquitous in secular contexts but also was subtly interjected into Judaism through the Septuagint, the Greek translation of the Hebrew scriptures.

---

[*] Lee Roy Martin (DTh, University of South Africa) is Professor of Old Testament and Biblical Languages at the Pentecostal Theological Seminary in Cleveland, TN USA. He also serves as Editor of the *Journal of Pentecostal Theology*.

[1] Gerald T. Sheppard, 'Biblical Interpretation after Gadamer', *PNEUMA: The Journal of the Society for Pentecostal Studies* 16 (1984), pp. 121–41 (139).

The hermeneutics of the apostles changed on the Day of Pentecost.[2] Although they continued to utilize many standard Jewish exegetical practices, their approach to biblical interpretation was altered by at least four new contextual factors: 1. the life, teachings, and resurrection of Jesus; 2. the gift of the Holy Spirit poured out on the Day of Pentecost; 3. the mission of the spreading the gospel, which demanded that the disciples go with haste into the world; 4. the eschatological nature of Jesus' kingdom, which required the disciples to wait patiently for the return of Jesus.[3]

In its radical re-ordering of reality, Pentecost might be compared to the divine encounters of the Old Testament prophets in their call narratives. The prophetic experience was an apocalyptic event that deconstructed previously held assumptions and created new theological perceptions and new possibilities for God's people.[4] Just as Moses was reborn at the burning bush, just as Israel was transformed at Mt. Sinai, and just as Isaiah was reshaped by his vision, so also the early disciples were changed at Pentecost. The comparison between Pentecost and the prophetic calling is strengthened further by Peter's interpretation of Pentecost as the fulfillment of Joel's promise that servants, sons, daughters, old, and young 'will prophesy' (Acts 2.17). Therefore, the gift of the Spirit is the gift of prophecy; and, consequently, Pentecost creates a community of prophets.[5] As John McKay has argued, the prophetic gift of the Spirit naturally leads to the prophetic interpretation of Scripture.[6] The sermons in the book of Acts as well as the New Testament documents demonstrate the outworking of that prophetic hermeneutic.

Like the early church, the first Pentecostals inherited a set of interpretive presuppositions; but while the apostles had been shaped by the hermeneutical assumptions of Judaism, the early Pentecostal movement was indebted to the conservative hermeneutical approaches of the late

---

[2] Cf. Sheppard, 'Biblical Interpretation after Gadamer', p. 132.
[3] Sheppard sees the tension between 'hurrying and waiting', along with the 'passionate personal experiences of the Holy Spirit, as the two features that form the 'heart of the Pentecostal tradition' (Sheppard, 'Biblical Interpretation after Gadamer', p. 140).
[4] See Rick D. Moore, 'The Prophetic Calling: An Old Testament Profile and Its Relevance for Today', *Journal of the European Pentecostal Theological Association* 24 (2004), pp. 16–29 (esp. pp. 18–21).
[5] See Roger Stronstad, *The Prophethood of All Believers: A Study in Luke's Charismatic Theology* (Cleveland, TN: CPT Press, 2010).
[6] John W. McKay, 'When the Veil Is Taken Away: The Impact of Prophetic Experience on Biblical Interpretation', *Journal of Pentecostal Theology* 5 (1994), pp. 17–40 (24–32). Cf. Larry R. McQueen, *Joel and the Spirit: The Cry of a Prophetic Hermeneutic* (Cleveland, TN: CPT Press, 2009).

nineteenth century. The Pentecostal movement emerged from a religious context that included the holiness movement, the healing movement, restorationist movements, revivalism, and millenarian movements,[7] all of which carried ramifications for biblical interpretation. Pentecostals, for the most part, practiced the common populist 'common sense approach'[8] that took the Bible at face value. They read the Bible literally,[9] collapsing the distance between the original context of Scripture and the context of the reader. Kenneth Archer identifies this early Pentecostal approach as 'the Bible reading method',[10] a method that consisted in searching the Bible for all Scripture references to a particular subject and then synthesizing those references into a theological statement. It is a harmonizing and deductive method.[11]

Also like the early church, the first Pentecostals found it necessary to revise their hermeneutics in light of their Pentecostal experience of the Spirit.[12] The baptism in the Holy Spirit was an apocalyptic inbreaking of God that altered their worldview. Jackie Johns writes, 'At the core of the

---

[7] Kenneth J. Archer, *A Pentecostal Hermeneutic: Spirit, Scripture and Community* (Cleveland, TN: CPT Press, 2009), p. 99. Cf. Jean-Daniel Plüss, 'Azusa and Other Myths: The Long and Winding Road from Experience to Stated Belief and Back Again', *Pneuma* 15.2 (1983), pp. 189–201 (191). For the impact of millenarian movements on Pentecostalism, see Grant Wacker, 'Functions of Faith in Primitive Pentecostalism', *Harvard Theological Review* 77 (1984), pp. 353–75 (369–73).

[8] Stephen R. Graham, '"Thus Saith the Lord": Biblical Hermeneutics in the Early Pentecostal Movement', *Ex auditu* 12 (1996), pp. 121–35 (124).

[9] Russell P. Spittler, 'Are Pentecostals and Charismatics Fundamentalists? A Review of American Uses of These Categories', in Karla Poewe (ed.) *Charismatic Christianity as a Global Culture* (Columbia, SC: University of South Carolina Press, 1994), pp. 103–16 (111–12). Cf. Wacker, 'Functions of Faith', who observes that the practice of snake handling is a result of literalism (p. 366). Early Pentecostal interpretation is described as 'precritical' by Archer, *A Pentecostal Hermeneutic*, p. 125; and by Timothy B. Cargal, 'Beyond the Fundamentalist-Modernist Controversy: Pentecostals and Hermeneutics in a Postmodern Age', *PNEUMA: The Journal of the Society for Pentecostal Studies* 15 (1993), pp. 163–87 (165, 170–71). Archer, however, prefers to describe Pentecostals as 'paramodern' (*A Pentecostal Hermeneutic*, pp. 28–45), a term that Archer attributes to Jackie Johns (p. 45, n. 137). Sheppard, however, suggests the term 'sub modern' ('Biblical Interpretation after Gadamer', p. 127).

[10] Archer, *A Pentecostal Hermeneutic*, pp. 99–127.

[11] Archer, *A Pentecostal Hermeneutic*, p. 102. Although a concordance was often used to gather the biblical references, the method was simplified by the use of 'chain reference' study Bibles that linked one verse to another through the use of marginal notation systems. The Bible reading method also formed the basis of reference works in which the Bible verses had already been collected into topical categories. One of the most popular of these was Orville J. Nave, *Nave's Topical Bible: A Digest of the Holy Scriptures* (Lincoln, NE: Topical Bible Publishing Co., 1903).

[12] Cf. Steven Jack Land, *Pentecostal Spirituality: A Passion for the Kingdom* (Cleveland, TN: CPT Press, 2010), pp. 1–9.

Pentecostal worldview is affective experience of God which generates an apocalyptic horizon for reading reality'.[13] Consequently, the addition of the baptism in the Holy Spirit to the aforementioned context of beliefs and experiences produced more than an addendum to conservative theology and hermeneutics; it transformed every element and shaped them into a new whole, which has been called the 'Full Gospel' or the 'Five-fold Gospel'.[14] As the 'central defining characteristic of the Pentecostal movement',[15] the Five-fold Gospel places Jesus at the center of Pentecostal theology and insists that Jesus is savior, sanctifier, Spirit baptizer, healer, and soon coming king.[16] The Five-fold Gospel is 'the theological grid' that 'provided a firm interpretive lens for the fluid Pentecostal community and their reading of Scripture'.[17]

Spirit baptism and the resultant Five-fold Gospel did not entirely negate the previously held theological commitments and hermeneutical assumptions of the early Pentecostals, but the new formulation of beliefs and affections generated subtle (and not so subtle) alterations of older, established paradigms. Although early Pentecostals were by no means monolithic in their approaches, there was a 'fundamental' difference between Pentecostal and non-Pentecostal hermeneutics.[18] The hermeneutical paradigm that developed in early Pentecostalism can be described in a variety of ways, but I would suggest several significant characteristics.

First, early Pentecostals viewed the Bible as a single unified narrative of God's redemptive plan, whose central message may be summarized in the Five-fold Gospel.[19] Herholdt explains:

---

[13] Jackie David Johns, 'Pentecostalism and the Postmodern Worldview', *Journal of Pentecostal Theology* 7 (1995), pp. 73–96 (87).

[14] Land, *Pentecostal Spirituality*, pp. 6, 38. Some non-Wesleyan Pentecostals omit sanctification from the formulation, which results in a 'Four-fold Gospel' or a 'Foursquare Gospel'.

[15] M. Nel, 'Pentecostals' Reading of the Old Testament', *Verbum et Ecclesia* 28.2 (2007), pp. 524–41 (526–27).

[16] Marius D. Herholdt, 'Pentecostal and Charismatic Hermeneutics', in Adrio König and S.S. Maimela (eds.), *Initiation into Theology: The Rich Variety of Theology and Hermeneutics* (Pretoria: Van Schaik, 1998), pp. 417–31.

[17] Archer, *A Pentecostal Hermeneutic*, p. 137. Herholdt remarks that the elements of the Full Gospel 'serve as broad hermeneutical categories within which Pentecostals will interpret everything that they read in Scripture' ('Pentecostal and Charismatic Hermeneutics', p. 426).

[18] Nel, 'Pentecostals' Reading of the Old Testament', p. 525.

[19] Like all conservative groups, Pentecostals assumed the inspiration and authority of Scripture. See Renea Brathwaite, 'Seymour on Scripture' (38th Annual Meeting of the Society for Pentecostal Studies; Virginia Beach, VA; Feb. 29–Mar. 3, 2012), pp. 12–17.

Thus, the purpose of the Bible is to bring humanity into harmony with God's salvific purposes... and here I mean salvation and a comprehensive sense of making all things new and whole. Consequently, interpretation of the Bible serves understanding, and understanding is part of the process of becoming whole... Thus the interpretation of the Bible is part of a process that answers to the criteria of becoming whole and all that it entails.[20]

As heirs of the restorationist movements, the Pentecostals believed that the gift of the Spirit was an indispensible characteristic of the true Church that must be experienced in contemporary times. The doctrine of justification by faith had been restored by the Reformation; sanctification had been restored by Wesleyanism; divine healing had been restored by the healing movement; and belief in the return of Jesus had been restored by the millenarian movements. Spirit baptism was the last piece of the puzzle, completing the restoration of primitive Christianity and preparing the bride of Christ for his return. The twentieth-century restoration of Spirit baptism to the Church came in fulfillment of Joel's prophecy that God would pour out both the 'early rain' and the 'latter rain' (Joel 2.23). The early rain fell on the Day of Pentecost and the latter rain began to fall during the Pentecostal revival and will continue to fall until Jesus comes.[21]

Second, viewing the Bible as one grand unified story led the Pentecostals to utilize intertextuality as 'a justifying mark of a faithful reading'.[22] The above-mentioned Bible reading method was a way of tracing Pentecostal themes from Genesis to Revelation. 'They found themselves called to work their way along the "figural pathways of a biblical text" so that for them the event of scriptural interpretation was itself always a kind of exodus, a pilgrimage, a journey into God'.[23]

Third, the Pentecostals' appreciation for the narrative quality of Scripture meant that they became a part of the story. Therefore, they no longer looked at the Bible from the outside; instead, they entered the world of the Bible, and the world of the Bible shaped their world.[24] At a time when

---

[20] Herholdt, 'Pentecostal and Charismatic Hermeneutics', p. 425.
[21] See Archer, *A Pentecostal Hermeneutic*, pp. 136–49; and Graham, ' "Thus Saith the Lord": Biblical Hermeneutics in the Early Pentecostal Movement', p. 127.
[22] Chris E.W. Green, ' "Treasures Old and New": Reading the Old Testament with Early Pentecostal Mothers and Fathers' (41st Annual Meeting of the Society for Pentecostal Studies, Virginia Beach, VA, Mar. 29–Apr. 3, 2012), p. 15.
[23] Green, ' "Treasures Old and New" ', p. 15.
[24] H.M. Ervin, 'Hermeneutics: A Pentecostal Option', *PNEUMA: The Journal of the Society for Pentecostal Studies* 3 (1981), pp. 11–25 (22). Cf. McKay, 'When the Veil Is Taken Away', who likens biblical interpretation to the production of a drama, which includes the actors on stage and the critics in the audience. Biblical scholars are equivalent to the drama critics,

modern scholarship (both liberal and conservative) excluded consideration of the supernatural and personal experience from the legitimate means for measuring truth claims,[25] the Pentecostals were testifying to ongoing experiences of the supernatural in the form of healings, miracles, and the charismata. According to Grant Wacker, 'Pentecostalism offered invincible certitude that the supernatural claims of the gospel were really true, not the old-fashioned gospel of the 19th century, but the awesome, wonderworking gospel of the first century'.[26] Furthermore, the Pentecostal experience altered their epistemology, giving them 'existential awareness of the miraculous in the Biblical world view'.[27]

Fourth, the Pentecostal experience of the supernatural not only affirmed the truthfulness of the supernatural components of the biblical story, but it also suggested a broader approach to knowing the truth. The charismata often included an element of divine revelation, and Pentecostals soon realized that the same Holy Spirit who moved upon the prophets to write Holy Scripture (2 Pet. 1.21) could move upon them to reveal the meaning of Scripture as well. For Pentecostals, the role of the Holy Spirit in biblical interpretation goes beyond the reformed concept of 'illumination'.[28] According to Cargal, Pentecostalism's 'emphasis upon the role of the Spirit in interpreting/appropriating the multiple meanings of the biblical texts is an important contribution as the Western church seeks to reclaim its sense of mysticism and the immanence of the transcendent which was diminished by rationalism'.[29] Furthermore, Russell Spittler argues that even though both Pentecostals and Fundamentalists pursued a literal approach to the Bible, the Pentecostal criteria for truth was somewhat different. The fundamentalist approach is based on rationalism whereas, in the Pentecostal approach, religious experience is more valuable than

---

who examine but do not participate. Pentecostals, however, are like the actors, who get on stage and enter into the story (pp. 32–35).

[25] See Sheppard, 'Biblical Interpretation after Gadamer', pp. 125–26. Sheppard argues that both liberals and Fundamentalists, 'because they both laid claim to the same historicism and theory of intentionality, represent' modernity (p. 126).

[26] Wacker, 'Functions of Faith', p. 361. Cf. Archer, *A Pentecostal Hermeneutic*, p. 95.

[27] Ervin, 'Hermeneutics: A Pentecostal Option', pp. 11–25 (24). On the role of experience in Pentecostal hermeneutics, see Cargal, 'Beyond the Fundamentalist-Modernist Controversy', pp. 178–81; and Roger Stronstad, 'Pentecostal Experience and Hermeneutics', *Paraclete* 26 (1992), pp. 14–30.

[28] See John Christopher Thomas, 'Women, Pentecostalism and the Bible: An Experiment in Pentecostal Hermeneutics', *Journal of Pentecostal Theology* 5 (1994), pp. 49, 55; and French L. Arrington, 'Hermeneutics', in Stanley M. Burgess and Gary B. McGee (eds.), *DPCM* (Grand Rapids, MI: Eerdmans, 1988), p. 382.

[29] Cargal, 'Beyond the Fundamentalist-Modernist Controversy', p. 186.

human reason.[30] 'The truthfulness of Scripture', writes Kenneth Archer, 'was discovered relationally, personally, and experientially more so than "scientifically"'.[31] Like the early Church in Acts 15, the first Pentecostals included their own experiences as a means of discerning the guidance of the Holy Spirit.[32] Spittler writes, 'Fundamentalists and neo-orthodox Christians mount arguments...Pentecostals give testimonies...There is a profound difference between the cognitive fundamentalist and the experiential Pentecostal'.[33]

Fifth, viewing the Bible as a lived story led also to a theological approach to narrative parts of the Bible.[34] That is, biblical narratives were seen as examples that the Church should follow, and the book of Acts, in particular, became the ideal model for the true Church.[35] After all, if even the Old Testament stories are 'examples...written for our admonition, upon whom the ends of the ages have come' (1 Cor. 10.11); and if all believers are to do the 'works' of Jesus (Jn. 12.14), who is our 'example' (1 Pet. 2.21), then surely the story of the early Church in the book of Acts must be a pattern that we should follow. 'These narratives are understood literally, and taken to be repeatable and expected, and Biblical characters' experiences are to be emulated. In this way Pentecostalism shares the primitivism of movements such as Montanism and the Anabaptists'.[36]

Sixth, for Pentecostals, the biblical story has its beginning, center, and goal in Jesus Christ. Herholdt argues that 'Christ is the picture that serves to bring the pieces of the puzzle together into a coherent whole'.[37] This means that the Old Testament was read Christologically—sometimes through the lens of allegory or typology.[38] Chris Green explains:

> Hence, the key to unlock a particular OT passage's hidden treasure is to discover how it speaks of Christ, how it casts him and his mission into relief...Pentecostals of the first generation stood convinced that because

---

[30] Spittler, 'Are Pentecostals and Charismatics Fundamentalists? A Review of American Uses of These Categories', p. 108.
[31] Archer, *A Pentecostal Hermeneutic*, p. 97.
[32] See Thomas, 'Women, Pentecostalism and the Bible', pp. 41–56.
[33] Spittler, 'Are Pentecostals and Charismatics Fundamentalists? A Review of American Uses of These Categories', p. 108. Cf. Ervin, 'Hermeneutics: A Pentecostal Option', p. 33; and Archer, *A Pentecostal Hermeneutic*, p. 97.
[34] Cf. Cargal, 'Beyond the Fundamentalist-Modernist Controversy', pp. 182–84.
[35] Cf. Graham, '"Thus Saith the Lord": Biblical Hermeneutics in the Early Pentecostal Movement', pp. 126–28.
[36] Nel, 'Pentecostals' Reading of the Old Testament', p. 527.
[37] Herholdt, 'Pentecostal and Charismatic Hermeneutics', p. 429.
[38] Brathwaite, 'Seymour on Scripture', p. 21. Cf.

Christ is the *import* of OT Scripture, the OT can and should be allowed to inform theological reflection and ecclesial practice.[39]

Seventh, early Pentecostals believed that the work of the Holy Spirit is to restore the last-days Church to its primitive capacity, and that the activity of the Holy Spirit (including biblical interpretation) takes place within the context of the Church.[40] The presence of God was manifested in the community by signs, wonders, and gifts of the Holy Spirit; and God's presence legitimated the community as the people of God.[41] Most often, the setting for biblical interpretation was the act of preaching, while the congregation would respond with vocal and physical signs of affirmation (or with silent protest).

Eighth, the eschatological expectations of the early Pentecostals compelled them to an urgent pursuit of world evangelization. Pentecostals believed the end to be near—it was the 'evening light' (Zech. 14.6–7),[42] and the 'night is coming when no one can work' (Jn. 9.4). The message of the Bible was that all the world must be saved, sanctified, filled with the Holy Spirit, healed, and prepared for the return of Jesus, the soon coming King; and time was growing short. Thus, for Pentecostals, the Bible functioned to form and equip the Church for its mission of evangelization, and it functioned as the content of their message to the world. Therefore, they would read the Bible 'with the end result in mind'.[43]

Early Pentecostals attempted to discern the implications of Spirit baptism and the Five-fold Gospel for biblical interpretation, and we must continue forward in that process of discernment. Our goal should be to produce a Pentecostal hermeneutic that is faithful to our theology and ethos and appropriate for our present context. The contributors to this volume have attempted precisely this kind of constructive approach. Their work has led to widespread agreement on the general contours of a Pentecostal hermeneutic. Scott Ellington summarizes the present consensus in terms of

> five distinctive accents in a Pentecostal reading of Scripture; that Pentecostal readings are narrative rather than propositional, that they are dynamic

---

[39] Green, '"Treasures Old and New"', pp. 12–13.
[40] Cf. Herholdt, 'Pentecostal and Charismatic Hermeneutics', p. 422.
[41] Cf. Nel, 'Pentecostals' Reading of the Old Testament', pp. 533–35.
[42] The *Church of God Evangel*, the official periodical of the Church of God (Cleveland, TN), began in 1910 as *The Evening Light and Church of God Evangel*, but the title was shorted to *The Church of God Evangel* in 1911.
[43] Cf. Herholdt, 'Pentecostal and Charismatic Hermeneutics', p. 430.

rather than static, that they are experience-based, that they seek encounter more than understanding, and that they are pragmatic, emphasizing transformation and application.[44]

Chris Green expands the list to eight points of general agreement:

1. The work of the Spirit in making faithful interpretation possible, inspiring the readers to make gospel sense of the texts.
2. The authority and sufficiency of the Scriptures' final, canonical form.
3. The role of the worshipping community in the process of interpreting the Scriptures.
4. The need for confessional, theological readings concerned primarily with how the Scriptures work as God's address to God's people here and now.
5. Respect for the irreducible diversity of theological and literary 'voices' in the *Scriptures*.
6. Regard for the over-arching 'story' of the history of salvation as a hermeneutical key.
7. The priority of narrative, literary readings of a text over against historical-critical readings.
8. The significance of the history of effects for the contemporary interpretative process.[45]

As Green acknowledges, most of the contemporary discussions regarding Pentecostal interpretation can be summarized under a triadic paradigm consisting of the Scripture, the Holy Spirit, and the community of faith.[46] This threefold framework is explicated in the chapters that follow, and it continues to be refined in light of changing contexts and global Pentecostal insights. Pentecostalism is a richly diverse movement with a variety of expressions, and each expression is deserving of its own particular version of Pentecostal hermeneutics.

---

[44] Scott A. Ellington, 'Locating Pentecostals at the Hermeneutical Round Table', *JPT* 22.2 (2013), forthcoming.
[45] Chris E.W. Green, *Toward a Pentecostal Theology of the Lord's Supper: Foretasting the Kingdom* (Cleveland, TN: CPT Press, 2012), pp. 182-83.
[46] See, for example, Rickie D. Moore, 'Canon and Charisma in the Book of Deuteronomy', *Journal of Pentecostal Theology* 1 (1992), p. 75, n. 1; Land, *Pentecostal Spirituality*, pp. 28-34; Thomas, 'Women, Pentecostalism and the Bible', pp. 49-56; and Archer, *A Pentecostal Hermeneutic*, pp. 212-60.

CHAPTER TWO

A PENTECOSTAL APPROACH TO SCRIPTURE*

Rickie D. Moore**

How should Scripture be approached? On this question we believe Pentecostals have some decisive insights which no one else can offer. We Pentecostals bear distinctive witness to a reality and dimension of life in the Holy Spirit, out of which a uniquely Pentecostal approach to Scripture emerges. Some of the key aspects of this reality of life in the Spirit and their import for a Pentecostal approach to Scripture are described in the following:

1. *The Holy Spirit addresses us in ways which transcend human reason*

We see this especially in the gifts of the Spirit (I Cor. 12.14) but also in more subtle ways (Rom. 8.1–27). Thus we know that there is a vital place for emotion as well as reason, for imagination as well as logic, for mystery as well as certainty, and for that which is narrative and dramatic as well as that which is propositional and systematic. Consequently, we appreciate Scripture not just as an object which we interpret but as a living Word which interprets us and through which the Spirit flows in ways that we cannot dictate, calculate, or program. This means that our Bible study must be open to surprises and even times of waiting or tarrying before the Lord.

---

* This chapter was first published as 'A Pentecostal Approach to Scripture', *Seminary Viewpoint* 8.1 (November 1987), pp. 4–5, 11. Editor's Note: This statement was drafted by Rick Moore in connection with his work on a committee authorized by the General Executive Council to look into the development of a comprehensive Bible study program for the Church of God. As such, this statement was included in the committee's report to the Executive Council in September and reflects the synthesis and consensus of those on the committee, including Chris Thomas, Cheryl Johns, Jackie Johns, and Steve Land, who chaired the committee.
** Rickie D. Moore (PhD, Vanderbilt University) is Chair of the Department of Theology at Lee University in Cleveland, TN, USA.

2. *Experience is vital to knowing the truth*

Pentecostal faith is not, as some have caricatured, an experience based faith. Yet we Pentecostals do see an inseparable interplay between knowledge and lived-experience, where knowing about God and directly experiencing God perpetually inform and depend upon one another. This accords with the biblical vs the common secular understanding of knowledge. In the Old Testament this is seen in the very word for knowledge, *yada*, which points beyond the conceptualization of an object to the actualization of a relationship. This is why *yada* is used for marital lovemaking (e.g. Gen. 4.1) and covenantal intimacy (e.g. Jer. 1.5; 22.16; 31.34). This understanding of knowledge is carried forward into the New Testament, so that, as 1 John teaches, 'he who does not love does not know God' (4.8). We Pentecostals have appreciated this biblical emphasis upon lived-experience by including testimony in our times of gathering around the Word and by expecting not just information but transformation. What would Pentecostal preaching be without the altar call? And by the same token, what would Pentecostal Bible study be without explicit recognition and overt responding to the transforming call of God's Word? Can our approach to Bible study be Pentecostal if the question 'What then shall we do?' is left unexpressed and unanswered or otherwise loses that urgency which marks a people of last-days expectancy and global mission?

3. *The Spirit calls every individual believer to be a witness of the truth (cf. Acts 1.8)*

The priesthood (1 Pet. 2.5, 9) and prophethood (Num. 11.27–29; Joel 2.28–32; Acts 2.16–20) of *all* believers has distinct reality among Pentecostals in our experience of the Spirit being 'poured out upon all flesh' (Acts 2.17). The Spirit gives to some the special gift of teaching but calls every believer to walk in the light for themselves (1 Jn 1.7; 2.27; cf. Eph. 4.7–17) and to be a Christ-like witness of that light before others (1 Jn 4.13–17; Mt. 5.14). These concerns claim deep roots in our Pentecostal heritage. We see them in the enduring adage, 'one should walk in the light as it shines upon his/her path' (the tradition underlying the *Lighted Pathway*), and in our expectation that every convert should be a firsthand partaker and bearer of the word, thereby edifying the congregation and evangelizing the lost.

4. *Knowledge of the truth is inseparable from active membership in the localized body of Christ*

The corporate experience of the faith has been especially vital to us Pentecostals. Pentecostal faith is born out of a gathering together of believers (Acts 2.1–4) and continues to be nurtured and sustained by this same communion of the saints (Acts 2.42–47). We have long testified to the special revelation of Christ 'where two or three are gathered together' in His name (Mt. 18.20). We have decried 'forsaking the assembling of ourselves together', for here we experience the indispensable ministry of 'exhorting one another, and so much the more, as we see the day approaching' (Heb. 10.25). In other words, here we experience the reality of being the body of Christ, bound together as a particular historical community with the holy bonds of mutual interdependence and accountability. Here the Holy Spirit speaks as nowhere else, bestowing and blending gifts among all the members in order to make manifest God's Word in the edification of the whole body (1 Corinthians 12; 14; Ephsians 4; Romans 12). The first general assembly of the Church of God in 1906 grew directly out of this commitment to gathering around the Word in the Spirit with explicit appeal to the Jerusalem Council of Acts 15, and this same conviction remains a mark of truly Pentecostal gatherings to this day.

Ironically, while certain cutting-edge trends in recent theology have moved closer to these Pentecostal emphases (e.g. narrative theology, theology as praxis, the community's role in interpretation, etc.), we Pentecostals have tended to move further away from these emphases as we have adopted the approaches, methods, and, in some cases, the curricula of other (non-Pentecostal) traditions. We believe that the Pentecostal content which we have been attempting to infuse secondarily into our Bible study is being effectively sabotaged by the powerful and pervasive teaching impact of non-Pentecostal methods. We consider the pursuit of a distinctly Pentecostal approach to Scripture to be absolutely essential right now if we are to survive and our children are to become Pentecostal. We submit that there is a crying need and a divine mandate before us right now to recover an approach to Scripture which will 'quench not the Spirit!' (1 Thess. 5.19).

CHAPTER THREE

CANON AND CHARISMA IN THE BOOK OF DEUTERONOMY*

Rickie D. Moore**

As everyone knows, biblical study is experiencing a revolution. Interpretation has been thrown wide open as new voices have entered the discussion and new eyes have encountered the text, as the historical-critical establishment and its rationalist-fundamentalist counterpart have increasingly given way to the recognition that what is brought to the text makes a decisive difference in what is found there.[1] The shifting methodological landscape is no doubt unsettling for many of us, even for those of us representing new perspectives. One might well wonder what gaining a voice means if the polity is to be anarchy. Yet amidst such humbling uncertainty

---

* First published in the *Journal of Pentecostal Theology* 1 (1992), pp. 75–92.
** Rickie D. Moore (PhD, Vanderbilt University) is Chair of the Department of Theology at Lee University in Cleveland, TN, USA.
[1] Of course there are those who would go further and say that what is brought to the text makes *all* of the difference—that interpretation, after all, is essentially the 'creating' of meaning. This brings us to the vast chasm of hermeneutical debate which has opened in our time. While I am not prepared here to take on such expansive matters, I would say that Pentecostals would seem to have a unique vantage point to bring to the discussion. To put the issue somewhat, perhaps even too, simplistically, it seems to me that Pentecostals, in their claims for a substantive ongoing revelatory role for the Holy Spirit, find themselves located in the crossfire between, for want of better terms, the liberal-critical tradition of biblical interpretation and the conservative Evangelical tradition. It seems that both of these traditions approach interpretation as a matter which is essentially limited to the reader and the text. Whereas the former tradition sees this finally in terms of an open and merely human process, whether focusing on the text or, as is more common nowadays, on the reader, the latter sees everything finally in terms of a closed divine deposit. Pentecostals, on the other hand, would want to approach interpretation as a matter of the text, the community, and also the ongoing voice of the Holy Spirit. And this opens up a view of interpretation which can appreciate both the necessary place of human subjectivity in a dynamic process (seen to be at work in the interpreting community *and* in the biblical text), as well as the place of the final authority of God manifested in and through the process (see the overview of F.L. Arrington, 'Hermeneutics, Historical Perspectives on Pentecostal and Charismatic', in *Dictionary of Pentecostal and Charismatic Movements* [ed. S.M. Burgess, G.B. McGee and P.H. Alexander; Grand Rapids, MI: Zondervan, 1988], pp. 376–89). Such an approach draws dismissals from both sides—as a relativizing of divine authority from the conservative Evangelical side and as an absolutizing of human process from the liberal-critical side.

there arises still the hope that a new voice will be heard—a voice from the text which will be much better than our own.

I approach this study as a Pentecostal and as one who is consciously attempting to integrate my Pentecostal vocation and perspective with critical Old Testament scholarship. Such integration is not easy for me, for I spent many years learning to keep these things mostly separate from one another. And now that I feel the need to pursue this interface, the way ahead is far from clear. In terms of examples, there is little for one to follow.[2] Thus the present effort is of necessity exploratory and experimental.

I propose here to look at the way in which the book of Deuteronomy sets forth the place and role of both inscripturated word and prophetic utterance. Not only does Deuteronomy evidence repeated emphasis on the establishment of each of these revelatory dimensions, but in chapters 4 and 5 there is seen sustained reflection, I would suggest, on the dialectical and complementary relationship between canonical word and what I would term charismatic revelation.

My Pentecostal perspective (or testimony) on Spirit and Word obviously parallels and is certainly informing my perceptions on the Deuteronomy passages. Yet these perceptions, it seems to me, surface elements in the text that have been hidden and suppressed by other perspectives of long standing. Briefly stated, the noticing of such dialectical possibilities in Israel's testimony of revelation has not been served by a historical-critical tradition that has legitimated the attribution of any tension or shift in emphasis to different literary sources or redactional layers.[3] More-

---

[2] Yet I would note John W. McKay, 'The Old Testament and Christian Charismatic/Prophetic Literature', in *Scripture: Meaning and Method. Essays Presented to Anthony Tyrrell Hanson for his Seventieth Birthday* (ed. B.P. Thompson; Hull: University of Hull Press, 1987), pp. 200-17; and 'The Experience of Dereliction and of God's Presence in Psalms: An Exercise in Old Testament Exegesis in the Light of Renewal Theology', in *Faces of Renewal Studies in Honor of Stanley M. Horton* (ed. P. Elbert; Peabody, MA: Hendrickson, 1988), pp. 3-13.

[3] Interestingly, a similar point has been made in certain quarters of Jewish biblical scholarship, which appreciates the dialectical dimensions of revelation in a way that is different, albeit not entirely unrelated, to my own. Note the following quote of S. Talmon, 'Revelation in Biblical Times', *Hebrew Studies* 26 (1985), p. 60:
> Such a separation of the sources in biblical literature [with respect to revelatory notions] is entirely unacceptable not only to Jewish exegetes who are considered 'pre-critical', such as S.D. Luzatto and D. Hoffmann—not to speak of the medieval commentators. Scholars trained in critical method such as Benno Jacob, Umberto Cassuto and M.H. Segal also categorically refuse to divide the concepts of the biblical belief in God and revelation into the particular formulations of the Elohistic, Jahwistic, Priestly, Deuteronomistic, Prophetic or Chronistic schools. The various names and epithets of God and the various forms of divine revelation and their multifarious

over, discernment of these possibilities has been equally impeded among conservative Evangelical scholars, the primary opponents of the historical-critical mainstream, insofar as they have been committed to a larger theological scheme that sees a radical and dispensational break between charismatic utterance and completed canon.[4]

My treatment approaches Deuteronomy in its final form—a course that needs little justification in this day of crumbling consensus.[5] Of course, I realize that where so little justification is needed, little justification can be claimed.[6] For the moment, any deeper justification will have to wait, perhaps for all of us.

The starting point for this treatment of revelation in Deuteronomy is 18.9–22. This text sets forth the office of the prophet in ancient Israel, with the words,

> Yahweh, your God will raise up for you a prophet like me from your midst, from among your kindred; him you shall heed (v. 15).[7]

Peter's Pentecost sermon in Acts 3, of course, takes this passage as a prophetic reference to Jesus (v. 22)—an eschatological move that Deuteronomy

---

content are regarded not as expressions of different concepts of Deity but as manifestations of the sole and only God who reacts to man's deeds in many different ways and allows himself to be perceived by men in sundry modes of revelation.

For a prime example of the more typical way that historical criticism has been applied in this area, and one involving one of the passages on which I will focus, see A. Rofé, 'The Monotheistic Argumentation in Deuteronomy IV 32–40: Contents, Composition and Text', *VT* 35 (1985), pp. 434–45.

[4] This relates primarily to the doctrine of the cessation of the *charismata* after the completion of the New Testament canon, as developed by Benjamin B. Warfield, but the doctrine has implications for the broader view of biblical revelation. This point has been developed more fully in an earlier version of this paper which I presented at the 20th Annual Meeting of the Society for Pentecostal Studies, 1990. For an extended biblical and theological challenge of Warfieldian cessationism, see J. Ruthven, *On the Cessation of the Charismata: A Critique of the Protestant Polemic on Post-Biblical Miracles* (JPTSup, 3; Sheffield: JSOT Press, 1996).

[5] See, e.g., J.G. McConville, *Law and Theology in Deuteronomy* (JSOTS, 33; Sheffield: JSOT Press, 1984), who challenges Pentateuchal criticism on a position no less central and pivotal than the linkage between Deuteronomy and Josiah's reformation. The call to shift focus to the final form of the text—in large part because of historical-critical scholarship's incapacity to sustain consensus on the prior compositional history of the text—was, of course, sounded first and most influentially by B.S. Childs, *Biblical Theology in Crisis* (Philadelphia, PA: Westminster Press, 1970); and his, *Introduction to the Old Testament as Scripture* (Philadelphia: Fortress Press, 1979). See also D.J.A. Clines, *The Theme of the Pentateuch* (JSOTSup 10; Sheffield: JSOT Press, 1978).

[6] Put differently, where any reading can be justified, *no* reading can be justified. And does this not bring us precisely to deconstructionism?

[7] Translations of the Hebrew in this chapter are my own.

itself sets up by its closing acknowledgement that 'a prophet like Moses' had not yet arisen in Israel (34.10).[8] Still the reference clearly points in the first place to an ongoing succession of prophets, situated as it is beside the other laws concerning the continuing leadership institutions of ancient Israel.[9]

Deuteronomy not only sets forth the prophetic office as a continuing medium of charismatic revelation but also explicitly sets forth the abiding place of the written canon in Israel. We see this establishment of canon in the leadership section just mentioned:

> When he (the king) sits on the throne of his kingdom, he shall write for himself in a book a copy of this law, obtained from the Levitical priests. It is to be with him, and he should read it all the days of his life (17.18-19).

We see this again in the summary section of the book:

> Moses wrote this law and gave it to the priests, the sons of Levi, who carried the ark of the covenant of Yahweh, and to all the elders of Israel. Moses then commanded them, 'At the end of every seven years, at the observance of the year of release, at the feast of booths, when all Israel comes to appear before Yahweh your God at the place he will choose, you shall read this law before all Israel in their hearing' (31.9-11).

Thus the two revelatory channels, those of canonical writing and charismatic speech, are both explicitly set forth in the book of Deuteronomy and projected forward into Israel's future life. Moreover, a rather close relationship is suggested when the stated effects, which Deuteronomy posits for these two modes of revelation, are compared.

The continuing impact of written revelation is spelled out clearly in chapter 31.

> When all Israel comes to appear before Yahweh your God at the place he will choose, you shall read this law before all Israel in their hearing... that they may heed and learn to fear Yahweh your God, and that they may be careful to do all the words of this law. Their children, who have not known it, should then heed and learn to fear Yahweh your God all the days you live in the land that you are crossing the Jordan to possess (31.11-13).

And this echoes the role seen for written revelation in the law of the king.

---

[8] This point is perceptively made by P.D. Miller, '"Moses My Servant": The Deuteronomic Portrait of Moses', *Int* 41 (1987), pp. 245-55 (p. 249).

[9] See the summary argument of M.G. Kline, *Treaty of the Great King* (Grand Rapids, MI: Eerdmans, 1963), p. 101.

He should read it all the days of his life, that he may learn to fear Yahweh his God, by keeping and doing all the words of this law and these statutes (17.19).

These same themes of heeding God's word and fearing him are likewise evident in the passage that introduces the office of prophecy. 'Whoever does not heed my words which he (the prophet) shall speak in my name, I myself will require it of him' (18.19). The intended goal of heeding God's words is presupposed here by this solemn warning against failure to do so. Similarly the expectation of responding to the true prophet with solemn fear is presupposed by the concluding disclaimer that the disproven prophet need not evoke such fear (v. 22).[10]

This equivalence of canon and prophecy in their stated goals of engendering fear of and obedience to God suggests a close linkage. On the other hand, the distinction between canon and charismatic utterance would seem to presuppose that each revelational medium would have its own respective function. Perhaps Deuteronomy could be seen addressing this implicitly in the way it accentuates the *enduring* character of the written word, while indicating the *occasional* nature of the prophetic word. Thus, the written law must be read *'every seven years'* and passed on to the children *'as long as you live in the land'* (31.10,13). By contrast, the prophet is someone whom God *'will raise up for you'* (18.15). The expression 'raise up' is plainly linked in biblical usage to the transitory and timely responsiveness of God, as becomes clear in the book of Judges (see 2.16, 18; 3.9, 15).

Of course, as soon as the contrast between written revelation and prophecy is drawn in terms of permanent vs. occasional, some might be inclined to conclude from this that prophecy was understood here in Deuteronomy as nothing other than temporary revelation on its way to becoming permanent written revelation.[11] Yet Deuteronomy offers nothing in explicit support of this view, nor does the view seem to square with

---

[10] It is true that the root גור (*gur*) is used instead of the more common word for fear, ירא (*yara*), yet 33.8 parallels these two roots in a couplet. One might argue that the object of fear in Deut. 18.22 is the prophet rather than, as elsewhere, God. However, the Hebrew syntax is ambiguous, using (after the verb) the preposition מן (*min*) with the third masculine singular suffix, for which NEB proposes the translation, 'it', in reference apparently to the word spoken. But could the suffix not also refer to God? Or, rendering מן differently, could not the entire phrase be translated, 'You shall not fear *because of* him [i.e. the prophet]'?

[11] This would follow from the assumptions of those who would see the New Testament *charismata* as being limited to the revelatory function that led to and was eclipsed by the written canon.

presentations of the prophetic tradition in other parts of the Old Testament. While it is true that there is much prophetic utterance which eventuates in written canon,[12] it is also clear that the Old Testament bears witness to a number of manifestations of divinely inspired prophetic speech that do not eventuate in the canonical recording of the verbal content. Indeed we see this even within the traditions of Moses. We read in Numbers 11.25, 'Yahweh came down in a cloud and spoke to him (Moses), and took some of the spirit that was upon him and placed it upon the seventy elders; and when the spirit rested upon them, they prophesied'. Then, after this act of prophesying, *for which no record of contents is given*, there follows the 'unrecorded' prophesying of Eldad and Medad, the two men upon whom 'the spirit rested' after the rest of the elders had departed. And with memorable words, Moses checks the intent of his follower to discredit this prophesying that took place outside of his presence, 'Would that all Yahweh's people were prophets; that Yahweh would place his spirit upon them!' (11.29).

Other examples of 'unrecorded' prophetic utterance[13] include the two occasions when Saul encounters prophetic bands and begins prophesying among them (1 Sam 10.10–13 and 19.20–24).[14] The second occasion is actually a succession of three episodes in which two groups of messengers precede Saul in encountering the prophets and prophesying. Then there are the one hundred 'prophets of Yahweh' whom Obadiah hid from Jezebel and Ahab (1 Kgs 18.3–4), presumably to silence their prophesying.

---

[12] Indeed, a consensus of modern scholarship on Old Testament prophecy is that most of the prophetic 'writings' originated as speech and not as literature. See the review article by W.E. March, 'Prophecy', in *Old Testament Form Criticism* (ed. J.H. Hayes; San Antonio, TX: Trinity University Press, 1974), pp. 141–77. See also C. Westermann, *Basic Forms of Prophetic Speech* (trans. H.C. White; Philadelphia, PA: Westminster Press, 1967).

[13] Some helpful insights on this subject were provided by my colleague, John Christopher Thomas, who has taught a section on the Holy Spirit in the Old Testament as part of his seminary course, 'Theology of the Holy Spirit'.

[14] While my interest here is the theology within, rather than the history behind, the text, I would, nevertheless, note in passing that the conventional move to relate these references to an ecstatic (typically Canaanite) tradition of prophecy, disassociated from classical Israelite prophecy, so-called (see the classic statements S. Mowinckel, '"The Spirit" and "Word" in the Pre-exilic Reforming Prophets', *JBL* 53 [1934], pp. 199–227), is undoubtedly informed by the same presuppositions which have left modern scholarship so ill-prepared to perceive the integration here noted between canon and charisma. For a recent historical reconstruction of Israelite prophecy which stresses the continuity of a charismatic dimension, see K. van der Toorn, 'From Patriarchs to Prophets: A Reappraisal of Charismatic Leadership in Ancient Israel', *JNSL* 13 (1987), pp. 191–218.

Here again, we encounter evidence of inspired utterance, which finds no record in the canonical writings.[15]

In addition to all of this evidence against the idea that prophetic speech was ever seen as only a phase in a revelatory process which ended with inscripturated canon, there is the story in 2 Kings 22–23. Here, the prophetess Huldah is called upon to confirm that the law book found in the temple is indeed the word of God (22.14–20). It is remarkable how that in this instance, what could be regarded as an already-canonized revelation is seen to depend in some sense upon a subsequent charismatic revelation.

All of these examples serve to strengthen the impression that prophetic utterance, in addition to its role in generating certain portions of the written canon, was seen to have a place and function in Israel's revelatory experience that stood on its own alongside that of inscripturated revelation. Thus we come back again to this issue of Israel's theology of revelation, and there seems to be good reason to look once again to the book of Deuteronomy, where, as was previously noted, the place of written canon and the office of charismatic utterance are explicitly and emphatically set forth. Moreover it seems promising to look in particular to Deuteronomy's sustained reflection upon the theophany of Yahweh at Horeb (Deut. 4 and 5), since this is the decisive moment from which Deuteronomy is careful to trace both of these revelatory provisions.[16] So in reference to God's institution of prophecy we read,

> you asked of Yahweh your God at Horeb on the day of the assembly, 'Let me not hear again the voice of Yahweh my God, or see this great fire any more, so that I will not die'. Then Yahweh said to me, 'What they have spoken is good. I will raise up for them a prophet like you from among their kindred; I will put my words in his mouth, and he shall speak to them all that I command him' (18.16–18).

And in reference to Israel's canonical origins we read,

---

[15] Perhaps the 'sons of the prophets', mentioned throughout the Elisha cycle (2 Kgs 2.3; 4.1; 5.22; 6.1; 9.1), should be seen as another biblical testimony to prophesying which does not eventuate in recorded revelation, especially in view of the strong probability that the term 'sons' here denotes representatives of the prophetic vocation and not mere followers of a prophet. See J.R. Porter, 'בני־הנבאים', *JTS* 32 (1981), pp. 324–29.

[16] Whereas S. Talmon ('Revelation in Biblical Times', pp. 55, 65) has recently stressed that nowhere in 'ancient Hebrew literature does one find either a systematic or a comprehensive description of "revelation,"' he goes on to argue forcefully that the 'Sinai Theophany is the foundation upon which rests the subsequent biblical concept of revelation'.

> On the day you stood before Yahweh your God at Horeb... he announced to you his covenant, which he commanded you to perform, that is, the ten words; and he wrote them upon two stone tablets (4.10a, 13).

Thus it is perhaps appropriate to find light on the complementary relationship between prophecy and canon in Deuteronomy's extended reflection upon the revelation at Horeb, which is presented in chapters 4 and 5. I would suggest that this is precisely what we begin to find as we look to the passage that leads into the Horeb testimony. Moses says,

> See, I have taught you statutes and ordinances as Yahweh my God commanded me, to do accordingly in the land that you are entering to possess. Keep them and do them, for that is your wisdom and your understanding in the eyes of the peoples, who will hear of all these statutes and say, 'Surely this great people is a wise and understanding nation'. For what great nation is there that has a god so near to it as Yahweh our God is to us whenever we call to him? And what great nation is there that has statutes and ordinances so righteous as all this law that I am placing before you today? (4.5–8).

The last two verses in this passage seem especially significant. Verse 8 most emphatically points to the vital and incomparable character of Israel's *canon*, which is denoted here by the words 'statutes and ordinances so righteous'. Yet v. 7, with parallel wording, points to the equally vital and incomparable endowment of having 'a god so near'. And this latter phrase, I would suggest, relates implicitly to *prophecy*, for it is precisely this matter of divine nearness that Deuteronomy uses to characterize the nature and origin of prophetic revelation.[17] For chapter 4 moves quickly from here to recall when Israel *'came near* and stood' before Yahweh at Horeb (v. 11), where Yahweh, Moses reminds them, 'spoke to you out of the midst of the fire' (v. 12). Then chapter 5 quickly takes up Israel's initial reaction to the ensuing experience of divine nearness. Expressing to Moses their

---

[17] See L. Boadt, *Jeremiah 1–25* (Wilmington, DE: Michael Glazier, 1982), pp. 190–91, who is one scholar to recognize prophecy's central concern with divine nearness. Boadt links Deut. 4.7 with Jer. 23.23, which reads, 'Am I a God at hand, says Yahweh, and not a God afar off?' This latter verse falls within an extended discussion of prophecy. Here the fundamental association of prophecy with divine nearness is assumed, even while Jeremiah is wanting to uplift Yahweh's transcendence as well. Boadt goes on to point out the emphasis among Israelite prophets on divine nearness through the frequently used phrase, 'Yahweh is with us' (Isa. 7.14; Hos. 11.9; Amos 5.14). I am indebted to my graduate assistant, Marcia Anderson, for sharing this reference with me. P.D. Miller (*Deuteronomy* [Interpretation; Louisville, KY: John Knox, 1990], pp. 56–57), however, argues that divine nearness in Deut. 4.7 is identified with God's law, drawing support from Deut. 30.11–14. However, contra Miller, the nearness stressed in this latter passage seems to depend upon the immediacy of Moses' role of *speaking 'to you this day'* (v. 11).

extreme fear of being consumed by the divine presence, the Israelites say to Moses, 'You *go near* and hear all that Yahweh our God will say, then you yourself can speak to us all that Yahweh our God will speak to you; and we will heed and do it' (5.27). This is, of course the precise moment that 18.16–17 recalls as the originative point of Moses' prophetic role and also of Israel's prophetic office. Thus Deuteronomy grounds prophecy in this concern for an ongoing revelatory manifestation of divine nearness.

By lifting up the unique phenomenon of Yahweh's nearness, Deuteronomy 4.7 not only points in the direction of prophetic utterance but also begins to illuminate its distinctive role in Israel's revelatory experience. The occasional and responsive nature of prophetic revelation, which I noted earlier in connection with the verb 'raise up' and which is here reflected in the phrase, 'whenever we call to him',[18] is now shown to be vitally significant for its role in manifesting 'a god so near'.

Deuteronomy 4.7–8, then, seems to constitute an important testimony to the complementary relationship of written word and charismatic word. God's people are called here to recognize and to hold together the law 'so righteous', which is firmly and *continuously* manifest in their written canon, and the God 'so near', which is dynamically and *continually* manifest in Yahweh's prophetic revelation.[19]

This dialectic, I would propose, is a primary focus of chapter 4, which elaborates a call for Israel to remember the revelation of Horeb (vv. 9–40), for this is precisely where the *law so righteous* and the *God so near*, indeed where written word and charismatic word, were first experienced *together* by Israel. Attention is called to this union right away in v. 13, which says, 'He [Yahweh] announced to you his covenant, which he commanded you

---

[18] The 'occasional' force of 'whenever' is generated in Hebrew, of course, by the temporal use of the preposition before the infinitive construct. See *BDB*, p. 91. Whereas it is common to think of prophecy more in terms of a unilateral divine initiative than a divine response to Israel's call, it is important to realize that God's prophetic initiative through Moses, which is the very one emphasized in the book of Deuteronomy, comes as a response to the people's request. Furthermore divine responsiveness to Israel seems inherent in the usage of 'raise up' (e.g. Judg. 3.15) and in the whole context of the law setting forth prophecy in Deut. 18, since it is preceded by the prohibition of seeking the help of pagan mediaries. A later explicit example of God sending a prophet in response to Israel's cry can be seen in Judg. 6.7–8, 'When the people of Israel cried to Yahweh...Yahweh sent a prophet to the people of Israel'.

[19] See W. Brueggemann, *Creative Word: Canon as a Model for Biblical Education* (Philadelphia, PA: Fortress Press, 1982), pp. 113–17, who appreciates the dialectical relation of these verses along other lines of emphases, yet lines which do not seem irrelevant to the interplay that I have noted between canonical and charismatic revelation. I will comment on this later.

to perform, that is, the ten words; and he wrote them upon two stone tablets'. This *declaring* and *writing* of Yahweh, which would later give way to the *declaring* and the *writing* of Moses and those who would follow after him, clearly represent the written word and the charismatic word and the fact that they were seen to be held together from this foundational moment of Israel's covenant. Furthermore, the hortatory force of the entire recollection of Horeb in Deut. 4 and 5 reflects the concern to continue to hold together these revelatory aspects against what seems to be considered the primary threat and tendency of Israel to displace or diminish the *God-so-near* (the charismatic-word) side of the dialectic.

Thus v. 12, after recalling that, 'Yahweh spoke to you out of the midst of the fire', emphasizes, '*you were hearing* (שׁמע, *shama*) *the sound* (קול, *qol) of words*[20] but saw no form, *there was only a voice* (קול)'. Verses 15–24 then go on to develop an extended warning against Israel's choosing a form (i.e., an idol) to the neglect of the voice of God (vv. 15–24). Here the idolatrous form is contrasted with Yahweh's word, the dynamism and untamed nearness of which is represented and manifest in the fire.[21] This section begins,

> Take heed to yourselves, for you saw no form on the day Yahweh spoke to you out of the midst of the fire, beware lest you...make a graven image for yourselves, in the form of any figure... (vv. 15–16).

Similarly, the section ends,

> Take heed to yourselves, lest...you make a graven image in the form of anything which Yahweh your God has forbidden you. For Yahweh your God is a devouring fire (vv. 23–24).

Against Israel's temptation to displace Yahweh's lively presence with a lifeless form, this passage insists upon heeding Yahweh's word as manifested in the fire. For the second time we hear, 'You saw no form' (cf. v. 12),

---

[20] My translation here accentuates the presence of the participle. The emphasis upon *hearing*, not only here but throughout chs. 4 and 5 (e.g. 4.1 and 5.1), reminds one of Samuel Terrien's argument for the oracular orientation of Israelite faith (*The Elusive Presence* [New York: Harper & Row, 1978], pp. 112, 121, 172, 182, 201, 279)—an orientation which has also been noted in Pentecostalism. See M.B. Dowd, 'Contours of a Narrative Pentecostal Theology' (paper presented to the 15th Annual Meeting of the Society for Pentecostal Studies, 1985).

[21] One is reminded here of Jeremiah's later appropriation of this same imagery of fire to characterize the overpowering immanence of the prophetic word within himself (Jer. 20.8; also 23.29). One might also be reminded of the fire of Acts 2.

but, as v. 36 will later summarize the counterpoint, 'He let you see his great fire, and you heard his words out of the midst of the fire'.

It is important how that the next section (vv. 25–31) extends this same struggle between static form and dynamic word into the context of Israel's future history, where Yahweh's dynamic word, we know, was to be manifest through the institution of prophecy rather than direct theophany. In the future, we are told, Israel will face the same temptation. And if Israel makes 'a graven image in the form of anything' (v. 25), Yahweh promises to scatter Israel and make them 'serve gods of wood and stone, the work of men's hands, that neither see, nor hear' (vv. 26–27). While Yahweh was earlier seen representing his covenant in tablets of stone (v. 12), the people of Israel are here shown the bankruptcy of any attempt on their part ever to reduce divine revelation to stone or any other static form. Yet if the Israelites, after experiencing this bankruptcy, then seek Yahweh 'with all (their) heart and with all (their) souls', Yahweh promises (in line with 4.7—'whenever we call upon him') that Israel can 'return unto (על, *al*) Yahweh and hear (שמע, *shama*) his voice (קול, *qol*)' (vv. 29–30).[22] With parallel wording, the hearing of the voice here is linked to the hearing of the voice at Horeb (v. 12). And the 'God so near' at Horeb parallels the restoration to Yahweh's presence here. Quite appropriately, then, the ending of this section grammatically parallels the ending of the previous section on Horeb. The earlier conclusion declared, 'Yahweh your God is a devouring fire' (v. 24), while v. 31 concludes, 'Yahweh your God is a merciful God'.

The summary section which now follows (vv. 32–40) immediately brings together these elements of devouring fire and divine mercy: 'Did any people ever hear the voice of a god speaking out of the midst of the fire, as you have heard, and still live?' (v. 33). This statement is especially significant for the way it seems intentionally and once again to link the divine voice, which the preceding section had just projected into Israel's future, with the divine voice at Horeb. The inference is registered that through future prophetic word, as through past theophanic word, Israel is mercifully kept alive.

---

[22] My translation here brings out the important parallel with 4.12.

The summary pushes on to the decisive point that Israel's hearing (from heaven) and seeing (upon earth)[23] of Yahweh's words and deeds[24] have been provided *'in order that you might know* that Yahweh is God,[25] there is no other besides him' (v. 35). The point is repeated with imperative force and with accent on the present, post-Horeb moment:[26] 'Know therefore this day, and lay it to your heart that Yahweh is God in heaven above and on the earth beneath; there is no other' (v. 39). Here again, Moses is setting the revelation of Yahweh's dynamic word over against Israel's temptation to idolatry. Throughout the chapter we have seen how Israel is warned against substituting forms from earth and/or heaven (cf. vv. 17–19) for the living voice of God, substituting artificial 'gods so near', as it were, for the true manifestation of Yahweh's nearness. Now God's living word, which Israel hears and sees, is given as the basis of the revelation which rules out all of these other gods 'in heaven above and on the earth beneath'.[27]

Having affirmed the 'God-so-near' aspect of Yahweh's revelation against being displaced by a static form, this chapter concludes with a verse that turns attention to the other aspect of Yahweh's revelation, the 'law so righteous' (cf. vv. 7–8):

---

[23] 4.36 reads, *'Out of heaven*...he let you *hear* his voice...and *on earth* he let you *see* his great fire...'

[24] Both word and deed, which significantly are held together in the Hebrew term, דבר (*davar*, cf. Deut. 8.3), are stressed in this section. We see this in the appeal to both the voice, which is heard, and the fire, which is seen, at Horeb (see 4.36). Moreover, the 'fire which is seen' is augmented in this section with the 'signs and wonders' that Israel 'was shown' (vv. 34–35) in the exodus and that Israel *will see* in the future conquest of Canaan (v. 38). All of this suggests that Israel's hearing and seeing, and that Yahweh's dynamic word, are not being relegated to past history. In addition to this passage, Deut. 34.10–11 also makes a strong linkage between 'signs and wonders' and prophecy. Discussing all of the occurrences of the phrase 'signs and wonders' in the Hebrew Bible and pointing up the phrase's connection to prophecy is D.N. Fewell, *Circle of Sovereignty: A Story of Stories in Daniel 1–6* (Sheffield: Almond Press, 1988). That miraculous signs as well as words belonged to prophetic ministry is abundantly clear throughout the OT, especially in the Elijah and Elisha stories. See my study, *God Saves: Lessons from the Elisha Stories* (JSOTSup 95; Sheffield: JSOT Press, 1990).

[25] Cf. the comments on 'a biblical way of knowing' offered by J.D. Johns and C.B. Johns, 'Yielding to the Spirit: A Pentecostal Approach to Bible Study', *JPT* 1 (1992), pp. 109–34.

[26] It is not insignificant that this point directly follows a reference to *still future* manifestations of divine revelation in the conquest (v. 38). This post-Horeb generation is made responsible for what Israel has seen and heard in the past, because Israel is presently seeing and hearing, and will continue to see and hear, the same living word of Yahweh.

[27] In making this point, I am struck by how 1 John begins with emphasis upon the living word that has been heard and seen (1.3; cf. 2.27) and ends with a call to renounce idolatry. Is it possible that this oft-puzzling ending of 1 John is to be illuminated by the same theological move as we see in Deut. 4?

> Therefore you shall keep his statutes and his commandments, which I command you this day (v. 40).

Interestingly, this statement turns our attention to the *past* words of God but does so in relation to the *present* words of (the prophet) Moses. 'This day' involves emphasis upon the present moment, especially since it has just been heard in verse 39. It is as if the *nearness* of divine revelation needs to be reinforced even with respect to the 'law so righteous'. A look at chapter 5 would indicate that this suggestion is on target.

Chapter 5, which is well known for its presentation of the core text of Israel's 'law so righteous', the decalogue, surrounds this core text with special stress on the fact that these *written words* (cf. 5.22) were originally given and are now continuing to be given in relation to *spoken words* which address Israel in the present. The section preceding the decalogue (vv. 1–5) is especially concerned that the written word not be left in the past. Moses says,

> *Hear*, O Israel, *the statutes and the ordinances* that I *speak in your hearing this day*,... Yahweh our God made a covenant[28] with *us* in Horeb. Not with our fathers did Yahweh make this covenant, *but with us*, who are *all of us here alive this day* (vv. 1–3, emphasis mine).

The section following the decalogue (vv. 22–33) is especially concerned with future revelation beyond this initial giving of the written word. Moses recalls,

> These words Yahweh spoke to all your assembly at the mountain out of the midst of the fire, the cloud, and the thick darkness, with a loud voice; and he added no more. And he wrote them upon two stone tablets and gave them to me... and you said... if we hear the voice of Yahweh our God any longer, we shall die... Go near, and hear all that Yahweh our God says; and speak to us all that Yahweh our God speaks to you (vv. 22, 25, 27).

God's positive response to Israel's specific request here opens the way for further revelation, not only through Moses' prophetic role at Horeb (v. 31) but also through the ongoing prophetic institution that stems from this moment, as seen in 18.15–18. In this latter part of chapter 5, concern for the future is registered especially in God's express desire that Israel's initial fear at hearing his spoken word (vv. 23–26) would continue.

---

[28] Here the 'covenant', as in 4.13, is used specifically to introduce the decalogue.

Oh that they had such a mind as this *always*, to fear me and keep all my commandments, that it might go well with them and with their children forever! (v. 29).

Thus, Israel's fearing before Yahweh's revelation here in chapter 5 (see also v. 5) parallels Israel's hearing and seeing of Yahweh's revelation in chapter 4. Each of these responses to God's *dynamic* word are made crucial for keeping God's *enduring* word.

In summarizing our look at the Horeb testimony of Deuteronomy 4–5, it is clear that Israel's having of a 'god so near' (as Yahweh is through his ongoing, dynamic prophetic utterance) is an urgent theological concern in Deuteronomy. Chapter 4 shows this revelatory provision to be crucial in resisting the temptation to *draw near* to idolatrous images of stone. And chapter 5 shows this provision to be crucial in resisting the tendency for Israel to *draw away* from God's word, reducing it to past inscriptions of stone, which do not continue to live in Israel's present or future.

Charismatic word is thus shown here to have a vital, ongoing role alongside written word. Deuteronomy here seems to see the essential and distinct contribution of charismatic revelation in terms of the manifesting of God's nearness in a way that counters an idolatrous manufacturing of divine presence, on the one hand, and a legalistic distancing of divine word, on the other. Thus, without charismatic revelation, Israel is prone both to violate Yahweh's first word[29] and to antiquate his entire word.

In the light of the foregoing considerations, I would suggest some broader implications. The concerns I have traced in chapters 4 and 5 would seem to be significantly related to the thrust of Deuteronomy as a whole. In this pivotal book, Moses addresses his last words to the new generation. He is concerned that God's word, which had been given and heard *before*, be heard, seen and kept *now*—and not just now but on and on into Israel's future. Deuteronomy, it could perhaps be said, is itself a prophetic word on Israel's canon—a word through which God makes himself and his canon present to the new generation. Thus, Deuteronomy *remembers* the paradigmatic revelatory moment of Horeb where God both wrote and spoke his word, in order for this same revelatory synergism to be *manifest in the present and carried forward into the future*. Is it

---

[29] I refer here, of course, to the decalogue's command against idolatry, which is surely the *first command*, even though it is possible to be understood as the *second word*, the first being, 'I am Yahweh your God who brought you out of the land of Egypt, out of the house of bondage' (5.6). See W. Harrelson, *The Ten Commandments and Human Right* (Philadelphia, PA: Fortress Press, 1980), p. 7.

too much, then, to say that Deuteronomy in general and chapters 4 and 5 in particular offer a *past basis, present model and future projection of the complementary relationship* between written word and charismatic word in the Old Testament?

Reinforcement for this last point could perhaps be found in the very terminology by which Israel expressed some of its primary epistemological and revelatory concepts. I would offer here a couple of suggestions that might merit further exploration. An especially important term for God's revelation is דבר (*davar*). While this is commonly translated as 'word', it is well known that it expresses much more than our term 'word', often requiring the translation 'event'. This vocabulary would accord with the argument above for seeing divine revelation as bringing closely together the notions of written word, spoken word, even manifested or embodied word. Complementing this, an important term for Israel's knowing is ידע (*yada*). Here again, the common translation, 'to know', falls short of the Hebrew notion, for our term 'know' points to the conceptualization of an object, whereas the Hebrew term resists such a subject-object dichotomy and points more to the actualization of a relationship between knower and known.[30] Again the Hebrew terminology seems to correspond in a striking way to the foregoing case for seeing Israel's apprehension of divine revelation as including ongoing relationship to the manifest presence of God. Thus God's word (דבר) and Israel's knowing (ידע), terms which come together in Deuteronomy 4.35, are terms which appear to correspond profoundly to one another and to the dynamic, integrative paradigm of revelation pointed to above.

A few concluding remarks are now offered. I have sought to show that Deuteronomy exhibits an urgent concern to observe a dynamic integration of canon and charisma in Israel's ongoing revelatory experience— a concern developed in Deuteronomy 4 and 5 and expressed most succinctly in the theological juxtaposing of 'a god so near' and 'a law so righteous'. Walter Brueggemann, as noted earlier, has appreciated the dialectical relation between these theological affirmations in Deut. 4.7–8. He sees this reference holding together a 'delicate and difficult balance' that rejects a 'God-less Torah (legalism)', on the one hand, and a 'Torah-less God (romanticism)' on the other.[31] In view of the foregoing discussion, I would suggest that the tension be posed in terms of a Spirit-less Word

---

[30] See Johns and Johns, 'Yielding to the Spirit'.
[31] Brueggemann, *Creative Word*, pp. 113–17.

(rationalism), on the one hand, and a Word-less Spirit (subjectivism), on the other. This may bring matters closer to home in seeing what is at stake in holding together the canonical-charismatic revelatory paradigm heretofore considered.[32] Obviously, to put the issue this way is to point forward from the text of Deuteronomy to the theological and hermeneutical concerns of Pentecostalism—a move which may not appear to be so overdrawn when one considers the historical and theological connections between the Sinai event (the Horeb theophany) in the Old Testament and the Pentecost event in the New Testament.[33]

Within this tension of canon and charisma—a tension that the hermeneutical traditions of modern Western theology have found ways to eliminate—Pentecostals must find their way. This tension will provide no easy place to stand—Sinai didn't either—but it just may provide the way for a new voice to be heard, one that we all need to hear.

I return at last to my starting point, where I suggested that my look at the final form of the text needed little justification in this day when longstanding formulations and the forms of study which they have represented have lost their absolute sway. We talk of paradigm shifts, but the biblical texts that we study would undoubtedly pose such a matter in terms of idolatry. Aren't we now witnessing the crumbling of our idols? And I refer not just to the canons of historical criticism but even to our claims upon the *final form* of the text. Would not Moses warn us against even these, when he says, 'Take heed to yourselves, since you saw no form on the day that Yahweh spoke to you at Horeb out of the midst of the fire' (Deut. 4:15)?

While some would want to read our present hermeneutical revolution in terms of the triumph of deconstructionism, the biblical texts which we study would bear witness to the ultimate deconstructionist, Yahweh, whose word (דבר) deconstructs *all* of our 'final' forms—even the enterprise of deconstruction itself, which makes an idol of the smashing of idols (cf. Jehu in 2 Kgs 10). Could all the deconstructing which is going on in contemporary Western hermeneutics be a disclosure of what we

---

[32] I would add that the dialectical relation between canon and charisma, between prescribed righteousness and divine nearness, and between Torah and God, suggests an interpenetration rather than a dichotomization of terms, so that, for example, canon can be seen to manifest divine nearness (cf. Deut. 30.11-14) and charismatic revelation can be seen to manifest prescribed righteousness (cf. 2 Kgs 22.15-17), but only as each is inseparably related to the other.

[33] On this see R. Stronstad, *The Charismatic Theology of St. Luke* (Peabody, MA: Hendrickson, 1984), pp. 58-62.

are essentially and finally capable of doing apart from a word which truly comes forth from the mouth of a living God? Unfortunately, this question of our deconstructive potential has implications not just for our literature but also for our politics. Within this context, I would want to approach the final form of the text, but in the light of the consuming fire. Let every reader[34] decide for him or herself whence this fire comes.[35]

---

[34] In place of 'reader' I could have put 'worshipper', for aren't we all? And hasn't the time come for us all to be more honest about what it is or who it is that we are worshipping in our reading and in our writing?

[35] I gratefully acknowledge the help of my colleagues in the preparation of this study, especially John Christopher Thomas, Cheryl Bridges Johns, Steven J. Land and James M. Beaty for their theological insight and their spiritual discernment and support.

CHAPTER FOUR

YIELDING TO THE SPIRIT:
A PENTECOSTAL APPROACH TO GROUP BIBLE STUDY*

Jackie David Johns and Cheryl Bridges Johns**

What, if anything, should be the distinctive characteristics of Pentecostal group Bible study? Bible study materials published by Pentecostals seem to assume they are Pentecostal because they contain frequent references to the baptism of the Holy Spirit, the gifts of the Spirit, and Acts 2.4.[1] This assumption implies that one has only to take theologically conservative, Scripture-based curricula, remove any objectionable material, add to it the doctrinal distinctives of Pentecostalism and the results will be Pentecostal Bible study.[2] It is ironic that a movement that laid claim to the restoration of biblical Christianity with a corresponding denunciation of creeds should so easily take an essentially creedal approach to evaluating study materials.

There exists among Pentecostals a certain inclination toward a false dichotomy between content and process. The dichotomy is frequently expressed in terms of the eternal nature of Scripture and the supposed temporal nature of methods. Methods are considered value-free tools which do not affect the truths they mediate and therefore may be borrowed from any number of sources, the social sciences being currently favored. Consequently, Pentecostals have failed to consider the implications of their dynamic belief system for issues of epistemology. The end result of this failure is that we may actually be using methods which negate

---

* First published in the *Journal of Pentecostal Theology* 1 (1992), pp. 109–34.
** Jackie David Johns (PhD, Southern Baptist Theological Seminary) is Professor of Discipleship and Christian Formation at the Pentecostal Theological Seminary, Cleveland, TN USA. Cheryl Bridges Johns (PhD, Southern Baptist Theological Seminary is Professor of Discipleship and Christian Formation at the Pentecostal Theological Seminary, Cleveland, TN USA.
[1] This generalization is based upon examinations of Sunday school and elective curricula published by four leading North American Pentecostal denominations: Assemblies of God, Church of God (Cleveland, Tennessee), Pentecostal Holiness, and Church of God of Prophecy.
[2] Several Pentecostal denominations are currently editing and publishing Sunday school curricula developed by evangelical publishers such as David C. Cook.

the very message we are attempting to communicate. We may be operating out of a hermeneutic that is inconsistent with or even in opposition to our very identity. Specifically, our methods may be militating against the experiential and relational dimensions of our faith.

Pentecostals are only now beginning to formulate a hermeneutic which takes seriously the dynamics of the Pentecostal faith. We have found the rationalism of twentieth-century evangelical Christianity to be an inadequate vehicle for passing on a faith which honors the active presence of the Holy Spirit in the contemporary world. Walter Hollenweger has highlighted this difficulty and noted that Pentecostal theologizing has often been ignorant of its own distinctive ethos.[3] William MacDonald has also highlighted the dynamic, oral witness of Pentecostalism in which testimonies of encounters with the living word are affirmed in relation to the written word, which serves as a check.[4] Michael Dowd has aptly described the dilemma facing Pentecostals attempting to formulate a Pentecostal hermeneutic: 'When the only "language game" in town is rationalism it is not hard to understand why an experiential, relational, emotional and moral faith would choose not to play by the rules'.[5]

Dowd called for a Pentecostal approach to Scripture that would incorporate both the mind and the affective-spiritual dimensions of existence. Francis Martin added that it is only through 'exegesis of the Spirit' that true understanding and appropriation of Scripture is possible.[6] While dialogue and study are rapidly emerging,[7] it is evident that much work is yet to be done to clarify the relationship between Pentecostal beliefs and Pentecostal processes.

The objective of this paper is to contribute to the ongoing discussion a paradigm for a Pentecostal approach to small group Bible study. We have

---

[3] In particular see W.I. Hollenweger, 'Creator Spiritus', *Theology* 81 (1978), pp. 32–40, and his 'Flowers and Songs: A Mexican Contribution to Theological Hermeneutics', *International Review of Mission* 60 (1971), pp. 232–44.

[4] W.G. MacDonald, 'Pentecostal Theology: A Classical Viewpoint', in R. Spittler (ed.), *Perspectives on the New Pentecostalism* (Grand Rapids: Baker Book House, 1976), pp. 58–74.

[5] M.B. Dowd, 'Contours of a Narrative Pentecostal Theology and Practice' (paper presented to the 15th Annual Meeting of the Society for Pentecostal Studies, 1985).

[6] F. Martin, 'Spirit and Flesh in the Doing of Theology' (paper presented to the 15th Annual Meeting of the Society for Pentecostal Studies, 1985).

[7] Note J.K. Byrd, 'Formulation of a Classical Pentecostal Homiletic in Dialogue with Contemporary Protestant Homiletics' (PhD dissertation, The Southern Baptist Theological Seminary, 1990), and 'Paul Ricoeur's Hermeneutical Theory and Pentecostal Proclamation', *Pneuma* 15.2 (1993), pp. 203–14. Also, R.D. Israel, D.E. Albrecht, and R.G. McNally, 'Pentecostals and Hermeneutics: Texts, Rituals and Community', *Pneuma* 15.2 (1993), pp. 137–61.

attempted to build this paradigm upon a Pentecostal epistemology[8] that is grounded first in the biblical understanding of coming 'to know' God and second in a dialogue with the epistemology of *praxis*.

Yada, the Paraclete, and the Scriptures: Basis for a Pentecostal Epistemology

It was suggested above that contrary to the experiential and relational nature of their faith, Pentecostals routinely dichotomize the content of Scripture from the learning processes which are reflected in Scripture. Such a dichotomy fails to see the unity between the God who is to be known and how that God wishes to be known. However, Scripture itself is clear that the two cannot be disjoined. Their unity may be clearly seen in the meaning of 'to know' in both the Old and New Testaments, the Johannine portrait of the Paraclete as teacher, the nature of the Church as covenant community, and the nature of Scripture as the word of God. In these the foundation for a Pentecostal epistemology is established.

Yada: *A Way of Knowing*

There exists in the Old and New Testaments a relatively consistent understanding of how one comes 'to know'. This understanding is rooted in Hebrew thought and may be contrasted with Greek approaches to knowledge. In the Old Testament the Hebrew word for 'to know' is *yada* (ידע). In general *yada* is treated as knowledge which comes through experience.[9] O.A. Piper has added that this knowledge implies an awareness of the specific relationship in which the knower stands with the object being experienced so that 'full comprehension of the object manifests itself in

---

[8] We have chosen the phrase 'Pentecostal epistemology' in order to convey our belief that there is an approach to knowledge that is consistent with Pentecostal faith, experience, and practice. What follows is an attempt to describe such an approach. It is not our intention to imply that Pentecostal experience gives rise to a special form of knowledge unavailable outside of the baptism in the Holy Spirit. As the text reveals, our true concern is for a biblical epistemology, an approach to knowing God that is consistent with the character of his personal self-disclosure as offered in Scripture.

[9] J.P. Lewis, 'ידע', in R.L. Harris (ed.), *Theological Wordbook of the Old Testament* (Chicago: Moody Press, 1980), I, pp. 366–68. It is not our intention to imply the existence of a static definition for the term *yada*. As with all literature, precise meaning is determined by context. James Barr has highlighted the diverse meanings *of yada* in the Old Testament. See his *Comparative Philology and the Text of the Old Testament* (Oxford: Clarendon Press, 1968), pp. 19–23. However, the evidence is overwhelming that the Hebrews operated out of an epistemology which emphasized encounter and response.

action which corresponds to the relationship apprehended...[10] Thomas Groome has concluded that *yada* is knowing 'more by the heart than by the mind, knowing that arises not by standing back from in order to look at, but by active and intentional engagement in lived experience'.[11] It is significant that *yada* was used as an euphemism for lovemaking and that the past participle of *yada* was used for a good friend or confidant.

This dynamic, experiential, relational knowledge stands in stark contrast to the Greek approach to knowledge characteristic of the word *ginoskein* (γινώσκειν), which involved a standing back from something in order objectively to 'know it'. In comparing *ginoskein* to *yada*, Rudolf Bultmann states, 'the OT usage is much broader than the Greek, and the element of objective verification is less prominent than that of detecting or feeling or learning by experience'.[12]

With this understanding, if a person knew God, he or she was encountered by one who lived in the midst of history and who initiated a covenant relationship which called for a response of the total person. Knowledge of God, therefore, was not measured by the information one possessed but by how one was living in response to God. A person was ignorant or a fool not because of the lack of awareness of facts about God but rather because of a failure to do the will of God.[13] Ignorance, then, implies guilt as Bultmann explains:

> Thus knowledge has an element of acknowledgement. But it also has an element of emotion, or better, of movement of will, so that ignorance means guilt as well as error... To know Him or His name is to confess or to acknowledge Him, to give Him honor and to obey His will.[14]

---

[10] A. Piper, 'Knowledge', *IDB*, III, pp. 42–48.
[11] T. Groome, *Christian Religious Education* (New York: Harper & Row, 1981), p. 141.
[12] R. Bultmann, 'γινώσκω', *TDNT*, I, pp. 689–719.
[13] G.J. Botterweck, 'ידע', *TDOT*, V, pp. 448–81.
[14] Bultmann, 'γινώσκω', p. 698. In his treatment of Old Testament theology from a canonical context, Brevard Childs also reached similar conclusions concerning knowledge of God in the Old Testament.
   To know God is to know his will. In the Old Testament to know God is not a mystical experience or merely an inter-personal relationship. Nor is it a feeling of spirituality. Rather, the knowledge of God is defined throughout as obedience to his will which has a content... Knowledge of his person and will are identical. and both are grounded in his self-revelation. To lack knowledge of God is described as disobeying his will and therefore evokes his anger (*Old Testament Theology in Canonical Context* [Philadelphia: Fortress Press, 1985], p. 51).

The New Testament, while employing Greek terms, continues the Hebraic understanding of 'to know'.[15] Knowing the Lord is still viewed as the result of encountering God in a manner that results in submission to his will but with the focus being on knowing God through Jesus Christ. To know God requires obedient and grateful acknowledgment of the deeds and commandments of Jesus. Therefore, 'Christian knowledge is not a fixed possession but develops in the life of the Christian as lasting obedience and reflection'.[16]

John's first epistle provides a rich illustration of the epistemological grounding of the New Testament. He seems intentionally to play against the Greek understanding of knowledge and attacks its implications for the Christian life, that is, that it is possible to know Jesus without conforming to him. For John, knowledge of God is grounded in a loving relationship (1 Jn 4.3, 16, 20), and this knowledge is manifest through obedience to the known will of God (2.3–5; 5.1–5). God is known through his entering into human history as flesh, and knowledge of him is inseparable from the manifestation of his lordship over life (5.6–12). Thus we know that we know him if we obey his commands (2.3).

The Paraclete: A Means of Knowing

If the first Johannine epistle describes the nature of knowing God through Christ Jesus, the Paraclete sayings in the Gospel of John describe the means of attaining that knowledge. There are five sayings (14.16–17, 25–26; 15.26–27; 16.7–11, 12–15), each of which could be isolated as literary units but could also fit within the larger text of the 'Final Discourse' of Jesus to form a homogeneous and coherent unit. Raymond Brown has demonstrated that Jesus and the Paraclete represent a tandem relationship of two salvific figures in the pattern of Moses and Joshua, and Elijah and Elisha.[17] The Paraclete was understood to be a 'second Jesus' through whom Jesus was to be experienced. Eskil Franck has further demonstrated that the primary character of these sayings was didactic rather than forensic as is often assumed.[18] The Johannine portrait of Jesus as rabbi or teacher is

---

[15] Piper, 'Knowledge', p. 44.
[16] Bultmann, 'γινώσκω', p. 707.
[17] R.E. Brown, 'The Paraclete in the Fourth Gospel', *NTS* 13 (1967), pp. 120–24.
[18] E. Franck, *Revelation Taught: The Paraclete in the Gospel of John* (Lund: Gleerup, 1985), pp. 13–68.

thus extended to the Paraclete so that Jesus offered to the disciples what might be called a pneumatic epistemology. He and the Father would be known through the teaching activity of the Spirit.

Three pneumatic epistemological themes, relevant to this present study, emerge from the Final Discourse.[19] *First, the Spirit would teach by bringing experiential knowledge of God.* Jesus taught that to know him was to know the Father (Jn 14.7) and that when the Paraclete came the disciples would know that Christ is in the Father, they are in Christ, and Christ is in them (14.20). Thus, the indwelling of the Paraclete would actualize the indwelling of the Father and Son and fulfill the prayer of Christ for the unity of the disciples and their unity with the Godhead (17.21). The role of the Spirit would be to cause believers to know the Lord God in the sense of knowing by intimate encounter.

Secondly, the central focus of the didactic function of the Paraclete was that the Spirit would communicate the words of Jesus. In the second Paraclete saying (14.25–26) Jesus asserted that the Paraclete would teach the disciples all things and remind them of everything he had said. These teaching and reminding activities of the Spirit would center around the historic words of Jesus. The task of the Spirit would be to bring the fullness of those teachings to the consciousness of the disciples. This would be a representation of his words in a living manner so that his commands would be freshly and appropriately applied to the experiences of the disciples.[20]

According to the final Paraclete saying (16.12–15) the Spirit would speak after Christ his ongoing message to the disciples. The content of the ongoing message would certainly be consonant with the historic life and teachings of Christ but would not be limited to them. The Spirit would bring new information, information the disciples would need to continue to exist in the sphere of all truth. This teaching activity would center on the glorification of Christ by communicating, or literally 'making known', that which is 'of Christ', that which belongs to Christ and the Father.

The thrust of both passages was to assure the disciples of the continuation of the teaching ministry of Jesus in spite of his physical removal from them. The words of Christ were of utmost importance and the Paraclete

---

[19] For a more thorough treatment of the teaching ministry of the Holy Spirit see J.D. Johns, 'The Pedagogy of the Holy Spirit according to the Early Christian Tradition' (EdD dissertation, The Southern Baptist Theological Seminary, Louisville, Kentucky, 1987), now available on www.amazon.com.

[20] Brown, 'Paraclete', p. 129.

as a personal presence would assure proper reception of and response to them; both to the glory of Christ. But the true significance of the words was that they were of Jesus and of the Father.

Thirdly, the Spirit would serve as an internal impetus for the standards of relational life in Christ. In the discourses, the teachings of Jesus were refined into the central command to love one another (13.34; 15.9, 10, 12, 17). Love was the essential characteristic of a disciple and the motivational force behind obedience to Jesus (14.15, 21, 23; 15.13). Love as expressed in obedience was to be the disciples' means of communion with the Father (14.21, 23; 16.27). Even the relationship of Jesus and the Father was described in terms of love (14.31; 15.10). Further, the witness of the disciples before the world was dependent upon their love for each other (13.35; 14.31). In as much as these functions (i.e. obedience to Jesus, communion with the Father and bearing witness) were attributed to the Paraclete, it follows that the Spirit would serve to actualize within the disciples this new standard of living.[21] Thus the Spirit brought communion with God and the corresponding knowledge of God was linked to knowledge of and loving relationship with the members of the new covenant.

The Covenant Community: Context for Knowing

The covenant community forms the context for encounter with God and the context for interpretation of the resulting transformation. The covenant which God offers to people is a covenant to be the people of God. He dwells in the midst of his people so that the church, being grounded in covenant relations, operates within an epistemology not of detachment and manipulation (which is a result of operating only with facts and principles) but rather *of participation and accountability*.[22] The community of the Spirit gives a corporate history to the knowing of God, and it judges and is judged by individual experiences. There is therefore the avoidance

---

[21] Likewise, the Spirit may be linked to the fulfillment of the teachings of Jesus concerning joy (15.11; 16.20–22) and peace (14.27; 16.33). These were gifts from Jesus through his words (15.11; 16.33) and presence (16.22, 33) and hence, it may be deduced, would be received through the Spirit.

[22] For an insightful treatment of a relational epistemology, see P. Palmer, *To Know as We Are Known: A Spirituality of Education* (New York: Harper & Row, 1983). Palmer calls for a departure from the 'information transmission' model to one that is grounded in an epistemology that honors the personalness of the knowing process. In such a context education becomes spiritual formation in which there is community and obedience to the truth.

of privatized subjectivism on the one hand and totalitarian objectivism on the other.

Bible study in this context is an avenue of communion with God and with others. It is not to be merely an exercise of individual interpretation in which the private self reigns. In the community of the Spirit there is no room for private knowledge as expressed in the slogan 'one truth for you, another for me, and never mind the difference'. Neither is there room for 'objectivist tyranny' in which concern for the *Truth* gives rise to the slogan 'there is one truth for me, the same for you, and I mind very much the difference'.

Knowledge, therefore, in the community of the Spirit is both a desire to know and to be known. As we are known by that which we desire to know we advance to the very heart of truth. This type of knowledge is frightening. Like the Israelites at Sinai, we are inclined to shrink from being known and exposed for who we are in light of who God is. However, the Holy Spirit offers to us a personal but corporate hope of transformation and relationship with the one who knows us and yet loves us, so that we can offer to others a relationship that both knows and loves.

Role of Scripture

Having discussed the nature, means, and context for knowing God, there remains the question of the place of Scripture in the process. Pentecostals are 'people of the Book'. Their allegiance to the Bible as the word of God and therefore the authority for Christian living is unwavering. Like Evangelicals they proclaim with Donald Bloesch that their

> supreme authority is the Word of God revealed and embodied in Jesus Christ and attested and recorded in sacred Scripture. This Word is not simply a past event but a living reality that meets us as we encounter Scripture and the kerygmatic proclamation of the Church. It cannot be reduced to words, but it is communicated primarily through words.[23]

However, for many Evangelicals and Pentecostals, encounter with God has a tendency to be climaxed at some faith experience so that subsequent use of the Bible takes on a utilitarian goal of building an objective support system for that experience. This relegation of experience to the

---

[23] D.O. Bloesch, *Essentials of Evangelical Theology* (San Francisco: Harper & Row, 1979), p. 239.

past enables them easily to dichotomize Bible study into aims of knowing (intellectually), aims of feeling (emotional), and aims of doing (volitional). While many scholars have attempted to balance these goals, a common result is to place emphasis on one above the others.[24] For some the Bible becomes primarily an answer book for the curious questions of life, a source of intellectual stability in a world often void of meaning. For others, there has been a tendency to spiritualize the Bible as a means of communion with God, that is, a feeling. In that atmosphere it is possible to downplay the objective aspect of the word of God, taking away its historical dimension and replacing it with mystical individualism.[25] For others the Bible is reduced to serving as a motivational textbook on Christian lifestyle. It is either a rulebook or a course on principles for Christian living rather than the authentic word of God that gives rise to continued transformation. Each of these approaches fails to appreciate the essential nature of Scripture as eternal word of God.

The model offered here takes seriously the notion that Scripture is the word of God, not word about God nor even word from God (if 'from' implies distance from God). God is always present in his word. The Spirit who breathed upon the prophets to speak forth the word continues to abide with the word. Inscripturated word is 'out of' God only in the sense that it proceeds from God but never in the sense that it can be cut off from God. The word is always holy unto the Lord. Yet in it God is reaching out to touch the profane. In Scripture God offers himself to humanity, inviting creation to know the creator. It expresses his nature and will in the 'language' of humanity. Therefore, Scripture is an objective, conceptual fountain out of which knowledge of God flows. It is the standard by which experience is to be interpreted and judged. But the study of Scripture must always be approached as sacred encounter with God.

---

[24] The best example of trying to balance the approach is no doubt F.B. Edge's *Teaching for Results* (Nashville: Broadman Press, 1956). This work has remained in print for over 35 years.

[25] John Wesley seemed to have achieved a balance between the subjective-objective nature of biblical interpretation. For Wesley, 'Scripture can only be understood through the same Spirit whereby it was given' (see his suggestions for Bible study in the 'Preface' to *Explanatory Notes upon the Old Testament* [1765], I, p. viii). Wesley gave admonition to 'Read the Scripture, with the single purpose of knowing the whole will of God, and with a fixed determination to do that will'. There must be prompt and total obedience to the light of Scripture. Early Methodism proceeded upon this conviction. The bands and societies therefore were places where believers were closely examined as to how they were measuring up to the light of God's word.

Summation

In summary, both the OT and the NT make it clear that in order to know God one has to be related to God in such a manner as to live in response to his known will. One does not move, however, from theory (ideas, facts about God which have been derived from an objectification of material relating to God) to practice (decision to follow God's commands). This approach employs a Greek epistemology rather than a biblical one and negates the covenantal grounding of our knowledge which encompasses the total person. One therefore learns about God by encountering God and responding appropriately out of that encounter. The Holy Spirit is the presence of God, the means of encounter. The church as community of the Spirit forms the context of the encounter. The Scriptures are objective, conceptual, personal word of God and as such govern the processes by which he is known. Utilizing Johannine imagery, one is instructed by the Spirit in all things, and this instruction comes via divine-human encounter as defined and facilitated by the Scriptures. Furthermore, this instruction takes place within the context of covenant relationships governed by love.[26]

A Dialogue with Praxis

Praxis has come to be a common epistemological term in the field of Christian education, especially among those who are within the tradition of liberation theology.[27] Basically, the term means 'reflection-action' and expresses a linking of knowing and doing. Current usage represents a move from the traditional theory-to-practice paradigm. A *praxis* epistemology shares many characteristics with the process of knowing inherent in the meaning of *yada*, yet it fails to capture some of the vital dimensions

---

[26] James Loder speaks of knowledge which is convictional, meaning that one is transformed in the knowing event. This transformation occurs when 'the Holy Spirit transforms all transformations of the human spirit'. See *The Transforming Moment* (New York: Harper & Row, 1981), p. 92. For Loder such a knowing event follows a fourfold pattern involving conflict, scanning, release, and mundane ecstasy and verification. Christ is the one who initiates, mediates, and concludes the process. Convictional knowing experiences are regulatory of both the self and the world and call forth further transformation. These experiences are integrated into our personal histories and become interpretive keys for any future knowing.

[27] Representatives of a *praxis* approach to Christian education would be Thomas Groome, who has already been cited, and also Daniel Schipani, the author of *Religious Education Encounters Liberation Theology* (Birmingham, AL: Religious Education Press, 1988).

found in the biblical pattern. We will attempt a dialogue between *praxis* and *yada*, lifting up areas of commonality and areas of divergence. Finally, we will discuss how insights from *praxis* as a way of knowing can be integrated into a Pentecostal approach to Bible study.

Historical Overview of the Term

In order for one to understand *praxis* there must first be a conscious move away from dichotomizing theory and practice, and toward seeing them as twin moments of the same activity that are united dialectically. Instead of theory leading to practice, theory becomes, or is seen in, the reflective moment in *praxis*. Theory arises from *praxis* to yield further *praxis*.

Aristotle saw *praxis* as a way of knowing which was basically related to one's reflective engagement in a social situation.[28] It was one of three ways of knowing, the other two being *theoria* (θεωρία) and *poesis* (ποίησις). *Theoria* was the highest form of knowledge which utilized only the intellect. *Praxis* merged thought with doing in the sense of interaction with society. *Poesis* merged thought with making, for example, the artisan's shaping of material objects. While *praxis* was beneficial and useful for moral training, it failed to allow one to attain the highest form of wisdom, *sophia* (σοφία). Only *theoria* could do this. Therefore, Aristotle retained the essence of the Platonic system which elevated pure reason above the material realm.

G.W.F. Hegel re-introduced the term *praxis* in modern times. Hegel took the term and adapted it to the Enlightenment's emphasis on critical reason. He placed theory and practice together in a manner even more dialectical than Aristotle. Hegel saw *praxis* in relation to *Geist*, the all-powerful and encompassing Spirit which guided the universe toward the actualization of itself. *Praxis*, according to Hegel, became the *praxis* of *Geist*. Human knowing was not realized by speculative theorizing apart from the world but rather was attained through reflection on and participation in the *praxis* of *Geist* within history.

Groome points out that Hegel's understanding of *praxis* left little room for self-initiated active/reflective engagement in the world. Knowledge comes instead by phenomenological observation of *Geist's* activity in

---

[28] The following brief historical overview of *praxis* is a condensed version of a more detailed account given by Groome. See *Religious Education*, in particular ch. 7, 'In Search of a Way of Knowing'.

the world. Thus, Hegel remained functionally caught in a Greek theory-centered manner of knowing.[29]

Karl Marx was influenced by Hegel's concept of *praxis*. He, however, put humankind in the place of *Geist*, calling for humans to influence and shape their own history. Thus, *praxis* became totally an endeavor within nature, devoid of any transcendent authority. Human critical reflection and action would be sufficient for the ongoing revolution of social reality.

Paulo Freire is a Catholic humanist who has most recently popularized *praxis* as an educational term. He has worked extensively in Latin America and around the world developing a *praxis* approach to education, both secular and religious. For Freire, *praxis* is necessary for a person to be fully human.

Freire bases a great deal of his understanding of *praxis* upon Marx. He divides the world into economic categories and calls for human activity in transforming these structures. People are to be active subjects in the historical process, not passive objects caught in a world in which they have no control.[30] While Freire considers himself a Christian, he leaves most of the responsibility for *praxis* up to humanity. At best God is a subjective presence in the historical process.[31]

The Limitations and Problems of Praxis

There are problems and limitations with a *praxis* epistemology, especially when compared to a biblical understanding of knowledge. In general these are grounded in its origin in Hellenistic thought. In spite of all efforts to join theory and practice into a singular moment, there remains in *praxis* a fundamental dualism between matter and reason. Because of this dualism, *praxis* assumes an unbridgeable distance between the knower and the known. The entire system elevates theory (in the form of reasoning

---

[29] Groome, *Religious Education*, p. 166.

[30] Freire is critical of Pentecostalism. He sees it as a religion which is ahistorical and passive, fostering cultures of silence and dependency. For Freire the process of concientization would move one beyond Pentecostalism toward a less 'opiate religion'. See his 'Education, Liberation and the Church', *Religious Education* 79.4 (1984), pp. 524–36. See also C.B. Johns, *Pentecostal Formation: A Pedagogy among the Oppressed* (JPTS, 2; Sheffield: JSOT Press, 1993). This monograph brings into dialogue the ideas of Freire and the Pentecostal faith.

[31] P. Freire, 'Letter to a Theology Student', *Catholic Mind* 70.7 (Sept. 1972), pp. 6–8.

skills) above all other forms of knowledge.[32] This objectification of others is an unavoidable aspect of this knowledge and the power of transformation is of necessity grounded in the 'spirit' of the individual.

Praxis is therefore an insufficient means of knowing God and achieving human transformation. Human reflection-action, while important, is distorted and may become self-serving, and thereby hinder true knowledge of God. Without an authority beyond the self that transcends and even negates reflection-action, we are left, in spite of our worthy intentions for the transformation of society, with sinful *praxis*. In contrast, there is within the meaning of *yada* a basis for the grounding of the self in a personal God who defines the nature and outcome of the knowing event. This grounding does not relegate human knowing to the passive posture found in Hegel's paradigm. Neither does it limit God to the role of a subjective partner in human historical processes.

Another problem with *praxis* springs from our inability, also due to sin, truly to know ourselves as subjects in the world in which we live. Transformation of the knower has to occur before that person can contribute to the righteous transformation of the world. This transformation requires the knowing person to be known and exposed and changed, thereby becoming an object as well as an active subject in the historical process. There is no room for passiveness or resistance toward critical reflection upon the world. If the basic nature of persons remains unchanged and human *praxis* remains separated from responsiveness to revelation, a self-serving, sinful *praxis* will emerge. This seems to be the case in histories of revolutions which began with transforming *praxis* but soon became hardened by dogmatic ideology which prevented further *praxis*.

While Pentecostals have historically emphasized that we are the objects of God's transforming grace, we have often neglected to acknowledge that via transformation we become partners with God in the redemptive process. We have failed to respond appropriately in obedience as historical subjects.[33] The solution may well rest in the integration of *praxis* methodology into the epistemology of *yada*.

---

[32] C.B. Johns, 'Affective Conscientization: A Pentecostal Response to Paulo Freire' (paper presented to the 21st Annual Meeting of the Society for Pentecostal Studies, 1991).

[33] Theodore Runyon and others have pointed out that John Wesley's concept of sanctification included an anthropology which saw humans as active agents in life and as partners with God in the redemptive process. For Wesley, Christianity was a social religion set in a world that was to be critically analyzed and acted upon. He strongly criticized the mystics for their advice to cease outward action and to withdraw from the world. See

The Integration of Praxis with Yada

Realization of the inherent limitations of *praxis* has caused some liberation theologians to speak of an 'epistemological break' which 'consists in the existential and historical following that yields a *praxis* knowing which is distinct from "natural understanding" as well as contrary to it'.[34] Daniel Schipani has reformulated liberationist *praxis* into an 'epistemology of obedience', which is characterized by discipleship as 'the dynamic, dialogical, and discerning following of Jesus'.[35] He asserts that the liberationist's view of *praxis* must be evaluated in light of the criteria derived from revelation, and from biblical revelation especially, 'lest doing the truth becomes equivalent to making the truth through historical *praxis*, rather than practicing the truth which is ultimately being revealed to us'.[36]

It is evident that a *praxis* epistemology must be modified in order to be incorporated into the Pentecostal faith tradition. Schipani's revision would come close to capturing the necessary dynamics. God must be understood to be the ultimate source and judge of all truth. Knowledge of God involves encounter with and participation in the divine nature which results in the transformation of the knower. The *praxis* that would flow out of such encounter would generate a fresh vision of the kingdom of God, a vision that incorporates an ethic that is consistent with an epistemology which joins knowing and loving.

Since a Pentecostal epistemology understands the knowledge of God to be experiential and relational, and it facilitates loving obedience to the known will of God, it should be seen as compatible with human *praxis* that is judged and transformed by the word of God. Still the nature and goals of biblical knowledge are best seen in the Hebrew word *yada*; to know is to encounter. *Yada* stresses the interrelatedness of the knower and the known. *Praxis*, on the other hand, offers the modern, Western mind a practical approach to the encounter. The best solution seems to be the integration of a *praxis* methodology into the broader epistemological grounding of *yada*.

T. Runyon (ed.), *Sanctification and Liberation* (Nashville: Abingdon Press, 1981). A Wesleyan-Pentecostal faith should take seriously this social dimension of redemption.

[34] J. Sobrino, *The True Church and the Poor* (trans. M.J. O'Connell; Maryknoll, NY: Orbis, 1984), p. 25. See also his *Jesus in Latin America* (trans. R.R. Barr; Maryknoll, NY: Orbis, 1987), esp. ch. 5, 'Following Jesus as Discernment'. For the most comprehensive treatment to date on the epistemological grounding of liberation theology, see C. Boff, *Theology and Praxis: Epistemological Foundations* (trans. R.R. Barr; Maryknoll, NY: Orbis, 1987).

[35] Schipani, *Religious Education*, p. 125.

[36] Schipani, *Religious Education*, p. 136.

An Approach to Bible Study

Drawing upon the above consideration of a Pentecostal epistemology and the dialogue with *praxis* and using the historic language of Pentecostalism, we have proposed an approach to Bible study which includes four interactive movements: Sharing Our Testimony, Searching the Scriptures, Yielding to the Spirit, and Responding to the Call.[37] The four movements are structured around the functions of the Paraclete as set forth in John's Gospel and should be viewed as interactive moments. While each movement logically leads into the next in the order given, all four must be held in dialectic tension as the entire learning experience is surrendered to the Spirit. Thus, the four movements are best understood as interdependent organic functions of a dynamic system.

---

[37] This approach is primarily the result of interaction with evangelical Christian education theorists. Perhaps the greatest influence upon our thought was our time spent with Lois LeBar while working on our Master of Arts degrees at the Wheaton Graduate School of Christian Ministries. LeBar proposed a three-movement approach to Christian teaching. Stated in two different forms (Way-Truth-Life, Boy-Book-Boy), her process stressed beginning where the learners are by addressing 'felt needs' as a means of surfacing 'real needs'. The teacher is then to lead the learners into the truth of God's written word where they will discover the living word, Christ Jesus, who is the answer to all human needs. In the third step the learners are led into changes of their lives appropriate to the truth they have just discovered. See L.E. LeBar, *Education that is Christian* (Old Tappan, NJ: Fleming H. Revell, 1958). LeBar's appeal to us was no doubt influenced by her personal charisma and skills as a teacher, but her ideas were especially cogent for us as Pentecostals. She believed in a resurrected Lord who could be known intimately and who would give direction to those who seek for it from him. She understood Bible study to be a means of personal encounter with God.

Other Evangelicals have suggested four-movement approaches to Bible study. Donald Joy addressed the need for *Meaningful Learning in the Church* (Winona Lake, IN: Light and Life Press, 1969), by suggesting the teacher move from Intersection to Investigation to Inference to Implementation. Larry Richards insisted that the need was for *Creative Bible Teaching* (Chicago: Moody Press, 1970), and titled his movements 'Hook, Book, Look, Took'. The major publishers of evangelical Sunday school curricula have adopted similar models. However, in our opinion these approaches have all moved to varying degrees away from LeBar's commitment to the living, personal presence of Christ.

Another significant influence upon our thought was Thomas Groome's *Christian Religious Education*. Cheryl had the privilege of studying with Groome and Paulo Friere during an intensive Summer term at Boston College. We found in Groome's application of Friere's thought on shared *praxis* a system complementary to LeBar and in harmony with our Pentecostal faith. Many of the ideas expressed in this article were first expressed in a paper we jointly submitted to F.B. Edge during our doctoral studies at The Southern Baptist Theological Seminary in Louisville, Kentucky. We are grateful for his ongoing encouragement in this quest. Titles for the four movements were the result of a group project with colleagues from the Pentecostal Theological Seminary. Members of the group included Steve Land, Chris Thomas, Rick Moore, and ourselves. The atmosphere and relationships of the Seminary have been especially helpful for the refinement of this ongoing undertaking.

Sharing our Testimony—Yada *of Life in the Community*

The first movement calls for the participants to share of themselves through the giving of personal testimony. In this movement the individual and the group are challenged to know themselves individually and corporately as subjects of history. Each participant brings to the study a personal knowledge of what it means to be human in a fallen, sinful world. Each brings expectations of what life could be like. Each is caught in a struggle for full humanity. Yet there is a commonness to everyone's knowledge, struggles and expectations, a shared sense of incompleteness in time.

The Paraclete sayings were given against the backdrop of the disciples' pending aloneness in the world; Jesus was going to leave them (13.31–14.4). Before his departure he raised critical issues concerning their relationships with himself and the Father, their relationships with one another, and their relationships with the world. It is significant that Jesus, the first Paraclete, defined the issues facing the disciples as products of the limitations of time and presence; he could not teach them the things he wanted them to know because he had to go away. Their relationship was incomplete. The disciples were caught in a maze of dialectic tensions: they knew (14.4) but did not know (14.5), they were in the world but were not of the world (17.6–18), they will be hated (15.18–25) but must themselves love (15.12, 17), they will be troubled but they will have the peace of Christ (14.27), etc. The second Paraclete will guide them through these tensions but will not remove the tensions. On the contrary, he will intensify the believers' conflicts with the world (15.18–27; 16.7–11). Indeed, the entire set of discourses (chs. 13–17) may be viewed as a call to confront the uncertainties of following Jesus and a promise of divine assistance in that endeavor.

What we mean by the sharing of our testimony is the giving of a personal account of the ongoing confrontation of the uncertainties of life in Christ. This is far more than the telling of a story or the recounting of disengaged facts. It is for us an act of interpersonal engagement in which individuals offer themselves with their limited knowledge of God and life to the group for shared critical reflection in a process that confronts the common tensions of following Christ and thereby contributes to the corporate testimony.

The sharing of testimony is a present action involving memory, reflection and interpretation. Memory is the pulling of the past into the present. The events being remembered may be temporally distant or near. They may even involve the immediate situation or the ideological constructs of the individual's belief system. The details may be distorted or accurate. In any case, memory is a present reality and is therefore an expression of the present self with its feelings, values and understandings.

Testimony also involves reflection and interpretation. Remembering is by its very nature a process of reflection. Associations with other events and relationships are unavoidable. Testimony is a selective act in which specific events of the past are brought to bear on specific aspects of the present in an effort to give meaning to the present. It thus involves an interpretation of the present through a reinterpretation of the past. It is a confrontation of the present with the past and thereby a confrontation of the past with the present. Thus the sharing of testimony is an act of engagement with one's own past and present.

Furthermore, the sharing of testimony is the offering of the self for the purpose of ministering to the body of Christ and giving glory to God. It is a confessional movement of self-denial in which the members of the group acknowledge (implicitly or explicitly) the incompleteness of their existence and therefore their need for ongoing transformation. The individual offers the self for interpretation by others and God. In the reception of a testimony the group members enter into critical reflection upon and interpretation of what they have heard. Members thereby interpret their own memories and situations. As they confess their existence as finite, historical beings in need of transformation they create a corporate consciousness with a shared memory and testimony.

Testimony also carries a sense of participation in the future. Past and present are confronted in an effort to appropriate coming realities. The dissonance of living in the kingdom of God while waiting on the full reign of God is thereby addressed. Experiences, feelings, values, understandings and expectations, etc., are shared in anticipation of God's response which will be discovered in his word. Thus testimony is given in expectation of dialogue with the Scriptures.

The role of the teacher is that of a guide, one who leads people toward the life-changing power of the word of God. The human teacher is a partner with the Paraclete-teacher who is leading the followers of Christ into the realm of all truth. But human teachers remain incomplete in their own existence. They are 'first among learners', and not depositors of truth. In preparation for this first movement the teacher must complete a thorough study of the passage to be considered and must reflect upon the life issues of the group members. By reflecting on the manner in which the passage and the needs of the people interact, the teacher is able to select an appropriate focus for the testimonies to be given.

In calling forth testimonies the teacher may pose a question, raise an issue, or open the discussion in any manner that invites the participants to enter into shared reflection upon their own experiences. Methodologically, testimony requires personal expression which may be given through a variety of media such as art, mime, role-play, monologue, dialogue, or the simple telling of one's story. Responses to these expressions should surface similarities in life experiences and help to create critical awareness of common issues facing the participants. These should be carefully articulated. The central issue is that the members of the group have the opportunity to reflect upon their present in light of their past and with anticipation of their future.

Searching the Scriptures—Yada *of the Word*

The second movement involves the searching of the Scriptures under consideration in an effort to know the word of God. It is here that the issues of epistemology must be clearly brought into dialogue with the task of hermeneutics. How is biblical interpretation to be done so as to facilitate a dynamic, relational, and obedient knowledge of God? The traditional hermeneutical approach leaves much to be desired inasmuch as it assumes that one can objectively understand the text by utilizing certain scientific tools. This approach ignores the subjective 'pre-understanding' that the interpreter brings to the text, and through its own subjective pre-understanding (i.e. a false assumption of objectivity) discounts any reliance upon the Holy Spirit as subjectivism.

The new hermeneutic as developed by Bultmann and others emphasizes the pre-understandings we bring to the text, but fails to honor the objective nature as well as the unity of the text. Certainly our approach acknowledges the presuppositions we bring to the text. The first movement, 'Sharing our Testimony', involves a confession of pre-understandings. However, we are committed to the objective authority of the text to judge all of life, including these presuppositions. Our approach is to bring life to the text so that the word of God might interpret us. The key element in understanding the text is the power of the Holy Spirit to work in spite of and even through our subjective nature.

Francis Martin has dealt with the issue of the role of the Holy Spirit in biblical interpretation by calling for a 'critical hermeneutics of the Spirit'.[38]

---

[38] Martin, 'Spirit and flesh', p. 1.

Utilizing Paul Ricoeur's categories of 'explaining' and 'understanding', Martin has constructed guidelines for 'exegesis according to the Spirit', which 'presupposes that the reader is in living contact with the same realities about which the author in the Sacred Text is speaking'.[39] The Scripture is to be understood, therefore, via the Holy Spirit who unveils the mystery of God's plan of salvation.

Martin's work is consistent with the teaching functions of the Paraclete as presented by John. The second Paraclete saying (14.25–27) addresses the need of the disciples for a deepened knowledge of the teachings of Christ. As in the first saying, the Paraclete is identified with the Spirit, and the Spirit's role in continuing the ministry of Jesus is reiterated. But here the Paraclete will be sent in the name of Jesus and will teach 'all things' and 'remind' the disciples of everything Jesus has said. These two clauses are parallel thoughts, that is, the reminding of everything Jesus has said is synonymous with the teaching of all things.[40] But the 'all things' which the Spirit will teach (v. 26) also stand in contrast to 'these things' which Jesus has already taught (v. 25), so that the role of the Spirit as teacher will be to add to what Jesus has taught. Jesus as teacher in human flesh has been limited to the time of his 'abiding with' the disciples but the Spirit will not be limited.[41]

But what is the intended extent of 'all things' (v. 26)? What will the Spirit add to what Jesus has taught? Will the Spirit teach quantitatively more than Jesus, literally 'all things'? Since the teaching of all things is synonymous with the reminding of everything Jesus has said, the answer is no. Rather, the function of the Spirit-teacher will be to interpret the sayings of Christ so as to enable the disciples to see the full meaning of Jesus' words.[42] His reminding will be a representing in a living manner; the words of Jesus will, through the Spirit, be freshly applied to the lives of the disciples.[43] The Paraclete will bring the words of Jesus to bear in a meaningful way on all the situations of life.

Rick Moore has offered exegetical grounding for a Pentecostal approach to God's word. His exegesis of Acts 15 (the Jerusalem Council) has yielded the following aspects of the hermeneutical process involved in the passage:

---

[39] Martin, 'Spirit and flesh', p. 1.
[40] R.E. Brown, *The Gospel according to John* (xiii–xxi) (AB; Garden City, NY: Doubleday, 1970), pp. 650–51.
[41] D. Moody, *Spirit of the Living God: The Biblical Concepts Interpreted in Context* (Philadelphia: Westminster Ptess, 1968), p. 166.
[42] Brown, *John*, p. 650.
[43] Brown, 'Paraclete', p. 129.

(1) comprehending God's word entailed attending to the testimony of God's activity in human experience; (2) comprehending God's word entailed affirming the participation of each and every believer; (3) comprehending God's word entailed a corporate process of discernment which went beyond individual perception and human reason; (4) comprehending God's word was bound to the eschatological mission of edifying the church and extending the gospel. Moore further points out that the new covenant's emphasis on the outpouring of the Spirit on all flesh (Jer. 31.31–34) calls for everyone to receive the word (דבר) of God and thereby come to full knowledge (ידע) of the covenant.[44]

We have concluded that searching the Scriptures in a group should bear certain characteristics. It should be personal. Each person must engage the text as one called to hear and receive the word of God. It should also be corporate and interactive. Individual interpretations should be submitted to the group for critical reflection in an attempt to achieve a consensus of understanding. Also, the text must be approached in a manner consistent with its nature as the word of God. It is an objective, historical reality which cannot properly be understood outside of the bounds of reason. Yet, it is a personal, subjective word that is carried along by the Holy Spirit. Out of the text flows the infinite presence of God which addresses the finite limitations of humanity. The Scriptures must be approached as an avenue for personal and corporate engagement with God. The knowing of the word involves the engagement of the whole person. It is an act of reason but is not limited to reason. Because of these considerations we suggest that the study of Scripture be inductive in nature.

The inductive approach assumes that the interpreter has a spirit of openness and is willing to do a thorough analysis of the text before drawing general conclusions. This approach elicits a deep personal engagement with the text in a manner that gives the text integrity by allowing it to 'speak for itself'. The power of transformation is realized when Scripture is honored and allowed to address us. Francis Martin describes this process as having a 'liberating power' because of the distance established between ourselves and the text.[45]

The inductive process first overviews the text in order to gain an understanding of the larger picture (main divisions, major themes, historical

---

[44] R. Moore, 'Approaching God's Word Biblically: A Pentecostal Perspective' (paper presented to the 19th Annual Meeting of the Society of Pentecostal Studies, Fresno, CA, 1989).
[45] Martin, 'Spirit and Flesh', p. 33.

and literary context, and relation of the individual parts of the whole). Observations are made on relationships between events, characters, ideas, etc., and finally conclusions are derived based upon these observations. The inductive process is based upon the assumption that the books of the Bible contain good literary structure and that this structure reveals the thought of the author. This process of interpretation when illumined by the Holy Spirit puts us in touch with the source realities of the Scripture so that we know ourselves to be addressed by the author himself. It is critical that the students receive the text unto themselves and dialogue with it.

Primarily the role of the teacher is to guide the participants in the inductive process of interpretation and thereby invite and facilitate discovery. In order to encourage engagement instead of detachment, lecture is not to be the predominant mode of this movement. Of course, there will be lectures given, especially when there are gaps in knowledge of textual issues or when the participants' exposure has been limited. But the teacher must avoid any posture, method, or terminology that tends to separate the learners from the text. Once the learners have become skilled in the method, the teacher serves as a facilitator of dialogue, making sure all points of view have been heard and the central issues have been addressed.

As the group searches the Scripture they will be prompted to reflect on their own life issues. Reflection should be ongoing throughout the four movements of the Bible study. However, movement to life should not keep the participants from thoroughly studying the text. The focus of this movement should be to attend to the Scripture.

Yielding to the Spirit—Yada *of the Spirit*

Parker Palmer's observation that 'we may bring truth to light by finding it and speaking its name, but truth also brings us to life by finding and naming us'[46] aptly describes the dynamics of this third movement. Yielding to the Spirit is that transforming encounter between the truth of Scripture and the truth found in our own selves.

Typically, Bible study materials written from the objectivist theory-to-practice stance take a deductionist tone of 'now here is the truth, go and

---

[46] Palmer, *To Know*, p. 60.

do likewise'. Such an approach is based on the Platonic assumption that if one knows the truth (reflectively) one will do the truth. *Theoria* must first be apprehended, for only then can it be actualized in the world.

These study materials tend to reduce the Holy Spirit to a prompter or mild-mannered coach. He is often portrayed as a quiet voice that will speak to the heart, urging one to live in the truth. The role of the teacher is to give out the objective truth (the word of God) and the Holy Spirit will take that word and make sure it does not return void. Unfortunately, we often go out from Bible study without any real change having taken place in our lives.

The Holy Spirit cannot be tamed and domesticated. In John's description of the Paraclete, the Spirit is understood to be the living presence of the sovereign God. The Spirit is an authoritative presence leading the church in its confrontation with the world.[47] Specifically, the Spirit bears witness to Jesus (15.26–27). Eskil Franck has described this function as revealing 'an actual, living, and authoritative knowledge about Jesus, which provokes response in people'.[48] The Spirit also 'convicts' the world of sin, righteousness and judgment (16.4–11). To convict means 'to expose'[49] with the sense of proving wrong.[50] The Spirit makes clear the presence of sin. In the final Paraclete saying (16.12–15) the Spirit is portrayed as guiding the disciples into all truth by speaking what he receives from Christ and the Father. The context suggests a meaning of guiding into and within the whole sphere of truth.[51] However, in this case the message of the Spirit is extended beyond the confines of the words of the historical Jesus. He will receive (*lambanein*) words directly from Jesus and deliver them to the disciples.[52] He will proclaim what is yet to come. Thus the Spirit will bring the mission and being of the resurrected Christ into the present reality of the church.

This epistemology demands that the church be responsive to God's critique of the individual and the church. The Holy Spirit is the agent of encounter with the holy God which results in transformation. The Spirit is not a domesticated cultivator of good works. As God's word becomes known, the individual and the group are known and named for who they are. They

---

[47] Brown, *John*, p. 690.
[48] Franck, *Revelation Taught*, p. 56.
[49] C.K. Barrett, *The Gospel according to St John: An Introduction with Commentary and Notes on the Greek Text* (London: SPCK, 1960), p. 405.
[50] D.A. Carson, 'The Function of the Paraclete in John 16.7–11', *JBL* 98 (1979), pp. 549–51.
[51] Barrett, *St John*, p. 408.
[52] Barrett, *St John*, p. 407.

are exposed and have the choice of obedient response with its resulting transformation or denial of the truth with its resulting degeneration.

But God is also critiquing the world. Yielding to the Spirit means attending to the Spirit's living presence in the world. The Spirit contextualizes the Scriptures, working within the believer to interpret the world. As God's word becomes known, the world is also known and named for what it is. To yield to the Spirit is to join oneself to the presence and mission of Christ in the world.

In this movement the task of the teacher is to assure that the group is called into accountability for living in the light of God's word.[53] In essence the objective is for the members of the group to renew their covenant to live under the lordship of Christ by surrendering to the transforming power of God's Spirit. The basic method is to place the testimonies of the group into dialogue with the discovered truth of the word. Critical memory is to be surfaced and engaged with the fresh knowledge flowing from the text. The core question of the movement is 'What is the Spirit saying to the church through this passage about our lives and the world in which we live?'

Specific methods should recognize the need for individual and corporate response. Creative expression through the writing of prayers, songs, poems, or letters is appropriate, as is the offering of other creative talents. The key is that these expressions flow from the soul that is surrendered to the Spirit. In that atmosphere the Spirit is free to engage the believers as he chooses. As the group attends to the Spirit he may choose to make himself known through the charismata or through a quiet voice from within the individuals. But we must allow him to set the boundaries of his activities. The task of the teacher is to yield to the Spirit so that the group is invited to do the same.

Responding to the Call—Yada *of the Father's Glory*

The ultimate objective of Bible study is to know God and live in his presence. Jesus understood the knowledge of God to be synonymous with

---

[53] We are using the term 'accountability', in the sense of encouraging the individuals and the group to take account of themselves as opposed to requiring that an account be settled. In general this responsibility is observed by keeping prior knowledge of God fresh in the memories of the group members.

eternal life (Jn 17.3). He also associated this life with the glory of God when he added

> I have brought you glory on earth by completing the work you gave me to do. And now, Father, glorify me in your presence with the glory I had with you before the world began (Jn 17.4–5 NIV).

It is the task of the Paraclete to bring glory to Christ. He will do this by receiving that which belongs to Christ and proclaiming it to the disciples. But that which he would receive of Christ was also of the Father (16.14–15). The glory of the Father and Son is one glory just as they are one. Thus the Holy Spirit causes believers to know the glory of God and to return that glory unto him. Just as Jesus understood the process of giving glory to flow out of the completion of the work of God, so we must give God glory through submission to his will.[54]

As we yield to the word of the Spirit we are convicted and transformed and thereby become a people of conviction, a people who have experienced what Craig Dykstra terms 'imaginal insight'.[55] A new testimony emerges, one in which we confess what we have seen and what we have heard and what we are compelled to be and to do. If we truly want to know God we must respond in loving obedience to the light he has shed upon our paths. The question of this movement is 'Lord, what would you have us do in response to your word?'

The role of the teacher in this movement is to provide opportunity for response and to lead the group in processing the personal and corporate call of the Spirit. As in the other movements, this response is both individual and corporate. By testifying to the conviction we have received, we give to the community our experience for verification and interpretation. In such a context the power of the word of God is both particular and general. Through shared accountability a consensus of the Spirit arises and with it a sense of corporate journey. No one should be left to 'go it alone'.

---

[54] The theme of giving glory to God through works that grow out of grace is often repeated in the New Testament. Consider especially Rom. 12.1–8; Eph. 4.1–16; Phil. 2.1–13; 1 Pet. 1–2.

[55] Dykstra defines imaginal transformation as moral growth through those 'events that give our lives their particular shape and quality, and out of which our responses to life often seem to flow'. In these experiences 'the deepest patterns of the nature of reality and existence, and of our relationship to them, are revealed, and our own essential convictions are rooted in them' (*Vision and Character* [New York: Paulist Press, 1981], pp. 87–88).

CHAPTER FIVE

WHEN THE VEIL IS TAKEN AWAY: THE IMPACT OF PROPHETIC EXPERIENCE ON BIBLICAL INTERPRETATION*

John W. McKay**

It is now nineteen years since I was baptized in the Holy Spirit. For the first nine of these I was still lecturing in biblical studies at Hull University and so inevitably was much occupied with trying to fit my new-found experience together with the sort of biblical and theological study we do in our universities. It was no easy task.

I found the two uncomfortable companions, like neighbours who acknowledge each other's existence but prefer to live separate lives, not interfering with one another, as it were on opposite sides of a garden wall. It could not be so with me, for in my life critical theology and committed prophetic/charismatic/Pentecostal experience had come together under the same roof and the ensuing tensions proved impossible to live with. The result was initially a lot of very deep rethinking and a total reassessment of what we are doing in teaching the Bible to Spirit-filled believers. The following discussion presents some of the conclusions.

My motivation is mainly to help students searching for a Pentecostal approach to studying the Scriptures, because I am convinced that there is an urgent need for a fresh approach to Bible teaching that will meet the needs of the revival of faith that today is running worldwide, almost all of it Pentecostal in origin and inspiration.

There are basically two ways of studying Scripture. One is objective and analytical, interesting in itself, but imparting little or nothing of the life of God to the student. The other, the way explored here, draws us to God

---

* This article is excerpted from a book with the same title, published by Kingdom Faith Ministries. It omits the book's chapters on shared experience of the life and ministry of Jesus, of the Lordship of Jesus and of the Fatherhood of God. Other chapters have been slightly abbreviated and only introductory and concluding paragraphs have been included in the sections on the biblical books as prophetic/charismatic literature and on the Drama of Salvation. Fuller treatment of individual books of the Bible can be found in McKay's *The Way of the Spirit* (available at http://www.thewayofthespirit.com).

** Before his death in 2001, John McKay (PhD, Cambridge University) was Director of Studies at Roffey Place in Horsham, England.

and gives life. When I discovered new life in Christ through the infilling of his Spirit, I knew nothing else would ever satisfy.

I wrote the first draft of the book from which this article is taken about eleven years ago. Its theological viewpoint has been well tested since then, both in preaching and teaching, but in that time much has also changed. Today there is far more dialogue between charismatics and biblical scholars than there was in the 1970s. In some ways that is good, but in others damaging, for compromise resulting from dialogue has so weakened the charismatic movement that the term 'charismatic' now prompts correspondingly weak notions about experience of the Holy Spirit. It is, however, hard to find a suitable alternative. 'Pentecostal' evokes thoughts of denominational streams, 'spiritual' is not specific; enough, 'revival' fails to highlight baptism in the Spirit and the spiritual gifts. I personally prefer 'prophetic', though to some that might imply limiting the Spirit's activity to one particular gift. In this discussion the terms 'prophetic', 'charismatic', 'Pentecostal', and 'spiritual' are for the most part used interchangeably, except when the specific reference of each is necessitated by the context.

Removing the Veil

> But whenever anyone turns to the Lord, the veil is taken away. Now the Lord is the Spirit... (2 Cor. 3.16–17)[1]

About the time when renewed faith was leading me out of academic theology to go and preach the gospel, the converse was happening with another Anglican priest/academic who said he had lost his faith. He felt it necessary to relinquish his holy orders, but did not feel any corresponding necessity to cease teaching theology in university. That is quite simply because academic theology can be taught and studied without faith. It is, after all, a purely mental discipline, in theory at any rate.

The Conflict of Theology and Faith

In a university theology department students are taught to analyse the text of Scripture as objectively and critically as possible. Efforts to stimulate faith are usually discouraged on the grounds that anyone, Christian, Muslim, Buddhist, atheist, agnostic or whatever, should be as free to study

---

[1] For convenience, biblical quotations are taken from the NIV, though I have occasionally retranslated an odd word or phrase (all acknowledged in footnotes).

theology as he or she is to study history or philosophy or any other degree subject. In practice most students, though by no means all, do have some kind of Christian faith, while the number of lecturers who would admit to active Christian commitment is also not negligible. However, the qualifications required for studying theology are not belief or religious devotion, but so many A-levels, as is only right and proper in an academic institution. The debate as to whether this state of affairs is also right from a Christian viewpoint is an old one and I do not wish to get involved in it here. My concern is simply to discuss the problems it raises for Spirit-filled Christians.

In contrast to my ex-priest colleague, I found it increasingly difficult to be purely academic about my faith, because the Spirit was speaking to me about loving, setting captives free, opening blind eyes, and glorifying Jesus, which are hardly the sort of exercises one usually associates with university departments. It is often said that charismatics are strong on praise, but weak on theology. I would rather say that they are strong on praise and strong on their own brand of theology, but unhappy about the sort of dispassionate, uncommitted theology one frequently encounters in an academic setting. In theory a Pentecostal theologian should have no problem about teaching in a seminary, but in practice much of the theology taught in ministerial training centres differs little in approach from that found in universities. There is clearly a tension that needs to be resolved. It is with such matters that I am here concerned.

Dialogue without Compromise—the Analogy of Drama

It seems to me that the two things, academic biblical study (whether pursued by liberal or conservative scholars makes little difference) and prophetic Christianity, operate at two very different levels. I see a kind of analogy with the world of drama, the academic being in some ways like the reviewer whose task is to analyse, criticize, and comment on the play, the charismatic more like the producer or the performer on stage. One individual may attempt to handle each of these functions separately at different times, but he or she will have great difficulty in doing them both together. Inevitably there must be a great deal of tension between the two, though it is hoped that in the end they might function to each other's mutual benefit, even if at times criticism and hurt may be the more apparent marks of their relationship.

Since my training is in biblical theology, I shall limit myself to this area. Whether my views apply equally to wider areas of theological study, I must leave others more competent than myself to judge.

Now in this context of biblical theology I should be quite unhappy with any theological position that is based on compromise or ideas about a middle way. Indeed I should regard such a theology as being as worthless as the opinion of a person mid-way between an actor and a drama-critic, for he or she would be neither one nor the other and equally useless to both. However, if compromise is unacceptable, there is the obvious danger that the academic's arguments might so undermine the faith of the charismatic that he or she would cease to function as one, or conversely that the charismatic might so dogmatically oppose the academic's opinions that he or she would become unwilling even to countenance rational, theological assessment. We see both tendencies operating from time to time among theological students in particular, but also among Christians in general. In the field of drama responses like these would either cause the play's performance to deteriorate from lack of attention to criticism, or to collapse altogether through defection of the actors.

Charismatics and academic theologians must somehow learn to live together, even if in a state of tension, like actors and their critics. That may prove not too difficult so long as the academic and the charismatic are two different people, but the problem takes on a totally different appearance when they become one and the same person. That was my own particular problem, but it is one that is becoming more widespread as the influence of prophetic Christianity grows. So in a sense this is an autobiographical essay, since it is written from personal experience as well as from academic reflection. As such it should be of some value to others who are either charismatics or academics, even if they are not both, especially since they tend, increasingly in our time, to brush shoulders with each other.

Biblical Scholarship and Revelation from the Spirit

In reading the views expressed in this discussion, it should be borne in mind that they are not all based on the findings of academic scholarship. Many of them are based on realizations that have resulted from my own experience of the Holy Spirit. 'Revelation' is the only word I know that adequately expresses their source, even if that may sound pretentious to some people; but at the same time it would be quite untruthful for me to deny a considerable amount of intellectual reflection as well. A much better way of explaining what I mean is to use an expression of Paul's, the one that furnishes the title of this article, concerning the removal of a veil. In 2 Cor. 3.14–18 he contrasts the understanding with which the Bible (the

Old Testament only in his day) is read before and after 'anyone turns to the Lord'. He says that beforehand it is read as it were with a veil over the mind, but afterwards with the veil removed. He attributes the change to the action of the Spirit, for, he says, 'the Lord is the Spirit', and he goes on to speak about contemplating the Lord's glory, presumably in the reading of Scripture, since that is what the paragraph is all about.[2] Then he reiterates emphatically that this 'comes from the Lord, who is the Spirit'. The message seems clear enough: the Spirit enables us to read the Bible with some new clarity that could not be possible without his aid.

Now charismatics commonly do speak of some disclosure experience similar to Paul's when they read the Bible after baptism in the Spirit. They tell of passages illuminated in new ways, of texts that take on new meaningfulness, of verses that burn themselves into the memory, of completely new appreciations of whole books of the Bible, of a positive urge to read page after page of the text, of exciting new discoveries about God's self-revelation in Scripture, and so forth. Charismatics who speak enthusiastically of their latest insights from reading Habakkuk or Jude will tell how before baptism in the Spirit some months earlier they did not even know these books existed, or certainly that they had no idea what was in them, let alone that they held such spiritual treasures.

For my own part, I well recall, for example, having spent three years as a PhD student mulling over Deuteronomy (among other things), and then, on re-reading it some years later in the light of my experience of the Holy Spirit, being surprised to discover the immense spiritual treasures in it that I had simply failed to appreciate before. Indeed I can honestly say that I came to understand more, not just about the content of Deuteronomy, but about the content of almost every other book in the Bible, and particularly in the New Testament, in the months following my own experience of Pentecost, than I had in all my years of theological study. There was certainly some kind of veil removed, for it was one of the most exciting and memorable experiences of my life re-reading the Bible from cover to cover, genealogies, statistics, priestly regulations and all, and finding in it, chapter after chapter, treasures I never realized existed. Furthermore, where before there had been only dim perception of the Bible's meaning as a whole, or no perception at all, now it all seemed to make excellent sense.

---

[2] NIV translates 'reflect the Lord's glory'. NIV footnote suggests 'contemplate', cf. RSV 'beholding'.

Biblical Literalism, Biblical Criticism and Biblical Experience of the Prophetic Dimension

> We have not received the spirit of the world but the Spirit who is from God, that we may understand what God has freely given us. This is what we speak, not in words taught by human wisdom but in words taught by the Spirit, expressing spiritual truths to spiritual men (1 Cor. 2.12–13).[3]

It is often said that charismatics have no adequate doctrine of Scripture, which is in some ways true, though perhaps it would be more accurate to say that they have problems with all existing doctrines of Scripture. That is not always because they consider them wrong, but rather because they find them insufficient for explaining their own appreciation of God's word. Since charismatics are drawn from a wide variety of backgrounds, some of them are fundamentalists, others are rationalists or liberals, and others are of every shade of opinion in between. Most, however, would express some frustration about the inadequacy of the traditional modes of interpretation they have inherited for describing their own views. Now this problem arises mainly because prophetic understanding operates on a different plane from all others.

The Academic Approach

The fundamentalists maintain a doctrine of literal inspiration of Scripture in all its detail, whether theological, historical, or scientific, and so, for example, would argue that the world was created literally in six days, that there actually was a first-created pair named Adam and Eve who originally lived in a garden called Eden which must at one time have been geographically locatable, that people really did begin to speak different languages when a tower project at Babel collapsed, and so forth. To the fundamentalists the laws of Israel were dictated word for word by God to Moses on Mount Sinai, and in a similar fashion the utterances of the prophets are the very speeches of God himself. Thus every word of Scripture is cherished as an infallible word of God to be read, studied, learned and obeyed, but not criticized or questioned.

By contrast the rationalists maintain that everything in the Bible should be open to criticism. They hold that it contains the depositions of people who were poets, philosophers, theologians, historians, and the like, and that

---

[3] So NIV footnote, cf. RSV. NIV text reads 'in spiritual words'.

their writings should be read and analysed in much the same way as those of any other poets, philosophers, theologians, and historians. Thus the Bible is seen as a record of the reflections of religious individuals about God, rather than of the revelations of God himself to people, and it is sacred not because it is God-given, but because it has become hallowed by centuries of tradition and use. According to this view the laws of Israel were simply accumulated over the generations, but, because of the sanctity of the memory of Moses, became attached to his name. Similarly, the utterances of the prophets are the collected poems and sayings of literary persons, well trained in the art of poetry, and to a lesser extent in prose-writing, people who also had some shrewd insight into matters political and theological. Thus, for example, Amos was probably no simple shepherd receiving messages from heaven, but a man of some culture and learning, perhaps a leisured sheep-farm owner, who had the time and freedom to devote to theological speculation. His writings should therefore be read with the same open critical eye with which one might read the works of any modern-day Bonhoeffer or Barth.

Between these extremes of interpretation lies a whole array of intermediate opinions that tend to one side or the other. Views that lean towards fundamentalism are usually called 'conservative', while the rationalist tendency is known as 'liberal'. The conservative tendency is sometimes also referred to as 'literalist' and the liberal as 'critical', or even 'radical'. Conservative opinion tends to be strongest in the evangelical wing of the churches, liberal in the non-evangelical. Set side by side these varied views form a complete spectrum of biblical interpretation. It may therefore seem surprising that the charismatic, or indeed anyone else, should find no place in its modulating shades of opinion where he or she feels entirely happy and at home.

This spectrum is, however, a fairly modern one. While it is possible to detect precursors to it in the writings of particular theologians through the centuries, particularly since the Reformation, it is only one that has held centre stage in the past 150 years. Liberal theology only began to become influential in the second half of the last century and fundamentalism was born as a reaction to it at the beginning of this century. In earlier times the liberal-conservative debate would have attracted little attention.

There is an older form of interpretation, popular before the Reformation and still sometimes used today, that sits loose to such questions about literal, historical value, neither affirming nor denying the Bible's accuracy at these levels. This kind of interpretation is almost entirely occupied with tracing hidden, spiritual meanings in the text. For example, it would see the real value of the flood story not in the fact that it preserves a record of something that happened long ago, but in the fact that it symbolizes or foreshadows the saving work of the church. In this view the ark carrying Noah and his family through the flood-waters to safety becomes a prototype of the church carrying Christians through the water of baptism to salvation. In a similar way the restored Jerusalem of the Old Testament prophets' visions becomes a portrayal of the heavenly Jerusalem of Christian end-time hope. Among the more common terms used to denote such spiritualizing interpretation are 'typology', 'allegory' and 'anagogy'. Limited examples of these methods are found in the New Testament itself, for instance in Paul's figurative use of the stories about Sarah and Hagar in Gal. 4.21–31, or Peter's use of the flood story in 1 Pet. 3.20–21, or Hebrews' use of the laws of temple, priesthood, and sacrifice in chs. 7–10. However, this form of interpretation is rarely used today, except occasionally in preaching, and to the modern mind it seems esoteric and antiquated.

Charismatics would also find such older methods rather awkward, for they are as much contemporary Christians as any. They may indeed be spiritually very sensitive, but they are also historical realists and would tend to start from the literal sense of the text in much the same way as the present-day conservatives or liberals. It is not because of any desire to retreat into spiritualizing that charismatics feel uncomfortable in the company of modern biblical interpreters. What then is their problem?

The Prophetic Mentality

The answer to that question is quite simply that charismatics are prophets, or at least prophetically sympathetic, and so read the Bible with the eye and intellect of prophetical persons. Let me illustrate what that means. Once in a conversation about a lecture course on mysticism a colleague remarked to me in some frustration, 'How can our students ever hope to understand mysticism? Surely only mystics themselves can properly appreciate the records of mystical visionaries. It must take a mystic to understand the mystics!' Charismatics might expostulate similarly about the Bible (or much of it), that only prophetical persons can properly appreciate the records of prophetical figures. Or again, another academic, a New Testament scholar with Pentecostal sympathies, once spoke to me of his exasperation when reading the works of fellow New Testament scholars who have no clear appreciation of the prophetic mentality of people like Luke or Paul or John.

Of course, to the non-charismatic such an attitude will seem exclusivist and arrogant, but it is very much in tune with similar viewpoints expressed by prophetical individuals in other times. For example, Tertullian in the early third century spoke of a division between the 'spiritual' Christians of his own (Montanist) church and the 'natural' believers *(psychici)* in the other churches and claimed that only the former truly appreciated what the Spirit of God was saying to the faithful.[4] Similar sentiments are found in the writings of Irenaeus in the late second century,[5] but even before that we find something much the same in the New Testament itself. Indeed Paul appears to have been the one who first introduced the distinction when he wrote to the Corinthian church:

> The man without the Spirit *(psychikos)* does not accept the things that come from the Spirit of God, for they are foolishness to him, and he cannot understand them, because they are spiritually discerned. The spiritual man *(pneumatikos)* makes judgments about all things'

(or perhaps better 'has the measure of them all'; 1 Cor. 2.14–15). Jude also draws a distinction between those who 'follow mere natural instincts' and those who 'have the Spirit' (Jude 19).

This is the context in which the charismatics' dilemma must be understood. From this view the bulk of current biblical interpretation, whether conservative or liberal, is the work of the natural mind searching for meaning in God's word using the common techniques of scholarship shared with other secular disciplines, such as history, literary criticism, or philosophy. This kind of investigation has immense value and it would be totally misguided to underrate it, but charismatics find themselves frustrated in the face of it, since it bypasses and fails to recognize a complete dimension that they see so very clearly in their Bible, indeed the one they regard as the most important of all, in the light of which they would wish all else to be viewed, the dimension they might call the spiritual *(pneumatikon)*, or the charismatic, or the prophetic.

As I try to give this dimension more concrete conceptual definition, I feel, very much like Paul, that that would be more effectively done 'not in words taught us by human wisdom but in words taught by the Spirit' (1 Cor. 2.13). In its light I sometimes find the conservative view easier to sustain, occasionally the liberal, but more frequently neither. It would be wrong to think of it only as a yardstick for measuring opinions of liberals and conservatives against each other, for it operates at a different level altogether and often has nothing to say about the arguments of scholarship

---

[4] Cf. Tertullian, *Against Praxeas*, 1.
[5] Irenaeus, *Adv. Her.* 5.6.1 (cited in Eusebius, *Eccl. Hist.* 5.7.2).

at all. Conservatism is a theology of biblical literalism, liberalism a theology of biblical criticism, but I would call the charismatic approach a theology of biblical experience—or, perhaps better, 'shared experience'. That aptly expresses the charismatics' awareness of the similarity between their own experience and that of the prophets, apostles and Jesus, and also their awareness of being active participants in the same drama in which the biblical personages were involved, of playing the same sort of part as they played in it, and of doing so in the same prophetic manner. All will become clearer as I proceed.

Shared Experience of the Power of the Holy Spirit

> And you will receive the gift of the Holy Spirit. The promise is for you and your children and for all who are far off—for all whom the Lord our God will call (Acts 2.38–39).

On the day of Pentecost Peter invited his hearers with these words to share in the apostles' experience of the Holy Spirit. Pentecostals claim that the invitation is still open and that acceptance of it radically changes a Christian's view, not only of his or her own faith, but also of the faith of the early New Testament church, and even of the prophetic personalities of the Old Testament.

Prophetic Appreciation of the Gifts of the Spirit[6]

In the early 1970s I came into contact with an ever-increasing number of Christians who claimed a spiritual endowment that gave them access to similar gifts today. Then I experienced some of these gifts myself and I vividly remember being quite startled by my discovery of what they really were. That, however, is another tale for another time. The important point here is perhaps best summarized in a Job-like confession that to that point I had heard of these things with my ears, but now I could say, 'My eyes have seen' (cf. Job 42.5). That is to say, before that time I had a theological or intellectual attitude to such matters, however confused or dimly perceived, but now they had become a living part of my own experience. Or, to put it another way, I had accepted Peter's invitation and was beginning to learn something of the extent of its implications.

---

[6] This, of course, relates to the spiritual gifts spoken about not only in the book of Acts, but also in other New Testament passages such as Rom. 12.6–8 and 1 Cor. 12.7–11.

Quite apart from being surprised to discover just how different the spiritual gifts looked from the inside than they had formerly appeared from the outside, I was now for the first time, in a fairly elementary way, made aware of the challenge that shared experience presented to traditional biblical interpretation. To begin with, I could no longer acquiesce in the views held by non-charismatics about the gifts and found myself instantly dissatisfied with almost every commentary on the subject that I read. Since I now knew for myself that the gifts were a living part of Christian experience available today as well as in the first century, I could no longer even discuss the possibility that they might be simply an expression of primitive religion or of a lost idyllic age of the church's early history, and certainly not the view that they were unintelligible. Of course, the mere experience of such phenomena as tongues, prophecy, supernormal knowledge, and healing was in itself no guarantee that these were the same gifts as those known to the earliest Christians, but at least the possibility was now worth exploring, and the further I looked, the more convinced I became that I was indeed sharing experiences of the same genre as those, not only of the early Christians, but also of the Old Testament prophets and of Jesus himself.

The miraculous and the supernatural in Scripture readily become part of charismatics' shared experience. They dream significant dreams that are more than mere phantoms of the night, but tell of God and his will. They see mystic visions of the Lord in his holiness and they hear the voice of God speaking, sometimes audibly, but more normally in the silence of their hearts. I refuse to recognize mere psychological explanations for these experiences, because, like the similar phenomena of which Paul speaks in 1 Corinthians 14, they edify and build up the believer and the community of believers in their faith in God and their love for one another.

Of course there can be a quite human element in all this, even a spurious one. That has led many to dismiss charismatic Christianity as counterfeit, but the same problem was present in ancient times and the Bible's answer to it is certainly not to reject the Spirit's work. On the contrary it bids us sift and discern what is of God and hold on to that: 'Do not put out the Spirit's fire; do not treat prophecies with contempt. Test everything. Hold on to the good' (1 Thess. 5.19–21). John tells us to test the spirits to see whether they glorify the incarnate and risen Christ (1 Jn 4.1–3), and when that is done it becomes immediately clear that present-day charismatic activity is indeed genuine.

Prophetic Views of Biblical Experience

Now that all sounds exceedingly dramatic, as indeed it is, but the effects of such shared experience for biblical interpretation are also dramatic, though in a very different way. It becomes increasingly difficult, for instance, for a liberal theologian who experiences this new dimension to view the miraculous and supernatural elements in the Old and New Testaments in terms of mythology or legend, and one immediate temptation for such a person is to jettison all his or her scholarship and become a fundamentalist. Some do fall to this temptation, though the step is not a necessary one. Fundamentalists make doctrinal claims, charismatics experiential. No charismatic could ever appeal to his or her shared experience to uphold such doctrines or prove such facts as the fundamentalist cherishes, for example the scientific veracity of the creation narrative in Genesis 1, or the literal existence of a fish that could carry Jonah in its belly without harming him. Prophetic insight has very little to say about such matters, though it does warm instantly to the emphasis on God's goodness in the creation story or to the message in the book of Jonah about the need for obedience in a prophet. Prophetic experience does not destroy or bypass one's reasoning faculty! It is still possible for charismatics to remain fairly liberal in their theological views, as some actually do.

Nonetheless, the major effect of shared experience is to make the charismatics treasure parts of the biblical record they might beforehand have viewed with much scepticism. Not only the miracle stories in the Gospels, but those actions attributed to the power of the Spirit in Acts and the prophetic narratives in the Old Testament also become particularly precious.

One area where shared experience completely transforms biblical interpretation is that of the prophetic word. The liberal views prophecy as something inspirational only in a very loose and vague sense, relating it more to natural sagacity, shrewd insight, and inherited traditions than to anything else. Prophetic experience, however, encourages a very different view, for the mediation of messages directly received is of the very essence of charismatic prophecy. Sometimes these messages are delivered in verse form, sometimes in prose, sometimes only the gist of the message is given and not in any particularly marked style, but always there is something received, some direct revelation that is passed on. Sometimes it will be communicated immediately, at other times it will be kept for a later occasion when the congregation is assembled together to hear it. Charismatic prophecy is something like the rehearsing of a conversation with a friend, only in this instance the friend is the Lord himself. 'Thus says the Lord' means literally that to charismatics, and so to them the liberal view of prophecy must remain entirely inadequate.

Equally, however, charismatics would find it hard to acquiesce in the fundamentalist view of literal, mechanical inspiration, as though God had precisely dictated every single word that is spoken. On some rare occasions it may seem like that, but generally the dictum of Paul holds good, that 'the spirits of prophets are subject to the control of prophets' (1 Cor. 14.32). Charismatics will tell that a prophecy is spoken in faith, that is, that it is indeed a word from God. Pressed about such an utterance charismatics would normally admit that, while they believe it comes from God, it is not always possible to draw an absolute line of demarcation between what is from God and what is from oneself. The utterance is certainly inspired, but it is filtered through a human channel, with the result that it is in the end only a near, hopefully very near, approximation to what God wants to communicate. Or, as Paul puts it in 1 Cor. 13.9, 'we prophesy in part' (i.e. imperfectly). That helps us understand why George gives his prophecy in King James's English, Mary hers in her local dialect, William his in cultured speech; or why Isaiah spoke with a Hebrew style quite different from Ezekiel's. The prophet's rehearsal of what God has said will have a degree of precision similar to the degree of exactitude which that individual might attain in reporting some important conversation, a degree that will vary from person to person, and will even vary according to the mood of the speaker.

Now at this point we are confronted with the problem of determining how much any prophecy is of God and how much of the prophet himself or herself. That is to say, we find ourselves acutely involved in the problems of discerning true and false prophecy. That, however, simply attests further to the reality of shared experience in charismatic/Pentecostal and biblical traditions, for the same problem was as acute in both Old and New Testament times as it is today (cf. 1 Kings 13; 22; Mt. 7.22; 1 Jn 4.1).[7]

---

[7] The prophetic writings in the Bible have stood the test of time and have been fully recognized as authentically inspired of God in a way that is unique, and hence are accepted as sacred scripture. They do, however, still reveal the individual personalities of the prophets themselves in considerable measure.

The Bible as Prophetic Literature

> In the past God spoke to our forefathers through the prophets at many times and in various ways, but in these last days he has spoken to us by his Son (Heb. 1.1–2).

All charismatics are convinced that in some way or other God does actually speak to people, whether to individuals, church groups, whole congregations, or even to some in the wider non-church community, through visions, auditions, prophecies, dreams, or 'in various ways', as Hebrews puts it, but certainly that he does speak. And so they find no need to dismiss as merely legendary the stories of God's conversations and communications with Abraham, Moses, Samuel, Solomon, Peter, Paul, or whomever. From their own experience and their conversations with other Spirit-filled Christians they know that such things are not uncommon, and so they view the literature that tells of them somewhat differently from liberal scholars, who would tend to use words like 'myth' or 'legend' in their discussions about it. The expression I myself prefer is 'charismatic (or prophetic) literature', because the biblical books are often very similar to the sort of writing we find in contemporary charismatic *(auto)biographies*, accounts of church renewal, records of healing and revival ministries, and the like, of which there are plentiful examples in our bookshops today.

It is clearly impossible to discuss all the books in the Bible here, or to maintain that they all contain the same level of charismatic literature though it is surprising how much of it one finds in the most unexpected places, such as in Numbers, Deuteronomy, Proverbs, Song of Songs, 2 Chronicles, or Ezra and Nehemiah.[8]

On this point the prophetic books hardly need any comment, for they are unquestionably charismatic literature, or at least to the charismatic they are. Collections of prophetic utterances are not commonly found in print today, but the exiled Camisards in London and their English converts at the beginning of the eighteenth century published many such books which they entitled *Prophetical Warnings*. However, present-day charis-

---

[8] Comments here are of necessity brief and representative. The prophetic/charismatic thrust of each book in both Old and New Testaments is fully discussed in my four-volume work, *The Way of the Spirit*. See also J.W. McKay, *The Old Testament and Christian Charismatic/Prophetic Literature*', in B.P. Thompson (ed.), *Scripture: Method and Meaning: Essays Presented to Anthony Tyrrell Hanson* (Hull: Hull University Press, 1987); *idem*, 'The Experiences of Dereliction and of God's Presence in the Psalms: An Exercise in Old Testament Exegesis in the Light of Renewal Theology', in P. Elbert (ed.), *Faces of Renewal: Studies in Honor of Stanley M. Horton* (Peabody, MA: Hendrickson, 1988); *idem*, 'My Glory-A Mantle of Praise', SJT 31 (1978), pp. 167–72; *idem*, 'Psalms of Vigil', ZAW 91 (1979), pp. 229–47.

matics have heard and probably uttered many prophecies themselves and so from their experience of the spoken word recognize the literary category instantly. Since I have already discussed how a charismatic's view of prophecy differs from that of the liberal or the conservative, there is no need to say more on the subject at this point.

The New Testament presents fewer problems in this context than the Old. The Synoptic Gospels can be read as charismatic biographies, particularly Luke's, in which a greater emphasis is put on the action of the Spirit in the initiation of Jesus' ministry (4.1–30), on his and his followers' experiences of joy in the Spirit (cf. 10.17, 21), on prayer (cf. 6.12), and on teaching to prepare the disciples for receiving the Spirit themselves (11.1–13; 24.49). John's Gospel is also very full of teaching about the Spirit and about the Christian's need to receive him, particularly in chs. 3–7 and 14–16.

Acts, especially in the first half, is replete with charismatic hero stories, tales of outpourings of the Spirit, of healings and other miracles, of visions, of praise and rejoicing, of power-filled ministries, of divine guidance. It is not without reason that this book has sometimes been nicknamed 'the Acts of the Holy Spirit'.

Revelation is the only book in the New Testament that actually calls itself 'prophecy' (1.3; 22.7, 10, 18). It was written about a visionary experience of the author when he was 'in the Spirit' on one occasion (1.10) and is certainly to be described as prophetic literature. It could almost be said that every single book in the New Testament is about some aspect of life in the Spirit. There is scarcely a chapter in which the charismatic does not find echoes of things he or she might want to say about his or her own experience of life in the Spirit or of things that other charismatics have told, whether in print or by word of mouth, about their experiences.

There is little doubt in my mind that the majority of the books of the Bible, in both testaments, are, in their very different ways and to different degrees, classifiable under the general title of charismatic or prophetic literature. But if that can be said about individual books, how far can it be said about the Bible as a whole? It is to that question we must now address ourselves.

The Drama of Salvation, or Creating the End-Time Church of the Spirit

> And afterward,
> I will pour out my Spirit on all people.
> Your sons and daughters will prophesy,
> your old men will dream dreams,
> your young men will see visions.

> Even on my servants, both men and women,
> I will pour out my Spirit in those days (Joel 2.28–29).

The question raised at the end of the last section touches on the long debated issue of whether or not there can be found any overarching thematic unity in Scripture. Some say the Bible has no consistent theological theme at all, but only many varied strands, and so they speak of diversity in the Bible rather than unity. They maintain that there is no need to look for a common theological interest in such different materials as laws of sacrifice, prophetic utterances, hymns of praise, wisdom sayings, and historical narratives. Perhaps this question of theological unity will never be resolved, but it is my belief that there is a coherence, though it is one that I would prefer to call experiential or charismatic rather than academic or theological, and I believe that this coherence can be grasped when we view the biblical records in the light of shared experience.

In the book from which this article is taken I have sketched, on the model of a theatrical drama, what I believe could serve as an expression of the operative sense of coherence to be found in a charismatic approach to the biblical corpus. The essential drama, as it unfolds from Genesis, has to do with the restoring of paradise or Eden. In the garden there were two special trees: the tree of the knowledge of good and evil and the tree of life. Driven from the garden humankind now has access to neither. They had tasted of one and that left them in a condition of sin, in need of forgiveness. Deprived of the other, their only future is death. These two trees represent the twin poles or foci of our drama, which is about God restoring humanity to a right relationship with both, first through his patriarchs, priests, prophets and kings, then more fully through Jesus and the church, and finally in his New Heaven at the end of time. At every turn prophetic/charismatic experience points the way forward to the fulfilment of God's purpose in restoration.

The essential message of the New Testament story is that the age of the Spirit has come, first in Jesus and then in his disciples, who prove themselves to be persons like the Old Testament prophets, persons such as the Old Testament believed God would raise up to fulfil his purpose in bringing blessing to all the families of the earth. Eden is not exactly restored, but there is an Eden-like quality about life in the early Christian community, where joy is one of the chief characteristics of its members. Since the world as a whole still remains under God's curse and in need of redemption, our drama continues to be played out with many of the same tensions and uncertainties as before, but there is now a new factor in it, for the followers of Christ have been granted access again to the source of life, lost since Eden, from which they can draw strength for the role they must play in the continuing outworking of God's purpose. Sin with respect to the tree of the knowledge of good and evil is now atoned for by the sacrifice of Christ, 'the Lamb of God, who takes away the sin of the world', and the wholesome virtue of the tree of life is now embodied in the gift of Christ, 'who will baptize with the Holy Spirit'. (Jn 1.29, 33). In the power of the grace and Spirit he supplies, his followers now live the Eden-life in considerable measure, as Ezekiel and other prophets had said they would. And that is very much a charismatic or prophetic quality of life.

Such a view of the Bible's coherent message is far from complete. Today almost 2000 years have passed and the hard truth is that Eden has still not been restored. History is littered with evidence of humanity's continuing unfaithfulness. And the record of the Christian church has not always been that good! So we are compelled in all honesty, even. at this stage, to raise once more the question that runs through the entire drama: can God's purpose ever really be fulfilled?

But again we can approach it with hope. At the end of the first century, John, one of Jesus' original disciples, was granted a vision, in which he saw the course of history to come, through many times of trial, to God's final hour to the blessings of Eden fully restored and humankind in Christ reigning at the last as was intended at the beginning. It is towards the hope engendered by this further vision of Eden's final accomplishment in what John calls the New Jerusalem that the drama tends. That, however, is in itself a further indication of the prophetic quality of New Testament faith, for it is of the very essence of prophecy to have some such future vision. Hence this final act is, and must always be, one led and dominated by the eschatological race of prophets, those who in some measure share in the vision and experience of the ancient prophets, persons such as those whom today we would commonly call Pentecostal or charismatic. Their vision, like that of the Old Testament prophets, is still an urgent and excited one, still forward looking, and still one of hope for a glorious finale. It is surely significant that as the curtain falls on the New Testament stage we hear John's voice say, 'He who testifies to these things says, "Yes, I am coming soon." Amen. Come, Lord Jesus' (Rev. 22.20).

In the time that has passed since then the gospel has indeed reached many peoples and the end John saw is now nearer than most care to imagine. The power of God's Word and his Spirit that worked in creation, which has upheld God's purposes through history, which motivated his prophets, which lived in Christ, which gives us a foretaste of Eden today, still works for the final recreation of all things.

The Charismatic, the Academic, and the Word of God

> But you will receive power when the Holy Spirit comes on you; and you will be my witnesses (Acts 1.8).

Such a drama-outline could hardly cover every aspect of Old and New Testament teaching, theology, and literature. Sometimes the literature, rather than illustrating charismatic experience, depicts the responses of those who have not appreciated it, as in the case of Job's counsellors, for instance. Our Bible is no simple-minded manual containing naive descriptive outlines of what prophetic religion should be like, but rather a dramatic account of the lives, experiences, and insights of men and women who themselves came into living experience of that kind of religion or into contact with other living exponents of it. It is essentially the story of the dynamic activity (the Spirit) of God and of people's varied responses to that. Hence it tells not only of prophets, but also of judges and sages, of kings and warriors, of craftspeople and fishermen, indeed of all sorts and conditions of people. It paints pictures of individuals who acted by the power of the Spirit, but equally of persons who did not; it paints pictures of times when the Spirit was very active in history, but equally of times when religion was decadent or arid. But always the measure or the ideal is that picture of the eschatological church of the Spirit, that race of prophetical persons whose purpose is to see Eden restored. It is to that end that the whole drama moves, and so it finds its apex in the life-story of the one who ushered in the final age of the Spirit, Jesus Christ.

Its contemporary value derives from the observation of the continuity of his work in the apostolic church and the implication of the whole drama that that work should still be continued today. It bids us align ourselves with Jesus and the apostles, to share their experience, to come out of the audience, and join the players in the final act, to wait in our own Jerusalems until we too are endued with the same power from on high. Once we do that, we find the curtain (or the veil) removed altogether and ourselves on stage holding hands with the apostles and seeing everything from their Pentecostal perspective.

For a biblical scholar, acceptance of that invitation creates an immediate problem. The academic task requires that one stand, as it were, off-stage, like a critic or reviewer, so that one can observe the drama with the more objective eye of scholarship, whereas the Holy Spirit draws one on stage with the actors. Thus such persons find themselves pulled in two directions, the one calling them to stand back and analyse what they see, the other urging them forward to participate in the action. Ideally, I suppose, it ought to be possible to do both, especially in ministerial training institutions, but in the critical atmosphere of academic theology the tension is considerable, often even unbearable.

Communicating Spiritual Truths in Scholarly Language

There is another aspect to this dilemma, one that is perhaps best illustrated through a brief autobiographical comment. I was myself attracted to the life of scholarship in the first instance by what I then called 'the riddle of the Bible'. To me, as indeed to so many others, the meaning of Scripture was by no means as evident as it has now become. While it attracted me as God's Word, the book itself was an enigma. It purported to be a deposit of revelation, but for the most part all that was revealed to me in it was a series of puzzles, albeit exceedingly fascinating ones. And so I spent many hours discussing the problem of Deuteronomy, the problem of Mark's Gospel, the problem of Christ, the problem of faith, and so forth. The essential message of Scripture quite simply eluded me, as it did everyone else with whom I discussed these problems, or at least as it seemed to do, since no one was able to provide me with answers that satisfied. And so, failing to find anyone who could guide me through the maze, I came to regard scholarship as a tool which might somehow unearth the Bible's hidden meaning, but only gradually and after many years of hard study by many hard-working, highly educated individuals. The field was far too vast for anyone scholar to handle alone. My own part must therefore be that of making some small contribution to a sum total of international scholarship that might some day produce something like a satisfactory solution to the riddle of the Bible. I must, however, admit to having experienced an increasing sense of despondency; the more I pursued this quite limited objective, the more aware I became of the confused complexity of theological debate, and proportionately I despaired of scholarship's ever discovering a solution.

It was for reasons almost entirely unrelated to these that lone day asked God to baptize me with his Holy Spirit just as he had done for his early disciples and seemed to be doing for an ever-increasing number of Christians in our time, but subsequent to that, and to my own great surprise, I found myself reading my Bible with completely new understanding. The veil Paul spoke about had been lifted and for the first time in my life I discovered that it all made very good sense. The riddle had quite simply vanished-yes, in a moment of time—and over the days and weeks that followed, as I watched the jigsaw of the various books and chapters of the Bible progressively reforming themselves into a coherent whole, I marvelled that I had not seen it all before.

It was an exhilarating discovery, but also a painful one, for it deprived me of most of my former scholarly purpose. It could no longer be my aim to help resolve the riddle of the Word of God; the Holy Spirit had done that for me. My studies had now manifestly to change focus, from my search for meaning to clarification of my new understanding. Similarly, the focus of my teaching had to change, from presenting the current state of scholarly opinion and debate to communicating my new discoveries.

Now, this is precisely the point at which the real acuteness of my dilemma becomes manifest. Since my insight into the coherence of Scripture has not come by purely academic processes, it is difficult to communicate it in purely academic terms. In a sense there is an analogy with romantic love. Anyone who loves his or her partner will understand what I mean when I say that I love my wife, but I find it well-nigh impossible to explain the nature of my love to anyone else. The words I use may convey an impression of something good, intimate, happy and worthwhile, but will scarcely satisfy someone who persists in asking for definitions. Similarly, those with spiritual experience comparable with my own will usually understand what I say without my having to explain too much, whereas others will mostly fail entirely to grasp my meaning. In other words, I realize that the Spirit of truth is more capable of leading others into all the truth than I can ever hope to be, even with my accumulated wisdom and learning.

Here is no theoretical difficulty, but a very practical one. I have discovered over the past seventeen years, indeed to my great frustration at times, that baptism in the Spirit can often give less literate people a much better appreciation of the message of the Bible than three years of university education in a theology department can give to more intellectually capable undergraduates, or a similar period of study in a theological college or seminary to ordinands. However, this observation is not really much different from that made by Paul, for example, whose experience in this respect seems to have been remarkably similar to my own, for he was firmly convinced that the truth about 'Christ and him crucified' or 'God's secret wisdom' could never be communicated as successfully through careful and erudite presentations of the gospel message as through 'demonstration of the Spirit's power' or when 'God has revealed it to us by his Spirit' (1 Cor. 2.1–10). We may likewise recall how even Jesus' teaching was not so easily understood by his own disciples before their experience of the Spirit at Pentecost as after it.

Unfortunately statements of this kind can and do convey an impression of arrogance, particularly to those who are engaged in the work of biblical scholarship. As I have already noted, however, that in itself is part of the charismatic's dilemma, also shared with the early apostles, and so I can do little more about it than Paul did when he wrote to the Corinthians, namely apologize for not being able to express myself about it more acceptably and assure the reader that the intention is quite the converse (2 Corinthians 10). My own debt to biblical scholarship is very great and can certainly not all be laid aside.

The Spirit makes us Witnesses, not Analysts

A third major area of tension between charismatics' experience and their scholarship lies in the shared experience with the apostles and the prophets of a compulsion to speak about one's new vision. Just before the ascension, according to Acts 1.8, Jesus forewarned his disciples that receiving the Holy Spirit would turn them into witnesses. Now there is a world of difference between the activities of scholarly research and witnessing. Academics will probe and analyse, or debate and hypothesize, until they find a solution that seems reasonable. They may themselves be convinced of its rightness, though they will recognize that further research may cause them to modify their views, and so they will want to present their findings in print for wider, more public discussion and debate. Charismatics cannot adopt such an approach to their disclosures. Their conviction of their essential rightness is based on revelatory experience, the confirmation of the Word, and their own corresponding faith, not on experimental investigation or argument, and consequently is much more absolute. They feel little desire to proffer their beliefs simply for discussion, but feel more like an explorer who has discovered a new world and wants to tell everyone else about it, inviting them to come and see it and even to settle in it. Hence charismatic writing is seldom publication of ideas or theories for debate, but witness, the declaring of what has been 'seen and heard' (cf. Mt. 11.4; Acts 2.33; 4.20). Here is no mere dogged determination to do something about Jesus' commission to evangelize, but rather an eagerness to proclaim what the Spirit has revealed. If charismatics are unhappy about purely academic analysis of their visions, they are equally unhappy about evangelical pressurization. They do not see their function as one of persuasion, but simply of declaration. They are not trying to convince others of the rightness of a theory, but to tell them of their discovery, as explorers tell of a new country. There is nothing to debate, even if the audience is sceptical. They are quite simply witnesses.

Now witnessing, the declaring of what one has 'seen and heard', is not an academic exercise. It may claim to be a presentation of truth that has not been seen by other scholars, but in itself it has nothing scholarly about it. It is the audience, or the jury, that finds itself engaged in the academic work of testing the witness, but the witness can never change the story if he or she is to remain true to what has been seen and heard. The witness simply cannot engage in the academic task at that level any more, for if this happens there is the implicit admission that witness may not be true. And there also lies a dilemma.

Much of what I have written here may seem to add to the impression alluded to earlier, that there is something anti-intellectual in the prophetic mentality. The impression is an unfortunate one, for their experience usually stimulates charismatics to very deep thought about God, the Bible, and the needs of society. It is not that charismatics cease to think theologically; quite the contrary. However, their theological perspective has changed, and changed so radically that they find their views no longer fit with those of the majority of today' s biblical theologians, and furthermore that they fail to find much satisfaction from participating in their debates. It is my convinced opinion that a charismatic's view of the Bible must be different from everyone else's, be they fundamentalists, conservatives, liberals, radicals, or whatever. Their views are based on doctrines, assumptions and hypotheses, albeit sometimes diametrically opposed ones, about the nature of Scripture and revelation. Charismatics' are based on what they discover themselves thinking after they have been baptized in the Holy Spirit. And as we have seen, this discovery is itself more in the realm of experience than of doctrine, for it is a discovery that one has stepped out of the audience into the play where one shares in so many, if not ultimately all, of the experiences of the actors, particularly of the charismatics/Pentecostals of the last act in the New Testament church.

The Wealth of the Witness of the Spirit

It is for these reasons that this article contains no weighing of the viewpoints of other scholars and no listing of the works of others with whom I am in agreement or disagreement. In one sense there is no debate. Prophetic experience leads me to treasure the biblical records with a new love that makes me less willing to dismiss as much as the liberals tend to do, but it does not persuade me therefore to accept all the historical conclusions of fundamentalism. But then, it tells me of things about which neither of these speak, and there lies its great attraction. The word that comes most readily to mind for describing these things is not fundamentalism, nor radicalism, nor any other '-ism', but truth. The witness of the Spirit, as Jesus says in John's Gospel, is essentially to truth—not to any truth about technical, historical or scientific data and statistics, which are properly subjects for scholarly research, but to the truth about the word of God, and that speaks to me of salvation, forgiveness, blessing, hope, love, joy, peace, power, and the like. Pre-eminently that truth is about Jesus, who, as we have it in John's Gospel, is himself the Truth (14.6). So the Spirit shows me the truth of Scripture (or resolves the riddle of the Bible) and the truth of Jesus (or resolves the riddle of the incarnation), but perhaps the two are one, for even the Bible itself recognizes an interplay between the written word of God and the incarnate Word of God. Both speak of the same truth, and the Spirit witnesses equally to both. That is not to say there is no truth in the things that liberals or conservatives say, but that there is a more profound truth that neither of these, in the charismatic's eyes at any rate, have ever grasped. That alone comes from the Spirit of God, not by any human intellectual process.

Of course, charismatic experience offers no magical solution to so many of the problems that the scholars handle, such as the date of the Exodus, or the editorial arrangement of the book of Ezekiel, or the authorship of the Pastoral Epistles, but it does bear witness to the basic truth of the accounts of what the biblical personalities experienced in their relationships and encounters with God or his messengers, and to the essential truth of their aspirations and hopes for those who believe in Christ. The charismatic's main argument with biblical scholars of the academy is therefore about the nature of belief. Charismatics want scholars to begin believing that what they are analysing is not just myth, or legend, or the theological ruminations of pious intellects, if they are liberals, nor simply ancient history or doctrinal presentations, if they are conservatives, but living Christian experience as it was and as it still should be. Like Peter, they want the critic to lay aside his or her pen for a moment and to step on stage to see what this Spirit-life is really like. But then every scholar or student who accepts that challenge will find themselves, as I do, longing for some new kind of scholarship through which they can express these new-found revelations and understandings.

That, in the end, is the invitation of Scripture itself. Does not our Drama of Salvation end with such a call from the Spirit and the Bride (of Christ, the church) who say 'Come!'? It is those who are 'thirsty' who will come, and when they do, they will drink of the water of life freely given by God. And that water is the Spirit of God himself, flowing from his throne and the Lamb. Our calling is not so much to receive understanding as to receive life. But in the light of that life there is indeed a freshness of understanding unknown to and unknowable by the natural intellect. The Christian, who has tasted such things and knows that nothing else can satisfy in the same way, must inevitably become a witness—but not without understanding. And that is why the Spirit cuts through all our debates and scholarship to lead us into all truth, his truth.

CHAPTER SIX

WOMEN, PENTECOSTALISM, AND THE BIBLE: AN EXPERIMENT IN PENTECOSTAL HERMENEUTICS*

John Christopher Thomas**

I

Perhaps few topics have generated the kind of discussion amongst Pentecostal scholars over the past few years than that which has emerged around the issue of 'Pentecostal Hermeneutics'. Scholars who have entered into this debate range from those who deny the need for a distinctive Pentecostal hermeneutic, preferring to follow certain evangelical models, to those who are in dialogue with a number of methodologies that have emerged within the last couple of decades. While no consensus has emerged as of yet, it appears that many scholars working within the Pentecostal tradition are less content to adopt a system of interpretation that is heavily slanted toward rationalism and has little room for the role of the Holy Spirit.

Several reasons account for the desire on the part of some Pentecostal scholars to identify and articulate a hermeneutic that is representative of the tradition and its ethos. Disappointment with the results of rationalism is one major factor in the emergence of this trend. Owing to the promises made for rationalism, growing out of the Enlightenment, many western thinkers became convinced that pure reason was the key to interpretation of any literature, both biblical and non-biblical. But the results of an unbridled rationalism have been anything but uniform, as witnessed in the diversity of current theological thought, which in and of itself suggests that there is more to interpretation than just reason.[1]

---

* First published in the *Journal of Pentecostal Theology* 5 (1994), pp. 41–56.
** John Christopher Thomas (PhD, University of Sheffield) is Clarence J. Abbott Professor of Biblical Studies at the Pentecostal Theological Seminary in Cleveland, TN USA and Director of the Centre for Pentecostal and Charismatic Studies at Bangor University, Wales.
[1] This assessment is true even of evangelical theology, where an extremely high view of Scripture has brought little consensus on a variety of interpretive matters.

The dearth of serious critical reflection on the role of the Holy Spirit in the interpretive process has also whet the appetite of several Pentecostal scholars for an approach which seeks to articulate what the Spirit's role is and how the Spirit works specifically. It is, indeed, one of the oddities of modern theological scholarship that both liberal and conservative approaches to Scripture have little or no appreciation for the work of the Holy Spirit in interpretation.[2] Obviously, such a hermeneutical component is of no little interest to Pentecostal scholars.[3]

Another contributing factor to this recent surge of hermeneutical activity amongst Pentecostals is the belief of several scholars that the role of the community in the interpretive process is extremely important. Given the community orientation of Pentecostalism, on the one hand, and the excesses of a somewhat rampant individualism among interpreters generally (both liberal and conservative), on the other hand, reflection on the place of the community in the hermeneutical process would appear to be a natural next step in the development of a Pentecostal hermeneutic.

Finally, the recent paradigm shift(s) in the field of hermeneutics generally has encouraged some scholars that the time is right to enter into a serious discussion about Pentecostal hermeneutics. Not only have insights from recent hermeneutical discussions confirmed the appropriateness of certain Pentecostal interpretive emphases (such as the importance of experiential presuppositions in interpretation and the role of narrative in the doing of theology), but also the insights gained from a diversity of approaches to the biblical text have given some Pentecostals courage to believe that they too have some contribution to make to the current hermeneutical debate.

While it might sometimes be thought, or even charged, that Pentecostals desire to articulate their own hermeneutical approach just to be distinctive, in point of fact, it would appear that just as Pentecostals have been able to help the church rediscover a number of biblical truths with regards to pneumatology, so they may also have gifts to give when it comes to the interpretive process itself.

But what would a Pentecostal hermeneutic look like and, more importantly, how would it function? What would be the essential components

---

[2] C. Pinnock, *The Scripture Principle* (San Francisco: Harper & Row, 1984), p. 155.

[3] One of the few serious treatments of this topic amongst Pentecostals is the work of J.W. Wyckoff ['The Relationship of the Holy Spirit to Biblical Hermeneutics', (PhD, Baylor University, 1990)], who after a historical survey proposes a model regarding the Spirit's role based largely on an educational paradigm of teacher.

of such an interpretive approach and how would one settle on them? These are just the beginning of a multitude of questions which this topic raises.

This short study does not seek to offer an exhaustive overview of the topic of Pentecostal hermeneutics, nor to articulate in a detailed fashion a sophisticated theory of interpretation.[4] Rather, it seeks to explore one possible paradigm, which is derived from the New Testament itself. After a brief discussion of this interpretational paradigm, the approach will be tested by attempting to gain leverage on a particularly difficult issue by the use of insights derived from this biblical paradigm.

II

It is possible, of course, to find a number of different hermeneutical approaches in the New Testament and several full-length studies have been devoted to the use of the Old Testament by various New Testament writers.[5] Of these many interpretive approaches, one in particular has had a special appeal for many Pentecostals especially at the popular level. This

---

[4] For some recent attempts at Pentecostal hermeneutics, cf. the following: G.T. Sheppard, 'Pentecostalism and the Hermeneutics of Dispensationalism: Anatomy of an Uneasy Relationship', *Pneuma* 6 (2, 1984), pp. 5–33; M.D. McLean, 'Toward a Pentecostal Hermeneutic', *Pneuma* 6 (2, 1984), pp. 35–56; H.M. Ervin, 'Hermeneutics: A Pentecostal Option', in *Essays on Apostolic Themes* (ed. Paul Elbert; Peabody, MA: Hendrickson, 1985), pp. 23–35; F.L. Arrington, 'Hermeneutics', *Dictionary of Pentecostal and Charismatic Movements* (ed. Stanley Burgess, Gary B. McGee; Grand Rapids: Zondervan, 1988), pp. 376–89; R. Stronstad, 'Trends in Pentecostal Hermeneutics', *Paraclete* 22 (3, 1988), pp. 1–12; R. Stronstad, 'Pentecostal Experience and Hermeneutics', *Paraclete* 26 (1, 1992), pp. 14–30; J.D. Johns and C. Bridges Johns, 'Yielding to the Spirit: A Pentecostal Approach to Group Bible Study', *JPT* 1 (1992), pp. 109–34; A.C. Autry, 'Dimensions of Hermeneutics in Pentecostal Focus', *JPT* 3 (1993), pp. 29–50; R. Israel, D. Albrecht, and R.G. McNally, 'Pentecostals and Hermeneutics: Texts, Rituals and Community', *Pneuma* 15 (1993), pp. 137–61; T.B. Cargal, 'Beyond the Fundamentalist-Modernist Controversy: Pentecostals and Hermeneutics in a Postmodern Age', *Pneuma* 15 (1993), pp. 163–87; R.P. Menzies, 'Jumping Off the Postmodern Bandwagon', *Pneuma* 16 (1994), pp. 115–20; G.T. Sheppard, 'Biblical Interpretation after Gadamer', *Pneuma* 16 (1994), pp. 121–41; J. McKay, 'When the Veil Is Taken Away: The Impact of Prophetic Experience on Biblical Interpretation', *JPT* 5 (1994), pp. 17–40; R.D. Moore, 'Deuteronomy and the Fire of God: A Critical Charismatic Interpretation', *JPT* 7 (1995), pp. 11–33; R.O. Baker, 'Pentecostal Bible Reading: Toward a Model of Reading for the Formation of Christina Affections', *JPT* 7 (1995), pp. 34–48; and K.J. Archer, 'Pentecostal Hermeneutics: Retrospect and Prospect', *JPT* 8 (1996), pp. 63–81.

[5] On this topic cf. especially E.E. Ellis, *The Old Testament in Early Christianity* (Grand Rapids: Baker, 1992); R.B. Hays, *Echoes of Scripture in the Letters of Paul* (New Haven: Yale University Press, 1989); C.A. Evans and J.A. Sanders, *Luke and Scripture: The Function of Sacred Tradition in Luke-Acts* (Minneapolis: Fortress, 1993).

approach is that revealed in the deliberations of the Jerusalem Council as described in Acts 15.1–29, which has recently shown up in certain academic discussions on Pentecostal hermeneutics.[6]

As is well known, the Jerusalem Council came together to determine if Gentile believers in Jesus must convert to Judaism in order to become full-fledged Christians. Luke relates that when Paul and Barnabas arrived in Jerusalem with the report regarding the conversion of the Gentiles, certain believers who were members of the religious party of the Pharisees (τινες τῶν ἀπὸ τῆς αἱρέσεως τῶν Φαρισαίων) demanded that the Gentile believers 1) be circumcised and 2) keep the law of Moses. As a result of this report and its somewhat mixed reception, the apostles and elders gathered together to look into this matter (ἰδεῖν περὶ τοῦ λόγου τούτου).

The first person to speak, Peter, begins by noting the actions of God among them. It was God who chose to allow the Gentiles to hear the Gospel (through the mouth of Peter) and believe. It was the God who knows all hearts who testified as to the validity of their faith by giving them the Holy Spirit. God had made no distinction between Jew and Gentile either in the giving of the Spirit or in the cleansing of hearts. In the light of such experience, Peter reasons that to place the yoke (of the Law?) upon these Gentiles would be tantamount to testing (πειράζετε) God. In contrast to the bearing of this yoke, Peter says it is by faith that all are saved!

This speech is followed up with a report by Barnabas and Paul, which also places emphasis upon God and the things that he did through them among the Gentiles, such as signs and wonders.

James now takes center stage and addresses the group. He not only interprets Peter's testimony to mean that God has received the Gentiles as a people unto his name, but he also goes on to argue that this experience of the church is in agreement with the words of the prophets, citing Amos 9.11–12 as evidence. Therefore (διό), in the light of what God had done and the agreement of these actions with the words of the prophets, James concludes that the Gentiles who are turning to God should not have their task made more difficult by requiring of them the observance of circumcision and the keeping of the Law of Moses. Rather, these Gentile converts are to be instructed to 'abstain from food polluted by idols, from sexual immorality, from the meat of strangled animals and from blood'. In the letter written to communicate the findings of this meeting to the church

---

[6] Cf. the discussion by F.L. Arrington, 'Hermeneutics', pp. 387–88 and R.D. Moore, 'Approaching God's Word Biblically: A Pentecostal Perspective' (A Paper Presented to the 19th Annual Meeting of the Society for Pentecostal Studies, Fresno, CA, 1989).

at large, the decision is described as resulting from the Holy Spirit, for v. 28 says, 'It seemed good to the Holy Spirit and to us not to burden you with anything beyond the following requirements'.

Several things are significant from Acts 15 for the purposes of this inquiry. First, it is remarkable how often the experience of the church through the hand of God is appealed to in the discussion. Clearly, this somewhat unexpected move of God in the life of the church (the inclusion of the Gentiles) was understood to be the result of the Holy Spirit's activity. It is particularly significant that the church seems to have begun with the church's experience and only later moves to a consideration of the Scripture.

Second, Peter's experience in the matter of Gentile conversions has led him to the conclusion that even to question the Gentile converts' place in or means of admission to the church draws dangerously close to testing God. Apparently Peter means that to question the validity of the Gentile believers' standing before God, in the face of what the Spirit has done, is to come dangerously close to experiencing the wrath of God for such undiscerning disobedience. In this regard it is probably not without significance that earlier in Acts (5.9) Peter asked Sapphira how she could agree to test the Spirit of the Lord (πειράσαι τὸ πνεῦμα κυρίου) through her lie. The results of her testing are well known. Is Peter implying a similar fate for those who stand in the way of the Gentile converts?

Third, Barnabas and Paul are portrayed as discussing primarily, if not exclusively, their experience of the signs and wonders which God had performed amongst them as a basis for the acceptance of the Gentiles. That such a statement would stand on its own, says a great deal about the role of the community's experience of God in their decision-making process.

Fourth, James also emphasizes the experience of the church through the activity of God as a reason for accepting the Gentile converts. It is clear that Luke intends the readers to understand that James adds his own support to the experience of the Spirit in the church, for James does not simply restate Peter's earlier words, he puts his own interpretive spin upon them.

Fifth, it is at this point that Scripture is appealed to for the first time in the discussion. One of the interesting things about the passage cited (Amos 9.11–12) is that its appeal seems primarily to have been that it agreed with their experience of God in the church.[7] But how did James (and the church with him) settle on this particular text? Did Amos intend

---

[7] As L.T. Johnson [*Scripture and Discernment: Decision Making in the Church* (Nashville, TN: Abingdon, 1996), p. 105] observes, 'What is remarkable, however, is that the text is confirmed by the narrative [events previously narrated in Acts], not the narrative by Scripture'.

what James claims that the text means? Could not the believers from the religious party of the Pharisees have appealed with equal or greater validity to other texts that speak about Israel's exclusivity and the Gentiles' relationship to Israel (cf. esp. Exod. 19.5; Deut. 7.6; 14.2; 26.18–19)?

When one reads the Hebrew text of Amos 9.11–12, or a translation based upon the Hebrew text, it becomes immediately obvious that there is no explicit reference to the inclusion of Gentiles as part of the people of God. In point of fact, in the Hebrew text, Amos says that God will work on behalf of the descendants of David 'so that they may possess the remnant of Edom and all the nations, which are called by the name, says the Lord that does this'. Although it is possible to read the reference to Edom and the other nations in a negative or retaliatory sense, it is also possible to see here an implicit promise concerning how Edom (one of the most hostile enemies of Israel) and other nations will themselves be brought into the (messianic) reign of a future Davidic king.[8] Whether or not such a meaning was intended by Amos is unclear.

By way of contrast, the LXX rendering of Amos 9.11–12 seems to intend a message about the inclusion of other individuals and nations who seek to follow God. At this crucial point, the text of Acts is much closer to the LXX, which reads, 'That the remnant of men and all the Gentiles, upon whom my name is called, may seek after (me), says the Lord who does these things'. The difference in the Hebrew text and the LXX seems to have resulted, in part, from reading Edom (אדום) as Adam (אדם) and taking the verb 'they shall possess' (יירשו) as 'they shall seek' (ידרשו).[9] Whatever may account for this rendering,[10] it is clear that James, as described in Acts 15.17, shows a decided preference for the LXX's more inclusive reading.

But why did James choose this particular text for support when other Old Testament passages appear to offer better and clearer support for the inclusion of Gentiles within the people of God? Such a choice is difficult

---

[8] So argues W.C. Kaiser, 'The Davidic Promise and the Inclusion of the Gentiles (Amos 9:9–15 and Acts 15:13–18): A Test Passage for Theological Systems', *JETS* 20 (1977), p. 102.

[9] C.F. Keil, *Minor Prophets* (Grand Rapids: Eerdmans, 1975), p. 334 n. 1 and D.A. Hubbard, *Joel & Amos* (Leicester; IVP, 1989), p. 242.

[10] Some argue a Hebrew text that challenges the MT at this point lies behind the LXX. Cf. M.A. Braun, 'James' Use of Amos at the Jerusalem Council: Steps Toward a Possible Solution of the Textual and Theological Problems', *JETS* 20 (1977), p. 116. R.J. Bauckham ('James and the Jerusalem Church', in *The Book of Acts in Its First Century Setting*, vol. 4; *Palestinian Setting* [ed. R.J. Bauckham; Grand Rapids, MI: Eerdmans, 1995), pp. 415–80) argues that the composition and interpretation of the Scriptural quotation in 15.16–18 is the result of 'the skilled use of contemporary Jewish exegetical methods and...' (how) '...the quotation is exegetical linked with the terms of the apostolic decree' (p. 453).

to understand until one views it within the broader context of the Lucan narratives. Specifically, Luke seems concerned to demonstrate that the promises made to David are fulfilled in Jesus and thus have implications for the church.

In the gospel, Joseph is identified as a descendant of David (1.27). The angel speaks to Mary regarding Jesus saying, 'The Lord God will give him the throne of his father David, and he will reign over the house of Jacob forever; his kingdom will never end' (1.32–33). Zechariah (apparently) speaks of Jesus when he says, 'He has raised up a horn of salvation for us in the house of his servant David' (1.69). Joseph and Mary go to the city of David for the census because Joseph is of the house and line of David (2.4). Later, the angels direct the shepherds to the city of David to find Christ the Lord (2.11). In Luke's genealogy of Jesus, David is mentioned (3.31). In a dispute over the Sabbath Jesus appeals to the actions of David (6.3). The blind beggar near Jericho addresses Jesus as the Son of David when he calls for help (18.38–39). In a discussion with the Sadducees and teachers of the Law Jesus says that although the Messiah is called Son of David, David calls him Lord (20.41–44).

This same emphasis continues in the book of Acts. Peter states that the Holy Spirit spoke Scripture through the mouth of David (1.16). In the Pentecost sermon Peter attributes scripture to David again (2.25) and says that he foretold the resurrection of Jesus (2.29–36). A little later in the narrative David is again identified as one through whom the Holy Spirit spoke (4.25). In Stephen's speech David is described as one who enjoyed God's favor (7.45). Several references to David are found in chapter 13 in Paul's sermon at Pisidian Antioch. David is said to have been a man after God's own heart whose descendant is the Savior Jesus (13.22–23). Jesus is said to have been given 'the holy and sure blessings promised to David' (13.34) and his death is contrasted with that of David (13.36).

That Luke would continue his emphasis on David should surprise no one. It would appear then, that part of the reason for the choice of this particular text from Amos is to continue the emphasis on the continuity between David and Jesus. It may also be significant that the first citation of Amos (5.25–27) in Acts (7.42–44) speaks of exile, while Acts 15 speaks of restoration.[11] Consequently, to cite the rebuilding of David's fallen tent

---

[11] For a comprehensive discussion of this approach cf. P.-A. Peulo, *Le problème ecclésial des Acts à la lumière de deux prophéties d'Amos* (Paris: Cerf, 1985).). Cf. also J. Dupont, ' "Je rebâtirai la cabane de David qui est tombée" (Ac 15, 16 = Am 9, 11)' in *Glaube und Eschatologie* (ed. E. Grässer and O. Merk; Tübingen: J.C.B. Mohr [Paul Siebeck], 1985), pp. 19–32.

as the context for the admission of Gentiles into Israel was perhaps the most effective way of making this point.

Sixth, James rather clearly speaks with authority as he discloses his decision. That the decision is closely tied to the previous discussions is indicated by the use of therefore (διό). That James has the authority to render a verdict is suggested by the emphatic use of the personal pronoun I (ἐγὼ κρίνω). But as the epistle itself reveals (v. 24), the decision was one that involved the whole group and the guidance of the Holy Spirit.

Seventh, several stipulations were imposed upon the Gentile converts. Most significant is the omission of a reference to circumcision. Aside from the directive to abstain from sexual immorality, the other commands refer to food laws. Their intent is a bit puzzling. Are they to be seen as the lowest common denominator of the Torah's dietary laws or as the true meaning of the food laws? Are they intended to be seen as universally valid? The practice of the later church (and perhaps Paul's own advice in 1 Cor. 8.1–13) has not viewed the food laws as binding, however.[12] Perhaps it is best to view them as (temporary) steps to ensure table fellowship between Jewish and Gentile believers. When the composition of the church changed to a predominately Gentile constituency, it appears that these directives regarding food were disregarded.

III

What sort of hermeneutical paradigm may be deduced from the method of the Jerusalem Council and what are the components of this model? Of the many things that might be said perhaps the most obvious is the role of the community in the interpretive process. Several indicators in the text justify this conclusion. 1) It is the community that has gathered together in Acts 15. Such a gathering suggests that for the author of Acts it was absolutely essential for the (entire?) community to be in on the inter-

---

M. Turner (*Power from on High: The Spirit in Israel's Restoration and Witness in Luke-Acts* [JPTS 9; Sheffield: Sheffield Academic Press, 1996], pp. 314–15) argues strongly for a interpretation which emphasizes '... that Zion's restoration is *well under way* as a consequence of Jesus' exaltation to David's throne'.

[12] There is some evidence that the decree regarding food was still followed as late as 177 CE in Gaul. Eusebius' report (*E.H.* V.1.26) of one female Christian's response to her tormentor, shortly before her martyrdom, illustrates this point. She said, 'How would such men eat children, when they are not allowed to eat the blood even of irrational animals?' (cited according to the translation of K. Lake, *Eusebius, Ecclesiastical History* I [London: Heinemann, 1926], p. 419.

pretive decision reached. 2) It is the community that is able to give and receive testimony as well as assess the reports of God's activity in the lives of those who are part of the community. 3) Despite James' leading role in the process, it is evident that the author of Acts regarded the decision as coming from the community under the leadership of the Holy Spirit. All of this evidence suggests that any model of hermeneutics which seeks to built upon Acts 15 cannot afford to ignore the significant role of the community in that process.

A second element which must be mentioned at this juncture is the role the Holy Spirit plays in this interpretive event. In point of fact, appeal is made to the action of God and/or the Holy Spirit so often in this pericope that it is somewhat startling to many modern readers. For not only is the final decision of the Council described as seeming good to the Holy Spirit, but the previous activity of the Spirit in the community also spoke very loudly to the group being in part responsible for the text chosen as most appropriate for this particular context. Such explicit dependence upon the Spirit in the interpretive process clearly goes far beyond the rather tame claims regarding 'illumination' which many conservatives (and Pentecostals) have often made regarding the Spirit's role in interpretation. While a model based on Acts 15 would no doubt make room for illumination in the Spirit's work, it would include a far greater role for the work of the Spirit in the community as the context for interpretation. While concerns about the dangers of subjectivism must be duly noted, the evidence of Acts 15 simply will not allow for a more restrained approach.

The final prominent component in this interpretive paradigm is the place of the biblical text itself. Several observations are called for here. First, the methodology revealed in Acts 15 is far removed from the historical-critical or historical-grammatical approach where one moves from text to context. On this occasion, the interpreters moved from their context to the biblical text. Second, the passage cited in Acts 15 was chosen out of a much larger group of Old Testament texts which were, at the very least, diverse in terms of whether Gentiles were to be included or excluded from the people of God. It appears that the experience of the Spirit in the community helped the church make its way through this hermeneutical maze. In other words, despite the fact that there were plenty of texts that appeared to teach that there was no place for the Gentiles as Gentiles in the people of God, the Spirit's witness heavily influenced the choice and use of scripture. Third, scripture was also apparently drawn on in the construction of certain stipulations imposed upon the Gentile converts to ensure table fellowship between Jewish Christian and Gentile Christian believers. This step seems to have been a temporary one and these stipulations in no way treat the Gentile converts as less than Christian nor as inferior to their Jewish-Christian brothers and sisters. These points unmistakably reveal that the biblical text was assigned and functioned with a great deal of authority in this hermeneutical approach. However, in contrast to the way in which propositional approaches to the issue of authority function, Acts 15 reveals that the text's authority is not unrelated to its relevance to the community, its own diversity of teaching on a given topic, and the role which the scripture plays in the constructing of temporary or transitional stipulations for the sake of fellowship in the community.

In sum, the proposed Pentecostal hermeneutic built on Acts 15 has three primary components: the community, the activity of the Spirit, and the Scripture. In order to gauge the usefulness of this paradigm, it will now be tested by addressing a specific particularly difficult issue currently facing the church.

IV

Perhaps one of the most significant current debates within the ecclesiastical world is that regarding the role of women in the ministry of the church. A number of problems complicate the issue, not least of which is the fact that the New Testament evidence ranges from texts that describe women as active participants in ministry to those that advocate the (complete) silence of women in the church. Although various approaches to these texts have been followed, for many interpreters the question comes down to one, did Paul (or someone writing in his name) mean what he said regarding silence? Normally, one of three interpretive decisions is made. 1) One possibility is that Paul intended for women to remain silent and, therefore, outside the ministry of the church. The passages which appear to advocate a leading role for women must mean something else or, at the least, be interpreted in a fashion that would not contradict the silence passages. 2) Another option is to say that Paul meant what he said regarding silence but did not intend these statements to be taken as universally applicable. Rather, they were directed to specific situations and have nothing, or very little, to contribute to the broader question. 3) Still another approach is to say that Paul simply did not mean what he seems to have said. Therefore, these texts do not contradict those which assign a leading role to women in the ministry of the church.

Each of these interpretive options, regardless of the theological orientation of the interpreters, is grounded in a somewhat rationalistic approach to the biblical text, which seeks to determine, primarily through historical-critical investigation, the meaning of these passages and how it is that they might fit together. For the most part, Pentecostals have followed the lead of others in attempting to come to a decision regarding this crucial issue. Unfortunately, there exists at present a logjam in most Pentecostal groups that shows few signs of breaking up. It is to this issue that the paradigm contained in Acts 15 is now applied.

The Pentecostal Community

As with the approach found in Acts 15, the appropriate place to begin this discussion is with the community in which this attempt at interpretation is to take place. Pentecostals should have little trouble with this component for the movement itself has been one in which community has played a leading role. For our purposes, the community is here defined as those individuals called out of the world by God who have experienced salvation through Jesus Christ and are empowered by the Holy Spirit to do the work of ministry in this present world. This community could be a single, local Spirit-filled body or a group (or denomination[s]) of such congregations. One of the crucial elements would be the presence of a sufficient level of knowledge of one another, accountability, and discernment within this community to safeguard against the dangers of an uncontrolled subjectivism and/or a rampant individualism. It would be a community whose shared experience of the Spirit would allow for testimony to be given, received, and evaluated in the light of Scripture. Therefore, as far as this issue is concerned, interpretation is no private affair, in the sole possession of scholars, but is the responsibility of the community. This observation remains valid even if, as in Acts 15, a group of leaders representing the larger group is called upon to perform such a function.

The Work of the Holy Spirit

It is within such a community that the experiences of the Spirit, or the acts of God, are manifested. As in Acts 15, the activity of God is made known to the larger community through testimonies about the work of the Holy Spirit. What sorts of testimonies would such a Pentecostal community hear regarding the role of women within the movement, and from whence would they come? The testimonies from the past found in the pages of publications from around the world like the *Apostolic Faith, Bridegroom's Messenger, Church of God Evangel, Pentecostal Holiness Advocate, Pentecostal Evangel*, and many others would bear witness to the fact that God has gifted women to do the work of ministry in the Pentecostal revival. The ministerial records from various denominational archives would reveal the ways in which the Spirit has endowed sons *and daughters* with gifts for ministries that circle the globe and manifest themselves in the planting of churches, founding of schools and orphanages, publishing newsletters and magazines, working with the poor and oppressed, as well as singing, preaching, teaching, and supporting the church financially. In addition to these forms of testimony, would not those converted, sanctified, Spirit Baptized, healed and called into the harvest through the ministries of our sisters join in the raising of their voices as to God's actions among us?

In the face of such powerful testimonies to the activity of God in the church, is a response like Peter's not appropriate—why do you wish to test God by placing restrictions upon the ministry of our Pentecostal sisters? If indeed God is giving gifts to women for ministry, are we not in danger of divine wrath if we test God by ignoring his actions? What if there are some in the broader community who object that *they* have not seen such ministry among women? One could only respond that most of those in Jerusalem had not seen Gentile converts with their own eyes, but in the end were willing to accept the testimony of others who had witnessed such conversions. At least within the Pentecostal community, the work of the Spirit would lead most to the conclusion that God does intend for women to take a leading role in ministry. But what about the biblical texts? Do they not, at least in some respects, contradict what the Spirit appears to be doing in the community? How should these texts be approached and what exactly do they tell us about women in ministry?

The Role of the Scripture

The dilemma at this point is the nature of the biblical evidence itself. For, in truth, the New Testament seems both to affirm and deny a leading role for women in the ministry of the church.

On the one hand, it must be acknowledged honestly that there are passages which state that women are to remain silent in the congregation (1 Cor. 14.33b–35) and under no circumstances are they permitted to teach or have authority over a man but must be silent (1 Tim. 2.11–12). Both texts have proven to be notoriously difficult to interpret in part because they seem to be contradicted or at the least modified by other passages in the same epistle (1 Cor. 11.5) or group of epistles (Titus 2.4).[13]

---

[13] One Pentecostal scholar goes so far as to suggest that the passage found in 1 Cor. 14.33b–35 is a later interpolation into the text. This somewhat radical decision is based

On the other hand, there are a number of texts which appear to assume a prominent role for women in the church's ministry. These texts indicate that: 1) it was expected that women had the gift of prophecy (Acts 21.9) and/or would pray and prophesy in the community's public worship (1 Cor. 11.3–16); 2) women were regarded as co-laborers in ministry by Paul (Rom. 16.3, 12; Phil. 4.3); 3) somewhat technical terminology for ministry functions could be assigned to women, note in particular the term διάκονον (Rom. 16.1) and the use of ἀπόστολος in Rom. 16.7;[14] 4) a woman could take the lead in instructing a man more fully in the way of the Lord (Acts 18.26), and 5) women hosted house churches (Acts 12.12; Rom. 16.3; 1 Cor. 16.19; Col. 4.15), which no doubt included more than simply providing space for worship.[15]

In the light of the experience of God in the community, there can really be no doubt which texts are most relevant to Pentecostals on the question regarding the role of women in the ministry of the church. Simply put, it would appear that given the Spirit's activity, those texts which testify to a prominent role for women in the church's ministry are the ones which should be given priority in offering direction for the Pentecostal church on this crucial issue. To the objection that might be raised on the basis of the silence passages, one can only respond that this objection is quite similar to the one that some of those present in Acts 15 could have produced regarding the exclusion of Gentiles. Despite the fact that a couple of silence passages do indeed exist, the powerful testimony of the Spirit in the life of the church coupled with numerous New Testament passages that clearly support a prominent role for women in ministry necessitate a course of action which not only makes room for women in the ministry of the church but also seeks to enlist all the talents of these largely under utilized servants of the Lord in the most effective way possible for work in the harvest.

A final way in which the Scripture might function in grappling with this issue concerns the possible need for the adoption of temporary stipulations in order to preserve the 'table fellowship' of the broader community. As with those adopted in Acts 15, these stipulations should be grounded

---

almost wholly on internal considerations. Cf. G.D. Fee, *First Corinthians* (Grand Rapids: Eerdmans, 1987), pp. 699–705.

[14] There may even have been an order of widows in the early church (1 Tim. 5.9–10).

[15] Cf. the relevant discussions in D. Birkey, *The House Church: A Model for Renewing the Church* (Scottdale, PA: Herald Press, 1988), and V. Branick, *The House Church in the Writings of Paul* (Wilmington, DE: Michael Glazier, 1989).

in the biblical tradition, in no way serve to undermine the legitimacy of women as ministers, and most likely be looked upon as temporary stipulations for the sake of genuine sensitivities on the part of some, both male and female, in the larger community of faith. However, it must perhaps be observed from the outset that the cultural and social context of a given community will be quite important in determining the specific stipulations adopted and could very well mean that stipulations might vary some in different parts of the world.

CHAPTER SEVEN

PENTECOSTAL BIBLE READING: TOWARD A MODEL OF READING FOR THE FORMATION OF THE AFFECTIONS*

Robert O. Baker**

Introduction

James sits quietly in his room. He stares blankly out of his window. His slackened face yields no awareness of the world around him. During his bad spells he will go days without speaking or acknowledging that he is spoken to. On a good day, those times when he will interact with those around him, he speaks with a passionless, flat voice, never betraying any emotion. Like most chronic schizophrenia patients, James suffers from *anhedonia*, a syndrome that is thought to be caused by damage to the brain's neural reward mechanism, rendering the afflicted individual unable to experience joy, affection, desire, pride, or humor.[1] With the exception of the loss of pride, much New Testament criticism today would seem to be like the work of a schizophrenic on a good day.

New Testament scholarship in general has displayed at least one of the major symptoms of paranoid schizophrenia. It lacks emotion. In their attempt to arrive at a scientific objective understanding of the text, scholars have inadvertently distorted the meaning of the texts they seek to explain. To seek to understand the ideational/rational content of a text without also seeking to experience and reflect upon its emotive effect is to skew the text's message. A rational approach to the biblical text is in effect, then, a schizophrenic one. By committing to read the text objectively from a critical distance, the professional reader subverts the text's evocative power or is at least unable to express the feeling that the text evokes in him or her.

---

* First published in the *Journal of Pentecostal Theology* 7 (1995), pp. 34–38.
** Robert O. Baker (PhD, Baylor University) currently resides in Bradenton, FL USA.
[1] M.E. Walsh, *Schizophrenia: Straight Talk for Family and Friends* (Warner Home Medical Library; New York: Warner, 1985), pp. 39–49.

Probably all of us have experienced certain affective responses as we have read biblical narratives, but these subjective feelings have not generally been seen as the domain of critical scholarship. Commenting upon the rational focus of contemporary reader-response criticism, Stephen Moore quoting Jonathan Culler has noted:

> The experiences that modern audience-oriented critics ascribe to their hypothetical readers are in contrast to their ancient or Renaissance counterparts, 'generally cognitive rather than affective: not feeling shivers along the spine, weeping in sympathy, or being transported with awe, but having one's expectations proved false, struggling with an irresolvable ambiguity, or questioning the assumptions upon which one has relied.[2]

To focus on the affective impact of a text places the critical scholar into the subjective realm of the emotions, decentering him or her from the objective distance that the biblical studies guild values so highly.[3]

Pentecostal scholars are in a unique position to deconstruct the Enlightenment myth and ideal of critical and passionless objectivity. As Pentecostals, we focus not only on orthodoxy (right belief), but also on orthopraxy (right action), and orthopathy (right feeling). Steven J. Land rightly notes that this threefold emphasis collapses the false dichotomy between reason and feelings.[4] Pentecostal readings, being informed by such a synthesis, are more holistic than has traditionally been the case in scholarly circles. In the present intellectual climate of postmodernism and deconstruction, where there is a breakdown of metaphysical hierarchies—object/subject, content/form, body/soul, scholarly/confessional—it would seem that the biblical studies guild is now more open to the holistic readings that Pentecostal scholars can bring to the field. Our agenda includes pushing at the edges of traditional concerns, moving beyond the discovery of a history behind the text, or the ideology of biblical discourse, toward an articulation of the formative rhetoric of the Christian canon. In this paper, I hope to take a few modest steps toward articulating how reading the Bible affects readers in their entire person.

I realized the importance of the emotional impact of the Scriptures on a particularly painful occasion. Word came to my family that my pater-

---

[2] J. Culler, *On Deconstruction: Theory and Criticism after Structuralism* (Ithaca, NY: Cornell University Press, 1982), p. 39, quoted in S.D. Moore, *Literary Criticism and the Gospels* (New Haven: Yale University Press, 1989), p. 96.

[3] Moore, *Literary Criticism*, p. 97.

[4] S.J. Land, *Pentecostal Spirituality: A Passion for the Kingdom* (JPTSup, 1; Sheffield: Sheffield Academic Press, 1993), pp. 13–14.

nal grandfather was near death. I was a teenager at the time and it had been several years since I had seen my grandparents. It was of singular importance to be with my grandfather one last time. A flurry of activity ensued: the purchase of plane tickets, the hurried packing of bags, a rush to the airport, and a desperate wait to see if we would even be allowed on the last flight that evening. When we arrived at the small regional airport, a family member was waiting and took us directly to the hospital. As we approached the nursing station, a nurse held up her hand, signaling us to wait until she finished her phone conversation. As we stood and waited she said into the phone, 'Doctor, I wanted to inform you that Mr Baker just expired.' Those words crushed me. All of the hurry then seemed pointless.

My father asked the nurse to refrain from notifying my grandmother, as he preferred to tell her himself. We arrived at my grandparents' home at about 3 am. My grandmother was awake, waiting for us. As I walked into the living room to give her a hug I saw her worn Bible open to John 14, 'I go to prepare a place for you'. She had been reading in her chair before our arrival, drawing comfort from the Scriptures. My father told her, 'Dad's gone.'

'I know,' she said, 'they called me.'

'I told them not to call, I didn't want you to be by yourself when you found out.'

'I wasn't alone.'

That simple affirmation and the knowledge that she had been reading from John evoked in me an awareness of the comforting presence of God. There was no decrease in sorrow, but I knew that God was with us in our sorrow. 'I go to prepare a place for you.' It is ironic. A passage that ostensibly communicates the absence of Jesus communicated to my family in that time of loss the presence of Jesus. My reading of Jn 14.1–2 perhaps did not reflect the *straightforward* meaning of the text, but it certainly was an affective reading.

My example points out some of the problems of reading the Scriptures for affect: problems that this paper will by no means completely overcome. Emotional response is both highly subjective and contextual. Whether or not the readers have had their morning cup of coffee or how they are getting along with their spouse affects their affect. Different readers will feel differently when reading the same text. The same reader may feel differently when performing a second reading of a text. It is this subjectivity of reading for affect that makes it a difficult topic to examine and discourse upon critically.

In this paper I will attempt to outline an approach to doing an affective reading in the New Testament. I will then seek to apply it to the passion of Jesus in John as a test case. It is important however to examine first some theoretical and methodological presuppositions for performing such a reading.

Roland Barthes

Roland Barthes in *The Pleasure of the Text* proposes that reading is an erotic activity that can result either in pleasure or bliss. The text of pleasure is defined as follows:

> The text that contents, fills, grants euphoria; the text that comes from culture and does not break with it is linked to a comfortable practice of reading.[5]
> On the other hand, the text of bliss is defined as follows:
> The text that imposes a state of loss, the text that discomforts (perhaps to the point of a certain boredom), unsettles the reader's historical, cultural, psychological assumptions, the consistency of his tastes, values, memories, and brings to a crisis his relation with language.[6]

Simply stated, the former affirms the reading subject. The latter confronts and affronts the reading subject.

Roland Barthes is a semiotician. As such his theory of criticism focuses on societal myths and the nature of language itself. For Barthes a myth is that which makes social structures appear natural, the way things are meant to be. Therefore texts that challenge our social assumptions or demythologize them could function as blissful texts. An example of a myth is the view of women in the 1950s. At that time it seemed natural to many persons that a husband should go to work and a wife should stay at home and care for the couple's children. In retrospect Barthes would argue that there was nothing natural about this arrangement at all. What made the arrangement seem natural was the ideology by which males oppressed females. The text of bliss then unmasks ideology for what it really is: not nature but social power.[7] The text that challenges our social assumptions, our ideologies, is blissful. The end of bliss is anarchy because in the blissful text the reading subject experiences an abrupt loss of his

---

[5] R. Barthes, *The Pleasure of the Text* (trans. R. Miller; New York: Hill & Wang, 1975), p. 14.
[6] Barthes, *Pleasure*, p. 14.
[7] R. Barthes, *Mythologies* (trans. J. Cape; New York: Noonday Press, 1972), pp. 118–31.

or her relationship to society resulting in complete solitude.[8] The bliss of the reader is the contemplation of the destruction of all culture and his or her selfhood.[9]

As a semiotician Barthes is also concerned with the reader's relationship to language. The text of pleasure confirms the reader's relationship to language. Such discourse is 'obedient, conformist, and plagiarizing'.[10] The text of bliss on the other hand affronts the reader, it represents the death of language.[11] The text of pleasure is a 'readerly' text; that is, it maintains the reader's comfortable relationship to language. The text of bliss however is a 'writerly' text; that is, there is a rupture or disfiguration of language.[12] The author is dead,[13] there is no definite correspondence between the signifier and the signified, the reader himself or herself infuses his or her own meaning into the sign from the reading side.

The above synthesis of Barthes' position represents an extreme simplification of his views. He is difficult to understand and often seems to revel in contradicting himself. While Barthes' approach to literature is not appropriate to the type of reading that I would like to perform, there are a few attractive features to his work.[14] He speaks about language and literary texts with a passion that is refreshing when compared to the sterility of much Anglo-Germanic discourse in the New Testament arena. A second strength of his work is that he speaks of a text's power both to affirm and to confront, to comfort, and to challenge. In addition he lays down certain criteria for determining what makes a text pleasurable or blissful. Although one may not entirely agree with Barthes' approach to affective reading, his work makes one point clear: alternative reading of texts can be done in a scholarly manner.

While Barthes' approach to reading literature has some attractive features it has some drawbacks as well. Barthes' views on language are not helpful for a discussion of the New Testament. It is difficult to see how the blissful state of complete isolation from society and from the meaning

---

[8] Barthes, *Pleasure*, p. 6.
[9] Barthes, *Pleasure*, p. 14.
[10] Barthes, *Pleasure*, p. 6.
[11] Barthes, *Pleasure*, p. 6.
[12] Barthes, *Pleasure*, p. 36.
[13] See Barthes' essay, 'The Death of the Author', in *Image Music Text* (trans. S. Heath; New York: Noonday Press, 1977), pp. 142–48.
[14] Barthes has in fact shown some interest in studying biblical texts. For an example see 'The Struggle with the Angel: Textual Analysis of Genesis 32.32–33', in *Image Music Text*, pp. 125–41.

of language can advance our understanding of literature that purports to reveal God. If language is meaningless, then there is no meaningful revelation and the effect of Scripture is to show that there is no signification, no meaning, no God.

The second deficiency of Barthes' work for my purposes is his erotic use of language. The word translated 'bliss' is the French word *jouissance*, an everyday polite term for orgasm. I do not care to do an orgasmic reading of the New Testament, nor do I think such a reading would be appropriate. Barthes' language is unabashedly erotic, and many of his examples are highly suggestive.[15] Using sexually charged language is not the most appropriate means of speaking about biblical texts. Most biblical texts are not erotic, therefore it would seem appropriate to use another terminology for its affective impact.[16]

Finding an Appropriate Affective Terminology

It is not unreasonable to assume that the Bible contains texts designed to evoke not just proper understanding (orthodoxy) or just proper actions (orthopraxy) but also proper feeling (orthopathy[17] or orthokardia).[18] To get at the affective impact of Bible reading it is important to use language that is consonant with the language of the Scriptures themselves. Gregory S. Clapper offers a framework that is more suitable than Barthes' approach for discussing the affective impact of the Scriptures in his book *John Wesley on Religious Affections: His Views on Experience and Emotion and their Role in the Christian Life and Theology*.

There are two advantages to utilizing Clapper's terminology. First of all he speaks of Christian affections as being more stable and enduring than just mood and emotion; he proposes that Christian affections are more like virtues.[19] Steven Land, who argues for a similar view of Christian affections, offers the following explanation:

> Love in particular and Christian affections in general are not passing feelings or sensate episodes. Affections are abiding dispositions which dispose the person toward God and the neighbor in ways appropriate to their source

---

[15] Among Barthes' favorite literary examples is the Marquis de Sade.
[16] Two possible examples of erotic biblical texts might be Song of Songs and Revelation.
[17] Land, *Pentecostal Spirituality*, p. 41.
[18] G.S. Clapper, *John Wesley on Religious Affections* (Pietist and Wesleyan Studies, 1: Metuchen: Scarecrow Press, 1989), pp. 154-56.
[19] Clapper, *John Wesley*, p. 85.

and goal in God. Feelings are important but they come and go, are mixed and of varying degrees of intensity. Moods too are variable, but affections characterize a person. One might, with adrenaline flowing, heart pumping and mood considerably elevated, breathe a silent thanks after a near miss on the highway. But this does not mean that one is a grateful person, much less a thankful Christian.[20]

So it may be seen that focusing on affections offers a distinct advantage for doing an affective reading. Affections are less variable and less context-dependent than are emotions or moods. Reading for affections frees the reader to focus on the features of the text rather than on the variable contexts of the reading audience.

The second advantage is that the language used by Clapper to describe Christian affections is more akin to the language used in the New Testament itself. Clapper enumerates the Christian affections as follows: thankfulness or gratitude; faith, which is more like personal trust than an affirmation of propositions; hope, the assurance of God's present work in believers and of future glory; love, 'the sum of all religion, the genuine model of Christianity'; fear, a holy awe that leads to repentance; joy, which the believer can experience even in sorrow or abject circumstances; and temperance, an abstinence from pleasures that do not lead to God.[21]

The similarity of affective language between the Gospel of John and Clapper is striking. Note the following examples from John:

Love
This is my commandment, that you love one another as I have loved you. No one has greater love than this, to lay down one's life for one's friends (15.12–13).[22]

Peace and Courage
I have said this to you, so that in me you may have peace. In the world you face persecution. But take courage; I have conquered the world! (16.33).

Fear or Awe expressed in worship
He said, 'Lord, I believe.' And he worshiped him (9.38).
Thomas answered him, 'My Lord and My God!' (20.28).

These few examples make it clear that while there is not an exact correspondence, the affective language provided by Clapper, at least in the

---

[20] Land, *Pentecostal Spirituality*, p. 136.
[21] Clapper, *John Wesley*, pp. 86–87.
[22] All quotations from the Bible are from the NRSV unless otherwise specified.

case of John's Gospel, offers a closer analogy than Barthes for describing the affective response anticipated by the implied author of John.

A Reader-Response Theory

The reader-response theory of Wolfgang Iser offers an avenue for performing an affective reading of a biblical text that avoids the weaknesses of Barthes' approach while affirming that the reading experience can be affective as well as cognitive.

Iser's View of the Text

Iser views the literary text as a communicative object. This object is intended by an author and is filled with indeterminacies or gaps.[23] The text contains instructions on how those gaps should be correctly filled.[24] The text does not refer to some hidden meaning that the interpreter is to dig out; rather the text is a potential experience that is realized by a flesh-and-blood reader. The role of the interpreter then is to experience the text by reading according to the rules of reading contained in the text.[25]

The Reader

Iser argues that literary texts are so structured that actual readers may properly fill in the indeterminacies of the text, that is, they may realize the communication intended by the author.[26] Iser defines the implied reader as 'those predispositions...necessary for a literary work to exercise its effect', or as a 'network of response-inviting structures which impel the reader to grasp the text'.[27] Stated simply the implied reader is a reading role offered to the actual reader of the text.

The implied reader is a set of rules in the text by which the reader can form a gestalt from the various perspectives in the text. These perspectives include the perspectives of the narrator, the characters, the plot, and

---

[23] W. Iser, *The Act of Reading* (trans. D.H. Wilson; Baltimore: Johns Hopkins University Press, 1978), p. 21.
[24] Iser, *Reading*, p. 38.
[25] Iser, *Reading*, p. 67.
[26] Iser, *Reading*, pp. 107-108.
[27] Iser, *Reading*, p. 34.

the reader. The convergence of these perspectives is where the meaning of the intended communication lies.[28]

The implied reader and the real reader are separate entities. The real reader is never able fully to suspend his or her disbelief, nor would such a state be desirable. Just as the literary work lies in a dialectic between the text and the reader so also the realization of the implied reader lies between the actual reader reading and the implied reader encoded in the text.[29] It is this reality that makes for multiple readings. Each reading is 'a selective realization of the implied reader'.[30]

For Iser the implied reader is a transcendental identity and it is therefore inappropriate to use outside sensibilities as an interpretive prism. The interpreter's lens should be ground from the text itself. That is not to say that real readers do not rely on personal experience to actualize the text; rather, what Iser objects to is the self-conscious use of qualifications such as Freudian psychology that are determined before one's encounter with the text.[31]

Therefore to perform an affective reading from the perspective of Wesley's understanding of Christian affections would clearly place me outside of Iser's approach to reader-response criticism. What I propose to do however is to read the text from the perspective that there are certain affections highly valued by the implied reader in John's narrative world. It is my argument that the implied reader views the formation of certain Christian affections as a rhetorical goal of the text. It is the goal of the implied author that the intended readers should not just have the correct beliefs, or perform the right actions, but also experience the appropriate affections.

Iser's View of Concretization

Concretization is 'the activity by which the text is put together in reading which leads to the reader's cognition of it as meaningful experience'.[32] The schematic text contains gaps. It is these gaps that the real reader fills in to create consistency from the literary text.[33] By filling in the meanings,

---

[28] Iser, *Reading*, pp. 35–36.
[29] Iser, *Reading*, p. 37.
[30] Iser, *Reading*, p. 37.
[31] R.C. Holub, 'Implied Reader', in I. Makaryk (ed.), *Encyclopedia of Contemporary Literary Theory* (Toronto: University of Toronto Press), p. 562.
[32] M.J. Valdes, 'Concretization', in Makaryk (ed.), *Contemporary Literary Theory*, p. 527.
[33] Iser, *Reading*, p. 189.

the reader creates an aesthetic object, a literary work from the literary text.[34] R. Alan Culpepper sums up the process of concretization nicely:

> As the reader adopts the perspectives thrust on him or her by the text, experiences it sequentially, has expectations frustrated or modified, relates one part of the text to another, and works out all the text leaves for the reader to do, its meaning is gradually actualized.[35]

As the actual reader processes the literary text he or she is constantly seeking to form a consistent narrative.

An Affective Reading of Jesus' Death in John

My thesis is that the death of Jesus as it is recounted in the Fourth Gospel (Jn 19.30) is the culmination of two affective-narrative strands woven into the fabric of John's narrative. By means of a selective sequential reading, I will seek to show how John has structured the Gospel in order to inculcate the Christian affections of love and fear in the actual reader.

By the time the reader of the Fourth Gospel has created the literary work to the point of Jesus' death, she or he has formed certain assumptions concerning that event. What is it that the reader experiences as he or she stands at the foot of the cross with the beloved disciple and the women, those who love Jesus and rejoice at Jesus' return to the Father (14.28)? First of all it is a fearful experience.

The Death of Jesus and the Christian Affection of Fear

Fear, it will be recalled, is not a slavish fear, but is more akin to awe. It is a perception of God in his otherness, his transcendence, his incomprehensible greatness.[36] In John, this affection is expressed in a worshipful response to Jesus. In 9.38 the healed blind man worships Jesus after the revelation that Jesus is the Son of Man. Likewise Thomas worships Jesus when he is revealed as the resurrected Christ (20.28).

The awe or fear that the Johannine Jesus impresses in the hearts of believing readers begins in the Gospel's prologue (1.1–14). It is here that the reader comes to know the divine origin of Jesus. Before the incarna-

---

[34] Iser, *Reading*, p. 21.
[35] R.A. Culpepper, *Anatomy of the Fourth Gospel* (Philadelphia: Fortress Press, 1983), p. 209.
[36] Clapper, *John Wesley*, p. 87.

tion, Jesus was the Logos, coexistent and coeternal with God. It is this Logos who is the agent of creation. It is this Word who is the life and light of all humanity. It is this Divine Person who becomes flesh and effects salvation for those who believe in him. It is this One who becomes a human being and has been witnessed by the implied author of the text. The effect of the prologue is to give the reader a privileged view of Jesus' identity by which he or she can gauge the ensuing events and characters.

What follows the prologue is a variety of encounters between Jesus and characters in the story world. Mark Stibbe asserts that the primary characteristic of the Johannine Jesus is his 'mysterious elusiveness'.[37] Stibbe traces the elusive nature of Jesus sequentially through the Gospel. In chs. 1–5 Jesus' language is elusive. This elusiveness is reflected in his interaction with his mother (2.4), the Jews (2.19–21), Nicodemus (3.3–10), the Samaritan woman (4.10–15), his disciples (4.31–33), and a royal official (4.48).[38] In 5.1–10.42 Jesus is elusive in regard to his movement. Many attempts are made to capture Jesus, but he is able to evade all attempts at apprehension. In chs. 13–17 the elusiveness of Jesus is demonstrated by the opacity of his farewell discourse to his disciples. In chs. 18–19, Jesus gives himself to those he eluded previously.[39] When the reader comes to the crucifixion and death of Jesus, she or he has an understanding of Jesus as the elusive mysterious one, and this understanding creates awe in the reader.

In addition to the understanding of Jesus from the prologue and the subsequent characterization of him as the one beyond apprehension, the reader is also able to draw upon certain predictive statements concerning Jesus' death that color his or her understanding and experience of that event. Specifically, in 10.17–18, Jesus asserts that in his death, he will not be a victim of evil persons; rather the time, the manner, and the necessity of his death are subordinate to his own authority and the command of his Father. The reader's memory of these assertions gives the reader a perspective for understanding Jesus' yielding of his spirit not as a failure, but as a mighty act of God.

Finally, the death of Jesus is depicted as his glorification. In 12.23 Jesus refers to his impending death as the hour of his glorification, expounding further that it is a 'lifting up' by which he will draw all persons to himself.

---

[37] M. Stibbe, 'The Elusive Christ: A New Reading of the Fourth Gospel', *JSNT* 44 (1991), p. 20.
[38] Stibbe, 'The Elusive Christ', p. 36.
[39] Stibbe, 'The Elusive Christ', pp. 36–37.

The view of Jesus' death as a glorification instead of just a humiliating victimization gives the reader reason to worship Jesus, not to flee or hang his or her head in shame.

The combination of these four elements—the depiction of Jesus as God in the prologue, the characterization of Jesus as the mysterious elusive one, the portrayal of his death as an act of his own authority, and the representation of his death as glorification—create a picture of the crucified Christ as one who is worthy of the reader's holy awe and worship. A sense of this awe may be seen in the first stanza of the hymn 'In the Cross of Christ I Glory':

> In the cross of Christ I glory,
> > Towering o'er the wrecks of time:
> All the light of sacred story
> > Gathers round its head sublime.[40]

The Death of Jesus and the Christian Affection of Love

The Fourth Gospel is so configured that the integration of the death of Jesus with the events that have gone before fosters the affection of love in the reader with Jesus as its primary object. Once again in the prologue the reader is alerted that Jesus, the Logos become flesh, has come to make persons the children of God and to give them a new birth. These affirmations create in the reader a sense that whatever follows, Jesus is one who acts in their behalf.

As the readers create the narrative world, following the actions and words of Jesus through the story, they arrive at his death with an understanding that Jesus is on the cross yielding his life because they, the readers, are the objects of Jesus' love. Jesus' predictions and teachings are the main sources for forming such an understanding. In 6.50-51, Jesus makes an allusion to his death as the offering of his flesh and that those who partake of his flesh will never die. In 10.11-18 Jesus teaches that he lays down his life as a shepherd would for his or her sheep. He lays down his life because he knows and cares for his sheep. It becomes increasingly clear to the reader that whatever Jesus does, he does it in his or her behalf.

In his farewell discourse Jesus teaches his disciples and the readers concerning the significance of his death. Jesus makes it clear that his death not only reveals that they are the objects of God's love, but also necessi-

---

[40] J. Bowring, 'In the Cross of Christ I Glory', in M.E. Aubrey *et al.* (eds.), *The Baptist Hymnbook* (London: Psalms and Hymns Trust, 1962), p. 178.

tates that they are to be loving subjects as well. He shows the disciples and the reader that the greatest love imaginable is laying down one's life for one's friends (15.13), that they are loved by Jesus (14.21; 15.9) and the Father (14.21, 23; 16.27). Those who love Jesus are required to obey his commandments (14.15; 15.9). In fact, loving one another is requisite to abiding in the love of Jesus.

As Jesus suffers the humiliation of arrest, trial, crucifixion, and death, the reader understands the cross as the ultimate expression of love for him or her. As the reader stands there with the others and together they see him offer up his life, they love and worship him. They see Jesus as worthy of all their life and all their love. Isaac Watts expresses the sentiment well:

> But drops of tears can ne'er repay the debt of love I owe.
> Here Lord, I give myself away; 'tis all that I can do.[41]
> In the Place of a Conclusion: Some Reflections on Process and Method

I have sought to demonstrate that reading the Bible is not just a cognitive experience, but an affective one as well. As a test case, I offered a reading of Jesus' death in the Fourth Gospel. It is my argument that the death of Jesus is so narrated and so related to the rest of the story that it fosters the formation of the Christian affections love and fear. The question I pose to myself now is: how well have I succeeded in my task? This study raises many more questions than answers. I have had the feeling as I have reflected on the subject matter, researched sources and sought to organize my ideas into some sort of cogent argument that I am on to something significant: namely, that Bible reading is an affective experience and that this experience is the proper domain of critical biblical research. At this time, however, I have no sense that I have a handle on how to discourse on the affective impact of Bible reading.

I followed to the best of my ability the phenomenological approach of Iser. His model is more formalist than other reader-response approaches, which allows for reading a text more on its own terms. I question, however, whether or not I have read the text on its own terms. I drew my understanding of affections from a 1989 dissertation on John Wesley's views of Christian affections. While Wesley's terminology would seem to offer the possibility of performing a reading that would benefit the believing

---

[41] I. Watts, 'Alas and Did My Savior Bleed', in R.P. Job *et al.* (eds.), *The United Methodist Hymnal* (Nashville: The United Methodist Publishing House, 1989), p. 294.

community, nonetheless, I fear that I may have distorted the affective experience by the grid I have brought. What remains to be done is in-depth analysis of the affective language in the Fourth Gospel in order that its affective rhetoric might be understood on its own terms.

My final question is a methodological one. Iser views the text as nonreferential, in the sense that it does not refer to a hidden meaning. The text for him represents one half of a communication event. The text requires a reader to complete the circuit of communication. By constructing a narrative from the schematic text, the reader's view of his or her own world is then transformed. What is the relationship between participating in the formation of the story-world and the transformation of the reader? I do not know that Iser has an answer to this question. It may be that the unanswered question is a weakness of his model (or my understanding of it).

It is my hunch that it is important to focus on the referential function of the biblical text. The Gospels do not refer only to an imaginative story-world, nor primarily to the historical Jesus, nor to the historical communities that produced these documents. The primary referent of the Gospels is the resurrected Christ, who is present to those he loves. It is this transcendent referent that makes me doubt the maxim that there is 'no sharp distinction between sacred and profane hermeneutics'.[42]

Clearly the Scriptures are special texts, having been inspired by the Holy Spirit. Truly to *understand* the message of biblical texts, one must submit to the Spirit who breathed the Scriptures and indwells the reading process. A reading strategy that coheres with and is informed by Pentecostal spirituality is a treasure that Pentecostal scholars can offer the church and its scribes. Pentecostal Bible reading is a bridge to our non-charismatic family in Christ. Crossing that bridge will result in our informing and being informed by the history and present practices of biblical interpretation.

---

[42] F. Kermode, foreword to Culpepper, *Anatomy of the Fourth Gospel*, p. vi.

CHAPTER EIGHT

DEUTERONOMY AND THE FIRE OF GOD: A CRITICAL CHARISMATIC INTERPRETATION*

Rickie D. Moore**

This study proposes a fresh approach toward something scarcely seen in biblical scholarship until recently—a literary theological reading of the entire book of Deuteronomy.[1] My treatment finds the theme of the fiery revelation of God at Horeb at the heart of the book, something which modern biblical scholarship heretofore has hardly noticed.[2]

My subtitle has double meaning. On the one hand, I am offering and urging an approach to the biblical text that is critical and at the same time charismatic, in the sense of its self-conscious commitment to read the biblical text through the lens of Pentecostal experience and confession. On the other hand, I want to say that the book of Deuteronomy is itself an act of interpretation that is, in a similar way, both charismatic and critical. Indeed Deuteronomy is the biblical canon's first programmatic attempt to re-read or interpret the canonical tradition previously given,[3] and it surely

---

* First published in the *Journal of Pentecostal Theology* 7 (1995), pp. 11–33.
** Rickie D. Moore (PhD, Vanderbilt University) is Chair of the Department of Theology at Lee University in Cleveland, TN, USA.
[1] Literary treatment of the whole of Deuteronomy in its final form was scarcely attempted in academic scholarship until Robert Polzin's *Moses and the Deuteronomist* (New York: Seabury, 1980), but Dennis T. Olson, *Deuteronomy and the Death of Moses: A Theological Reading* (Minneapolis, MN: Augsburg Fortress, 1994), offered the first full-scale literary *theological* treatment. Olson acknowledges the scarcity of attempts to approach Deuteronomy in this manner, drawing attention to the mixture of genres and particularly its casting in terms of a speech, which make Deuteronomy less inviting to literary approaches than, say, the narrative materials of books like Genesis or Samuel (See Olson, p. 2).
[2] While it has been common to see the content of the decalogue, and particularly the first commandment as represented in the Shema, at the center of the book (see P.D. Miller, *Deuteronomy*, Interpretation Series [Louisville: John Knox Press, 1990], pp. 14–15, this has not done justice to Deuteronomy's fuller emphasis upon the theophanic dimension of the Horeb revelation.
[3] The clearest acknowlegement of this point that I know is Walter Brueggemann, 'The Case for an Alternative Reading', *Theological Education* 23 (1987), p. 96: 'The primal script is the Mosaic event and the Mosaic narrative of Exodus and Sinai. Deuteronomy is a reread-ing of this ancient script, a second reading (cf. Deut. 17.18, from whence comes the name Deuteronomy), a derivative reading which is done with authority and imagination'.

must be seen as a remarkably critical attempt, if criticism has anything at all to do with being rigorously open to perspectives which stand over against one's own standpoint, to voices which intrude, as it were, from the margin.

A self-consciously Pentecostal perspective comes to the table of modern biblical scholarship as a voice from the margin. Perhaps for this reason it is better prepared to see the starkly marginal location of Deuteronomy's own word, a context no less marginal than the wilderness and yet ultimately even more marginal than that. It is a word that comes, so Deuteronomy claims, from out of the midst of the fire of God. This claim may be more relevant to a critical understanding of Deuteronomy, and perhaps even to the dynamic of critical interpretation itself, than 'critical' scholarship has yet dared to entertain. I hope to show in this paper how I, at least, have come to believe so. Such an effort has prompted me to begin, like the book of Deuteronomy, with a story. It is a story that leads to my interpretation of Deuteronomy that I will then set within the context of current Deuteronomy scholarship. Yet it is a story that tells not only how I have come to interpret Deuteronomy but also how Deuteronomy has come to interpret me.

A Journey in the Study of Deuteronomy

I have been a student of the book of Deuteronomy for a long time. As a child growing up in a Pentecostal denomination, it was natural for me to take the first words of Deuteronomy, 'these are the words of Moses to all Israel', as a personal invitation to draw near and to listen with all God's people to this one who had stood before the very fire of God on the holy mountain. I had never seen this fire, but this old man's words were not difficult for me to trust, perhaps because of the elders gathered around me, whose faces at times seemed to reflect what I took to be the light from that same fire. I felt that I could somehow come close to this fire and close to these words'.[4]

Yet there was an awareness, even then, that out beyond the margins of our Pentecostal community there were other voices with which I would have to contend, voices which knew nothing of this fire and which stood ready to offer a fiery challenge to the credibility of *my* ever knowing it.

---

[4] The Hebrew name for the book of Deuteronomy is אלה הדברים (*ellah ha-debarim*), 'these are the words'.

I suppose I first learned to fear these other voices from the same source that had first made me to desire holy fire, that is, the faces of my elders.

I finally encountered these voices in their full force when, as a young man, I left my father's house and took a journey into a far (different) country, where I spent all I had on a graduate program in Old Testament studies. There I was directed once again to the first words of the book of Deuteronomy, but now a mountain of scholarship stood before these words and yielded a very different reading, namely, 'these are *not* the words of Moses'. I learned that to believe otherwise was to be *'pre-critical'*. And I knew, without it having to be explicitly stated, that to be seen as 'pre-critical' in this environment was a fate to be feared worse than death. Being relegated to the camp of the pre-critical was cursed; being admitted to the guild of the critical was blessed. I survived that time mostly by hiding in a wilderness between the curse that I feared and the blessing that I could not bring myself to embrace.

To be more specific, the treatment of Deuteronomy that I encountered in my 'critical training' placed this book at the very center of the canons of modern biblical scholarship (as in the JE*D*P hypothesis) with its elaborate body of writings and prevailing theories on the late dating and complex redactional history of the Pentateuch.[5] This towering fortress of scholarship, with its formidable conclusions about the text and methods used to reach them, was a far cry from the ethos and impulses of my Pentecostal confession. This was the case not only with respect to the book of Deuteronomy but across the entire range of my 'critical training'. In a way that went against my deepest and mostly unconscious longings, I was being relentlessly conditioned to experience criticism and confession as mutually exclusive opposites.

Then came the day that I was offered a teaching position at my denomination's Pentecostal seminary. And as Providence would have it, for the very first semester and on a recurrent basis thereafter I was expected to teach a course on the book of Deuteronomy. My initial reaction was anxiety. There was no area of study where I felt any wider gap between the critical approach in which I had been schooled and the confessional interests for which I was now to be responsible. To my relief, I soon discovered the work of certain Evangelical scholars who had found ways to defend

---

[5] A representative survey of the historical critical scholarship on Deuteronomy can be found in R.E. Clements, *Deuteronomy*, Old Testament Guides (Sheffield: Sheffield Academic Press, 1989).

against the skeptical critical conclusions as far as the late, post-Mosaic dating of Deuteronomy and had done so by re-employing the very methods developed by the mainstream of historical critical scholarship, namely a form-critical argument that links the structure of Deuteronomy to an international treaty form found to be extant during the time of Moses but not in later centuries.[6] In this I found a new way to survive. I came out of hiding, but not much more than that. My new occupation essentially amounted to trying not to offend a confession that still seemed threatened, while trying to defend against a criticism that continued to intimidate me.

As my journey in teaching Deuteronomy continued, the book that I had expected to be the last place for discovering an interface between Pentecostal confession and critical biblical scholarship started becoming for me the place of liveliest intersection and greatest potential. This took place under the impact of changes which were happening on several fronts: (1) in the field of biblical studies, (2) in Pentecostal scholarship, and (3) in my own relationship to both as a result of my return to a context of study within a Pentecostal community.

In critical biblical scholarship there was the growing impact of the paradigm shift from moderism to post-modernism, which is now the rage in Western culture. The undermining of modernity's foundation upon an epistemology claiming neutral objectivity eliminated any credible basis for keeping marginal perspectives, such as my Pentecostalism would represent, from being given a hearing in the academic arena. I encountered a new permission to look at the biblical text through Pentecostal eyes.

Furthermore this was reinforced by the related shift in academic scholarship away from the dominance of historiographical concerns and toward literary approaches and interest in narrative and story.[7] In Pentecostal scholarship this encouraged a conscious interest in the narrative orientation of Pentecostalism's own theological heritage. Story or testimony had been the prime vehicle and mode of discourse in Pentecostal faith from its beginnings, long before it had become fashionable in academic circles.[8]

---

[6] M.G. Kline, *Treaty of the Great King: The Covenant Structure of Deuteronomy* (Grand Rapids, MI: Eerdmans, 1963) and K.A. Kitchen, *Ancient Orient and the Old Testament* (London: Tyndale Press, 1966), pp. 90–102.

[7] The literature is voluminous, but the shift is well represented by G.W. Stroup, *The Promise of Narrative Theology* (Atlanta, GA: John Knox Press, 1981). See also the seminal article of S. Crites 'The Narrative Quality of Experience', *JAAR*, 39 (1971), pp. 291–311.

[8] See M. Dowd, 'Contours of a Narrative Pentecostal Theology and Practice', (paper presented to the 15th Annual Meeting of the Society for Pentecostal Studies, 1985), and

Still the turn toward narrative and literary concerns in critical scholarship was undoubtedly important in helping Pentecostal scholars like myself to get in touch with their native 'tongue'. I began teaching Deuteronomy at a time when Robert Polzin's work had made a significant case for the value of pursuing literary study of this book as well as biblical literature in general.[9]

Alongside of these important changes in academic biblical study and in Pentecostal scholarship, however, there was for me the even more decisive change of becoming part of a community of Pentecostals where I began daily to be challenged and helped toward bringing my own faith perspective into conscious, thoroughgoing dialogue with my biblical scholarship for the first time. It was not that my own life experiences had been without relation to my critical studies before this time. Part of the discovery was that they had been having a great deal of effect on my research, but in ways that were largely in the background and out of conscious view. I found out that although I had spent many years being trained to interpret texts, I had learned very little about interpreting my own story.[10]

I believe I can honestly say (or testify!) that this conscious move to begin bringing my own faith confession into interaction with my technical work on the text, instead of a compromise or contamination of my critical study (which is what I had been led to expect from such a move), was actually encountered as the most *critical* step I had ever taken in studying biblical texts. It is precisely what enabled me and forced me to realize that many of my earlier research choices and conclusions, which had passed for *critical* scholarship,[11] had actually been the product of largely *uncritical* impulses, such as social conformity and intellectual intimidation. I encountered a great deal of self-discovery, some of it unwelcomed and painful, which made biblical study more critical and yet at the same time

---

J.-D. Plüss, *Therapeutic and Prophetic Narratives in Worship: A Hermeneutic Study of Testimony and Vision* (Bern: Peter Lang, 1988).

[9] *Moses and the Deuteronomist*, cited earlier.

[10] A book which focused this insight for me at the time was C.V. Gerkin, *The Living Human Document: Re-Visioning Pastoral Counseling in a Hermeneutical Mode* (Nashville, TN: Abingdon Press, 1984). Far more important than this book, however, was the person who recommended it to me, Robert D. Crick, an elder on my faculty who took a personal interest in me in those early years and 'read me like a book' with his brilliant pastoral counseling skills and fathering compassion. He was to me what Morrie Schwartz was to Mitch Albom in Albom's wonderful autobiographical account, *Tuesdays With Morrie* (New York: Doubleday, 1997). I will be forever grateful.

[11] I refer here mainly to papers written for courses in my graduate program at Vanderbilt University, 1976–1981.

more confessionally invigorating for me than it had ever been. As I continued teaching Deuteronomy in this vein and in this setting I became more and more convinced that it was opening me toward a fresh approach to the biblical text that could prove very significant and helpful to both Pentecostalism and biblical scholarship as a whole. I did not see some great new hermeneutical formula. What I saw instead were more and more instances in the particular text of the book of Deuteronomy where Pentecostalism's narrative orientation and instincts seemed capable of freshly informing and benefiting from a literary-theological approach to the book of Deuteronomy.

First, I was struck by the way that Deuteronomy went beyond merely utilizing narrative (a great deal of the literature of the biblical canon does this) to commending it as the prime means of expressing and keeping the faith. No urging of the book is more prominent than the call to remembrance.[12] What's more, as the Hebrew canon's own paradigm for passing the faith to a new generation,[13] Deuteronomy succeeds through its own example in elevating narrative to a place of primacy and centrality for the whole canon. The work of Walter Brueggemann was especially important in helping me begin to see 'narrative as Israel's primal mode of knowing' and the significant implications which flow from this.[14] Yet I knew another means of access to such insights. I knew from my own background as a Pentecostal what it was like to be on the inside of a testifying, witnessing community where narrative was the central mode of theological expression. I began to sense that Pentecostals had significant insights to offer as well as receive in the study of this important aspect of Deuteronomy.

Specific elements in the narrative content of Deuteronomy began to appear especially relevant as I continued to pursue what seemed like a convergence of critical and Pentecostal perspectives on the text. Foremost here was the emphasis given in the book to the theophanic experience and revelatory testimony of Mount Horeb. The striking feature was not just that Deuteronomy repeatedly recalls this event (1.6; 4.10–15; 5.2–33; 18.16–20; 34.10) but also that it seems to strive to make it available and

---

[12] Especially prominent examples are seen in chapters 4 and 8. For a full survey see Edward P. Blair, 'An Appeal to Remembrance: The Memory Motif in Deuteronomy', *Interpretation* 15 (1961), pp. 41–47.

[13] On this see especially D.T. Olson, *Deuteronomy and the Death of Moses* (Minneapolis, MN: Fortress Press, 1994), pp. 7–14.

[14] See especially his *The Creative Word: Canon as a Model for Biblical Education* (Philadelphia, PA: Fortress Press, 1982), pp. 15–27.

present to the new generation (see especially 5.2–4). Once again I encountered something that seemed familiar in the light of my experience as a Pentecostal. I knew something first-hand about a community called to gather around a root experience of visionary and revelatory encounter with God in a way that expects the ushering of the present into that encounter.[15] It became apparent that the role of the Pentecost event (cf. Acts 2) in my own faith tradition suggested important parallels with the role of the Horeb event in the book of Deuteronomy, parallels of spiritual and experiential dynamics which went beyond the historical evidence which modern scholarship had turned up for linking the Feast of Pentecost to the commemoration of the giving of the Law at Horeb or Sinai.[16]

I do not think it is going too far to say that I sensed the affirmation of a *charismatic dimension* in Deuteronomy that scholarship was ill equipped to probe. I found one Old Testament scholar who had seen the category of charisma and the notion of a charismatic tradition as being decisive for understanding the book of Deuteronomy. Joseph Blenkinsopp, in his book *Prophecy and Canon*, argues that the book of Deuteronomy along with the three divisions of the Hebrew canon were formed in response to an ongoing conflict of authority claims between an institutional tradition of 'normative order' and a charismatic tradition of 'free prophecy'.[17] Blenkinsopp links these traditions and categories of analysis on the one hand to Old Testament scholarship's longstanding debate on the relationship between law and prophecy and on the other hand to Max Weber's sociological typology of institution versus charisma.[18] The view of Deuteronomy that emerges in Blenkinsopp's treatment appreciates the strategic impact of a charismatic tradition on the book, but sees this tradition as a social threat which the book of Deuteronomy was fashioned to mitigate and control. Blenkinsopp sees a book 'deeply indebted to prophecy', but nevertheless shaped by an opposing clerical scribalism that sought to neutralize charismatic

---

[15] For a recent attempt to develop this insight into a central thesis for Deuteronomy see J.G. McConville and J.G. Millar, *Time and Place in Deuteronomy* (Sheffield: Sheffield Academic Press, 1994).

[16] See R. Stronstad, *The Charismatic Theology of St. Luke* (Peabody, MA: Hendrickson, 1984), pp. 58–62.

[17] Prophecy and Canon: A Contribution to the Study of Jewish Origins (Notre Dame, IN: University of Notre Dame Press, 1977).

[18] Blenkinsopp, *Prophecy and Canon*, pp. 7–9, 39–46, and 147–52. Blenkinsopp cites translations of several of Weber's major works, originally published just before and after the sociologist's death in 1920: *Ancient Judaism* (New York: The Free Press, 1952); *The Sociology of Religion* (London: Methuen, 1965); and *The Theory of Social and Economic Organization* (New York: The Free Press, 1964).

claims by assimilating their insights and impulses 'within its own institutional grid'.[19] Rather than 'ascribing cynical self-interest to these Torah scribes', Blenkinsopp wants to respect 'that they were persuaded of their own legitimacy and of the inability of prophecy to provide a sound basis for the life of the community'.[20]

I do not know whether Blenkinsopp's analysis was consciously affected by the charismatic renewal that peaked on his campus of the University of Notre Dame in the seventies, right before the time his book appeared.[21] However, I have come to realize, along with most of the scholars in this generation, I suppose, that where we stand profoundly affects our reading of the data. Scholars did not talk much about 'readings' back during the time when Blenkinsopp's volume appeared. However, things have changed dramatically since then. It is surely becoming much clearer to us all now that the historical critical methods of that day, though still very much in use, have themselves given decisive ground on their authority claims. In the end they too produce nothing other than 'readings'.[22]

Blenkinsopp offers *one reading* of a charismatic dimension in the book of Deuteronomy, one that is not neutral with respect to the sociological categories he utilizes. The modern Western academic tradition, which Blenkinsopp represents with his historical critical methodology and Weberian sociological analysis, is surely one that sides overwhelmingly with 'normative order' over against 'charisma'. Notwithstanding the rela-

---

[19] *Prophecy and Canon*, p. 8.
[20] *Prophecy and Canon*, p. 8.
[21] For an account of the Catholic Charismatic Renewal and the early role of the Notre Dame University campus as a center of this movement, see F.A. Sullivan, 'Catholic Charismatic Renewal', in S.M. Burgess and G.B. McGee (eds.), *Dictionary of Pentecostal and Charismatic Movements* (Grand Rapids, MI: Zondervan, 1988), pp. 110–26. It is perhaps confirming of my own lack of truly critical engagement at this time to admit that, despite my knowledge of and interest as a Pentecostal in this well-publicized event, the question of any relationship between the clash of institution and charisma on the Notre Dame campus and the discussion of such a clash in ancient Israel by this Notre Dame professor never entered my mind when I first encountered Blenkinsopp's book during this time.
[22] I make this latter point not in order to dismiss but rather properly to appreciate Blenkinsopp's contribution. I believe his analysis is seminal and helpful in pointing to a decisive charismatic dimension and tradition in the book of Deuteronomy. His application of Weber's sociological categories of charisma and institution has allowed him to get at larger dynamics and concerns in the literature than what one usually finds in historical-critical work of this sort, and this is to the benefit not only of the study of Deuteronomy but also of its application to matters of contemporary concern. Blenkinsopp, in fact, uses his canonical study to suggest a more positive appreciation for charisma in the life of established religion than one usually finds in modern Western scholarship (*Prophecy and Canon*, pp. 151–52), and as a Pentecostal I welcome this as a positive and long overdue step.

tive value he might ascribe to the latter, it is clear that he comes from a perspective that is defining and viewing charisma from the outside. How would the charismatic dimension in the book of Deuteronomy read to someone coming from the other side? I have become convinced that this latter question is worth pursuing to the potential benefit of all. At the same time, I recognize that any attempt on my part to do so immediately encounters some serious problems. First, there is the question of whether my life-long participation in a North American 'classical' Pentecostal denomination, not to mention my graduate training at a secular university, qualifies me to attempt a reading from 'the other side'. Margaret Poloma's sociological study of the leading North American Pentecostal denomination, *The Assemblies of God at the Crossroads*, utilizes the same Weberian categories to show that we North American Pentecostals have gone a long way already down the road of institutionalization and loss of our 'charismatic' identity.[23] Then there is the problem that even with *this* insight we find ourselves appropriating definitions, methods, and approaches to interpretation that derive from 'outside' sources.

Yet then does it not require precisely such sources 'outside' ourselves to make our interpretation something more than a self-serving projection of our own experience and ego, in other words, to make our interpretation *critical*? Is it the case, then, that any attempt to read the charismatic dimension of the biblical text from the inside, such as I am here proposing, will inevitably shut down the 'outside' perspective, or critical principle, which alone delivers us from self-serving subjectivity? Does a critical approach to interpretation invariably end where a confessional approach begins? It is at the heart of my purpose here to indicate how I have come to believe otherwise.

On the surface of things, it should not be surprising that modern thought has been so successful in training us to see criticism and confession as clear opposites. There is no doubt that the embrace of confession has too often served the avoidance of criticism, the stifling of voices different from or outside of our own. I say, 'no doubt', because I have seen this dynamic not just in others but also in myself. Biblical criticism helped me to get in touch with a lot of this. Yet I came to find another dimension of criticism that academic criticism, as I have experienced it, scarcely touches. It is a level of criticism that I find, if anything, *more critical* insofar as it

---

[23] *Assemblies of God at the Crossroads: Charisma and Institutional Dilemmas* (Knoxville, TN: University of Tennessee, 1989), pp. 232–41.

unleashes a starker challenge to the self-securing tendencies of my own interpretive standpoint. It is the criticism which I found and experienced when I pushed more deeply *into* rather than *away from* my Pentecostal confession and experience.

I began to encounter a voice from the text of Deuteronomy that was more critically demanding of me than critical scholarship ever had been. This was the voice that brought me to the self-effacing realization that my academic training as an Old Testament scholar had been dominated largely by suppressed embarrassment and fear. These two things had driven me *everywhere* in my study, but I was too *uncritical* to notice. I was secretly embarrassed about the uncredentialed heritage and humble status of my uneducated Pentecostal elders. Notwithstanding the fiery 'mountain top' experiences to which my elders bore witness, and perhaps more and more *because* of them, it was a past I wanted to forget and one which I was desperately trying to 'rise above'. As far as fear, I was afraid of scholars and smart people. I was constantly intimidated by them and in awe of them, never realizing at the time that this was the fear of which worship is made. I had a chance to recognize the power with which both of these passions were acting upon me one day when a friend and fellow graduate student, a Lutheran who had turned down an offer to study at Yale, asked me what church I attended. My face flushed with shame as he identified my denomination as Pentecostal and even asked me about speaking in tongues. I was so afraid of my friend's 'educated' opinion of me that I could do little more than stammer and grope for an awkward escape from the encounter. I shook off the potential self-revelation of this moment and went right back to my study carrel that day, suffering no loss of faith in my critical access to how the ancient authors came to compose the biblical writings, even though I was completely out of touch with the decisive factors at work behind *my* scholarly writing, right there in front of my nose.

When I finally made the turn toward a self-consciously Pentecostal approach to the text, Deuteronomy met my past-negating embarrassment with its sustained call for God's people to remember. Remember your background of homelessness in an extremely rural area where you depended on a welfare system of daily food allotments (e.g., 8.2–16); remember that your ancestors were known not for their education but for a lack of knowledge (8.3,16); remember that your pedigree traces not from the upper class, middle class or even lower middle class but rather from slaves (5.15; 15.15); remember even that your background reveals a humiliating negation of national honor (9.7,13, 25).

Deuteronomy met my fear of intellectual giants with its condemnation against fear of all the giants that faced God's people (1.28–35; 7.17–18).

In fact the very context of Deuteronomy is determined by a lamentable episode of capitulation to this fear (ch. 1). The fear of an old generation postponed entry into the land, so that a new generation had now to be addressed with the same covenant choice. This kind of fear is found thriving here in the absence of the one fear that is prominently commended in the book of Deuteronomy and one that, I had to admit, was virtually non-existent in the context of my academic training—the fear of God (e.g., 4.10; 5.29). Deuteronomy helped me to see the underlying issue whenever fear was directed to anything other than God. The issue was idolatry. I had never realized before how much fear had to do with worship.

To put it succinctly, in the face of Deuteronomy's principal call to have no other gods before Yahweh, I found that another fear had claimed my allegiance. Before the call to remember the past and to honor my father and mother, I found myself given over to repression, embarrassment and dishonor. Interpreting Deuteronomy through the grid of my Pentecostal experience and vice versa brought me to a new interpretation of myself—a rigorously critical interpretation.

I realized at the same time that the book featured a rather rigorous criticism of the people of Israel and even Moses, who repeatedly is seen acknowledging his own weakness, failure, and consequent debarment from the promised land.[24] In fact, I cannot remember ever seeing this degree of self-critical rigor anywhere in the discourse of modern criticism. Was this critical perspective of Deuteronomy achieved through bracketing out the 'inside' confession while opening to the scrutiny of 'outside' sources? Reading Deuteronomy in intersection with my Pentecostal experience led me to another possibility and explanation. For I found on the inside, indeed at the very heart, of my Pentecostal experience and, I believe, the charismatic dimension of the book of Deuteronomy as well, an overwhelming encounter with the ultimate 'outside' source, so that the most radical criticism is disclosed precisely at the core of this confession. Against modernity's longstanding dichotomization of confession and criticism, there is found here a surprising fusion. It may, in fact, be the constitutive fusion in the radical inaugural moments of charismatic experience and tradition. I am proposing that in such moments utter confession and utter criticism implode. It is an utterly confessional moment, for everything yields to the claim of a theophanic experience. The claim is not

---

[24] See J.G. McConville, *Grace in the End: A Study in Deuteronomic Theology* (Grand Rapids, MI: Zondervan, 1993), pp. 133–134, who is the only scholar I have found who acknowledges the remarkably critical thrust of this literature.

decided but evoked, so that it is not so much a matter of *making a claim* as a matter of *being claimed.* Yet because this is the case, it is a moment of utter criticism. To be thus claimed is at the same time to be disclaimed, to be seized, taken captive and dispossessed of everything previously claimed. It is to know what it is to stand stripped down to the nakedness and weakness of one's confession. It is to know how vulnerable one's claims were all along and ever will be. It is an experience so radically confessional that we, like Isaiah, can say nothing less than, 'I saw God!' Yet it is so radically critical at the same time that we cannot help but exclaim, 'Woe is me!' Over against this kind of experience I find the tradition of Enlightenment criticism somewhat trivial and not nearly critical enough.[25]

Coming from this kind of critical-charismatic experience opens up a different reading of reality and a different reading of Deuteronomy. The way I read it (*and the way it has read me!*), Deuteronomy is itself coming from this kind of experience, and it is grounded and driven by the theophanic encounter with Yahweh at Horeb. This overwhelming revelatory moment, I would contend, is the prime issue and theme of the book. This is where Moses is coming from and where he is insisting that the new generation, and by extension *every* new generation, must come from if they are to live, keep the faith, and inherit the promises of God.

The Death of Moses and the Fire of God

The quickest and clearest way for me to present the outline of this literary-theological interpretation of Deuteronomy is to do so in contrast to an alternative one that has recently been offered by Dennis Olson of

---

[25] At least one scholar within the critical guild has ventured to consider how that the witness to divine wonder in the biblical text represents a *critical* challenge to the sociology and epistemology of the Western academic establishment. See W. Brueggemann, *Abiding Astonishment: Psalms, Modernity, and the Making of History* (Louisville, KY: Westminster/ John Knox Press, 1991). 'Abiding astonishment' is a phrase and a formulation which Brueggemann takes up from Martin Buber (M. Buber, *Moses* [Atlantic Highlands, NJ: Humanities Press International, 1946], pp. 75–77). He follows Buber in acknowledging that regardless of how one thinks about the possibility of *supernatural* phenomena, the experience of 'wonder must be accepted as a datum' that cannot be explained away. Indeed wonder happens precisely at the point where *'explanation'* has been overwhelmed and overridden. Brueggemann seems to think that a modern hermeneutic which has dismissed 'wonder' in the name of critical objectivity has done so at the cost of blinding itself from the most decisive aspect of the literature and the people it has sought to understand, but even more than that, it has blinded itself from its own ideological stake in the dismissal, evading the key clue to a truly critical understanding of itself (pp. 41–53).

Princeton University. Olson's comprehensive treatment of Deuteronomy is the first thoroughgoing literary-theological approach to the book that has appeared in mainstream biblical criticism.[26] His grasp of the book's structure offers what I believe is a breakthrough insight. His convincing identification of the parts into which the canonical form of the book has been arranged sets the stage for identifying the theme that holds the parts together. Thus I follow Olson's literary insight into the book's structure in my own effort to identify the book's main theme. Yet our different theological perspectives, which surely have to do with different ways of perceiving and pursuing *critical* interpretation (and perhaps charismatic encounter as well), yield starkly contrasting understandings of Deuteronomy's primary theme. Olson argues that the book's governing theme is *the death of Moses*,[27] whereas I find it in the theophanic encounter with *the fire of God*. I will summarize Olson's interpretation before offering my own.

Olson introduces his reading of Deuteronomy with the observation that a series of parallel superscriptions mark the respective beginnings of all the major sections of the book in its present form.[28] The book itself begins

---

[26] Olson, *Deuteronomy and the Death of Moses*, pp. 4–5, presupposes some of the broad conclusions of historical critical scholarship as far as attributing the book to a Deuteronomistic school whose composition of Deuteronomy took place in multiple stages over a range of time that turned on two major events: (1) the fall of the northern kingdom, the place where the Deuteronomists were thought to have originated before being forced to migrate to the south when the fall of the north occurred (2) the fall of the southern kingdom, a crisis that provided the Deuteronomic tradition with a chance to offer the nation a viable way forward in the face of the collapse of the 'establishment' traditions of Judah. Olson does not offer any argument for these conclusions nor does his central argument depend upon these conclusions in any significant way, since he is treating the book in its final form. On the other hand, his central argument demonstrates such a thoroughgoing coherence, integrity and balance in the final shape of Deuteronomy that it would seem to have the unintended effect of posing a formidable challenge to the historical-critical claims for multi-staged, multi-layered composition. For a recent and *intentional* challenge to these long-held critical positions on the book of Deuteronomy see the historical-critical treatment of Oxford scholar J.G. McConville, *Grace in the End*, pp. 45–64.

[27] Olson, *Deuteronomy and the Death of Moses*, pp. 6–22, in presenting his argument for the theme of Moses' death, calls it 'an important recurring theme' (p. 7) and 'a central metaphor' (p. 17), seemingly careful not to overstate. However, his claims for the theme's integral relationship to the book's entire structure and theological movement (pp. 21–22) indicate nothing less than seeing the death of Moses as *the* leading theme.

[28] Olson, *Deuteronomy and the Death of Moses*, pp. 14–15. Olson points to other scholars who have noted the editorial structuring role of the superscriptions, as early as P. Kleinert, *Das Deuteronomium und der Deuteronomiker* (Leipzig: J.C. Hinrich, 1872), p. 167, but Olson breaks fresh ground in finding in these headings the key for grasping the overall literary shape of the book and the interrelationship of its parts. Here and in the following paragraphs I draw from Olson's own summary of Deuteronomy's structure, as presented on pp. 14–17.

with the most inclusive such superscription: *'these are the words of Moses'* (1.1). This phrase stands before not only the whole book but also the initial narrative section, which reviews the events leading up to the present context of Moses' address to the new generation.

In 4.44 we encounter the second superscription, *'this is the torah'*. It introduces what Olson takes to be the most defining section of the book. This is so since *torah*, Olson argues, is the most adequate genre term for Deuteronomy as a whole, and this short section, which recounts the giving of the decalogue or ten commandments, presents what Olson sees to be a nutshell summary of the entire book.

The next section begins in 6.1 with *'this is the commandment, statutes and ordinances'*. The singular noun 'commandment' refers, so Olson maintains, to none other than the great commandment of the *Shema*, which is presented right away in 6.4–5. This command, which only states in a positive way what the first commandment of the decalogue expresses negatively, is seen to be elaborated in the remainder of this longest section of the book. First there is commentary on the great commandment itself extending through chapter 11, argues Olson, and then comes the lengthy subsection of chapters 12–28, which begins by reiterating the second part of the earlier superscription, *'these are the statutes and the ordinances'* (12.1). These detailed laws which, as others have recognized,[29] expand upon the commands of the decalogue, are ultimately to be seen as expansions of the single great commandment.[30]

Chapters 29–32 form the next section and are introduced with, *'these are the words of the covenant'* (29.1)—not the one made with Israel at Horeb, the verse quickly qualifies, but rather the present one 'in the land of Moab'. These chapters feature three new measures, Olson argues, that are meant to provide for Israel's future covenant life: (1) a liturgy of covenant renewal (chaps. 29–30; cf. 31.10–13), (2) a transfer of leadership from Moses to Joshua along with the writing down of *torah* (chap. 31), and (3) the giving of the Song of Moses as a continuing witness (chap. 32).

The final superscription, *'this is the blessing'*, stands before the book's last two chapters. They present the last words of benediction that Moses

---

[29] See especially S. Kaufman, 'The Structure of the Deuteronomic Law', *Maarav*, 1.2 (1979, pp. 105–158, whose proposal for seeing the laws of Deut. 12–28 in terms of a series of legal expansions of the ten commandments in the same order of the decalogue has been widely accepted in recent scholarship.

[30] Olson, *Deuteronomy and the Death of Moses*, pp. 49–51, points to the long tradition of recognizing the inclusive role of the great commandment. He cites rabbinic comment as well as the words of Jesus (Mark 12.28–31).

pronounces over the children of Israel (chap. 33) and then the ensuing account of Moses' death, which includes a kind of eulogy of last words pronounced over Moses (chap. 34).

So the sections of Deuteronomy can thus be summarized:[31]

> **Chaps. 1–4**
> 'These are the words' (1.1) Past Story
>
> **Chap. 5**
> 'This is the torah' (4.44) Torah in a Nutshell
>
> **Chaps. 6–28**
> 'This is the commandment, Law for the Present statutes and ordinances' (6.1)
>
> **Chaps 29–32**
> 'These are the words New Covenant for of the covenant' (29.1) the Future
>
> **Chaps. 33–34**
> 'This is the blessing' (33.1) Blessing for the Future

The theme of Moses' death, which obviously dominates Deuteronomy's final section, is found by Olson in all the previous sections as well. He finds that it is not only present in each part but also strategically placed in a way that unites all the parts together.[32]

The first section (chaps. 1–4), which highlights the story of judgment upon the old generation (1.19–2.25), links this death outside the promised land with Moses' own death (1.37; 3.22-23). Furthermore, an additional reference to Moses' death seems to indicate that it somehow opens the way, pursued throughout the rest of the book, for the new generation to enter into life in the promised land (4.21-22).

As regards the second section (chap. 5) Olson acknowledges that there is no direct mention of Moses' death.[33] However, he argues that the theme indirectly 'creeps again upon the stage' when the people request that Moses go near and listen to God in their stead, so that they will not have to risk being consumed by further exposure to the fire of God (4.24-27). In their words, 'Why should we die? For this great fire will consume us, if we hear the voice of God anymore' (4.25). The shadow of death, suggests

---

[31] Olson, *Deuteronomy and the Death of Moses*, p. 16.
[32] Olson, *Deuteronomy and the Death of Moses*, pp. 17–22. Here Olson presents a preview summary of the theme's recurrence in each section. He elaborates this in the subsequent chapters of his study.
[33] Olson, *Deuteronomy and the Death of Moses*, p. 46.

Olson, is thus made to fall over the very essence of Moses' call and role as revelatory mediator.

In the following legal section, which elaborates 'the commandment, statutes and ordinances' (chaps. 6–28), Olson again finds indirect references to the theme of Moses' death. He points to the golden calf story (9.8–10.11) where Moses recalls his intercession on behalf of the people before God. Moses' 40-day fast, in which he relinquishes the necessities of life, together with his prostration before Yahweh, wherein Olson sees 'a posture resembling death',[34] these suggest for Olson a *kind of* demise, a *'death' in quotation marks*.[35] It is a mediatorial death, here again, by which the people of Israel are enabled to live.

Olson finds one more such reference to Moses' death in the law of 18.15–22, which anticipates God's future move 'to raise up a prophet' like Moses (18.15, 18). Not only does this passage point toward the time after Moses is gone, it also recalls once again how that the prophetic role of Moses was established at Horeb in the context of the people's reaction to the threat of death.

> You desired of Yahweh your God in Horeb on the day of the assembly, saying, 'Don't let me hear again the voice of Yahweh my God, neither let me see this great fire any more, so that I will not die' (18.16).

In addition to these references, Olson finds in many of the detailed 'statutes and ordinances' (chaps. 12–28) something that 'resonates with the theme of Moses' death'.[36] He shows how that numerous laws, such as the laws of sacrifice, sabbath or of slave and debt release, 'have to do with giving something up, letting go, dying, or acknowledging the limits of human abilities, knowledge, and laws'.[37] These injunctions follow the trajectory of Moses' own fate, thinks Olson, in their underlying assumption that life somehow comes through death.

The Moab covenant section of chapters 29–32 in its own way affirms this idea of life coming through death, argues Olson. This happens specifically in the way that the covenant mechanisms of the renewal liturgy of chapters 29–30 and the Song of Moses in chapter 32 provide for preservation of the community even beyond the anticipated curse of death

---

[34] Olson, *Deuteronomy and the Death of Moses*, p. 19.
[35] Olson, *Deuteronomy and the Death of Moses*, p. 61. Olson here uses quotation marks repeatedly in making his point, 'Moses "dies"'.
[36] Olson, *Deuteronomy and the Death of Moses*, p. 20.
[37] Olson, *Deuteronomy and the Death of Moses*, p. 20.

and exile outside the promised land (29.16–30.7; 32.26–43). Olson sees these two communal provisions for 'life through death' framing a central subsection, chapter 31, which explicitly and repeatedly emphasizes the urgency of the occasion of Moses' impending death (31.2, 14, 16, 29). Here the transfer of Moses' leadership to Joshua and Moses' words to writing provide vital means for life to go on.

As Olson sees it, all the foregoing 'allusions to Moses' death 'finally flow into' the final section of Deuteronomy (chaps. 33–34) and its account of the actual death of Moses. Moses pronounces his last words of blessing upon the individual tribes, which is itself an act of final passage (chapter 33), just before the closing scene. The act of passing on final words to the children characterizes not only this concluding section but also the book as a whole. And it is an act that from the beginning has been occasioned and overshadowed, as Olson would emphasize, by the death of Moses.

There is no doubt that Olson has succeeded in demonstrating a greater place in Deuteronomy for the theme of the death of Moses than has heretofore been recognized. To see it as the leading or governing theme, however, is not justified according to my way of reading the book. Olson's view is most vulnerable in his discussion of chapter 5. Granting Olson's point that this is the book's most defining section, nothing less than a virtual blueprint summary of the whole book in line with its introductory superscription, *'this is the torah'* (4.44), it should be quite telling that this key section offers no explicit reference to Moses' death. Olson finds no more than an *indirect* reference by way of the people's request for Moses to stand between them and the death that they fear before the fire of God. But is it not possible and even more likely that this reference to *encounter with divine fire* is not just an indirect allusion to the book's main theme but rather the main theme itself? It is surely the commanding theme of chapter 5, insofar as references to the fire of God and the people's response of fear frame the presentation of the decalogue (5.4–5; 22–29) and come to an unparalleled crescendo of divine longing in verse 29, *'Oh that they had such a heart as this always to fear me and keep all my commandments'*. If fear as well as obedience makes up the proper response to *torah*, then this living fire as well as the written commandments may be what this section has in view in announcing, *'this* is the *torah'*.[38]

---

[38] For an elaboration of this point see my earlier chapter, 'Canon and Charisma in the Book of Deuteronomy'.

This crucial chapter replays Israel's fearful encounter with the fire of God at Horeb, and identifies it with what *torah* is all about and what God longs for *'always'*. Even as it constitutes the sustained yearning of God, it can be seen as the sustained emphasis of Moses throughout the entire book in each of its major sections. Such emphasis belies the perpetual tendency of God's people to lose sight of the holy fire (cf. 5.24-27). I do not think that this is unrelated to modern scholarship's lack of recognition of the leading thematic role of the Horeb theophany in the book of Deuteronomy, which I now intend briefly to show.

Deuteronomy begins with reference to the revelatory event of Horeb (1.2-3).[39] The narrative immediately announces, 'Yahweh our God spoke to us at Horeb' (1.6). There unfolds from this announcement a story of how God's people then journey from this mountain, not just in a geographical way (cf. 2.3) but more importantly in a theological way. They soon journey away from the presence of Yahweh (1.29-33), who has promised, as Moses points out, 'to go before you' (1.30) even as he 'went in the way before you, as in the fire by night' (1.33). This, then, is a story about how the consuming fire of Horeb is illegitimately left behind, causing an unbelieving generation to be consumed (2.16). But this narrative that thus leads *away from* the Horeb theophany leads a new generation, and the reader of Deuteronomy, once again *back to* it. For the thrust and the heart of chapter four is a calling of Israel back to the overwhelming charismatic experience at the mountain of fire.

> Be careful and guard yourselves diligently lest you forget the things your eyes have seen and they depart from your heart, how that you stood before Yahweh your God at Horeb...You came near and stood before the mountain, and the mountain burned with fire unto the midst of heaven, with darkness, clouds, and thick smoke. Then Yahweh spoke to you from the midst of the fire. You heard the sound of the words but saw no form, only a voice (4.10-12).

The remainder of chapter 4 counters Israel's present and future tendencies to choose idolatrous forms over the living voice of Yahweh (cf. 4.15-16). This choice poses the burning issue of Deuteronomy: idol forms vs the formless and form-annihilating fire. As this chapter declares, 'Yahweh your God is *a consuming fire*' (4.24).

---

[39] One sees not only the geographical reference in verse 2 but also the theological reference in verse 3, which redefines '*these words* of Moses' in the superscription as those 'according to all that Yahweh had given him in commandment to them', pointing to Moses' mediatorial encounter at Horeb between 'Yahweh' and 'them'.

The opening section of Deuteronomy thus moves *from* Horeb and then *back to* Horeb in an effort to show God's people that the way to keep the word is to keep coming from the fire from which the word keeps coming.

If the first section of Deuteronomy intends to *take Israel back* to the Horeb theophany, then the second section (ch. 5), which is entirely devoted, as we have seen, to this revelatory event, aims to *bring the Horeb encounter forward* to God's people. As the introductory words of Moses flatly assert,

> Yahweh our God made a covenant with us in Horeb. Yahweh did not make this covenant with our ancestors, but with us, even all of us who are alive here today. Yahweh spoke with you face to face at the mountain from the midst of the fire (5.2–4).

It is obvious from this key passage, especially in view of its appearance in this most important section of Deuteronomy, that perpetual, living response to the fire of God is of central concern for the whole book. This verse provides for the perpetuation of Horeb's fire just as the recruitment of Moses in 5.31 provides for the extension of the decalogue revelation that we see in the legal section which comes next (chaps. 6–28).[40] The people may incline toward having statutes and ordinances without the fire, but Moses clearly strives here to bring the fire forward with the words.[41] This would, then, apply to the rest of his words in the book.

The legal section (chs. 6–28), however, is not without its own direct reference to the theme of the fiery theophany at Horeb. In fact the two most prominent *allusions to the death of Moses* in Olson's reading of this section appear as *explicit and direct references to the theophanic encounter* on the holy mountain. The second of these references (18.16–18) replays the scene at Horeb (cf. 5.24–31) when the people react in fear before the fire of God and ask for Moses to mediate. This time the scene stresses divine provision for continuing mediation even after Moses with Yahweh's promise 'to raise up a prophet' like Moses in the future (18.18). Thus the mediation of

---

[40] The relation of chapter 5 to chapters 12–28 is made explicit in the way that 5.31 recalls how Moses is commissioned to relay the 'statutes and ordinances', which are the very terms we meet in the superscription of 12.1. See Olson, *Deuteronomy and the Death of Moses*, p. 46.

[41] The same point can be seen in 4.7–8, which indicates that Israel is to be distinct from the nations not only in having 'statutes and ordinances so righteous' (v. 8) but also in having 'a God so near as Yahweh our God' (v. 7).

holy words *and holy fire*, it would seem, is not to be limited to the time of Moses nor to the book of Deuteronomy.[42]

The legal section's earlier reference to the Horeb encounter involves the golden calf narrative, featuring Moses' 40 days of prostration on the mountain before Yahweh (9.25), the longest narration of a single episode in the entire book (9.8–10.11). Whereas Olson seems to find the significance of this elaborate narrative in the way it subtly points forward to Moses's actual death, I find it much more likely that this life-and-death encounter on Horeb is *the main event*, to which Moses' final appointment with God on Nebo (chap. 34) becomes a mere echo (note 34.10). For where did Israel first and most deeply discover the truth that life comes through death—a truth that permeates the specific laws of chapters 12–28, as Olson has so convincingly shown?[43] Was it through the natural death of Moses and the natural succession of one generation giving way to the next, such as Moses' death depicts? I suppose that if this is the only kind of death that one takes seriously, then this is where the given truth must be sought. But another possibility emerges for those who would take seriously a theophanic encounter that could 'scare you to death' and yet amazingly leave you alive (cf. 5.26 and 9.19).[44] This is the kind of theophanic experience into which this testimony of Moses' intercession leads God's people even more deeply than before.

The next section, as we have seen, explicitly differentiates the past covenant encounter at Horeb with the present one in Moab (29.1 introducing chaps. 29–32). Yet a significant connection to the Horeb theophany occurs in what Olson recognizes as the central portion of this section. Olson, however, gives virtually no attention to it.[45] Surely it should be regarded as a major moment in the book when God, whose past words have until this point only been relayed and quoted, now, for the first time in the book, speaks for himself (31.14). God calls Moses to come with Joshua into the 'tent of meeting', where he 'appears' in 'a pillar of cloud' and speaks to Moses and then Joshua (31.14–23). This reference to the Horeb-like manifestation of God's own presence may not signify much to those who, here again, do not take such experiences very seriously, but for those who do, there is every reason to see in this theophanic account at this point

---

[42] Note how Jeremiah, who is often viewed as the Hebrew canon's prime example of a 'prophet like Moses', sees his prophetic word as divine fire (Jer. 20.9; 23.29).

[43] Olson, *Deuteronomy and the Death of Moses*, pp. 62–125.

[44] This kind of death experience just might be decisive enough to put 'natural death' in quotation marks.

[45] Olson, *Deuteronomy and the Death of Moses*, pp. 134–135.

in Deuteronomy a major dimension of God's provision for Israel's future covenant life. Alongside the provisions which Olson notices—a covenant liturgy (chaps. 29–30), a human successor and written canon (chap. 31), and a covenant song (chap. 32)—there is surely something to be said for the manifestation of divine presence itself, which is here both demonstrated presently at the 'tent of meeting' and given future significance in the divine threats ('I will hide my face' 31.17, 18) and promises ('I will be with you', 31.23) which are spoken within the 'tent of meeting'. And surely a 'tent of meeting' in and of itself presupposes a major place for continuing revelatory encounter, at least for those who have ears to hear and eyes to see.[46]

The final section of Deuteronomy (chaps. 33–34), though it has no extended reference to the Horeb theophany as we have found in all the other sections, does have two brief references that could not be more strategically located. One comes at the very beginning, the other at the very end. Moses's blessing on the tribes begins, 'Yahweh came from Sinai' (33.2). Just like the message of Deuteronomy as a whole (cf. 1.6), which altogether represents Moses' last words to Israel, these last words of benediction are seen to flow ultimately from Yahweh's revelation at Horeb. In the final paragraph of the book, concluding attention is brought to how Yahweh had known Moses 'face to face' (34.10). The narrator's accompanying comment that 'there had not arisen a prophet like Moses (in this regard) since', combines with Deuteronomy's earlier reference that God has promised 'to raise up a prophet like Moses' (18.18), and together these words prompt God's people forward toward the future prospect of 'face to face' encounter with the consuming fire.[47]

Conclusion

In the light of the foregoing interpretation, I would now offer some summary reflections and mention a few larger implications.

---

[46] It may be indicative of the negative national prospects which are emphasized in this chapter (31.16–18, 21, 29) that this people, who had earlier opted for their own tents rather than the burning mountain (5.30), now find themselves on the outside of the 'tent of meeting' looking on. Modern scholars, such as Olson, who scarcely acknowledge the theophanic significance of this meeting, seem to be looking on at an even greater distance. The 'classroom' can be a long way from the 'tent meeting'.

[47] On this eschatological effect at the book's conclusion see the perceptive comments of P.D. Miller, '"Moses My Servant": The Deuteronomic Portrait of Moses', *Interpretation* 41 (1987), pp. 245–55 (p. 249).

Approaching Deuteronomy from the inside of my Pentecostal confession has led me to the conclusion that the fiery theophany of Horeb is the central theme of the book. There are those who would criticize me for having read my own confessional experience into Deuteronomy. Yet would not the pronounced lack of attention to the Horeb theophany in Deuteronomy scholarship render the latter at least equally open to the criticism of having read the book through its own experience or lack thereof. It all becomes a matter of what experiences and indeed what criticism we are willing to take seriously.

My reading has pointed up a number of literary relationships and connections, which can be judged on their own merits. Yet I am forthrightly acknowledging that the coherence that I have discerned and uplifted in this reading involves more than literary observations. It has much to do with pursuing how things appear from the inside of such a confession as opens Deuteronomy, *'our God spoke to us'*. From the outside, such a confession is easily regarded as some primitive notion belonging to a pre-critical world-view where such notions are commonplace, and if commonplace, then not expected to be particularly noteworthy, much less central, in such literature as we have before us. However, from the inside, such a confession would easily point to the singular claim which evokes the given worldview, which divides time, and which commands and centers the deepest commitments of the heart. It would thus not appear surprising to find this claim occupying the thematic center of this writing, for it would point to the heart of the hermeneutic which is generating the writing. And if the heart of the hermeneutic, then not a mere buttress for some more fundamental claim or a means to reinforce a standpoint already occupied. We are dealing rather with the point where standing and understanding have their beginning, because this is where they have been completely lost and found anew. We are dealing, in other words, with the point where confession becomes profoundly critical.

The voice that comes to claim central position on the inside of this confession comes from the outside, from the wilderness, from 'otherness' itself. It comes from the margin and then marginalizes all who claim it, who are claimed by it. It will ever put marginal voices in a totally and radically new light—the voices of widows, orphans and aliens. Without the experience of the voice that comes from the midst of the fire, as it did on the day of Pentecost and as it did at Azusa Street, we may never become critical enough to affirm as we should the other voices from the margins.

CHAPTER NINE

PENTECOSTAL HERMENEUTICS: RETROSPECT AND PROSPECT*

Kenneth J. Archer**

> We are not fighting against people or churches, but we are seeking to replace dead forms of dogmas with living, practical Christianity.
> *The Apostolic Faith*, William Seymour

The Pentecostal movement emerged out of the intense Weslyan-holiness and Reformed evangelical revivals of the late nineteenth century. What specifically distinguished this movement from the other revival movements was the binding together of the biblical concept of the baptism of the Holy Spirit with the charismatic phenomenon of speaking in other tongues. However, we must recognize that even though the baptism in the Holy Spirit with the evidence of speaking in other tongues is the distinctive doctrine of Pentecostalism, it is not the central essence of Pentecostalism.

What is at stake in the present hermeneutical debate is *not* whether Pentecostals have correctly exegeted the Lukan corpus according to the traditional historical-critical methodologies, *but* Pentecostal identity. Thus, the purpose of this article is to identify the essence of Pentecostalism in order better to appreciate the contemporary debate concerning Pentecostals and hermeneutics. By doing this I hope to show that a promising hermeneutic can be extrapolated from the spiritual ethos of classical Pentecostalism.

The Essence of Pentecostalism

The essence of Pentecostalism is its persistent emphasis upon the supernatural within the community. G. Wacker, in his article 'The Functions

---

* First published in the *Journal of Pentecostal Theology* 8 (1996), pp. 63–81.
** Kenneth J. Archer (PhD, University of St Andrews) is Professor of Pentecostal Theology and Christian Studies Director of the Master of Arts in Theological Studies at Southeastern University, Lakeland, FL, USA.

of Faith in Primitive Pentecostalism', argues that the framework in which speaking in tongues should be analyzed is the thoroughly experiential supernaturalistic conceptual horizon.[1] This supernaturalistic horizon of Pentecostalism is 'marked by living in and from the eschatological presence of God'.[2]

Pentecostalism with its manifestation of the charismatic gifts (tongues, prophecy and healings) 'offered invincible certitude that the supernatural claims of the gospel were really true'.[3] Pentecostalism perceived itself as a revival movement that called the church to relive the apostolic experiences that are related in the New Testament.[4]

At the center of this supernaturalistic horizon stood Jesus the Savior, Sanctifier, Healer, and soon coming King.[5] The christological themes were rooted in the revivalistic movments of the late nineteenth century. To these christological themes Pentecostals added one more—Spirit baptizer, and they saw themselves as living in the latter rain (Joel and Acts).[6] They viewed this Holy Spirit outpouring as the final act in the drama of salvation, for the second coming of Jesus was going to happen very soon. Pentecostal identity was shaped from the beginning by an 'eschatological intensity and an existential identification with "the full gospel" of the New Testament Apostolic Christianity'.[7] Pentecostals, like other restoration groups, were certain that they had recaptured the essential features of the New Testament church[8] and that these supernatural features were available to all Christians.

This supernaturalistic worldview has been identified as the very reason for the overwhelming growth of the Pentecostal movement.[9] Margaret Poloma's recent sociological study of one of North America's largest Pentecostal denominations (the Assemblies of God) argues that Pentecostalism may be seen as an 'anthropological protest against modernity' by 'provid-

---

[1] *HTR* 77 (1984), p. 360.
[2] S. Land, *Pentecostal Spirituality: A Passion for the Kingdom* (JPTSup, 1; Sheffield: Sheffield Academic Press, 1993), p. 184.
[3] Wacker, 'The Functions of Faith', p. 361.
[4] F. Arrington, 'Hermeneutics', in S.M. Burgess and G.B. McGee (eds.), *Dictionary of Pentecostal and Charismatic Movements* (Grand Rapids: Zondervan, 1988), p. 381.
[5] Land, *Pentecostal Spirituality*, p. 56.
[6] See D. Dayton, *Theological Roots of Pentecostalism* (Peabody, MA: Hendrickson, 1987).
[7] M. Dempster, 'The Search for Pentecostal Identity', *Pneuma* 15.1 (1993), p. 1.
[8] Wacker, 'The Functions of Faith', p. 364.
[9] Wacker, 'The Functions of Faith', pp. 374–75.

ing a medium for encountering the supernatural'.[10] She characterizes the Pentecostal worldview by the 'belief in and experience of the paranormal as an alternate *Weltanschauung* for our instrumental rational modern society'.[11] She points out that this may be seen as an anomaly to the dominant scientific worldview of our day,[12] yet it is precisely this supernaturalistic worldview which propels the growth of Pentecostalism within the modernistic age.[13] In presenting the worldview of Pentecostalism,[14] I hope to convey that the essence of the movement is the belief in and encounter with the supernatural in the Christian life. This experiential worldview is at the heart of the present hermeneutical debate.

Classical Pentecostals and Scripture

The early Pentecostals' 'operative principle of interpretation was the conviction that exegesis is best when it is as rigidly literal as credibility can stand'.[15] An extreme example of literal interpretation is to handle snakes and drink deadly poisons based on a literal reading of Mark 16. This example serves further to illustrate that when Pentecostals interpreted the Bible in a literalistic fashion, they did so in order to apply it directly to their immediate context.[16] (Mark 16, then, was understood as indicating what 'signs' should be evident among the Pentecostal community presently, not as past 'signs' which took place within the New Testament church.) Thus, Pentecostal interpretation placed little or no significance upon the historical context of Scripture nor would it be concerned with the author's original intent (the historical-critical method). The Bible is the Word of God and understood at face value.[17] The horizons of past and present were fused, or from a critical perspective, confused.

---

[10] *The Assemblies of God at the Crossroads* (Knoxville, TN: University of Tennessee Press, 1989), p. 19; cf. p. xix.
[11] Poloma, *Assemblies of God*, p. xvii.
[12] Poloma, *Assemblies of God*, p. xvii.
[13] Poloma, *Assemblies of God*, p. xx; Wacker, 'The Functions of Faith', p. 374. Wacker makes the same point by saying 'the movement flourished, in short, not in spite of the fact that it was out of step with the times, but precisely because it was'.
[14] See J.D. Johns, 'Pentecostalism and the Postmodern Worldview', *JPT* 7 (1995), pp. 73–96.
[15] Wacker, 'The Functions of Faith', p. 365.
[16] G. Sheppard, 'Pentecostals and the Hermeneutics of Dispensationalism', *Pneuma* 16.2 (1984), p. 22.
[17] Arrington, 'Hermeneutics', p. 378.

This literal or face value interpreting of Scripture without any concern for the historical distance allowed Pentecostal preachers to emphasize the immediate meaning of Scripture. Joseph Byrd, after researching the first decade of Pentecostal preaching makes the following four descriptive conclusions about the sermons:

1. Preaching was spontaneous and *not* relegated to professional clergy.
2. Preaching participated in the overall trajectory of worship services, it was *not* necessarily the climax of the service.
3. The *congregation participated* in the sermon in terms of responding, but the sermon also allowed for participation of the congregation more fully in the 'altar call'.
4. The sermon reached for an *immediate experience* for the listeners and was not characterized by a hermeneutic that spent its time exegeting a text in a historical-critical manner. Put simply, the preacher focused on the immediate meaning of a text and not upon what a text meant in its original context.[18]

The Holy Scriptures for early Pentecostals were not viewed as a past 'static deposit of truth' but as the present 'primary source book for living the Pentecostal life'. The Pentecostal expects all the supernatural manifestations of the Scriptures to be realized during the present era.[19] This 're-experiencing' of the biblical text was further emphasized in the worship service by testimonies. These testimonies offered by laity provided evidence that God still was working miracles in the present.[20] The testimony not only served to provide evidence of God's miraculous power but also aided in the process of interpreting Scripture. The testimonies presented by the community helped to shape the understanding of those who were attending the worship service. Thus the Pentecostal community participated in the hermeneutical process.

Pentecostals (primarily from the white denominations such as the Assemblies of God) readily accepted the fundamentalist dispensational hermeneutic.[21] Some have argued that this is a sign of the Pentecostals'

---

[18] J. Byrd, 'Paul Ricoeur's Hermeneutical Theory and Pentecostal Proclamation', *Pneuma* 15.2 (1993), pp. 204–205 (emphasis added).
[19] Arrington, 'Hermeneutics', p. 383.
[20] Wacker, 'The Functions of Faith', p. 362.
[21] F. Arrington, 'Dispensationalism', in Burgess and McGee (eds.), *Dictionary*, pp. 247–48.

desire to find acceptance by the Fundamentalists.[22] Yet others argue that this adoption was a result of the Pentecostal self-identity as God's eschatological community.[23] This wedding of Pentecostalism to a fundamentalist dispensational hermeneutic has been complicated. Pentecostals who used dispensationalism had to modify it in order to preserve their emphasis upon the miraculous in this church age.[24]

A Summary of Classical Pentecostalism

Some general conclusions can be made about how classical Pentecostals have viewed Scripture. First, they have seen Scripture as the inspired Word of God which is authoritative and wholly reliable (cf. any Pentecostal statement of faith). The Bible not only represents a witness to God, but also it is the very word of God. Thus, the human authors of Scripture are seen as passive instruments. Inspiration, then, becomes dictation.[25]

Secondly, as a result of Scripture being received as the objective authoritative present word of God, they have not recognized a historical distance between themselves and the text. Biblical statements are understood at face value with no appreciation for the ancient context in which Scripture was first delivered.[26] This simple pietistic yet critical hermeneutic focused primarily upon their immediate context.[27] Ironically, this approach led to multiple dimensions of meaning.[28] However, this did not lead them to affirm relativism.

Thirdly, their interpretation was theologically colored by their christological 'full gospel' pre-understanding; therefore, their doctrine would be

---

[22] Sheppard, 'Pentecostals', p. 5.
[23] Arrington, 'Hermeneutics', p. 385.
[24] See Sheppard, 'Pentecostals', pp. 5–33.
[25] Arrington, 'Hermeneutics', p. 380. Classical Pentecostals never incorporated a theory of dictation into their Statements of Faith, they asserted that Scripture is authoritative and most did not even include 'inspired'.
[26] Arrington, 'Hermeneutics', p. 380. Cf. G. Walker, 'Playing for Keeps: The Primitivist Impulse in Early Pentecostalism', in R. Hughes (ed.), *The American Quest for the Primitive Church* (Chicago: University of Illinois Press, 1988), pp. 196–219.
[27] R. Spittler, 'Scripture and the Theological Enterprise: A View From the Big Canoe', in R.K. Johnston (ed.), *The Use of the Bible* (Atlanta: John Knox Press, 1985): 'I am not at all prepared to say that such simple pietistic use of Scripture is defective; it is not so much wrong as limited' (p. 75). Thus, he says that 'the historical-critical method is [necessary but] inadequate because it does not address piety' (p. 77).
[28] T. Cargal, 'Beyond the Fundamentalist-Modernist Controversy: Pentecostals and Hermeneutics in a Postmodern Age', *Pneuma* 15.2 (1993), p. 165.

consistent with evangelical Christianity in general.[29] The doctrinal position produced a stabilization and limitation to the multiple dimensions of meaning.

Fourthly, the prime interpreter and preacher was the local pastor. The 'Pentecostal clergy', as Russell Spittler put it, were for the most part 'lay people who quit their jobs'.[30] Christian Lalive d'Epinay's study of the Pentecostal movement in Chile points out this similar characteristic of Pentecostal clergy: 'Nothing in the pastor's social origins, recruitment or training separates them from the mass of church members' and 'the gradual abandonment of secular activities by the candidate pastor highlights the fact' that 'he is only a layman who specializes to the point of giving all his time to the church.'[31] The distinction between Pentecostal laity and clergy rested upon the latter being divinely called by God to proclaim the word of God to the people of God. Consequently, education was not necessary and at times seminary training was seen as a hindrance to effective preaching.

Thus far we have identified the historical beginning of Pentecostalism which came as a result of the evangelical revivals of the late nineteenth century, particularly the Wesleyan-holiness and Keswick higher life movements. Emerging from this context of American restoration revivalism came a distinct Pentecostal spirituality: 'it was the black spirituality of former slaves in the United States encountering the specific catholic spirituality of the movement's Grandfather, John Wesley'.[32] Pentecostalism's unique doctrine was the wedding together of the holiness concept of baptism in the Holy Spirit with speaking in other tongues as the physical evidence for such an experience. Thus, 'Pentecostals succeeded in doing what the Holiness Movement could not do in that it offered the believer a repeatable and unmistakable motor-expression which in effect, guaranteed his possession of the Spirit'.[33]

---

[29] W. Menzies, 'The Methodology of Pentecostal Theology: An Essay on Hermeneutics', in P. Elbert (ed.), *Essays on Apostolic Themes* (Peabody, MA: Hendrickson, 1985); M. McLean, Toward a Pentecostal Hermeneutic', *Pneuma* 6.2 (1984), p. 51: 'Most Pentecostals are fundamentalists in that they believe in the five fundamentals'.

[30] Spittler, 'Scripture', p. 75.

[31] *Haven of the Masses: A Study of the Pentecostal Movement in Chile* (London: Lutterworth Press, 1969), p. 95.

[32] Land, *Pentecostal Spirituality*, p. 35.

[33] V. Synan, *The Holiness-Pentecostal Movement in the United States* (Grand Rapids: Eerdmans, 1971), p. 122.

The essence of Pentecostalism is the emphasis upon the omnipotent God breaking into the everyday life of the believer. As Steven Land so concisely and accurately has explained,

> The faith, worldview, experience and practice of Pentecostals was thoroughly eschatological. They lived both in the tension of the already but not yet consummated Kingdom... Time and space were fused and transcended in the Spirit, and at the heart of testimony, expectation and worship was Jesus, the Savior, Sanctifier, Healer, Baptizer with the Spirit, and Coming King.[34]

This worldview was and still is antithetical to modernity's conception of reality.

Contemporary Pentecostal Hermeneutics

Walter J. Hollenweger's monumental study of Pentecostalism published first in German in 1968 opens with this dedication: 'To my friends and teachers in the Pentecostal movement who taught me to love the Bible and to my teachers and friends in the Presbyterian church who taught me to understand it.'[35] Hollenweger's chiding remark no doubt reflects a simplistic scholarship among early Pentecostals, even though there were a few competent scholars. This is no longer the case, however, for Hollenweger, in a 1992 article states that today 'one finds scores of first-class Pentecostal scholars' and these scholars 'deserve to be taken seriously'.[36] He concludes the article by saying,

> Pentecostalism has come of age. It is now possible to be filled with the Spirit, to enjoy the specific Pentecostal charismata and Pentecostal spirituality, to believe in Pentecostal mission, and at the same time to use one's critical faculties to develop them and to use them—as any other charisma for the Kingdom of God.[37]

Pentecostal scholarship has reached new levels of sophistication as the Fall 1993 issue of *Pneuma: The Journal of the Society for Pentecostal Studies* demonstrates. This issue contains essays on the theme of Pentecostal hermeneutics. 'Here we see social scientific research coupled with postmodern methodologies of interpretation and an ability to appeal to the

---

[34] Land, *Pentecostal Spirituality*, pp. 55–56.
[35] W. Hollenweger, *The Pentecostals* (London: SCM Press, 1972), p. xvii.
[36] W. Hollenweger, 'The Critical Tradition of Pentecostalism', *JPT* 1 (1992), pp. 7, 9.
[37] Hollenweger, 'Critical Tradition', p. 17.

most recent trends in biblical and theological studies.'[38] These Pentecostal scholars are utilizing the latest methods in order to represent valuable aspects of Pentecostal experience and tradition.

The following portion of this paper will focus upon the contemporary Euro-American Pentecostal discussion of hermeneutics. This topic has generated a lively debate amongst Pentecostal scholars. This can be attested to by examining the current contents of two prominent Pentecostal journals; namely, *Pneuma* and the *Journal of Pentecostal Theology*. Scholars are responding to a general call to develop a hermeneutic with which to construct a theology worthy of the name Pentecostal.[39]

Pentecostals have a distinct way of reading the Scriptures. They read them 'through Lukan eyes especially with the lenses provided by the book of Acts'.[40] This Luke-Acts perspective has led Pentecostals to the conclusion that the believer should have not only a salvation-regeneration experience but also a second subsequent Spirit baptismal experience. This is understood to be of considerable importance because with it comes an endowment of power for evangelism (Acts 1.8), and this experience of Spirit-baptism should be normative for all believers.

F.D. Bruner and James D.G. Dunn have provided important critiques of Pentecostal exegetical reading of Scripture. They both set out to evaluate the claim made by classical Pentecostals that the baptism in the Spirit is a second and subsequent normative experience for Christians.[41] Both scholars employ the historical-critical exegetical methodologies in order to recover the author's original intent.[42] Both scholars find Pentecostal exegesis incorrect in its presentation of a subsequent experience.

Dunn, however, is more sympathetic in his evaluations than Bruner. Bruner believes that the heart of the gospel is under attack because the

---

[38] G. Sheppard, 'Biblical Interpretation after Gadamer', *Pneuma* 16.1 (1994), p. 127.
[39] Land, *Pentecostal Spirituality*, p. 38.
[40] Dayton, *Theological Roots*, p. 23.
[41] Dunn, 'Baptism in the Spirit: A Response to Pentecostal Scholarship on Luke-Acts', *JPT* 3 (1993), p. 5, claims this is the thesis of his *Baptism in the Holy Spirit*; Bruner, *A Theology of the Holy Spirit: The Pentecostal Experience and the New Testament Witness* (London: Hodder & Stoughton, 1970), p. 78: 'Is the Pentecostal teaching on the experience of the Spirit in conformity with New Testament teaching?...should Christians seek a second...experience subsequent to their Christian initiation?...should I have the Pentecostal experience?'
[42] Bruner, *Theology*, p. 153: 'The final question at stake in our confrontation with Pentecostalism is not: was Luke right or wrong...but: does Pentecostalism rightly or wrongly understand Luke...?'

reformation doctrine of justification by faith alone has been impaired.[43] Bruner's comments reveal this concern:

> A principal error of Pentecostalism, shared by some of Pentecostalism's parents and relatives in conservative evangelicalism, is the conviction that the gospel is sufficient for the beginning but not for the continuing of the Christian life, for bringing the Holy Spirit initially but not fully...
> Christians not only once-and-for-all receive the Spirit through the message of faith apart from the fulfilling of conditions (Gal. 3:2) but they continue to be supplied fully with the Spirit and ministered miracles through the very same message without additional techniques or deeper messages or secret means (3:5)...
> The consequence for the Pentecostal doctrine of fullness must be the abandonment of any condition for the fullness of the Holy Spirit other than the one, initiating, sustaining, and powerful message of faith in Jesus Christ. There is for Christians no fuller, no more fulfilling gospel than the gospel that makes a man a Christian; to assert that there is, is to fall under Paul's severest censure (Gal. 1:6–9; 5:2–12).[44]

Two observations can be drawn from Bruner. First, he believes he has correctly interpreted Luke-Acts by utilizing the historical-critical exegetical method. Secondly, he reflects the general attitude of the Reformed tradition that Pentecostalism jeopardizes the gospel.[45] This second observation touches upon the issue of Pentecostal identity.

Mainline classical Reformed Protestantism has typically viewed Pentecostalism and the Holiness movement in terms of an evangelical 'subculture'. Pentecostalism and the Holiness movements did not come out of old-school Presbyterianism but are products of Wesleyan thought. The structures of Wesleyan thought are not characteristically those of the tradition of 'Protestant orthodoxy' and so 'these movements are not classical Protestantism but protest against it'.[46] Thus, there is more involved in Pentecostal hermeneutics than the exegesis of Luke-Acts. Pentecostal experiential spirituality is also at stake.

---

[43] H. Lederle, 'Pre-Charismatic Interpretations of Spirit-Baptism', in *A Reader on the Holy Spirit: Anointing, Equipping and Empowering for Service* (Los Angeles: International Church of the Foursquare Gospel, 1993), p. 33.

[44] Bruner, *Theology*, p. 240.

[45] D.G. Bloesch, *Essentials of Evangelical Theology*, II (San Francisco: Harper Collins, 1978), p. 236. Bloesch makes this charge against both the Holiness and Pentecostal traditions.

[46] D. Dayton, 'Yet another Layer of the Onion or Opening the Ecumenical Door to let the Riffraff in', *The Ecumenical Review* 40.1 (1988), pp. 98–99.

Dunn, according to the editors of the *Journal for Pentecostal Theology*, has been the most 'provocative and stimulating' dialogue partner for Euro-American Pentecostal biblical scholars.[47] Dunn's *Baptism in the Holy Spirit* in particular and his *Jesus and the Spirit* in general challenged the classical Pentecostal understanding of Spirit baptism while at the same time affirming the charismatic character of the early Church.[48] In response to Dunn's challenging work, a number of Pentecostals set out to overturn his conclusions.[49] I will focus upon one Pentecostal scholar in particular; namely, Robert Menzies, an Assemblies of God missionary, who is presently Professor of New Testament at Asia Pacific Theological Seminary in the Philippines.

The debate between Dunn and Menzies has been carried out in the *Journal of Pentecostal Theology*. Both Robert Menzies and Dunn use the same exegetical methods, yet Menzies' argument for a subsequent work of the Holy Spirit is strong, if not stronger than Dunn's (Dunn himself recognizes this). The charge of Menzies and others is that Dunn does not give Luke enough credence for a view of pneumatology that is distinct from Paul. Menzies argues that 'Luke describes the gift of the Spirit *exclusively* in charismatic terms as the source of power for effective witness', and it was Paul who was the first to attribute soteriological functions to the Spirit.[50] Therefore, the central issue concerning the debate between Dunn and Menzies is: 'Does Luke separate the outpouring of the Spirit on individuals from conversion initiation and see it as an empowering

---

[47] This comment made by the editors prefaces Dunn's article, 'Baptism in the Spirit', p. 3.
[48] R. Menzies, 'Luke and the Spirit: A Reply to James Dunn', *JPT* 4 (1994), p. 115.
[49] Dunn cites the following in his article, 'Baptism in the Spirit', p. 4: H.D. Hunter, *Spirit-Baptism: A Pentecostal Alternative* (Lanham, MD: University Press of America, 1983); H. Ervin, *Conversion-Initiation and the Baptism in the Holy Spirit: An Engaging Critique of James D.G. Dunn's Baptism in the Holy Spirit* (Peabody, MA: Hendrickson, 1984); R. Stronstad, *The Charismatic Theology of St Luke* (Peabody, MA: Hendrickson, 1984); F.L. Arrington, *The Acts of the Apostles* (Peabody, MA: Hendrickson, 1988); J.B. Shelton, *Mighty in Word and Deed: The Role of the Holy Spirit in Luke-Acts* (Peabody, MA: Hendrickson, 1991); R.P. Menzies, *The Development of Early Christian Pneumatology with Special Reference to Luke-Acts* (JSNTSup, 54; Sheffield: JSOT Press, 1991). Other scholars who have also recognized a distinctive character to Luke's pneumatology include H. Gunkel, *The Influence of the Holy Spirit* (Philadelphia: Fortress Press, 1979 [1888]); E. Schweizer, 'πνεῦμα', *TDNT*, VI, pp. 389-455; D. Hill, *Greek Words and Hebrew Meanings* (Cambridge: Cambridge University Press, 1967), G. Haya-Prats, *L 'Esprit force du l'eglise* (Paris: Cerf, 1975); and M.M.B. Turner, *Power from on High: The Spirit in Israel's Restoration and in Luke-Acts* (JPTSup, 9; Sheffield: Sheffield Academic Press, 1996).
[50] Menzies, 'Luke and the Spirit', p. 117.

gift rather than a soteriological gift?[51] Dunn argues 'no' and Menzies argues 'yes'.

These debates about what the author (Luke) intended his readers to understand will probably not be solved. Yet as a result of this debate Euro-American Pentecostal scholarship has demonstrated its ability to defend its doctrinal distinction with scholarly sophistication. Pentecostal scholarship has aided in elevating Acts from a purely historical narrative to a historical-theological narrative thus giving it the same doctrinal clout as Paul and John.[52] This would be consistent with the traditional Pentecostal approach to Scripture as a homogeneous whole. Therefore, R. Menzies (and other Pentecostals) argues for a distinct Lukan pneumatology, yet he also argues that it is complementary and not contradictory to Paul and/or the rest of the New Testament.[53] However, classical Pentecostal exegesis did not distinguish between a Lukan and Pauline pneumatology, but read Paul in light of Acts. Hollenweger was correct when he wrote, 'When we look for the biblical roots of the Baptism of the Spirit, we discover that the Pentecostals and their predecessors based their views almost exclusively on the Gospel of Luke and the Acts of the Apostles.'[54]

The Dunn-Menzies debate touched upon an important issue. Do Pentecostals need a unique hermeneutic in order firmly to establish their beliefs and practice in Scripture? Robert Menzies declares, 'The hermeneutic of evangelicalism has become our hermeneutic'.[55] This should come as no surprise since Robert's father, William Menzies, has argued this. W. Menzies regarded redaction criticism's emphasis upon the author/editor's original intention as a positive development within historical

---

[51] Dunn, 'Baptism in the Spirit', p. 6; Menzies, 'Luke and the Spirit', p. 117.

[52] I. Howard Marshall's *Luke: Historian and Theologian* (Exeter: Paternoster, 1970) marked an important shift in evangelical thinking recognizing Luke both as historian *and* theologian. See the important work of Pentecostal scholar Roger Stronstad, *Charismatic Theology*.

[53] R. Menzies, 'The Essence of Pentecostalism', *Paraclete* 26.3 (1992), p. 1; 'Coming to Terms with an Evangelical Heritage', *Paraclete* (1994), p. 22: 'Luke's pneumatology is *different* from—although complementary to—that of Paul'. Menzies acknowledges in 'The Essence of Pentecostalism', that D.A. Carson cannot accept two different pneumatological views in Scripture because it would create problems for an evangelical doctrine of inspiration (p. 7). What is different and complementary for Menzies and Pentecostals is different, contradictory and destructive for Carson and the evangelical Reformed tradition.

[54] *The Pentecostals*, p. 336. Even Hollenweger believes that James Dunn's *Baptism in the Holy Spirit* interprets Luke through 'Pauline' eyes, and Hollenweger himself believes that Catholics and Pentecostals have some justification from Luke but not from Paul for their beliefs (p. 350).

[55] R. Menzies, 'The Essence of Pentecostalism', p. 1.

critical hermeneutics. He believed that redaction criticism is the important exegetical key for 'the kind of hermeneutic required for a Pentecostal theology of Spirit-baptism initiation accompanied by tongues'.[56] Robert Menzies has utilized redaction criticism in demonstrating a Lukan pneumatology that is different from a Pauline pneumatology.

The Menzies represent the predominant Euro-American attitude within Anglo-Pentecostal scholarship. These scholars constitute a group which has turned to the evangelical wing of the Church in order to find 'particular hermeneutical assistance'.[57] Cargal correctly recognizes that North American Pentecostal scholars 'have tended to align themselves with evangelicals in their move toward adopting the methods of historical criticism'.[58] For Menzies, this 'assimilation of the modern Pentecostal movement into the broader evangelical world is an exciting and positive event'.[59] The Menzies hope that through this assimilation Pentecostalism will bring the church back to 'a fuller understanding of the theology of the Spirit, not an essentially different understanding'.[60]

Others, however, view this assimilation of Pentecostalism into Evangelicalism as destructive to Pentecostal identity and doctrine. Mark McLean highlights this concern:

> A strict adherence to traditional evangelical/fundamentalist hermeneutic principles leads to a position which, in its most positive forms, suggests the distinctives of the twentieth century Pentecostal movement are perhaps nice but not necessary; important but not vital to the life of the Church in the twentieth century. In its more negative forms, it leads to a total rejection of Pentecostal phenomena.[61]

A hermeneutic that focuses only upon what the original inspired author meant and/or intended first readers to understand will not completely satisfy the requirements of a Pentecostal hermeneutic. The essence of Pentecostalism asserts that 'the spiritual and extraordinary supernatural

---

[56] W. Menzies, 'Methodology', p. 8.

[57] R. Johnston, 'Pentecostalism and Theological Hermeneutics: Evangelical Options', *Pneuma* 6.1 (1984), p. 55. He recommends to the Pentecostal community to look to evangelicals for help in developing an evangelical hermeneutic with some Pentecostal aspects.

[58] Cargal, 'Fundamentalist-Modernist Controversy', p. 163. This is not the best move for Pentecostals: 'Any hermeneutic which cannot account for its loci of meaning within a postmodern paradigm will become nonsensical and irrelevant' (p. 187).

[59] R. Menzies, 'Luke and the Spirit', p. 119.

[60] W. Menzies, 'Methodology', p. 1. Notice the restorationist theme in his statement.

[61] McLean, 'Pentecostal Hermeneutic', p. 37.

experiences of the biblical characters are possible for contemporary believers'.[62]

This concern has led some scholars to articulate a hermeneutic that is more representative of the early tradition and ethos of Pentecostalism.[63] These scholars desire to move away from a hermeneutical system that is heavily slanted toward rationalism which tends to downplay experience and/or the role of the Holy Spirit.[64] These scholars are attempting to present a *holistic* Pentecostal hermeneutic which can also be used within the Christian community. French Arrington reflects this: 'The real issue in Pentecostalism has become hermeneutics, that is, the distinctive nature and function of Scripture and the roles of the Holy Spirit, the Christian community, grammatical-historical research, and personal experience in the interpretive process'.[65] The important role of the Holy Spirit and the impact of personal experience upon hermeneutics are the most frequently discussed dimensions. To these categories I now turn.

A common complaint against Pentecostals is that they eisegete their experiences into the text; thus, they experience something and then find it in Scripture.[66] Roger Stronstad challenges this charge by building upon the suggestions of MacDonald[67] and William Menzies[68] who argue that personal experience should be assigned to a certification or verification function at the end of the hermeneutic process. Stronstad contends that 'experience enters the hermeneutical enterprise at the beginning of the hermeneutical process'.[69] His article sets out to demonstrate that

---

[62] Byrd, 'Ricoeur's Hermeneutical Theory and Pentecostal Proclamation', p. 205; Arrington, 'The Use of the Bible by Pentecostals', *Pneuma* 16.1 (1994), p. 105.

[63] A hermeneutic which not only elucidates the original meaning of the biblical text (the *supposed* function of the historical critical exegetical methodologies) but also answers the question of what the text means today.

[64] J.C. Thomas, 'Women, Pentecostals and the Bible: An Experiment in Pentecostal Hermeneutics', *JPT* 5 (1994), p. 41.

[65] Arrington, 'Use of the Bible', p. 101.

[66] G. Fee, 'Hermeneutics and the Historical Precedent: A Major Problem in Pentecostal Hermeneutics', in R.P. Spittler (ed.), *Perspectives on the New Pentecostalism* (Grand Rapids: Baker Book House, 1976), p. 122.

[67] MacDonald, 'A Classical Viewpoint', in Spittler (ed.), *Perspectives*, p. 6, describes Pentecostal theology as a 'Christ-centered experience-certified theology'.

[68] W. Menzies, 'Methodology', pp. 12–13: 'Personal experience should not be a priority in establishing theology' yet 'testimony and exposition are equally handmaidens to truth' thus 'if a biblical truth is to be promulgated, then it ought to be demonstrable in life'. For Menzies, personal experience should verify or demonstrate the continuity between the biblical concept and experiential reality.

[69] R. Stronstad, 'Pentecostal Experience and Hermeneutics', *Paraclete* (Winter 1992), p. 16.

'charismatic experience in particular and spiritual experience in general give the interpreter of relevant biblical texts an experiential presupposition which transcends the rational or cognitive presuppositions of scientific exegesis'.[70] Stronstad contends that Pentecostal hermeneutics will have a variety of cognitive (Protestant grammatico-historico exegesis) and experiential elements (salvation and charismatic experience or at least openness to the reality of contemporary charismatic experience).[71] Stronstad recognizes that charismatic experience in itself will not enable one to become 'an infallible interpreter' of Scripture; yet, charismatic experience provides an important pre-understanding for Scripture.[72] By experiential verification Stronstad recognizes the need to move beyond an exegesis which leads to sound biblical theology. He, like all Pentecostals, desires to incorporate the theological truths into contemporary Christian experience which testify to the New Testament presentation of Scripture as ethical-spiritual, experiential theology.[73]

The emphasis on the important dimension of experience has resulted from the Pentecostal/Charismatic understanding of God's presence. Pentecostals recognize not only the fruit of the Spirit to be vital but also the gifts of the Spirit to be just as vital because the manifestation of God's presence has been continuous from creation down to this very day.[74] Thus the supernatural, experiential worldview of Scripture is our worldview; that is, an understanding of God who is above and beyond creation yet in and among his people and testified to by signs and wonders.

The role of the Holy Spirit is continually referred to by Pentecostals as an important element in hermeneutics. A fundamental principle is that 'Scripture given by the Holy Spirit must be mediated interpretively by the Holy Spirit'.[75] The Holy Spirit is viewed as both inspirer of Scripture as

---

[70] Stronstad, 'Experience', p. 17.
[71] Stronstad, 'Experience', p. 25.
[72] Stronstad, 'Experience', pp. 25–26.
[73] See J. McKay, 'When the Veil is Taken Away', *JPT* 5 (1994), pp. 17–40, who contends that Charismatic theology is a theology of shared experience. Shared experience expresses the Charismatic-Pentecostal 'awareness of the similarity between their own experience and that of the prophets, apostles and Jesus, and also their awareness of being active participants in the same drama in which the biblical personages were involved' (p. 26). These shared experiences enable Charismatics and Pentecostals to grasp the central theme of Scripture—God restoring humanity to a right relationship with him—and therefore call the person to participate in God's restoration of his creation. McKay reveals the restorationist motif, which views this era as God's final act in the drama of salvation.
[74] McLean, 'Pentecostal Hermeneutic', p. 38.
[75] Arrington, 'Use of the Bible', p. 104.

well as illuminator of Scripture; therefore, the Holy Spirit plays a vital part in elucidating the contemporary meaning of Scripture.[76]

Many Pentecostals would argue for a prominent role of the Holy Spirit in the interpretive process but I have found only one in my research thus far who has articulated how the interpreter would rely upon the Holy Spirit. Arrington suggests four ways in which the interpreter relies on the Holy Spirit:

> (1) submission of the mind to God so that the critical and analytical abilities are exercised under the guidance of the Holy Spirit; (2) a genuine openness to the witness of the Spirit as the text is examined; (3) the personal experience of faith as part of the entire interpretative process; and, (4) response to the transforming call of God's Word.[77]

The Holy Spirit enables the interpreter to bridge the historical and cultural gulf between the ancient authors of the Scriptures and the present interpreter.[78] This strong emphasis upon the Holy Spirit comes from the Scriptures which emphasize the role of the Holy Spirit as revealing God and God's will to his people (1 Cor. 2.9–10a).

These two dimensions (experiential and pneumatic) can lead to a subjectivizing interpretive process; however, it must be pointed out that Scripture has always stood as the objective standard to which Pentecostals must submit. Thus Bruner, whose work is sharply critical of Pentecostalism, recognizes that 'Pentecostalism quite openly declares that unless it can support its case biblically it has no final compelling reason to exist'.[79]

John Christopher Thomas has suggested a holistic Pentecostal hermeneutic which incorporates Arrington's concern for a pneumatic illumination and a dialogical role between Scripture and experience.[80] He deduces his paradigm from the Jerusalem council as recorded in Acts 15. Thomas points out that Acts 15 grants an important role to the community and to the Holy Spirit in the interpretive process of dealing with Gentile Christians.[81] Thomas makes several observations concerning this passage before proposing his Pentecostal hermeneutic. These are worth

---

[76] Arrington, 'Use of the Bible', p. 104. Cf. H. Ervin, who said, 'There is no hermeneutic unless and until the divine *hermeneutes* (the Holy Spirit) mediates an understanding' ('Hermeneutics: A Pentecostal Option', in Elbert [ed.], *Essays*, p. 27).

[77] Arrington, 'Use of the Bible', p. 105.

[78] Arrington, 'Use of the Bible', p. 105.

[79] Arrington, 'Use of the Bible', p. 63.

[80] Arrington, 'Dispensationalism', pp. 32–38; Thomas, 'Women', pp. 105–107.

[81] Thomas, 'Women', p. 49.

mentioning because in them we hear the concerns of some Pentecostals who find a pure historical-critical methodology to be an oppressive, alienating experience to the common laity. The danger is that the historical-critical methodology takes the Bible out of the hands of the Christian community, out of the hands of the ordinary person, and puts it in the laboratory of the expert who alone has the proper tools and training to interpret Scripture.[82]

First, Thomas argues that the methodology revealed in Acts 15 is one in which the interpretive process moves from the believing community's context to the biblical text. This particular biblical move is in reverse order to the historical-critical method, which starts at the text and moves to context. Secondly, the Holy Spirit in the community is seen to enable or illuminate the Christian community to overcome the difficulty of receiving Gentiles as Christians. There existed plenty of Old Testament passages which proclaim the impossibility of Gentiles becoming full-fledged members of God's covenant community. Thirdly, Scripture was used in this process, yet, as applied to the matter of rules for table fellowship, it generated only a temporary resolution.[83] This reveals that the text's authority is not unrelated to its relevance to the community or its own diversity of teaching on a given topic.[84]

Thomas's hermeneutic contains three primary components: the community, the activity of the Holy Spirit, and Scripture. These components are not static but in dialogue with each other. The community testifies to the experiences attributed to the Holy Spirit and then engages Scripture to validate or repudiate the experience or issue.[85]

Thomas applies this paradigm to the contemporary issue of women in ministry and in so doing demonstrates how the paradigm can work and can help to resolve an issue which Scripture in and of itself cannot resolve. Scripture with the aid of personal testimony through the guidance of the Holy Spirit can resolve this issue. His hermeneutic regards Scripture as authoritative and central for the rule and conduct of the church, because,

> ultimately the experience of the church must be measured against the biblical text and in that light, practices or views for which there is no biblical

---

[82] Arrington, 'Use of the Bible', p. 103.
[83] Thomas, 'Women', p. 50.
[84] Thomas, 'Women', p. 50.
[85] Thomas, 'Women', pp. 51–56.

support would be illegitimate...this includes respect for the texts' literary genre and diversity as well as the unity of Scripture.[86]

Thomas has thus far presented a hermeneutic which attempts to be consistent with the classical Pentecostal ethos which resists the complete adoption of an evangelical historical-critical method. The traditional evangelical historical-critical methods would be utilized in the hermeneutic process but would not monopolize the process. Contemporary Christian experience must also be included in the hermeneutical process.

In conclusion, Pentecostalism began among the poor and racially marginalized people in society. Even today Pentecostalism's greatest growth is in the so-called third-world countries. Pentecostalism in its classical beginning should not be viewed as pre-modern or pre-critical but as sub-modern. Pentecostals were never invited to be equal partners in the modernist debate, but they still ate from the crumbs which fell from the table of modernity.[87] They demonstrated a modernist mindset by arguing that they had scriptural empirical verification of their spiritual experience (Spirit baptism resulting in speaking in tongues). Yet, the Pentecostal worldview contains important concepts which are strikingly similar to postmodernism.[88]

Today some Pentecostals attempt to express themselves with a purely modernistic hermeneutic (the historical-critical method) yet if Pentecostalism desires to continue in its missionary objective while keeping in tune with its classical ethos, then Pentecostalism must have a postmodern accent; an accent which is both a protest against modernity as well as a proclamation to move beyond modernity; or better, after the modern.[89] For Pentecostal scholars a satisfying hermeneutic cannot be uncritical or even sub-modern, but it must move beyond the historical-critical methodology which has gradually transformed biblical writings into museum pieces without contemporary relevance.[90] Pentecostals believe that God still speaks today and when God speaks, God has more to say than just

---

[86] Thomas, 'Women', p. 55.
[87] Sheppard, 'Pentecostals', pp. 127–29.
[88] See Johns's article, 'Pentecostalism'. Also J.P. Martin, 'Toward a PostCritical Paradigm', *NTS* 33 (1987), pp. 370–85.
[89] See Cargal, 'Fundamentalist-Modernist Controversy'. Also B. Turner, *Theories of Modernity and Postmodernity* (London; Sage Publications, 1990), pp. 1–12.
[90] E.V. McKnight, *Postmodern Use of the Bible: The Emergence of the Reader-Oriented Criticism* (Nashville: Abingdon Press, 1988), p. 14.

Scripture,[91] yet it will be scripturally sound. This results from the Holy Spirit being immanent in creation and the community. Thus the Spirit will speak horizontally with a human voice or through human dreams. This is possible because humanity is created in God's image and God took upon God's self humanity; consequently, there exists an essential relatedness which makes communication possible.[92]

Thomas's hermeneutical paradigm captures both the dialogical and dialectical essence of Pentecostalism. Thus we recognize the interdependence between the Scripture, Spirit, and reader(s). 'There must be a constant dialogue between the interpreter and the text', because 'God's Word is not a dead letter to be observed coldly but a word which speaks to my situation...'; therefore, 'the hermeneutical circle is not only unavoidable but desirable'.[93] Pentecostalism's contribution to hermeneutics is in the area of community participation and experiential understanding. There exists a promising Pentecostal hermeneutic rooted in the classical spiritual ethos of Pentecostalism. This hermeneutic will speak with a liberating voice accented by postmodernity.

---

[91] C. Pinnock, 'The Work of the Holy Spirit in Hermeneutics', *JPT* 2 (1993), pp. 3–23. Pinnock, not a Pentecostal, argues for the same idea in this article: 'The Spirit helps us understand what was meant by the biblical authors with a view to our understanding what God wants to say to us today' (p. 9).

[92] F. Watson, *Text, Church and World* (Edinburgh: T. & T. Clark, 1994), pp. 107–23.

[93] G. Stanton, 'Presuppositions in New Testament Criticism', in I.H. Marshall (ed.), *New Testament Interpretation* (Carlisle: Paternoster Press, rev. edn, 1985 [1977]), p. 66.

CHAPTER TEN

PENTECOSTALISM AND THE AUTHORITY OF SCRIPTURE*

Scott A. Ellington**

'Is the Bible the Word of God?' I frequently ask students this question at the beginning of their study of the inspiration and the authority of Scripture. At the Mexican Bible Seminary, where I have taught for a number of years, the answer is invariably 'yes!' What is more, it seldom if ever occurs to any of my students to ask even the most basic qualifying questions, such as 'what do you mean by "Word of God"?', before answering. Such enclaves of non-critical acceptance of traditional doctrine are, however, increasingly rare in the Christian academic circles of our day, while seeming to flourish undisturbed in other parts of the Christian church, most noticeably in the developing countries of the world.

When, however, I follow this first question by asking '*how do we know that* the Bible is the Word of God?', the responses become far less certain and automatic, requiring as they do some level of critical thought. Answers tend to range from 'that's what the Bible teaches', to 'that's what my pastor taught us', to a suspicious 'don't *you* believe that the Bible is the Word of God?'. The problem is that, in this modern age of doubt, questioning and discovery, these types of answers, along with many more sophisticated proofs, are increasingly easy to question and invalidate. The fact is that Scripture does not attempt to set forth and defend a doctrine of inspiration and authority, but rather simply speaks authoritatively.

When pressed to provide an answer to my second question ('Why do you believe that the Bible is the Word of God?'), I noticed a persistent tendency among Pentecostal students to fall back on testimony of personal experiences. By that I mean stories taken from their own lives and experiences in which they understood God to speak to them, and indeed to 'come down' and meet with them, among other ways, in and through the medium of biblical text. I observed time and time again that it was possible to question and even cast serious doubts on traditional

---

* First published in the *Journal of Pentecostal Theology* 9 (1996), pp. 16–38.
** Scott A. Ellington (PhD, University of Sheffield) is Associate Professor in the School of Christian Ministries at Emmanuel College, Franklin Springs, GA USA.

understandings of and proofs for infallibility and inerrancy in Pentecostal groups without seriously challenging their understanding of the Bible as the authoritative 'Word of God'. This suggests to me that Pentecostals do not found their understanding of the authority of Scripture on a bedrock of doctrine, but that, in fact, their doctrine is itself resting on something more fundamental, dynamic, and resilient; their experiences of encountering a living God, directly and personally. Doctrines may be challenged and even overturned without striking at the very heart of Pentecostal faith because the central emphasis of Pentecostalism is not a teaching which must be believed or a proof which can be deduced and defended against all challenges, but a God who must be reckoned with in direct encounter. This understanding is not, of course, unique to Pentecostalism, but its centrality of emphasis and the influence which it has over the daily lives of adherents is. I believe that this emphasis has a dramatic and important impact on the way in which Pentecostals do theology.

Pentecostals are far less ready to fight and die in defense of doctrinal statements than many other theologically conservative Christian groups seem to be. This, I believe, is not because Pentecostals are less able to think critically than other Christian groups or that they find doctrine unimportant. Rather, I propose that, in fact, Pentecostals understand and utilize doctrine in a fundamentally different way from those traditions which are more thoroughly grounded in rationalist models[1] of considering the question of the authority of Scripture. For Pentecostals, doctrine is not essentially *generative* in function, but rather *descriptive*. A generative understanding of the way in which doctrine is utilized could, for example, begin with the statement the Bible is inspired by God and from that deduce that it is, therefore, inerrant. But Pentecostals, on the other hand, utilize doctrine to describe and verbalize *lived experience*. Formal doctrinal statements, which are deductive in nature, are, among Pentecostals, an attempt to organize and understand described experience and do not attempt to serve as proofs for those things which lie completely outside the realm of experience. Beliefs are not derived from understanding, but arise from intense individual and corporate experiences of the presence and action of God in the lives of Christian believers. Doctrine is descriptive of and, as such, arises out of experience. Pentecostalism begins

---

[1] The term 'rationalist' is intended here to refer to all theological models which rely largely or entirely on the use of reason as a means of approaching theological questions, while at the same time seeking to exclude all non-rational methodology. All theological methods are, to some extent, rational, but not all give an exclusive place to the faculty of reason, devaluing anything which is not primarily if not completely rational.

with intense experiences of encountering God. God reveals himself in the pages of the Bible, in signs and wonders, in worship and prayer in very real and powerful ways. Pentecostals base their faith *first* on the God that they have met and know in relationship, and only then do they attempt, with greater or lesser success, to articulate their experiences in normative, doctrinal ways. This is not to say that, for Pentecostals, doctrine is unimportant, but it is to recognize that the basic fodder of the doctrinal process within Pentecostalism is the experience of the community of faith.

The Church of God (Cleveland, Tennessee) has as its earliest official statement on the authority of Scripture a declaration published in the *Evangel*, August 15, 1910, which began by saying, 'The Church of God stands for the whole Bible rightly divided. The New Testament is the only rule of government and discipline.'[2] A more detailed statement of faith on the subject was not adopted until 1948, when the General Assembly of the church included the statement 'We believe in the verbal inspiration of the Bible' in its statement of faith.[3] J. Christopher Thomas implies that the adoption of a more detailed expression of faith concerning the authority of Scripture had more to do with the church's dialogue with the National Association of Evangelicals than with a felt need within the denomination. He says, however, that:

> Such a history (of the statement of faith) should not be taken to suggest that Pentecostals did not always believe wholeheartedly in the inspiration of Scripture, but that Pentecostals had their own concerns alongside the debates which were mostly going on elsewhere within the Evangelical community.[4]

C.M. Robeck, in an article on the National Association of Evangelicals, states that the association between Pentecostals and Evangelicals in the National Association of Evangelicals, founded in 1942, led to the 'evangelicalization' of Pentecostals. He notes that 'some Pentecostal groups have rewritten their statements of faith, and others have imported such "evangelical" issues as "inerrancy" into their theological arenas for the first time'.[5] Thomas[6] in particular notes the efforts on the part of Pentecostals to gain acceptance in evangelical circles through the National Association

---

[2] C. Conn, *Like a Mighty Army: A History of the Church of God* (Cleveland, TN: Pathway Press, 1911), pp. 111–18.
[3] Conn, *Like a Mighty Army*, p. 218.
[4] J.C. Thomas, 'The Word and the Spirit', *Evangel* 81 (7), p. 5.
[5] C.M. Robeck, 'National Association of Evangelicals', S.M. Burgess, *et al.* (eds.), *Dictionary of Pentecostal and Charismatic Movements* (Grand Rapids: Zondervan, 1990), pp. 635–36.
[6] Thomas, 'The Word and the Spirit', p. 5.

of Evangelicals, and he finds very telling the fact that the statement 'We believe in the verbal inspiration of the Bible' was not adopted by the Church of God until 1948, during this time of early association.

Thomas's and Robeck's observations suggest to me that formal doctrinal statements on the authority of Scripture among conservative churches in this century arose out of debates which were not immediately important within the Pentecostal church. Pentecostals adopted statements of scriptural authority which were essentially Evangelical as part of their effort to gain a wider acceptance in the conservative Christian community, and the Evangelical movement in the US has been and is today preoccupied with articulating their faith within the framework of modern rationalism. They are resisting the encroachment of modernity using the tools of modern scientific method and playing by the rules and within the restrictions of rationalism. One of the central arguments which I want to make in this paper is that, even today, doctrinal statements on the inspiration and, derivatively, the authority of Scripture are secondary in importance among Pentecostals to the experiences of an authoritative God in and through the Scriptures. Evangelicals use 'proofs' for inspiration to try to support a sagging argument for biblical authority, while Pentecostals begin with an authoritative encounter with God and then seek to describe biblical inspiration in the only terms available to them, those of conservative Evangelicalism.

For some, this suggestion that experience and not doctrinal statements are at the heart of Pentecostal faith might provoke a deep felt suspicion that I am proposing that we compromise or even abandon altogether doctrinal 'truths'. In a number of conservative circles, any deviation from the accepted view would fail the breathalyzer test of established orthodoxy. I am not trying to reject doctrinal statements, but I am suggesting that Pentecostals need to begin by asking a different set of questions. Instead of beginning with a declaration of what Pentecostal doctrine should and must be, I want to begin by observing what it, in fact, looks like and how it actually functions.

In this brief study, I would like to examine four proposals: first, that modern rationalism is limited by its very nature to a partial understanding of the nature and presence of God and that it has reached boundaries in its speech about God beyond which it cannot pass; second, that Pentecostals have failed adequately to formulate and articulate models of doctrine which are true to their tradition, choosing instead to adopt uncritically the doctrinal models of Evangelical Christians; third, that Pentecostalism is different from other branches of the Christian church in the way that it approaches theology and that, therefore, Pentecostals need to formulate a distinctly Pentecostal theology; and finally, that at the local church level, theology is frequently oral in form and some thought should be given to devising a theology which exploits the richness of testimony in the Pentecostal tradition.

Pentecostalism and the Pentecostal Use of Scripture

To a certain extent, it is misleading to speak of a 'Pentecostal' understanding of Scripture or 'Pentecostal theology' or a 'Pentecostal hermeneutic'. There is, in fact, nothing which is completely new and unique to the modern Pentecostal movement. All Christian churches have emphasized experience to a greater or lesser extent. Glossolalia, miraculous signs, and healings have been a part of the Christian experience for 2,000 years and, with the exception of glossolalia, of the faith of Old Testament Judaism before the time of Christ. Having stated, however, that Pentecostals have not invented or discovered a 'new thing', it is certainly fair to say that few if any other Christian churches today take so literally the New Testament accounts of experiences of lived relationship with God and empowerment by the Holy Spirit for ministry as do the Pentecostal and Charismatic movements. A faith which in no way attempts to express a personal encounter with a living God is deeply suspect for many Pentecostals, simply because it is a foreign concept. God is intensely interested in relationship with his creation, and Pentecostals understand God's invitation to relationship in very literal and concrete terms and have testimonies of encounters with God which form the basis of their faith and theology.

I admit freely my own frustration and inability adequately and fully to define 'Pentecostal experience', precisely because Pentecostalism is a movement within the Christian church and, therefore, cannot be wholly different from any other branch of the body. Having said this though, Pentecostals have a set of shared experiences which, if not wholly *different* from those felt by the larger family of Christ, are not universally shared by the body. All Christians have had some level of experience with God, but not all Christians share in some of the depths of experience and insight which have been a part of the modern Pentecostal movement. It is, therefore, difficult to describe an experience which is not held in common by all.

Personal and communal experience is, quite obviously, a precarious basis for faith, being more open to subjectivity and self-deception. Relationship with God, however, is not a closed system in which the individual believer is free to manipulate the data to satisfy his or her own desires, needs and expectations. It is precisely because God is so intrusively real that our subjective experience is constantly being challenged and proved. Nor is the Pentecostal understanding of the Christian faith strictly an internal experience and, therefore, beyond the reach of critical evaluation. Signs, wonders, and miracles in the Pentecostal community serve to make experiences a shared, community property because they are external evidence of the power and presence of God working within the community and the world. Biblical authority in the Pentecostal church rests, in part, on experiences of God in and through the Scriptures which constantly intrude on the realm of 'daily life'.

Within Pentecostal and charismatic circles, the Bible is the basic rule of faith and practice and supplies the corrective and interpretive authority for all religious experience. This belief is not a matter of dogma but arises from repeated observations of the way in which God utilizes Scripture interactively. The words of Scripture add language to the relationship which exists between the believer and God. Therefore, 'what the Bible says' is identical with 'what God says' in Pentecostal theology, so that the task of applying biblical teaching to the life of the believer and the community of faith is essentially an interpretive one, which seeks to understand in the clearest way possible what it is that God is saying to the Church in and through the biblical text. A central question in biblical study in Pentecostal circles is 'How do we live a Christian life according to the Scriptures?' Along with many more conservative branches of the Christian church Pentecostals approach the Bible with very practical questions, expecting to encounter in the Scripture the very words of God speaking directly to their needs and guiding them in the transformation which the Holy Spirit is actively carrying on in their lives. It is the transformative action of the Holy Spirit which persistently intrudes on Christian experience and prevents our interpretations from becoming simply a process of reading our own needs and wants into the text and hearing only that which we want to hear.

The Nature of Scripture

That the Enlightenment challenge to authority in all its forms which in turn has led to the modern critical studies of the Bible has seriously altered and, in some contexts, even destroyed any coherent notion of biblical authority is such a self-evident notion that I will not take time in this present work to document it.[7] A further and more extreme move in more recent times has been to subsume all external authority to the particular context of the individual responding to an authoritative claim. There are, according to such views, no external sources of authority which are universal absolutes. It is fair to say that in many, though by no means in all, northern and western churches, the authority of the Bible has been qualified in the extreme by questions of the reader's own context and background. In fact, some would argue that biblical authority in no way transcends the immediate context of the reader. Because I cannot establish any absolute, universal standards from Scripture, so the argument goes, the meaning of Scripture in my particular context is determined precisely by that context.

This assumption is one of several that has grown out of a worldview which demands that all experience be challenged and measured according to a set of 'objective' and 'scientific' measures. This scientific and rational worldview has narrowly defined the parameters within which the biblical text may be studied and has denied validity to all other approaches to the Bible. As a result, the modern, western worldview has become the exclusive measuring stick for interpreting Scripture and no room has been left for this basic understanding of the nature of reality to be challenged. The American Evangelical movement has chosen largely to defend its notion of biblical authority within the limits of modern rationalism, trying within the narrow restrictions of a scientific worldview to defend a Bible which will not be confined in such tight quarters, but which insists on making absolute and universal claims which cannot be adequately documented and verified by experimental method alone.[8]

---

[7] John Goldingay offers a brief but informative outline of this crisis of biblical authority in his *Models for Scripture* (Grand Rapids, MI: Eerdmans, 1994), pp. 117–21.

[8] Simply on a pragmatic level, this rationalist worldview is rapidly becoming a minority view. Explosive growth in the third world, particularly among the more doctrinally conservative churches, and most noticeably in the Pentecostal and Charismatic movements, has broken the modernist monopoly on biblical studies. That is to say, the majority of the Christian church today does not have the same worldview as western rationalism. The first world church has, it is true, been reasonably successful up until now at silencing these new voices, either by funding and controlling their educational structures and controlling the language which is available to them to articulate their faith or by simply denying access and voice in the church's political process. This has not always been done intentionally or even consciously, but the missionary movements of the western world have all too frequently exported their worldview as though if were inseparable from the gospel message, being themselves, at times, unable to distinguish the two. I hope to demonstrate in this paper the ways in which our worldview has been promoted and exported as though

Steve Land challenges the Pentecostal practice of adopting uncritically from evangelical circles their statements about the inspiration of Scripture. He understands the Scripture to be 'Spirit-Word', that is, the dynamic interaction of written text and the Holy Spirit.

> The Spirit who inspired and preserved the Scriptures illuminates, teaches, guides, convicts and transforms through the Word today. The Word is alive, quick and powerful, because of the Holy Spirit's ministry. The relation of the Spirit to Scripture is based on that of Spirit to Christ. Even as the Spirit formed Christ in Mary, so the Spirit uses Scripture to form Christ in believers and vice-versa.[9]

Doctrines of infallibility and inerrancy arose out of but regress from spiritualities which 'practiced a much fuller doctrine of the Word of God'.[10] Land places the authority of the Spirit ahead of the authority of Scripture, stating that 'The Spirit was over the church. The Spirit was prior to Scripture. So, the order of authority was Spirit, Scripture, church. Without the Spirit there would have been no Word, incarnate or written; without the Word, no church'.[11]

Clark Pinnock sees the sharp division between the original inspiration of Scripture and the present day illumination of Scripture by the Holy Spirit to be unnecessary. He states that:

> Both are crucially important and both belong to that larger process of inspiration in which the Spirit first gave the Scriptures and then repeatedly gives them again and again to readers. God's breathing ought to be recognised both in the formation and in the appropriation of the text.[12]

Thus, for Pinnock, 'If the Bible is to become the word of God in our lives, the letter is going to have to come alive by means of the Spirit'.[13] I would state it even more plainly. The book which we call the Bible is not of itself the word of God, but only becomes the word of God to the reader

---

it were part of the gospel and how this view is, at times, incongruous with the experiences of the Christian faith in cultures which do not share our own worldview. I would submit that throughout the world and even in many local US church communities the question of biblical authority is far more active and alive than modern scholarship would have us believe.

[9] Steven J. Land, *Pentecostal Spirituality: A Passion for the Kingdom* (Sheffield, England: Sheffield Academic Press, 1993), p. 100.

[10] Land, *Pentecostal Spirituality*, p. 74.

[11] Land, *Pentecostal Spirituality*, p. 106.

[12] Clark H. Pinnock, 'The Work of the Holy Spirit in Hermeneutics', *Journal of Pentecostal Theology* 2 (April, 1993), p. 4.

[13] Pinnock, 'The Work of the Holy Spirit in Hermeneutics', p. 5.

or hearer through the action and participation of the Holy Spirit in a continuation of inspiration. While many conservative Christians would affirm this understanding, Pentecostals place paramount importance on the Spirit's 'inspiring' of the biblical text as we receive it. The Pentecostal understanding of biblical authority depends primarily on experiences of the Holy Spirit speaking and guiding in and through the biblical text.

This has clear implications for a doctrine of the authority of Scripture. The Bible is not simply a text about whose propositions we can debate, it is the authoritative word of God *because* the same Holy Spirit who inspired its writers meets us today in its pages. For Pentecostals, biblical authority does not rest in the text we can justify, but in the God that we know in and through the text.

Cheryl Bridges Johns, in her book *Pentecostal Formation: A Pedagogy among the Oppressed*,[14] argues that the modern rationalist scientific worldview is based on a Greek philosophical understanding of reality, which sees the 'knower' as subject and the thing known as object. There is, according to Johns, an impenetrable barrier between the knower and the thing known in Greek philosophy. Greek philosophy is essentially dualistic, setting up a distinct and absolute barrier of separation between the knowing subject and the object of knowledge: that which is known. Johns maintains that this approach to knowledge is non-Hebrew and, therefore, non-biblical. Instead she argues for adoption of the Hebrew notion of *yada'*, or knowing in active relationship, as a biblical model for talking about knowledge of God. Thomas Groome describes *yada'* as knowing which 'arises not by standing back from in order to look at, but by active and intentional engagement in lived experience'.[15] Modern ways of knowing approach God as an object of knowledge and not as the subject which guides us in our discovery of reality. I seek to place the concept of biblical authority not in a doctrinal setting, but rather in a relational and experiential setting within the community of faith.

Susan Handelman makes the argument that our modern interpretation of biblical material has been distorted by the fact that we read the Scripture through Greek lenses.[16] She draws from Hans-Georg Gadamer's monumental work on the nature of truth and knowledge to illustrate the

---

[14] C. Johns, *Pentecostal Formation: A Pedagogy Among the Oppressed* (JPTSup, 2; Sheffield: Sheffield Academic Press, 1993).
[15] T. Groome, *Christian Religious Education* (San Francisco: Harper & Row, 1980), p. 141.
[16] S. Handelman, *The Slayers of Moses: The Emergence of Rabbinic Interpretation in Modern Literary Theory* (Albany, NY: State University of New York Press, 1982).

dramatically different use that words have within the Greek way of understanding. Gadamer tells us,

> In the earliest times the intimate unity of word and object was so obvious that the name was considered to be part of the bearer of the name, if not, indeed, to substitute for him... Greek philosophy more or less began with the insight that a word is only a name, i.e. that it does not represent true being.[17]

As a result, words were considered to be mere symbols of some higher truth and were themselves suspect in their ability to communicate truth. If this understanding is expanded and applied to the whole of language, Scripture becomes a place where we go to acquire information about God and not a place where we go to meet the person of God in a direct encounter through the words of the text. And if we cannot 'know' God through direct encounter, all we have is knowledge *about* God and all that we can do is merely encounter the idea of God. This God is a completely foreign notion in Pentecostal hermeneutics.

Yada', on the other hand, is a knowing in active relationship. We do not simply know about God, but we 'get to know' God experientially in direct encounter. Such knowledge can never be absolutized or reduced to a series of 'spiritual laws' or a pharisaic legalism, but it must arise from a constant interaction with the known one. Thus, both those who would reduce the Scripture to a set of abstract rational principles and those who would try to freeze it into a series of dogmatic moral laws which function quite independently of their divine author are operating under false models of knowing.[18]

Because our knowledge of God is relational and not merely informational, theology can be better expressed orally, because that is the primary mode of relational communication among ordinary people in the community of faith. Johns has pointed out that Pentecostal theology is essentially oral in nature. Pentecostalism arises out of experiences of the presence and action of God in the everyday life of the Christian, in constant dia-

---

[17] Hans-Georg Gadamer, *Truth and Method* (New York: Continuum, 1975), p. 366.

[18] Johns clarifies the type of relationship which we enjoy with the one whom we seek to know. Because God is sovereign, we can act as subjects of history, transforming the world around us, *only* after we have been acted upon as objects of God. Put another way, our ability as Christians to act transformatively depends first and foremost on God working in us an inner transformation, a sanctification from the power and effects of sin which would distort and disable our praxis. Thus, to *know* God is not an abstract and uninvolved kind of knowing, but is a knowing in dynamic relationship which changes an individual in the way that they act and speak and think.

logue with the biblical story, interpreted within the community of faith and through the guidance of the Holy Spirit. This last element assumes that our relationship with God can never simply be considered as past knowledge, but that it is ever a present and dynamic force as we seek to understand our story in the light of the larger biblical story and to integrate our experiences of God in the larger context of the experiences of the community of faith, both contemporarily in our present community and context and historically in the Church tradition and the Scripture itself.

Because this process is decidedly oral and experiential, it includes the uneducated and uninitiated, and, indeed, it puts the 'modern' person at a distinct disadvantage. The rationalist paradigm in which we have been so successfully indoctrinated has made it all but impossible for us to avoid 'demythologizing' and rejecting everything which does not fit the structure of reality in which we are immersed. We are robbed of our ability to imagine any reality outside of the physical, verifiable, predictable, domesticatable world which we have created for ourselves. Thus, the structural demand with which we approach God in relationship to a great extent defines the parameters of that relationship. This is not to say that God is simply a determined Being, but it is to recognize that our faith affects the shape of our relationship with God.

Testimony and oral expression lend themselves to the understanding and knowing of the God with whom we are in an active relationship, and it requires no 'special knowledge' or expertise in order to participate actively in the search to know God. As a result, access to God is not controlled by a few professionals, but is open to all. By encouraging each member of the community of faith to share testimonies of his or her experiences of God and to participate in illuminating these experiences in dialogue with Scripture, the church community, and the Holy Spirit, the opportunity and the responsibility to know God is shared equally by all. Because Pentecostal theologizing is oral and experiential, all participate on an equal footing, with no particular advantage for those who have special training or superior education. It should not seem strange, therefore, that testimony is at the heart of the speech about God in Pentecostal circles. The result of this theological approach for the question of biblical authority is that this authority is not imposed from 'above' by church leadership, but the Bible is experienced as authoritative as the Holy Spirit is found to be at work in and through Scripture in the lives of each member of the church community.

The *yada'* way of knowing directly challenges the fundamental assumption of the scientific method: objectivity. God has objective existence apart from us, but our ways of knowing God are subjective in nature. In scientific investigations, the knower attempts to separate herself from the thing known and to be an 'objective' observer, that is, to 'objectify' or treat as a distinct and separate 'object' of study the thing to be known. Although such absolute objectivity is, in fact, an illusion, at the very least an attempt is made to minimize the impact of the knower on the person or thing to be known.

In interpersonal relationships, on the other hand, knowledge depends on the knower offering him- or herself to that being which he or she wishes to 'know'. Thus, the person of the knower is an essential part of 'knowing'. The problem is that, as the knower offers more of herself or himself in the relationship, the safeguards against subjectivism begin to disappear. But I am suggesting that knowing God in a Pentecostal setting is, by its very nature, subjective. Subjectivism, far from being a bad thing, is both necessary and unavoidable in relationships. In fact, apart from entering into a subjective relationship with God through the person of the Holy Spirit, we cannot really *know* God. Clark Pinnock tells us that '... since to know God is to know a person, there is a subjective dimension in our interpretation which requires a living relationship with God and the operation of his Spirit'.[19] Knowledge of God outside of a relationship with God is inevitably a distorted knowing, and we can know God in a personal relationship only through the operation of the Holy Spirit. Subjectivism becomes a problem when it denies the relationship and seeks the good of the believer over and against God's will. Subjectivism is negative to the extent that it is non-relational and selfserving. A question with which Pentecostal scholars must wrestle is 'how can the Pentecostal approach to theology remain relational, while avoiding the distortions which are possible in subjective involvement?' Johns has suggested a dynamic balance between the individual, the Holy Spirit, the Scripture, and the community of faith.[20]

The person of the Holy Spirit acts as our guide and corrective. Apart from the active participation of the Spirit, the mere words of the text have no power to transform us. We are not free, as Ficht has suggested, to create God in our own image. If we try to domesticate God to our own pur-

---

[19] Pinnock, 'The Work of the Holy Spirit in Hermeneutics', p. 5.
[20] An additional element which is all too frequently overlooked in Pentecostal circles is the value and importance of tradition. Because many Pentecostal churches arose in a context which was deeply suspicious of creeds, they have often failed to value the 'testimonies' of the larger community of faith, both in our present day and historically throughout the ages.

poses or to force Him out of the process, we are left without the dynamic of interactive relationship. Johns claims that it is in the process of 'sharing our testimony' that we confess our subjective preunderstanding and that we make our objective claim. Subjectivism is not denied, as is the case with some rationalist models, but rather expressly vocalized, so that it may then be evaluated within the equally subjective community of faith and in light of Scripture.

Stanley Hauerwas's book *Unleashing the Scripture: Freeing the Bible from Captivity to America* defends the thesis that 'the Bible is not and should not be accessible to merely anyone, but rather it should be made available only to those who have undergone the hard discipline of existing as part of God's people'.[21] He goes on to say that:

> Most North American Christians assume that they have a right, if not an obligation, to read the Bible. I challenge that assumption. No task is more important than for the Church to take the Bible out of the hands of individual Christians in North America.[22]

His self-admittedly outrageous statement is based on the understanding that Scripture is only recognizable as such within the community of faith and that all who read it as Scripture must do so as a participating member of that community, under its authority. When this is not done, Hauerwas argues, the Bible is subverted to serve the political needs of the reader. Individualism in modern society has made much more real the threat of a destructive subjectivism, and active participation in a reading community is the best safe-guard against subverting the text to the service of individual self-interest. Biblical authority, then, incorporates the notion of involvement in the community of faith. Indeed, the Bible is authoritative for the church community, and to place oneself voluntarily outside of that community is to fail to recognize the Bible as authoritative.

The thesis of this study is that biblical authority in the Pentecostal community arises from personal and communal experiences of the transformative power of the Holy Spirit in the lives of individuals, in the community of faith and in the world. The Spirit utilizes and works in harmony with and through Scripture to transform the lives of individuals and to empower them supernaturally to become instruments of God's transformation and restoration of fallen creation. Because most formal doctrine

---

[21] S. Hauerwas, *Unleashing the Scripture: Freeing the Bible from Captivity to America* (Nashville: Abingdon Press, 1993), p. 9.
[22] Hauerwas, *Unleashing the Scripture*, p. 15.

is expressed through and bound up in a rationalist paradigm, the community of faith in a dynamic, experiential relationship with God, and not the academic community, is the proper setting for the discovery and exploration of a Pentecostal understanding of biblical authority. Pentecostal doctrine, in order to speak to and interpret experiences of encounter with God, must arise out of experience and be subject to examination and conceivably alteration by experience, Scripture, and the Holy Spirit. Scripture acts as a corrective for experience and the biblical text has the last word. This is not to say that biblical doctrine is inferior or non-essential, but it is to recognize that the Bible is not essentially a doctrinal treatise. Rather, it is a record of testimonies, a story of the relationship between God and his creation. As it moves through stories of creation, fall, trial, promise, preservation, deliverance, faithfulness, failure, exile, redemption, and restoration, the biblical forms (oracle, vision, narrative, song, command, theological treatise, etc.) reflect the diverse ways in which the biblical authors *experienced* the revelation of God. Indeed, leaving aside the question of whether the canon should be considered to be closed, it can be stated that the community of faith today should understand itself to be a continuation of the community of faith in which the Scripture was originally forged. Because the Scripture arose in the community of faith and can only be legitimately authoritative within that community today, it is correct to say that, while not originating with the community of faith, the Bible's authority nevertheless is formed and functions effectively only within that community. Although the historical, social, political, cultural, and economic contexts of each local community of faith are unique, I argue that the biblical text can only be entered into and *re-experienced* in the same setting in which it was originally formed, that is, in the community of faith. The text cannot be fully understood simply by analyzing it in a detached and objective way. The authority of Scripture can be adequately understood only by the community which has committed itself to live under the discipline of that authority because that authority arises from a living interaction between God and the community of faith. The biblical text offers a world of communal relationship to God, and one can fully enter that world only in the community of faith, because finally it is the community's story and not just the collected stories of individuals. Christian doctrine should arise from and describe the relationship between the individual, the community of faith, and God, as it is informed by Scripture.

I argue that, while church doctrines are vital to the preservation and articulation of the Christian gospel, they are essentially reductionistic and impersonal when cast in the form of inflexible dogma. A belief in an authority of Scripture which is doctrinally based and not founded in personal experiences of encounter with God in and through Scripture is, I believe, an inadequate source of authority. Indeed, the person that founds his or her faith on doctrine rather than personal experience informed by doctrine has chosen a singularly unstable foundation. Doctrines, which serve an important role in defining and guiding faith, are nevertheless not the foundation of faith. Faith, in order to be strong, must spring from and be nurtured by an encounter with God and not just knowledge about God. The biblical text was forged in (but not merely by) a community that was in dynamic relationship with the Self Revealing One, and it is the community of faith which provides the richest setting for the Holy Spirit's revealing of God to us through Scripture today. The worldview of such a community expects and looks for experiences of dynamic, life-changing encounter with a God who is intent on being known in relationship.[23]

It matters very much whether we see the Scripture as simply a series of good teachings or ideas and concepts or even as a sacred history, or whether we understand it to be a relational world of encounter with God and the historical community of faith into which we enter, with our intellect, but also with our emotions, intuitions and feelings. I submit that any reading of the Scripture which is devoid of experiences of encounters with God and which occurs in isolation from the community of faith is an inadequate reading which fails to comprehend Scripture's origin, function and, ultimately, what Scripture is. Thus, while doctrines are an essential tool in organizing biblical teachings and evaluating personal and communal experiences, for the Bible to be truly 'authoritative' in the life of an individual and community, God must be experienced and encountered by that person and community in and through Scripture.

Toward a Pentecostal WorldView

At the heart of the conflict which exists between traditional statements of the authority of Scripture and a Pentecostal understanding of that

---

[23] David Clines, in his book *The Theme of the Pentateuch* (Sheffield, England: Sheffield Academic Press, 1989), understands Scripture to provide a world which the reader is invited to enter. He says that 'The Pentateuch as a story therefore performs the function of creating a "world" that is to a greater or lesser extent unlike the world of the reader, and that invites the reader to allow the horizons of his own world to merge with those of the other world' (p. 102). For Clines it might be unimportant whether this world is real or imagined, but Pentecostals make the claim that the world of Scripture into which we are invited is real, because the God which we meet there is real.

authority is the question of worldview. Most modern theology attempts to bracket out subjective experience, whereas for Pentecostals, experiences of encountering God are the beginning point of theology and the constant companion of the theologian. Doctrinal statements are a product of and not the source of experiences of revelation and encounter.

Walter Wink criticizes modern critical method for its artificiality which separates the scholar both from the world of the biblical text and from the practical world of lived Christian experience as it is today. Modern historical-critical method requires a separation from and objectification of its focus of study, the biblical text. Wink maintains that the historical-critical method must practice a functional atheism, separating the text from the stream of existence and objectifying it. He states that, 'by detaching the text from the stream of my existence, biblical criticism has hurled it into the abyss of an objectified past'.[24] Thus a vast gulf is fixed between the reader and the text. Because of this, Wink claims that the fruits of critical study, which has made the biblical text into an abstract object, are not readily applied to practical situations of daily use.

Wink also notes that historical method, by its very nature, must exclude all consideration of the supernatural. In order for historical method to function, the historian must have a world in which outside interference and arbitrary divine intervention are excluded. Biblical history can only be studied and applied in the same way as secular history if we assume that both operate according to the same ground rules. Supernatural in-breakings into history do not fall within the realm of explainable cause and effect and are, therefore, disruptive to the formation of a history under the historical-critical model.[25] Thus, modern criticism is forced to exclude all consideration of the miraculous, both in the biblical history and in its application to the life of the church today. Interestingly, the result is that the supernatural is excluded from the conversation not so much for reasons of faith, but rather for reasons of expediency. The model just will not function in a world open to the supernatural.[26]

---

[24] W. Wink, *The Bible in Human Transformation* (Philadelphia: Fortress Press, 1973), pp. 3–4.
[25] Wink, *The Bible in Human Transformation*, p. 38.
[26] Jackie Johns ('The Covenant Community as Paradigmatic Context for Leadership Development in the Pentecostal Church. Part One: Pentecostalism and the Emerging Worldview'. A paper presented at the 23rd Annual Meeting of the Society for Pentecostal Studies, 1993) develops the notion that a predominantly rational approach to biblical studies is impoverished in that it limits our access to the text to the single human attribute of the intellect. He notes that Pentecostal theology is 'transrational' and that 'Pentecostals

David Kelsey[27] observes that the mode in which we understand God to be present in large part determines the resulting form of our theology. But by choosing one way in which to understand God to be present, there is a great temptation to eliminate all competing models of understanding. Biblical scholarship which relies on the methods of modern biblical criticism, tends, unfairly, to bracket out other ways of understanding God to be present. Thus, those ways of knowing God which are traditionally identified with rationalism are much less open to knowing God in other ways, such as emotionally, or in supernatural events which transcend a strictly scientific worldview. By limiting our imagined notions of the ways in which God is and is not present, what one effectively does is to bracket out a relational understanding of knowing God, settling instead for a more distant and distorted knowledge *about* God.

It is worth noting that the emotional and the supernatural are eliminated from 'scientific' discussions not because they can be invalidated using scientific method, but rather because they can be neither invalidated nor adequately evaluated using such methodology. To exclude the supernatural from the question of biblical authority is as much a faith statement as its inclusion.

Parker Palmer, in his classic work *To Know as we are Known: Education as a Spiritual Journey*, argues that the entire educational structure produces a scholarship and a knowledge which is essentially anti-communal. He describes the way in which we objectify that which we would know in order to manipulate and control it. This, of course, suggests that scientific method is not disinterested, but that it, in fact, can be motivated by a desire not simply to understand, but also to subjugate. 'We are well educated people', Palmer says, 'who have been schooled in a way of knowing that treats the world as an object to be dissected and manipulated, a way of knowing that gives us power over the world'.[28] He goes on to say that:

> Of course ownership and control are possible only in relation to objects or things. One cannot own a living being until, by a twist of mind, one turns it

---

do not limit truth to the realm of reason. For them the spectrum of knowledge includes cognition, affection, and behavior, each of which is fused to the other two' (p. 18). By narrowly defining the range of possible approaches that we allow the Holy Spirit to utilize in revealing God to us, we have greatly impoverished our experience of God.

[27] D. Kelsey, *The Uses of Scripture in Recent Theology* (Philadelphia: Fortress Press, 1975).

[28] P.J. Palmer, *To Know as we are Known: Education as a Spiritual Journey* (San Francisco: Harper & Row, 1993), p. 2.

into a piece of property, a slave, thus gaining the dominance modern knowing strives for.[29]

He maintains that education mediates the relationship between the knowing subject and the world, which is the object of knowledge, giving supremacy to the knowing self over the known world.[30] Palmer's startling conclusion is that knowledge is not amoral, but that it begins in a 'place of passion within the human soul'.[31] Thus, we must not only question the feasibility of objectivity, we must also be aware that, as we make the necessary move toward attempted objectivity in our evaluations, we are neither purely rational nor strictly amoral and disinterested.

Exploring a Pentecostal Paradigm

Charles Kraft's book *Christianity with Power: Your Worldview and Your Experience of the Supernatural* explores the ways in which worldview predisposes openness to experience God in the spiritual realm.[32] His basic argument is that those whose worldview is predominantly rationalist are much less available to supernatural revelation and that they have radically reduced the range of revelation which they will allow the Holy Spirit to utilize. Kraft maintains that, while we cannot fully escape from our worldview, because it is a part of our very identity, we are able to modify and change it.

Walter Brueggemann speaks of our worldview as not merely opening us to new ways of viewing the world, but he understands our speech actually to act to form and transform our reality, that is, to be world creating. Brueggemann says,

> our new intellectual environment acknowledges that human agents are in process of constituting reality, and that formative work is done through rhetoric. This means that speech is not merely descriptive, but it is in some sense evocative of reality and constitutive of reality.[33]

Speaking of the prayer language of the Psalter he says that

---

[29] Palmer, *To Know as we are Known*, p. 24.
[30] Palmer, *To Know as we are Known*, p. 21.
[31] Palmer, *To Know as we are Known*, p. 7.
[32] C. Kraft, *Christianity with Power: Your Worldview and your Experience of the Supernatural* (Ann Arbor, MI: Vine Books, Servant Publications, 1989).
[33] W. Brueggemann, *Texts Under Negotiation: The Bible and Postmodern Imagination* (Minneapolis: Fortress Press, 1993), p. 12.

in the Psalms the use of language does not describe what is. It *evokes* to being what is not until it has been spoken... In using speech in this way, we are in fact doing in a derivative way what God has done in the creation narratives of Genesis. We are calling into being that which does not yet exist (cf. Rom. 4.17).[34]

Brueggemann rejects a more traditional understanding of knowing, saying that

> in this post-Cartesian situation, knowing consists not in settled certitudes but in the actual work of imagination. By imagination, I mean very simply the human capacity to picture, portray, receive, and practice the world in ways other than it appears to be at first glance when seen through a dominant, habitual, unexamined lens.[35]

Reality for Brueggemann is a habit of imagining and not an immovable universal. 'The world we take as "given"', he says, 'is a long-established act of imagination that appeals to be and claims assent as the only legitimate occupant of the field'.[36] For Brueggemann, then, the biblical text is transformative in that it offers to the reader an alternative imagination, out of which a new reality can be constructed.

While Brueggemann would identify God as intimately involved in this process of transformation, he refuses to be pinned down on questions of the form which the presence and activity of God might take. While many Pentecostals would agree with Brueggemann's emphasis on the importance of speech and his criticism of our willingness to accept too readily the world we are offered as 'reality', they would want to identify the action of God in the direct, personal, and very involved relationship between the believer and the Holy Spirit. Although Brueggemann is not a part of the Pentecostal Movement, his concept of the creative imagination, in which the text of the Bible funds or stimulates belief in a world which does not yet exist and which we cannot yet see is somewhat similar to the Pentecostal notion of accepting the Scripture by faith and the words which it speaks to us and the promises which it makes to us as being spoken and made by God. By confessing and believing the words of God in Scripture, words which are couched in a worldview different than our own, we are invited to imagine a God that transcends our worldview, not so much destroying it as expanding it and transforming it to include the spiritual

---

[34] W. Brueggemann, *Praying the Psalms* (Winona, MN: Saint Mary's Press, 1986), p. 28.
[35] Brueggemann, *Texts Under Negotiation*, pp. 12–13.
[36] Brueggemann, *Texts Under Negotiation*, p. 13.

world. The Bible invites us to see beyond our own worldview and to catch a glimpse of the world as God sees it.

Because the Pentecostal worldview is not confined to the western world of scientific method and observable fact, it is open to hearing the voice of Scripture differently. The authoritative voice of the Bible can no longer be restricted and reinterpreted by the confines of the possible. Tongues, complete sanctification of the believer, miracles, and the supernatural intrusion of the Holy Spirit into the lives of believers are just as fully a part of what God is saying through Scripture to the church today as is the command to love, a preoccupation for the needs of the poor and oppressed, and the commission to preach the gospel. For Pentecostals, biblical authority need not be modified and contained by the possible, the practical, or the expedient.

Conclusion

The goal of this study has been to examine the ways in which the Pentecostal community of faith understands and utilizes biblical authority. I have challenged modern biblical criticism on a number of counts, not because modern criticism has nothing to offer us, but because modern scholarship frequently makes a number of assumptions about the nature of Scripture which are ill-advised and unnecessary. Modern rationalism, either for reasons of convenience or expediency, has chosen to bracket out fields of inquiry which they are unable to eliminate using scientific method. The exclusion, for example, of the supernatural is a decision which science simply cannot support. It can be neither fully proven nor disproven because it falls outside the realm of examination by experimental method and can be neither brought into a controlled environment nor reliably duplicated. The supernatural and miracles must, in such a model, be excluded as a statement of faith. Some would argue that this is necessary, desirable, and even justifiable. My point is simply that this decision is a faith statement and not the inevitable result of scientific method. A predominately rationalist worldview unnecessarily restricts both our approach to Scripture and the ways in which we make ourselves available to hear from God. By excluding the supernatural and focusing instead exclusively on the rational, much modern scholarship has become impoverished in the way that it understands God to be present and has distanced itself from that which millions of Christians experience as an important part of their faith.

My thesis is that biblical authority in the Pentecostal community of faith arises from personal and communal experiences of the transformative power of the Holy Spirit in the lives of individuals, in the community of faith and in the world. Pentecostals, I believe, found their belief in the authority of Scripture not on doctrinal beliefs or theological arguments, but on experiences of personal encounter with God in and through the biblical text.

As a result of this present discussion, I would like to make four observations. Firstly, biblical scholarship which is founded largely or entirely on a rationalistic understanding of faith and God has met its limits in today's world. Stepping back from something in order to obtain 'objective distance' is an essential step toward deeper growth and understanding. If, however, understanding stops at objectification, it must remain non-relational in nature and, therefore, limited in its application. Modern biblical criticism has made huge contributions to our understanding of Scripture and the Christian faith and we will continue to harvest its fruits for generations. If, however, we choose to cling doggedly to yesterday's discoveries and methods, the Christian church will pass us by. Modern biblical scholarship needs to reexamine and expand its vision. I believe that the Pentecostal movement offers an important way forward.

Secondly, it seems apparent to me that Pentecostals have allowed themselves to be drawn into a battle which is not their own. I do not wish to argue against inerrancy and infallibility, but I want simply to point out that such ways of articulating the question of biblical authority arise out of a worldview which is radically different from that into which Pentecostalism invites us. If it were somehow possible finally to disprove the doctrines of infallibility and inerrancy, the Pentecostal understanding of the authority of Scripture would not be noticeably changed. I am not suggesting that doctrine is not of vital importance, but I do believe that we are exhausting our ammunition and squandering our strength on the wrong battlefield. We cannot fully function within a rationalist framework because that framework can easily be at odds with that which is central to the foundation of Pentecostal theology, a lived experience of God. We need to formulate doctrines which rely not just upon that which we think, but which can accommodate that which we experience as well.

The division in Pentecostal method between academic and church worlds has led to a kind of theological schizophrenia. We practice one form of theologizing within the Pentecostal community and a quite different form when we discuss faith with those who do not claim the same set of Pentecostal experiences. This split has led some scholars to the conclusion that Pentecostalism and biblical scholarship are wholly incompatible. John McKay finds the kind of scholarship which is practiced in religious academic institutions today to be incompatible with a charismatic understanding of Scripture. Speaking both of liberal and conservative factions, McKay states, 'Their views are based on doctrines, assumptions and hypotheses, albeit sometimes diametrically opposed ones, about the nature of Scripture and revelation. Charismatics are based on what they discover themselves thinking after they have been baptized in the Holy Spirit.'[37] While the rift that McKay observes between Pentecostal and rationalist approaches to Scripture is certainly there, I do not see this separation as an uncrossable abyss.

Thirdly, with all the above mentioned qualifiers, I want to maintain that Pentecostal theology is fundamentally different from the other models of theology which are prevalent today. Notice I did not say that *Pentecostalism* is *fundamentally* different, but that the model of doing theology which we utilize can and must be different. We must find a way to articulate a theology which gives free range to our experiences of encountering God in dynamic and powerful ways. Pentecostal theology and hermeneutics are different because they arise not primarily out of rational reflection, but rather out of lived experience. Our theology must reflect that central element of our faith.

Lastly, in addressing the question of what a Pentecostal theology might look like, I would like to point to the centrality of testimony in Pentecostal churches. Because Pentecostal theology is descriptive and oral in nature, we have quite naturally chosen to do a great deal of our theology utilizing testimony. This is not a planned move on the part of the Pentecostal community, but it seems to be simply the best and most natural approach to articulating experiences. Perhaps the most pressing question that this present study raises is, what would a more formal theology that arises out of testimony in the Pentecostal community look like? I believe that the formulation of such a theology is a vital task for the Pentecostal community.

---

[37] J. McKay, '"When the Veil is Taken Away" The Impact of Prophetic Experience on Biblical Interpretation', *Journal of Pentecostal Theology* 5 (Oct. 1994), p. 39.

CHAPTER ELEVEN

HEARING WHAT THE SPIRIT SAYS TO THE CHURCHES:
PROFILE OF A PENTECOSTAL READER OF THE APOCALYPSE*

Robby Waddell**

1. *In(tro)duction to Pentecostalism: A Text to be Interpreted*

This chapter seeks to venture in a postmodern direction by unequivocally acknowledging my own socio-religious context, Pentecostalism.[1] There are distinctives within the worldview of Pentecostalism which have predisposed the manner in which I interpret the biblical texts.[2] Thus in this chapter, I sketch the contours of Pentecostalism and suggest a possible hermeneutic which is faithful to the ethos of the movement. Following the delineation of a Pentecostal hermeneutic, I examine the work on the role of the Spirit in the Apocalypse by a few Pentecostal scholars to see to what extent their theological persuasion has affected their work. The chapter ends with a turn toward the Apocalypse to see what additional insights the book might contain toward further development of the hermeneutic.

The previous chapters contained two latent methodological slogans which provide the impetus for the following characterization of the ethos of Pentecostalism. The first can be referred to as the 'contextualization of interpretation'. I.T. Beckwith acknowledges that the supposedly impartial exegeses of biblical texts, often showcasing 'the ingenuity of interpreters', have consistently been swayed by the scholar's circumstances, either political or ecclesiastical, and by the methodology and hermeneutic

---

* Chapter 3 of Robby Waddell, *The Spirit of the Book of Revelation* (JPTSup, 30; Blandford Forum: Deo Publishing, 2006), pp. 97–131.
** Robby Waddell (PhD, University of Sheffield) is Professor of Religion at Southeastern University, Lakeland, FL, USA.
[1] For a prospectus on the future of Pentecostal scholarship see the Society for Pentecostal Studies presidential address of J.C. Thomas, 'Pentecostal Theology in the Twenty-First Century', *Pneuma* 20 (1998), pp. 3–19; repr. in *idem, The Spirit of the New Testament* (Blandford Forum: Deo Publishing, 2005), pp. 4–22.
[2] S.A. Ellington has explored the relationship between a distinctive Pentecostal worldview and the Pentecostal appropriation of scripture (S.A. Ellington, 'Pentecostalism and the Authority of Scripture', *JPT* 9 [1996], pp. 16–38).

applied to the text.[3] Like the interpreters before me, I too have been influenced by my circumstances along with my presuppositions concerning the text of the Apocalypse. As a member of a Pentecostal community of faith, I acknowledge that I am influenced by a particular Gestalt or pre-text which predisposes my interpretation of the biblical texts. Any reading that is explicitly *pro nobis* must concede that the context of the community (in)forms the interpretation.[4] In a similar vein, E. Schüssler Fiorenza accentuates the 'plurality of meaning' (the second methodological slogan) when she observes that the imaginative language of Revelation need not be exegetically reduced to a one-to-one meaning but rather be allowed to evoke 'imaginative participation'.[5]

---

[3] I.T. Beckwith, The *Apocalypse of John* (Grand Rapids: Baker Book House, 1967, repr. of 1919 edn), p. 319. Surprisingly, as early as 1919, Beckwith foreshadows the emphasis within biblical studies that has recently been placed on the reception of the text. Noting the tacit subjectivism in his observation, Beckwith advises close attention to the historical situation of the original author and his or her audience as well as attention to the literary influences of the text, in the case of the Apocalypse primarily Jewish apocalypses and the Old Testament. I understand this advice to be Beckwith's attempt to set boundaries for the proper influences on the scholar in order to produce an accurate interpretation.

[4] For an excellent example of a Pentecostal *pro nobis* reading see F. Cimpean, 'From Margins to Center: Pentecostal and Orthodox Readings of Romans 8 in Romania', *JPT* (forthcoming). Cimpean argues that the theological crux of Romans is life in the Spirit as recorded in ch. 8, the center of the book. The Western interpretation which focuses on justification by faith is practically mute in the Eastern context of Romanian Pentecostalism and the Eastern Orthodox church. See also S.E. Fowl (ed.), The *Theological Interpretation of Scripture: Classic and Contemporary Readings* (Cambridge: Blackwell, 1997), a reader of theological interpretations of scripture; *idem*, 'The New Testament, Theology and Ethics', in J.B. Green (ed.), *Hearing the New Testament* (Grand Rapids: Eerdmans, 1995), pp. 394–410; S.E. Fowl and L.G. Jones, *Reading in Communion: Scripture and Ethics in Christian Life* (Grand Rapids: Eerdmans, 1991); S. Fish, *Is There a Text in This Class? The Authority of Interpretative Communities* (Cambridge, MA: Harvard University Press, 1980), pp. 303–71.

To refer to a Pentecostal reading as being *pro nobis* does not engender solipsism because the reading is formed by what God is presently saying through the scriptures. The participation between God and the community which is taking place when scriptures are interpreted is analogous to the synergistic involvement of God and the individual in salvation. S. Land writes that salvation requires an 'affective transformation', because, '[s]oteriology is not simply the exposition of redemption accomplished and applied, though it is grounded in what God has done for us. But the 'for us' is grounded in the 'in himself (the *pro nobis* in the *a se*)' (S.J. Land, 'A Passion for the Kingdom: Revisioning Pentecostal Spirituality', *JPT* 1 [1992], p. 201).

[5] E. Schüssler Fiorenza, The *Book of Revelation*, p. 22. Note the way in which Fiorenza's words resonate with Pentecostal theology. 'In the Spirit [Pentecostals] participate in the marriage supper but also live in the 'not yet' of a lost world...the Spirit acts...via the Word, enabling the believer to travel backward and forward in salvation history and to *imaginatively participate* in the events that have been and are yet to be' (S.J. Land, *Pentecostal Spirituality: A Passion for the Kingdom* (JPTSup, 1; Sheffield: Sheffield Academic Press, 1993), p. 98 [emphasis added]).

'Contextualization' and 'plurality' serve as a pair of shibboleths for a paradigm shift which has been hotly debated in the guild of biblical studies, a shift away from the diachronic historical-critical method toward more synchronic narrative methods. Historically, professional biblical scholars examined texts in terms of source criticism and subsequently redaction criticism, focusing on the *Sitz im Leben* of the author and/or the original audience. These historical methods seek to provide an *objective* ground where a critical distance between the scholar and the text can be maintained so that the exegesis is not tainted with the experience of the interpreter. Attempting to discover the historical and literary sources which produced the text, these traditional forms of criticism give little attention to the final form of the text.[6]

In a belated response to New Criticism, a movement within literary studies that concentrated solely on the final form of the text, biblical studies has produced volumes of scholarship concentrating on the narrative integrity of the biblical texts.[7] Although the dominance of the historical-critical approach within biblical scholarship has waned, narrative approaches, which are increasingly claiming a larger portion of the academic pie, continue to maintain a prominent place for the pursuit of objective meaning, albeit *within* the text, as opposed to historical criticism whose attention is primarily *behind* the text.[8] The emphasis on the

---

[6] An early example of an attempt to rescue a text from the unsatisfactory conclusions of historical criticism is D.J.A. Clines, *I, He, We, and They* (Sheffield: Sheffield Academic Press, 1976). Clines offers a 'rhetorical' reading of Isaiah 53, maintaining the passage's integrity as a poem and avoiding the historical temptation to crack the code.

[7] Very little work has been done on Revelation from a narrative-critical viewpoint with the exception of the very good work by David L. Barr, 'The Apocalypse as a Symbolic Transformation of the World: A Literary Analysis', *Int* 38 (1984), pp. 39–50; *idem*, 'The Apocalypse of John as Oral Enactment', *Int* 40 (1986), pp. 243–56; *idem, New Testament Story: An Introduction* (Belmont: Wadsworth, 1987). Also see R.J. Bauckham's work, which is not necessarily narrative-critical but does give due regard to the final form of the text. For the most part, narrative criticism in biblical studies seems oblivious to New Criticism's demise in its native discipline. Cf. S.D. Moore, *Literary Criticism and the Gospels* (New Haven: Yale University Press, 1989), pp. 108–30.

[8] For an explanation of narrative criticism in biblical studies see N.R. Peterson, *Literary Criticism for New Testament Critics* (Philadelphia: Fortress, 1978); M.A. Powell, *What is Narrative Criticism?* (Minneapolis: Fortress, 1990); G.R. Osborne, *The Hermeneutical Spiral: A Comprehensive Introduction to Biblical Interpretation* (Downers Grove: Inter Varsity Press, 1991), pp. 153–73. W.R. Tate offers an excellent introduction to biblical hermeneutics by dividing scholarship into three sections (the world *behind* the text, the world *within* the text, and the world *in front* of the text) (W.R. Tate, *Biblical Interpretation: An Integrated Approach* [Peabody, MA: Hendrickson, 1991]). The origin of modern narrative theory is traced back to T. Todorov, who coined the term 'narratology' in 1969: *Grammaire du Decameron* (The Hagne: Mouton, 1969). See also G. Genette, *Narrative Discourse*

text within narrative criticism has given way (at least in some parts of the academy) to an emphasis on the reader and his or her context (i.e. reader response and poststructural criticism).[9] These newer approaches, while not abandoning attention to the final form of the text, attach importance to what the reader brings to the text as a vital component in the interpretation of meaning.[10]

Despite the rise of synchronic methods and in the face of the popularity and acceptance of contextual readings (e.g. gender and racial interpretations), the debate continues concerning the extent to which biblical scholars should explicitly integrate their theological convictions[11] when they engage in biblical studies. Be that as it may, Pentecostals (especially those of the rank and file) read the Bible theologically as divinely inspired scripture which can and will speak directly to their present situations and will affect every aspect of their lives.[12] Thus, a Pentecostal reading

---

(Ithaca: Cornell University Press, 1980); *idem, Narrative Discourse Revisited* (Ithaca: Cornell University Press, 1988).

[9] Reader response criticism is so discursive that it may have been placed alongside narrative criticism; however, the juxtaposition of 'reader response' with 'poststructuralism' reflects the method's deconstructive accent. See Moore, *Literary Criticism and the Gospels; idem, Poststructuralism and the New Testament: Derrida and Foucault at the Foot of the Cross* (Minneapolis: Fortress, 1994); J.P. Tompkins (ed.), *Reader-Response Criticism: From Formalism to Post-Structuralism* (Baltimore: Johns Hopkins University Press, 1980).

[10] Examples of these contextual readings would include feminist readings, African American readings, psychoanalytical readings, liberation readings and many other voices from the margins which have taught that the view from the fringe is not always identical with the traditional interpretation of sacred texts.

[11] See R.D. Moore's testimonial introduction, where he deconstructs the binary opposites so prevalent in the academy of criticism and confession. Scholarship has long favored criticism relegating confession to the church, but Moore shows how these opposites are not as exclusive as previously thought. Cf. R.D. Moore, 'Deuteronomy and the Fire of God: A Critical Charismatic Interpretation', *JPT* 7 (1995), p. 20; *idem*, 'Canon and Charisma in the Book *of Deuteronomy*', *JPT* 1 (1993), p. 92. In the latter article, Moore brings together another binary opposite (written revelation and spoken revelation). Contrary to J. Derrida, Moore does not privilege writing nor does he privilege speech but rather holds the two in a continual tension, maintaining a harmony between *'a law so righteous'* (the inscripturated revelation) and the *'God-so-near'* (charismatic revelation). I will comment more on this later. Although he advocates a synchronic method, Moore questions the infatuation with the *'final form'* using the words of Moses as a warning, 'Take heed to yourselves, since you saw no form on the day that Yahweh spoke to you at Horeb out of the midst of the fire' (Deut. 4.15, the translation from the Hebrew is Moore's). In God there is no form, only the consuming fire. Moore concludes with a deconstruction of deconstructionism, calling into question the idolatry of 'smashing idols (cf. Jehu in 2 Kings 10)'. For Moore, God is the ultimate deconstructionist.

[12] Pentecostals do not have a monopoly on reading the Bible theologically. Indeed, Christians, particularly those not involved in professional biblical studies, have always read theologically. Therefore, the claim that a Pentecostal reading must be theological

would be both synchronic, focusing on the final form of the text, and theological, allowing the ethos and experience of the tradition to inform the interpretation theologically. Perhaps owing to the strong ecclesiastical commitments of most Pentecostal biblical scholars, theological implications have always been an implicit part of their hermeneutical *telos*, yet I am proposing that an explicit theological hermeneutic,[13] applied throughout the interpretive process and not restricted to *a posteriori* reflection, is essential in order to produce a Pentecostal reading of a text.

By proposing that a Pentecostal reading must be theological, I am not disparaging historical methods or non-theological interpretations, for they continue to offer vital insights into the biblical texts which serve to enlighten the academy.[14] Indeed it is possible for a Pentecostal scholar to address a topic of interest for Pentecostals without employing an explicitly Pentecostal method.[15] However, I wish to differentiate between the examination of a topic which interests Pentecostals and the explicitly Pentecostal examination of a topic. In this study, it is my intention to

---

is not exclusive, although a Pentecostal reading will look somewhat different from other theological readings owing to the differences in the respective socio-religious contexts.

[13] F. Watson, *Text Church and World, passim*, Watson builds on the work of B.S. Childs, *Introduction to the Old Testament as Scripture* (London: SCM Press, 1979); *idem, The New Testament as Canon: An Introduction* (London: SCM Press, 1984); H.W. Frei, *The Eclipse of Biblical Narrative: A Study in Eighteenth and Nineteenth Century Hermeneutics* (New Haven: Yale University Press, 1974). See R. Morgan with J. Barton, *Biblical Interpretation* (Oxford: Oxford University Press, 1988); and A.C. Thiselton's critical appreciation of Morgan's work in A.C. Thiselton, 'On Models and Methods: A Conversation with Robert Morgan', in *The Bible in Three Dimensions*, pp. 337–56.

[14] Hollenweger has argued that Pentecostals should embrace the findings of historical criticism in their congregations and not limit these historical insights to their seminaries (W.J. Hollenweger, 'Intellectual Honesty and Healing the Wounds of Division' [keynote address presented to the 28th Annual Meeting of the Society for Pentecostal Studies, 1999]). The value of historical criticism for a Pentecostal or any Christian congregation is debatable. See the dissident comment by S.E. Fowl, 'Until the historical-critical method becomes critical of its own theoretical foundations and develops a hermeneutical theory adequate to the nature of the text which it is interpreting it will remain restricted...to the guild and the academy, where the question of truth can endlessly be deferred' (S.E. Fowl (ed.), *The Theological Interpretation of Scripture*, p. 26).

[15] See J.C. Thomas, *Footwashing in John 13 and the Johannine Community* (Sheffield: Sheffield Academic Press, 1991). While not explicitly engaging in a Pentecostal method, Thomas did participate in process of formation within a worshiping and praying Pentecostal community that innately affected his research and interpretations, thereby leaving traces in the monograph of his Pentecostal theology and praxis. See also J.C. Thomas, 'Reading the Bible from within Our Traditions: A Pentecostal Hermeneutic', in J.B. Green and M. Turner (eds.), *Between Two Horizons* (Grand Rapids: Eerdmans, 2000), pp. 108–22. Thomas ends with an autobiographical conclusion in which he delineates the formation and impact provided from his faith community.

follow the latter method as I investigate the role of the Spirit in Revelation. The following section is a description of the origins and theological ethos of Pentecostalism which will serve as a contextual intertext[16] for both the development of a Pentecostal hermeneutic and the application of that hermeneutic to the text of Revelation. Beyond the conventional perfunctory justification, the preceding description of my interpretational context contains personal viewpoints.

2. *The Origins and Theological Ethos of Pentecostalism*

Since the birth of the movement at the beginning of the twentieth century, Pentecostalism has affected almost every facet of Christianity.[17] Despite its vast size and perhaps owing to the movement's demographics, the impact

---

[16] The notion of a Pentecostal ethos serving as an intertext has previously been discussed in the Fall 1993 issue of *Pneuma*. These articles encompass the conviction *a la* Gadamer (and Ricoeur) that the shared experience of a community may be envisioned as a text which in turn intersects with a literary text forming the crossroads (or roundabout) of meaning. Utilizing the popular hermeneutical metaphor of a 'fusion of horizons', these scholars envision the relationship between a text and an interpreter: R.D. Israel, D.E. Albrecht and R.G. McNally, 'Pentecostals and Hermeneutics: Texts, Rituals and Community', *Pneuma* 15.2 (1993), pp. 137–61; T.B. Cargal, 'Beyond the Fundamentalist-Modernist Controversy: Pentecostals and Hermeneutics in a Postmodern Age', *Pneuma* 15.2 (1993), pp. 163–87; J-D. Plüss, 'Azusa and Other Myths: The Long and Winding Road from Experience to Stated Belief and Back Again', *Pneuma* 15.2 (1993), pp. 189–201; J. Byrd, 'Paul Ricoeur's Hermeneutical Theory and Pentecostal Proclamation', *Pneuma* 15.2 (1993), pp. 203–14. See also the editorial, M.W. Dempster, 'Paradigm Shifts and Hermeneutics: Confronting Issues Old and New', *Pneuma* 15.2 (1993), pp. 129–35. The preceding issue of *Pneuma* contained four responses which to varying degrees serve as retorts to the articles previously cited. R.P. Menzies offered the most antagonistic retort: 'Jumping Off the Postmodern Bandwagon', *Pneuma* 16.1 (1994), pp. 115–20.

The acknowledgment of the relationship between the context of the reader and the literary text is not unique to theological studies but rather was derived from parallels in the discipline of literary theory. For a sampling, see A. Jefferson, 'Autobiography as Intertext: Barthes, Sarraute, Robbe-Grillet', in M. Worton and J. Still (eds.), *Intertextuality: Theories and Practices* (Manchester: Manchester University Press, 1990), pp. 108–29.

[17] To access the history and development of Pentecostalism, a good place to begin is V. Synan (ed.), *The Holiness-Pentecostal Movement in the United States* (Grand Rapids: Eerdmans, 1971); R.M. Anderson, *Vision of the Disinherited: The Making of American Pentecostalism* (Peabody: Hendrickson, 1972); W.J. Hollenweger, *The Pentecostals* (Peabody: Hendrickson, 1972); D.W. Dayton, *Theological Roots of Pentecostalism* (Metuchen: Scarecrow, 1987); Land, *Pentecostal Spirituality*; H. Cox, *Fire From Heaven: The Rise of Pentecostal Spirituality and the Reshaping of Religion in the Twenty-first Century* (Reading: MA: Addison-Wesley, 1995); D.W. Faupel, *The Everlasting Gospel: The Significance of Eschatology in the Development of Pentecostal Thought* (Sheffield: Sheffield Academic Press, 1996). For bibliographical resources see G. Wacker, 'Bibliography and Historiography of Pentecostalism (U.S.)', *DPCM*, pp. 65–76.

of Pentecostalism on biblical scholarship has been minimal in comparison to the movement's growth. The majority of Pentecostals are located on the margins of society, but nevertheless constitute twenty-one percent of organized global Christianity. According to a 1988 survey, seventy-one percent of the Pentecostals in the world are non-white. The same survey classifies Pentecostals as being 'more urban than rural, more female than male, more children (under eighteen) than adults, more third world than western world, more living in poverty than affluence, more family-related than individualist'.[18] The gender, racial, and socio-economic characteristics of the movement have been immanent since its inception.

The origins of Pentecostalism can be traced back to a revival held at the Bethel Bible School in Topeka, Kansas in January 1901, when a teenage girl by the name of Agnes Ozman became the first person in modern times to be 'baptized in the Spirit and speak in other tongues'. The Bethel Bible School was under the direction of Charles F. Parham who had been teaching that the chief distinctive which had been present at Pentecost as recorded in Acts 2 but was absent in the church of his day was glossolalia, popularly referred to as 'speaking in tongues'. The effect of the 1901 revival was not felt on a world wide scale until William J. Seymour, a one-eyed black holiness preacher who had been influenced by Parham's teaching, moved to Los Angeles, California. It was in Los Angeles that Seymour led a revival at the Azusa Street Mission which lasted for three years (1906–1909). Those who attended Azusa Street and the hundreds of other Pentecostal revivals that had sprung up around the world experienced a resurgence of the gifts of the Spirit as recorded in 1 Corinthians 12, which had only been practiced in the ecclesiastical margins, at least in the West, through the centuries.

In addition to the new emphasis on spiritual gifts, Pentecostalism was also experiencing a new-found equality that was cutting across traditional lines of race, gender, and socio-economic class.[19] Seymour attributed the diversity of the earliest participants to divine providence, offering an opportunity to experience the refreshing of the Spirit to those who were

---

[18] D.B. Barrett, 'Statistics, Global', *DPCM*, p. 811.
[19] Some observers outside the tradition have wrongly deduced that Pentecostalism primarily consisted of an escapist theology that appealed to the lower economic status: R.M. Anderson, *Vision of the Disinherited: The Making of American Pentecostalism* (Peabody: Hendrickson, 1972); L. Pope, *Mill Hands and Preachers: A Study of Gastonia* (New Haven: Yale University Press, 1965).

otherwise marginal in society. Seymour rejoices over the benefit of his eclectic congregation in his newspaper, *The Apostolic Faith*:

> If it had started in a fine church, poor colored people and Spanish people would not have got it, but praise God it started here. God Almighty says He will pour out His Spirit on all flesh... It is noticeable how free all nationalities feel. If a Mexican or German cannot speak in English, he gets up and speaks in his own tongue and feels quite at home for the Spirit interprets through the face and people say amen. No instrument that God can use is rejected on account of color or dress or lack of education. This is why God has so built up the work.[20]

Unfortunately, the unity of the early Pentecostal movement suffered from theological divisions centering on the nature of the Trinity and the essence of sanctification. The movement was further fragmented by racial divisions and a marginalization of women which infiltrated the movement as it evolved into separate denominations and was compromised by affiliations with non-Pentecostal organizations. This initial phase of Pentecostalism, dubbed 'classical Pentecostalism', is represented primarily in the U.S.A. by the Assemblies of God, Springfield, Missouri; the Church of God, Cleveland, Tennessee; the Church of God in Christ, Memphis, Tennessee; and the International Church of the Foursquare Gospel, Los Angeles, California.

Beginning in the late 1950's the spiritual renewal which marks Pentecostalism experienced a resurgence, this time in the mainline churches.[21] Unlike the classical Pentecostals, who for the most part left their parent Holiness denominations, those involved in the 'Charismatic Renewal' (as this phase is commonly labeled) remained within their churches of origin. This second phase gained national attention in the U.S.A. in 1959, when Dennis Bennett, the rector of St. Mark's Episcopal Church in Van Nuys, California, announced to his congregation that he had been baptized in the Holy Spirit and had spoken in tongues. Glossolalia, albeit a defining characteristic of the renewal, was only one of many charisms included in the worship of the Charismatics. The location of the Charismatic renewal was not limited to Protestant denominations but included

---

[20] W.J. Seymour, *The Apostolic Faith* 1.1 (1906), p. 1. Previously cited in Land, *Pentecostal Spirituality*, p. 17.

[21] P.D. Hocken, 'Charismatic Movement', *DPCM*, pp. 130–60; cf. the following: A. Bittlinger (ed.), *The Church Is Charismatic* (Geneva: Renewal and Congregational Life, World Council of Churches, 1981); R. Quebedeaux, *The Charismatics II* (San Francisco: Harper & Row, 1983).

scores of Catholics[22] as well as some in the Eastern Orthodox tradition.[23] Although the Charismatics were not primarily from lower socioeconomic classes, the adherents did share a desire with the classical Pentecostals to return to a more authentic New Testament experience.[24]

The differences between classical Pentecostalism and the Charismatic renewal have been delineated on two fronts, namely ecclesiology and eschatology. As mentioned above, the ecclesiology of the former movement was sectarian and therefore formed new denominations while the ecclesiology of the latter movement did not venture to establish any new organization, preferring to remain in the churches of origin. In matters of eschatology the classical Pentecostals have a distinctively greater emphasis on apocalypticism than those in the Charismatic renewal. Indeed, permeating every stratum of Pentecostal theology is an apocalyptic expectation that the parousia is imminent. The derivation of this apocalyptic accent is best equated with the Wesleyan Holiness revivals

---

[22] F.A. Sullivan, 'Catholic Charismatic Renewal', DPCM, pp. 110–26; cf. the following: N.A. Abbott (ed.), *The Documents of Vatican II* (New York: Guild Press, 1966); K. Ranaghan and D. Ranaghan, *Catholic Pentecostals* (paramus: Paulist Press, 1969); *idem, As the Spirit Leads Us* (Paramus: Paulist Press, 1971); E.D. O'Connor, *The Pentecostal Movement in the Catholic Church* (Notre Dame: Ave Maria Press, 1971); E.D. O'Connor (ed.), *Perspectives on Charismatic Renewal* (Notre Dame: University of Notre Dame Press, 1974); R. Martin, *The Spirit and the Church: A Personal and Documentary Record of the Charismatic Renewal and the Ways it is Bursting to Life in the Catholic Church* (New York: Paulist Press, 1976); K. McDonnell, *Charismatic Renewal in the Churches* (New York: Seabury Press, 1976); K. McDonnell (ed.), *Presence, Power, and Praise: Documents on the Charismatic Movement* (Collegeville: Liturgical Press, 1980).

[23] B.A. Stephanou, *The Charismatic Renewal in the Orthodox Church: 100 questions most frequently asked about the Orthodox Charismatic Renewal* (Fort Wayne: Logos Ministry for Orthodox Renewal, 1976).

[24] This brief sketch of the origin of Pentecostalism will suffice for this study. However, the movement has experienced additional rejuvenations. Called the 'Third Wave', as distinct from the 'first wave' (classical Pentecostalism) and the 'second wave' (the Charismatic renewal), the third phase of the movement, whose participants are primarily evangelical Christians, shares the emphases on healing, exorcisms, and prophetic speech with the first two waves, but wishes to distinguish itself in several areas. Third-wavers insist that the baptism in the Holy Spirit occurs at conversion, as opposed to the Wesleyan view of subsequence. Furthermore, they avoid such self designations as 'charismatic' and 'Spirit-filled' in order to accommodate those in their congregations who do not participate in the charismatic style of worship; cf. C.P. Wagner, 'Third Wave', *DPCM*, pp. 843–44; *idem*, 'The Third Wave', *Christian Life* (September 1984), p. 90. The most recent rejuvenation of Pentecostal motifs in the church has been associated with the so-called 'Toronto Blessing'. For a critical appraisal cf. the following: F.D. Macchia, 'Guest Editorial: 'The Toronto Blessing': No Laughing Matter', *JPT* 8 (1996), pp. 3–6; M.M. Poloma, 'The Spirit Movement in North America at the Millennium: From Azusa Street to Toronto, Pensacola and Beyond', *JPT* 12 (1998), pp. 83–107; L. Pietersen (ed.), *The Mark of the Spirit? A Charismatic Critique of the Toronto Blessing* (Carlisle: Paternoster, 1998).

of the nineteenth century. Pentecostalism was not created ex nihilo but rather was the product of several convergent streams within the religious landscape, creating a current whose impact has yet to be ultimately determined. In addition to the Wesleyan Holiness doctrine of the pre-millennial coming of Jesus, Pentecostals have also maintained the Wesleyan distinctives of healing and sanctification, to which Pentecostals added their own understanding of the baptism in the Holy Spirit. This final characteristic has been the most conspicuous benchmark for the collective Pentecostal-Charismatic movement.

The heart of Pentecostal theology is centered on five principal motifs which have comprised the major tenets of the so-called 'full gospel' (i.e. justification by faith in Christ, sanctification by faith as a second definite work of grace, baptism in the Holy Spirit evidenced by speaking in tongues, healing of the body provided in the atonement, and the pre-millennial return of Christ).[25] The emphasis these fundamentals have received throughout church history may be traced from Luther justification) through Wesley (sanctification) to Cullis (healing) and the prophecy preachers of the nineteenth century (pre-millennial second coming), culminating in the Azusa Street revival (baptism in the Spirit). The full gospel developed a distinctively Christological accent within Pentecostalism as its early adherents testified that Jesus Christ was their Savior, Sanctifier, Spirit Baptizer, Healer, and Coming King.

Often attempts to pigeon-hole the Pentecostal movement by locating it within the broader stream of Christianity err in a reductionistic fashion, either by delimiting the movement as being 'essentially fundamentalist Christianity with a doctrine of Spirit baptism and gifts added on... [or] as an experience which fits equally well in any spirituality or theological system—perhaps adding some needed zest of interest'.[26] Avoiding this reductionistic characterization, S.J. Land has offered a litany of paradoxical continuities and discontinuities between Pentecostalism and other streams of Christianity. Land writes:

---

[25] The extent to which the fivefold gospel has affected Pentecostalism can hardly be overstated, as is clearly demonstrated by Land, *Pentecostal Spirituality*; D.W. Faupel, The *Everlasting Gospel*; and D.W. Dayton, *Theological Roots if Pentecostalism*. Dayton represents a subtle difference in his work by focusing on a fourfold rather than a fivefold center by excluding any significant discussion on sanctification, though Dayton acknowledges the existence of the fivefold model.

[26] Land, *Pentecostal Spirituality*, p. 29.

[Pentecostalism] is more Armenian than Calvinist in its approach to issues of human agency and perseverance. It is more Calvinist than Lutheran in its appreciation of the so-called 'third use of the Law' to guide Christian growth and conduct. It is more Eastern than Western in its understanding of spirituality as perfection and participation in the divine life (*theosis*)...[it] is more Catholic than Protestant in emphasizing sanctification-transformation more than forensic justification, but more Protestant than Catholic in the conviction that the Word is the authority over the church and tradition for matters of faith, practice, government and discipline. In its origins Pentecostalism was more Anabaptist than the magisterial Reformation in its concern for peace and a covenanted believers' church where discipleship and discipline are essential features of congregational life. Pentecostalism has a more Holiness-evangelical hermeneutic than the fundamentalist evangelical tradition in terms of its actual use of Scripture and understanding of the role of reason.[27]

As Land has argued, the ethos of Pentecostalism, albeit distinctive, intersects with every branch of Christianity. Thus, although a Pentecostal reading will be sectarian (i.e. *pro nobis*), there will certainly be times when the interpretation will resonate with an ecumenical ring. Indeed it is my hope that others will be able not only to differentiate themselves from my interpretations but also to find places of self-recognition.[28] For I suspect that Pentecostals have a distinctive contribution to offer to the academic disciplines of biblical studies and hermeneutics.

3. *Toward a Pentecostal Theological Hermeneutic*

Discussions concerning hermeneutics have preoccupied Pentecostal scholars for almost two decades. A large portion of the attention given to 'Pentecostal hermeneutics' has been primarily theoretical, arguing on the one hand the validity of a Pentecostal distinctive in biblical interpretation, and on the other hand arguing to what extent postmodern literary theory

---

[27] Land, *Pentecostal Spirituality*, pp. 29–30.
[28] I have gleaned these sentiments from Land, *Pentecostal Spirituality*, p. 7. See the Society for Pentecostal Studies presidential address of C. Bridges Johns, 'The Adolescence of Pentecostalism: In Search of a Legitimate Sectarian Identity', *Pneuma* 17.1 (Spring 1995), pp. 3–17; P.D. Hanson, 'Scripture, Community and Spirit: Biblical Theology's Contribution to a Contextualized Christian *Theology*', *JPT* 6 (1995), pp. 3–12; D.T. Irvin, "'Drawing All Together in One Bond of Love": The Ecumenical Vision of William J. Seymour and the Azusa Street Revival', *JPT* 6 (1995), pp. 25–53. Cf. W. Brueggemann, 'II Kings 18–19: The Legitimacy of a Sectarian Hermeneutic', *HBT* 8 (1985), pp. 1–42.

should be employed by a Pentecostal interpreter.[29] The present contribution to the discussion is by no means new. The acknowledgement that Bible reading should be interwoven with theological convictions and insights was endemic to all premodern biblical interpretation (e.g. Tertullian, whose Montanist persuasion resonates quite nicely with Pentecostals).[30] Tertullian shunned the idea of anyone attempting to interpret the biblical texts by means of philosophy, for 'what indeed has Athens to do with Jerusalem? What concord is there between the Academy and the Church? What between heretics and Christians?'[31] According to Tertullian, coalescing philosophy and revelation would result in unfaithfulness to the latter. I do not suspect that the average Pentecostal sitting on a church pew

---

[29] For a bibliography see J.C. Thomas, 'Women, Pentecostals and the Bible: An Experiment in Pentecostal Hermeneutics', *JPT* 5 (1994), pp. 41–56, n. 4; see also K.J. Archer, 'Pentecostal Hermeneutics: Retrospect and Prospect', *JPT* 8 (1996), pp. 63–81. Cf. F.L. Arrington, 'Hermeneutics', *DPCM*, pp. 376–89; R. Stronstad, 'The Dynamics of a Pentecostal Pneumatology: Essays in Hermeneutics and Theology' (unpublished monograph); J.W. Wycoff, 'The Relationship of the Holy Spirit to Biblical Hermeneutics', PhD thesis (Baylor University, 1990); M.S. Clark, 'An Investigation into the Nature of a Viable Pentecostal Hermeneutic', DTh thesis (University of South Africa).

While the majority of material on Pentecostal hermeneutics has been theoretical, there have been a few pieces which have focused primarily on reading a particular text, though the larger task of defining a Pentecostal style of reading has been on the horizon. I would like to highlight four such contributions. (1) R.O. Baker, 'Pentecostal Bible Reading: Toward a Model of Reading for the Formation of Christian Affections', *JPT* 7 (1995), pp. 34–48. Baker offers a reading of the death of Jesus in the fourth Gospel which was influenced by his own experience of the death of his grandmother and the affections he was able to draw on because of his experience. (2) R.D. Moore, "'And Also Much Cattle?!": Prophetic Passions and the End of Jonah', *JPT* 11 (1997), pp. 35–48. Moore offers a reading of the book of Jonah based on an assumption that consideration of Jonah's passions will get at the *heart* of the text and parallel the *heart* of the Pentecostal experience. (3) Thomas, 'Women, Pentecostals and the Bible', pp. 41–56. Thomas renders a reading of Acts 15 and its record of the Jerusalem Council, offering the practice of the early church as an exemplar for the contemporary church to use during theological deliberations. Thomas continues by testing his theory with the topic of women in ministry. (4) L.R. McQueen, *Joel and the Spirit: The Cry of a Prophetic Hermeneutic* (Sheffield: Sheffield Academic Press, 1995). This monograph may be the most extensive attempt to read an entire book of the Bible in a Pentecostal manner. McQueen delves into his own experience of 'praying through' in order to tap into the idea of lament which permeates the book of Joel.

[30] J. McKay, 'When the Veil is Taken Away: The Impact of Prophetic Experience on Biblical Interpretation', *JPT* 5 (1994), p. 25. McKay acknowledges the partiality of Tertullian for 'spiritual' Christians of his own Montanist church as opposed to 'natural' believers (*psychici*) in other churches. McKay, who also refers to similar sentiments in Irenaeus (*Adv. Her.* 5:6.1), pushes further back to the comments in the New Testament. Paul writes to the Corinthian church, 'The man without the Spirit (ψυχικός) does not accept the things that come from the Spirit of God, for they are foolishness to him, and he cannot understand them, because they are spiritually discerned. The spiritual man (πνευματικός) makes judgments about all things' (1 Cor. 2.14–15 NIV translation, previously cited by McKay).

[31] *Prescription against Heretics*, 7 (*ANF*, 3:246).

makes a conscious effort to read his or her scriptures theologically, yet on the other hand, there is nothing that is non-theological about the expectation maintained by the Pentecostal reader that God will unfailingly speak through the scriptures. Thus, it is with a somewhat latent effort to be faithful to the Spirit in which the biblical texts have been written that Pentecostals read the Bible theologically.

Approaching the Bible theologically is certainly not restricted to Pentecostals. Indeed, a good deal of recent hermeneutical work has argued that the Bible should be studied outside of a community of faith whose scripture it is. The debate over the development of a theological hermeneutic can be seen by contrasting the work of F. Watson[32] and P. Davies.[33] Watson, on the one hand, argues that every biblical scholar should pursue theological issues while critiquing a biblical text; Davies, on the other hand, argues that professional biblical studies should be free of all theological discussion, discussion which he would regulate to the church. I disagree with Watson that theological issues are the only appropriate pursuit for biblical scholars but I also disagree with Davies that the university has no place for theological inquiry.[34] The key to the issue is that a 'neutral' approach does not exist; therefore, the most responsible way forward is for scholars to acknowledge the subjectivity of their perspectives.[35]

The reluctance to integrate biblical studies and theology is not limited to biblical scholars. Theologians as well question whether the technical analysis of biblical scholars can be relevant for systematic theology. B.S. Childs has pioneered readings and interpretations that bridge the gap between biblical studies and theology caused by the professionalization of these respective disciplines. Childs calls into question the ability of historical criticism to begin with the neutral task of description. Childs writes, 'It is commonly assumed that the responsible exegete must start with the descriptive task and then establish a bridge to the theological

---

[32] F. Watson, *Text, Church and World: Biblical Interpretation in Theological Perspective* (Grand Rapids: Eerdmans, 1994).

[33] P. Davies, *Whose Bible is it Anyway?* (Sheffield: Sheffield Academic Press, 1995).

[34] See also M.G. Brett, 'Four or Five Things To Do with Texts: A Taxonomy of Interpretative Interests', in D.J.A. Clines et al. (eds.), The Bible in Three Dimensions: Essays in Celebration *of* Forty Years of Biblical Studies in the University if Sheffield (Sheffield: Sheffield Academic Press, 1990), pp. 356–77.

[35] See I. Paul, 'The Value of Paul Ricoeur's Hermeneutic of Metaphor in Interpreting the Symbolism of Revelation Chapters 12 and 13', PhD thesis (Nottingham Trent University, 1998), p. 216.

problem. It is felt that the real problem lies with the second task. Rather, the reverse is true.'[36]

Before proceeding with a possible profile of a theological hermeneutic, I should perhaps digress by offering a clarification of how the word 'theological' is being used in this context. When juxtaposing 'theological' with 'Pentecostal', I am suggesting, in agreement with Watson, that Christian scholars ought to read from a confessional point of view. The intended meaning of 'theological' in this context is more akin to 'spiritual' (Revelation 11 the witnesses saw the city 'spiritually' and called it Sodom and Egypt). Spiritual is not mystical because the reality of the spirituality is in a concrete context of love and passion, pain and pleasure, happiness and sorrow. Thus, for Pentecostals, a spiritual reading is not a head trip nor solely a heart trip but rather an exercise in imagination that is grounded by the contextual realism of the spirituality. Instead of subsuming 'theological' under an Enlightenment rationalistic model, I wish to circumvent such a dependence, preferring in its place a more Hebrew notion. 'Theology', which means 'study of God', is flipped on its head in Judaism because God is not the object of study but rather the subject. When reading scripture (the Word of God) theologically, the reader/believer is encountering the living God. Following R.D. Moore, I choose to understand 'Word of God' as an event (דבר). A theological reading is not merely a deduction but rather a revelation (ἀποκάλυψις). This revelatory idea may be complemented with an understanding of another Hebrew word, ידע. Traditionally translated 'to know', 'the Hebrew term resists such a subject-object dichotomy and points more to the actualization of a relationship between knower and known'.[37] Thus, a Pentecostal theological hermeneutic has less to do with Greek philosophy than with theophany, a divine encounter, a revelation, an experience with the living God.[38]

---

[36] B.S. Childs, 'Interpretation in Faith', *Int* 18 (1964), p. 260.

[37] Moore, 'Canon and Charisma', pp. 90–91. See the discussion of ידע in J.D. Johns and C. Bridges Johns, 'Yielding to the Spirit: A Pentecostal Approach to Group Bible Study', *JPT* 1 (1993), pp. 109–34. See also the comments of C.H. Pinnock, 'The Work of the Holy Spirit in Hermeneutics', *JPT* 2 (1995), p. 13. Pinnock writes, 'Interpretation is about more than retrieving information—it is also about the effects on readers that texts can set in motion'.

[38] Pentecostal readings, even of the Old Testament, will often exhibit a Christological accent owing in part to the strong Christological emphasis in the fivefold gospel. F. Watson addresses the issue of the Hebrew scriptures being read with a Christological twist. Watson acknowledges that the New Testament and the Old Testament are 'distinct' but 'inseparable', being mutually shaped by the other. He writes, 'Either the Hebrew scriptures are the sole property of the Jewish community, in which case the Christian church should

Working with the above definition of 'theological', the discussion may now return to the delineation of a theological hermeneutic. Pentecostals are far more interested in the narrative of their spiritual experience than in the main concerns of modernity. Therefore, a theological reading will have some defining characteristics which reveal its recalcitrance toward not only the historical-critical method but modernity as well. The relationship between Pentecostalism and modernity is quite antithetical and yet the 'postmodern' label does not quite fit either. S.B. Fowl has suggested the use of the neologism, 'non-modern'.[39] Fowl lists four defining characteristics of a non-modern interpretation:

> First, it will be interested in premodern biblical interpretation. Second, it will shape and be shaped by the concerns of Christian communities seeking to live faithfully before the triune God rather than by the concerns of a discipline whose primary allegiance is to the academy. Third, theological interpretation of scripture will try to reject and resist the fragmentation of theology into a set of discrete disciplines that was a result of the conceptual aims of modernity and the practical result of professionalization. Finally, theological interpretation of scripture will be pluralistic in its interpretative methods; it will even use the interpretative methods of modernity to its own ends.[40]

Each of these characteristics of a non-modern approach finds substantial parallels within the ethos of Pentecostalism. An examination of these connections will provide the needed light to envision the contours of a Pentecostal theological hermeneutic.

---

denounce all claim on them; or they can also be read as the Christian Old Testament'. Watson is insightful to point out that tension with his conclusion is more often levied from the historical-critical approach than from the Jewish community (F. Watson, *Text Church and World*, p. 3).

Again Pinnock is helpful. He writes, 'The Old Testament is being read in the light of the new situation created by the coming of Jesus Christ and the Spirit is indicating meanings that do not correspond to the grammatical-historical meaning of the text'. He continues, the early theologians 'employed spiritual reading which allowed them to move in the midst of a kaleidoscope of biblical imagery... They knew that texts can cause dynamic things as the Spirit actualizes their message in our consciousness' (C.H. Pinnock, 'The Work of the Holy Spirit in Hermeneutics', p. 13).

[39] S.E. Fowl (ed.), *The Theological Interpretation if Scripture*, p. xvi. The term 'non-modern' is preferred over the more popular 'postmodern'. For the precarious relationship between Pentecostalism and postmodernity see J.D. Johns, 'Pentecostalism and the Postmodern Worldview', *JPT* 7 (1995), pp. 73–96. Johns may also be credited with the trope, 'para-modern', as an alternative to 'postmodern'.

[40] Fowl (ed.), *The Theological Interpretation if Scripture*, p. xvi.

The granting of a significant amount of credence to premodern interpretations and methods is easily justifiable in a postmodern society.[41] The decline of the theory that meaning is singular and the consequential crescendo of the voices from the fringe has deconstructed the historical-critical goal of discovering *the* meaning of a text.[42] Biblical scholarship by and large has treated premodern interpretations as a failure to obtain the single meaning of the text; however, the acceptance of a plurality of meaning rejects any such condemnation. Normally, Pentecostals read with an eye open towards the plain meaning of scripture; however, they are open to the multiple meanings in the texts which the Spirit can and does afford them when they read, a common testimony being 'every time I read, the Lord shows me something new'. Discovering the testimony of the early church will be a new experience for some Pentecostals. The restorationist theme so prominent in the movement has allotted little room for any acknowledgement of church history other than the New Testament stories. The lesson which may be learned from an acquaintance with premodern interpretation is that others too have struggled with the interpretation of scripture before God. The emphasis which Pentecostals have placed on testimonies may provide the vehicle needed with which our churches can learn to appreciate the premodern interpretations. In a post-critical society, non-modern and reassessed premodern interpretations will detemine not only the future of the church but perhaps the academy as well.

Historically, Pentecostalism has been suspicious of the academy. Anti-educational sentiments within the movement have been fueled by the rarity with which the concerns of the academy have paralleled the concerns of the community of faith. In a modern age, a scholar could claim to be pursuing objective truth so that concern (either academic or ecclesiastical) played little or no role in the pursuit. No longer may claims of objectivity hide the latent presuppositions which had already been shaping the scholar's vision of the truth, which lacked the intellectual honesty of the contextual nature of his or her perceived truth. Reading the text in the light of a present experience of the community may provide an

---

[41] D.C. Steinmetz, 'The Superiority of Pre-Critical Exegesis', *Theology Today*, 37.1 (1980), pp. 27–38.
[42] See the comments of C.S. Lewis on his novel *Till We Have Faces*, where he says 'an author doesn't necessarily understand the meaning of his own story better than anyone else' (W.H. Lewis (ed.), *Letters of C.S. Lewis* [New York: Harcourt, Brace and World, 1966], p. 273).

opportunity for the modern critic to cast the ultimate (historical) judgment against contextual reading (the charge of anachronism). However, inasmuch as it is in continuity with the testimony of the early church, the community continues to be a living organism and not merely an organization, thereby muting the perceived criticism.[43]

As mentioned above Pentecostalism is at its very heart an apocalyptic movement. The expectation of the return of Christ is paramount in Pentecostal theology. This eschatological theme resonates with Fowl's statement that the community in which a non-modern theological reading may take place must be living before the triune God.[44] Throughout history there have been segments of Christianity which have had a strong eschatological emphasis. It is with these groups that Pentecostalism will have the most continuity.

There are many contextual readings of scripture representing various segments of different communities of faith that are vying for the attention of the reader. The most popular readings which explicitly identify their contextual location have been feminist readings and African American readings.[45] Similar to these readings which contain sounds reminiscent of liberation theology,[46] Pentecostal readings will also be from the bottom or from the margins. Pentecostal readings are sympathetic to feminist readings for the majority of Pentecostals are female and although the political climate has digressed into a more chauvinistic model the original

---

[43] M. Cartledge, 'Empirical Theology: Towards an Evangelical-Charismatic Hermeneutic', *JPT* 9 (1996), pp. 115–26. Cartledge discusses the relationship of the current church with the testimony of scripture as a dialectic between consistency and innovation which allows room for both the idea that Spirit can speak fresh in today's church but also that the testimony from the past will not be violated.

[44] S.J. Land, 'The Triune Center: Wesleyans and Pentecostals Together in Mission', *WTJ* 34.1 (1999), pp. 83–100. Land defines the Pentecostal-Holiness community with five primary characteristics, all of which are framed with the general idea of being trinitarian eschatologically.

[45] F.F. Segovia and M.A. Tolbert, *Reading from This Place: Social Location and Biblical Interpretation in the United States* (Minneapolis: Fortress, 1994).

[46] Liberation theology has many points of contact with Pentecostalism. See C. Bridges Johns, *Pentecostal Formation: A Pedagogy among the Oppressed* (Sheffield: Sheffield Academic Press, 1993). For the relationship of biblical studies to liberation motifs see G. West, *Biblical Hermeneutics of Liberation* (Pietermaritzburg: Cluster, 1991); idem, 'Reading the Bible and Doing Theology in the New South Africa', in D. Carroll, D. Clines, and P. Davies (eds.), *The Bible and Human Society* (Sheffield: Sheffield Academic Press, 1995), pp. 445–58; R.S. Sugirtharajah (ed.), *Voices from the Margin: Interpreting the Bible in the Third World* (Maryknoll: Orbis, 1991); J. Levison and P. Pope-Levison, 'Global Perspectives on New Testament Interpretation', in J.B. Green (ed.), *Hearing the New Testament*, pp. 329–48; C. Rowland and M. Corner, *Liberating Exegesis: The Challenge of Liberation Theology to Biblical Studies* (Louisville: John Knox Press, 1989).

Pentecostal movement was able to blur the gender lines in relation to authority and leadership that mirrored the early church. Likewise the majority of Pentecostals are non-white, which places a Pentecostal interpretation in a sympathetic relationship to African American reading as well. The extent to which African spirituality has influenced Pentecostalism can hardly be overstated.[47]

Resisting the temptation to fragment theology into various subdisciplines has been a challenge for Pentecostalism owing to the overwhelming influence of the modern academy. One paramount exception is the work S.J. Land has done on the integral relationship between spirituality and theology. According to Land, spirituality is not separate from theology as a sort of appendix, but is the essence of theology in theory and practice. Spirituality shapes an epistemology and permeates through theology into an ethic that goes out into the world (missionary) because Christ is returning (apocalyptic). In agreement with Land, I see a connection not only between spirituality and the academic discipline of theology but the academic discipline of biblical studies as well. Land fuses together the responses of worship, prayer, and witness, responses that correlate with the central affections of gratitude, compassion, and courage (respectively). I also have found this fusion of affections and erasure of traditional lines between academic disciplines in the work of R.D. Moore and C. Bridges Johns.

R.D. Moore explains that the caricature of the Pentecostal faith as experienced-based is faulty. Pentecostal worship, albeit ardent, maintains 'an inseparable interplay between knowledge and lived experience, where knowing about God and directly experiencing God perpetually inform and depend on one another'.[48] Knowledge is here understood as pointing 'beyond the conceptualization of an object to the actualization of a relationship'.[49] C. Bridges Johns has appropriated postmodern theorizing and deconstruction to the ministries of homiletics and catechesis, emasculating Enlightenment constructs which formed the basis of evangelical

---

[47] See Hollenweger, *The Pentecostals*, pp. 21–28; idem, *Pentecostalism: Origins and Developments Worldwide* (Peabody: Hendrickson, 1997), pp. 18–40; Land, *Pentecostal Spirituality*, pp. 21–22; Cox, *Fire From Heaven*, pp. 139–60, 243–62.

[48] R.D. Moore, 'Pentecostal Approach to Scripture', *The Seminary Viewpoint* 8.1 (1987), p. 4.

[49] Moore, 'Pentecostal Approach to Scripture', p. 4.

models of preaching and teaching, whose 'whole paradigm has served to domesticate the mystery of faith'.[50]

The future relationship between the postmodern world and Pentecostalism is ambiguous. As C. Bridges Johns writes, 'Contemporary Christianity seems caught between a past life governed by institutional certitude and a future seemingly without instruments of control'.[51] She adopts an understanding of time as 'carnival time', a contribution from Mikhail Bakhtin, who described life as a fusion of binary opposites such as sacred/profane, lofty/low, great/insignificant, and wise/stupid. The deconstruction of modern theology will not be replaced by another monolithic system, but rather, a carnival sideshow, where various systems exist in tension.[52]

The ramifications for biblical studies of R.D. Moore's and C. Bridges Johns' observations are multiple, but I would like to note three. First, the difference between subject and object becomes blurred. In a time of carnival, the subject/object becomes a clown constantly changing masks but never surfacing unmasked. Deconstructing the modern notion of presence, the festival of Pentecost offers a presence which comes 'from the wilderness, from "otherness" itself. It comes from the margin and then marginalizes all who claim it, who are claimed by it.'[53] Secondly, C. Bridges Johns highlights the necessity of participation in the Spirit within the teaching/learning process. According to C. Bridges Johns, teaching 'involves an understanding that while critical reflection and dialogue are involved in learning, what is primary is not the critical side but the participatory side'.[54]

---

[50] C. Bridges Johns, 'Meeting God in the Margins, Ministry among Modernity's Refugees', in M. Zyniewicz (ed.), *The Papers of the Henry Luce III Fellows in Theology* (Atlanta: Scholars Press, 1999), p. 20.

[51] Bridges Johns, 'Meeting God in the Margins, Ministry among Modernity's Refugees', p. 7 (emphasis added).

[52] Another helpful definition of the theological significance of deconstruction comes from F. Watson, *Text, Church, and World*, p. 80. Watson writes that
> from a deconstructive perspective, the assertion that a text has a meaning, or meanings, tacitly assumes the transparency of language to that which lies behind it and which generates it; that is, it assumes that one can transcend language, eventually arriving at the reality to which the language is merely a helpful sign post... Once it is written the meaning never fully exists... The overt logic of the text will always already have been subverted by a covert logic or anti-logic, and the role of deconstructive analysis is to bring this paradoxical situation to light.

[53] Moore, 'Deuteronomy and the Fire of God', p. 33.

[54] Bridges Johns, 'Meeting God in the Margins, Ministry among Modernity's Refugees', p. 23.

Finally, C. Bridges Johns questions the ontological status of the text. Given the nature of text/textus, how are Pentecostals going to articulate their theology of scripture? She writes that 'the biblical text must be approached as an avenue for personal and corporate engagement with God... The written text has an objective, historical reality which cannot properly be understood outside of the bounds of reason. Yet, it is a personal subjective word that is carried along by the Spirit.'[55]

Pentecostals have traditionally maintained a very high view of scripture, albeit vaguely defined. In the August issue of the *Evangel* in 1910, The Church of God published its earliest official statement about scripture: 'The Church of God stands for the whole Bible rightly divided. The New Testament is the only rule for government and discipline.' Later, the Church of God adopted a more evangelical terminology when writing its Declaration of Faith: 'We believe in the verbal inspiration of the Bible'. In a postmodern world where the ontological status of the text has been questioned, evangelical models are being deconstructed.[56] However, the Pentecostal understanding of the relationship between the Spirit and the written text does not suffer the same fate as the fundamentalist doctrines. S.J. Land has discussed the relationship between the Spirit and the text as a dynamic interaction of 'Spirit-Word'.

> The Spirit who inspired and preserved the Scriptures illuminates, teaches, guides, convicts and transforms through the Word today. The Word is alive, quick and powerful, because of the Holy Spirit's ministry. The relation of the Spirit to Scripture is based on that of Spirit to Christ. Even as the Spirit formed Christ in Mary, so the Spirit uses Scripture to form Christ in believers and vice-versa.[57]

Musing about the work of these Pentecostal scholars has demonstrated Fowl's final point that the method of a theological hermeneutic will be pluralistic. Indeed there is not so much a single Pentecostal method but rather multiple strategies which are faithful to the tradition without doing

---

[55] Bridges Johns, 'Meeting God in the Margins, Ministry among Modernity's Refugees', p. 24.

[56] Cf. the comments of S.A. Ellington: 'The Bible is not simply a text about whose propositions we can debate, it is the authoritative word of God *because* the same Holy Spirit who inspired its writers meets us today in its pages. For Pentecostals, biblical authority does not rest in the text we can justify, but in the God that we know in and through the text' (Ellington, 'Pentecostalism and the Authority of Scripture', p. 24).

[57] Land, *Pentecostal Spirituality*, p. 100.

violence to the text.⁵⁸ In Pentecostalism, the hermeneutics of suspicion gives way to an open heart which is longing to be formed by God via the Spirit into the image of Christ. Understanding the Word of God requires a local hermeneutic that is sensitive to the spiritual context. Fowl's concluding comments in his introduction to his reader are insightful. Proficiency in performing theological interpretations of biblical texts 'is not simply reflected in increased intellectual capacities. Rather, for Christians proficiency in reading scripture theologically is ultimately reflected in a life that is transformed to conform more nearly to the image of Christ.'⁵⁹

It is possible to sum up a Pentecostal hermeneutic with the following motto: 'Unless we believe, we shall not understand'. These words are adapted from the works of Anselm who writes, 'For I do not seek to understand so that I may believe; but I believe so that I may understand. For I believe this also, that unless I believe, I shall not understand.'⁶⁰ I modified the words to read with a more communal tone for I have become increasingly convinced that only in the community will we hear the voice of God,⁶¹ or in other words, 'hear what the Spirit is saying to the churches' (Rev. 2.7).

---

⁵⁸ I owe this idea of multiple strategies as opposed to a singular method to K.J. Archer. Cf. K.J. Archer, *A Pentecostal Hermeneutic for the Twenty-First Century: Spirit, Scripture and Community* (JPTSup, 28; London: T. & T. Clark, 2004). Now available as *A Pentecostal Hermeneutic: Spirit, Scripture and Community* (Cleveland, TN: CPT Press, 2009).

⁵⁹ Fowl (ed.), The *Theological Interpretation of Scripture: Classic and Contemporary Readings*, p. xxvi.

⁶⁰ *Proslog.* 1 (trans. M.J. Charlesworth, *St. Anselm's Proslogion*, Oxford: Clarendon, 1965), p. 115.

⁶¹ Jack Deere offers his powerful testimony about how he learned to tell the difference between reading the Bible and hearing from God, in his book, *Surprised by the Power of the Spirit*. Deere writes: 'In the process of getting theologically trained and becoming a seminary professor, I developed an intense passion for studying God's Word. I found myself loving the Bible more than I loved the Author of the Bible. I was caught in this trap for more years than I would like to remember... It took me too long to learn that knowing the Bible is not the same thing as knowing God, loving the Bible is not the same thing as loving God, and reading the Bible is not the same thing as hearing God' (J. Deere, *Surprised by the Power of the Spirit* [Grand Rapids: Zondervan, 1993], p. 187, previously cited in J.K.A. Smith, 'The Closing of the Book: Pentecostals, Evangelicals, and the Sacred Writings', *JPT* 11 [1997], pp. 49–71). Smith argues that Pentecostalism, like the early church, is a 'people of the Spirit' rather than a 'people of the Book'. Smith warns Pentecostals that a certain understanding of the Bible can lead to a textualization that circumvents the present involvement of the Spirit in interpretation of the Biblical texts.

4. *Pentecostal Scholars and the Spirit of the Apocalypse*

Now that the Pentecostal ethos has been defined along with a possible hermeneutic, attention can be shifted toward two new questions. First, what contributions have been offered by Pentecostal scholars concerning the role of the Spirit in the Apocalypse? Second, do their interpretations fit the preceding description of the tradition? Three pieces of scholarship have been selected to represent Pentecostalism.[62]

4.1. *S.M. Horton*

Although Horton's work is not solely on the role of the Spirit in the Apocalypse, his thoughts are of importance to a history of interpretation of Pentecostal scholars owing to the magnitude of his influence in the tradition. In reference to the image of the seven spirits, Horton can easily be aligned with Victorinus of Pettau and the others after him who identified the seven spirits as a reference to the seven-fold Spirit of Isaiah 11, which was to rest on the Messiah.[63] Horton places the majority of his discussion of the Spirit in the Apocalypse in a chapter titled, 'The Spirit in the Ministry of the Church', where he sees a close relationship first between the Spirit and Jesus Christ and then between the Spirit and the church. However, given that his primary emphasis in the aforementioned chapter is on Paul's letters, there is little else to glean from Horton's work on this topic.

4.2. *R.H. Gause*

Similar to most commentaries on Revelation, Gause's work does not allot special attention to the role of the Spirit. Thus, his position on the Spirit's role must be extracted by giving attention to the texts which refer to the Spirit. Gause understands the symbol of the 'seven spirits' to be a reference to the Spirit of God. Likewise, he sees the phrase ἐν πνεύματι as a description of John's experience with the Holy Spirit. In regard to the hearing formula, Gause writes, 'The Lord's relationship to the Holy Spirit is fundamental to the Church. He forms His Church by the presence of

---

[62] S.M. Horton, *What the Bible Says about the Holy Spirit* (Springfield: Gospel Publishing House, 1976); R.H. Gause, *Revelation: God's Stamp of Sovereignty on History* (Cleveland: Pathway Press, 1983); F. Martin, 'Book of the Apocalypse', *DPCM*, pp. 11–13.
[63] Horton, *What the Bible Says About the Holy Spirit*, p. 61.

the Holy Spirit in it.[64] Furthermore, he states that the hearing formula is directed to all churches of all times as the Spirit continues to speak the words of Christ. Gause's work is helpful but somewhat limited given the popular nature of the commentary.

4.3. *F. Martin*

In the *DPCM*, Martin offers a succinct analysis of the Apocalypse focusing on two points that are of special interest to Pentecostals, namely the book's pneumatology and the millennium.[65] With regard to the pneumatology Martin discusses three aspects: (1) the role of the Spirit in the Act of Revelation; (2) the Spirit of Prophecy; and (3) the Spirit and the Church.

Under his first rubric, Martin addresses the phrase ἐν πνεύματι, arguing that the Spirit is the agent of revelation. Martin correctly sees John's appeal to the Spirit as a claim of prophetic authority. He also notes the close relationship between the Spirit in Christ evidenced by the hearing formula in the seven messages which instructs those in the church to hear what the Spirit is saying, despite the fact that Christ is identified as the speaker of the messages. Martin cites Jn 16.15, 'the Spirit will take from what is mine and make it known to you', as support that the Spirit and Christ are especially close in the Johannine literature.

Commenting on Rev. 19.10, he writes:

> Given the frequency with which the early rabbinic tradition designated the Spirit of God as the 'Spirit of Prophecy', it is clear that Revelation is asserting two things: (1) the role of the Holy Spirit is linked to the witness of Jesus, and (2) this witness is prophecy.[66]

According to Martin, when John identifies his work as 'prophecy', he is avowing dependence on the Spirit.

Finally, Martin addresses the Spirit and the Church. Focusing on the direct discourse of the Spirit in Rev. 14.13; 22.17, he asserts that the Spirit is closely related to the life of the church and is indeed the source of life in the resurrection (Rev. 11.11). He concludes the section on the Spirit with a brief discussion on the 'seven spirits', which he identifies as the Spirit, who possesses both the power and the knowledge of the Lamb (cf. Rev. 5.6).

---

[64] Gause, *Revelation: God's Stamp if Sovereignty on History* (Cleveland, TN: Pathway Press, 1983), p. 46.
[65] Martin, 'Apocalypse, Book of the', *DPCM*, pp. 11–13.
[66] Martin, 'Apocalypse, Book of the', *DPCM*, p. 12.

4.4. Summary

The contribution of these scholars may best be explained within the context of the history of Pentecostal scholarship. Pentecostal scholarship has been outlined in three distinct phases by the editors of the *Journal of Pentecostal Theology*, in the editorial of the journal's inaugural issue. The first generation includes the earliest Pentecostal scholars who completed postgraduate work despite 'an environment which did not encourage nor even perceive the viability of interaction between Pentecostal faith and critical theological scholarship'.[67] Within the theological subdisciplines of descriptive historical study and social-scientific analysis, a second generation of scholars experienced the 'opportunity for the first time to bring their Pentecostalism to bear upon their graduate research'.[68] With the rise of a third generation, Pentecostal scholars have been given the opportunity to integrate the distinctives of Pentecostal faith with their critical theological research. In the 1998 SPS presidential address, J.C. Thomas suggests that perhaps the rise of a fourth generation of Pentecostal scholarship is being experienced. This generation, according to Thomas, will benefit from the increasing number of Pentecostals within academia and the attention that accompanies any group with such extensive demographics, but more importantly this generation will have the 'opportunity to read, assess, and critique academic works by Pentecostal scholars, an opportunity largely impossible just a few short years ago'.[69] If this assessment of the history of Pentecostal scholarship is accurate, then I would most likely be identified as a member of the fourth generation.

The previous work, while being consistent with the ethos of the movement, has been the labor of earlier generations. Martin's work is somewhat of an exception as it shows tremendous foresight, hindered only by its brevity. The time has arrived for a new inquiry by a more recent generation which has the opportunity to integrate more deliberately the Pentecostal ethos and theology into an examination of the biblical texts. At times, Pentecostal scholars have avoided this more difficult task of developing a constructive theology, perhaps owing to an academic inferiority complex.[70] Although Pentecostalism has been historically

---

[67] R.D. Moore, J.C. Thomas, and S.J. Land, 'Editorial', *JPT* 1 (1992), p. 3.
[68] Moore, Thomas, and Land, 'Editorial', p. 3.
[69] Thomas, 'Pentecostal Theology in the Twenty-First Century', p. 5.
[70] C. Bridges Johns has suggested that '[t]here is inherent within the ranks of Pentecostal believers an inferiority complex which assumes that non-Pentecostals know more than we do and do things better than we can' (C. Bridges Johns, *Pentecostal Formation: A Pedagogy*

dubbed as an anti-intellectual movement, W.J. Hollenweger suggests that 'anti-intellectual' is a critique of Pentecostalism 'which can no longer be accepted without qualification'.[71] Hollenweger cites *EPTA Bulletin, Pneuma,* the conference papers from SPS and the European Pentecostal Research Conferences as proof of the scores of first-rate Pentecostal scholarship. The generations of Pentecostal scholars which have gone before me are a rich heritage which I am happy to claim; however, a problem persists, according to Hollenweger, because the scholarly Pentecostal publications 'are not read by Pentecostal leaders (not to speak of the rank and file) who in general have no idea what a mine of insight and dedicated scholarship they are missing'.[72] I regret that Hollenweger's final assessment concerning the minimal impact of Pentecostal scholarship on the leaders and the laity of Pentecostal denominations continues to ring true; however, as the creative and helpful work produced by Pentecostal scholars continues to increase, there are signs that the scholarship is beginning to have an effect. Nevertheless, the chasm between the scholar's study and the church pew is nowhere more evident than in the interpretation of the book of Revelation.

5. *A Pentecostal Hermeneutic for Revelation*

When the word 'revelation' is used in the title of this section it has a double meaning, for it refers not only to the Apocalypse but also to the event of revelation. Pentecostals would claim that the ability to interpret a revelation is prerequisite for a valid interpretation of the Revelation. Further, the Apocalypse seems to be a good place to pursue the development of a Pentecostal hermeneutic owing to the apocalyptic nature of the movement's ethos. Thus, attention is now turned toward the Revelation with an expectation that not only will the text be unveiled but a hermeneutic may be unveiled as well.

5.1. *Apocalypse or Revelation?*

The book of Revelation is the first piece of literature included in the apocalyptic genre to use the word 'apocalypse'. The Jewish apocalypses which

---

among the Oppressed [Sheffield: Sheffield Academic Press, 1993], p. 7; *idem,* 'The Adolescence of Pentecostalism: In Search of a Legitimate Sectarian Identity', pp. 3–17).
   [71] W.J. Hollenweger, 'The Critical Tradition of Pentecostalism', *JPT* 1 (1992), p. 7.
   [72] Hollenweger, 'The Critical Tradition of Pentecostalism', p. 7.

predate the book of Revelation do not even contain the word. It was not until after the Apocalypse of John that writers of apocalyptic literature began categorizing their works as apocalypses.[73] Therefore, my reading of Revelation takes its first pause after the initial phrase Ἀποκάλυψις Ἰησοῦ Χριστοῦ (the revelation of Jesus Christ), which stands in stark contrast to the title commonly given to the book, ΑΠΟΚΑΛΥΨΙΣ ΙΩΑΝΝΟΥ. Ironically, John is not using the word ἀποκάλυψις to identify his literary work with a particular genre but rather as a description of his experience. The extent to which experience should play a role in interpretation has been a hotly debated topic. Traditionally, Pentecostals have adopted an epistemology that was heavily influenced by their experience in the Spirit; and therefore, Pentecostals may easily identify with the experience of John recorded in the text (i.e. the experience of receiving a revelation).

'Apocalypse', which is a transliteration of ἀποκάλυψις, means 'unveiling or revelation', whence the popular title, the 'Book of Revelation'. When John wishes to identify the literary genre of his work, he refers to it as a prophecy, an identification he makes at least five times (Rev. 1.3; 22.7, 10, 18–19), possibly six (Rev. 19.10).[74] Furthermore, John refers to the prophets as his brothers. Since the Apocalypse of John plays such a vital role in defining the apocalyptic genre perhaps it should be included in the list of apocalyptic literature.[75] Nevertheless, the theological significance of the

---

[73] See J.J. Collins (ed.), 'Apocalypse: The Morphology of a Genre', Semeia 14 (1979), pp. 1–214; D.E. Aune, The New Testament in its Literary Environment (Philadelphia: Westminster, 1987), p. 242. and idem, 'The Apocalypse of John and the Problem of Genre', Semeia 36 (1986), pp. 65–96. The production of apocalyptic literature experienced a long and prolific climax from the second century BCE to the second century CE. The writers of the apocalypses wrote with pseudonyms, chosen strategically in order to give the literature more authority (e.g. Daniel, Baruch, Ezra, Isaiah, and Abraham). The genre is characterized by its eschatological outlook, which is fixed from an otherworldly perspective. The genre also contains an anti-establishment tone. Cf. L. Alexander (ed.), Images of Empire (Sheffield: Sheffield Academic Press, 1991). The Jewish apocalypses claim to be in the tradition of their prophets but include concepts of demonology and dualism. Apocalyptic sections can be found in many NT texts (e.g. Mark 13; 1 Thess. 4.15–17; 2 Thess. 2.1–12; 1 Cor. 15.20–28; 2 Cor. 5.1–5; Heb. 12.22–25). Some of the Jewish apocalypses seem to have been edited with a Christian flavor (e.g. 4 Esdras, Testaments of the Twelve Patriarchs, Ascension of Isaiah, the Christian Sibyllines) and some Christian apocalypses were written (e.g. Didache 16, the Apocalypse of Peter, and the Shepherd of Hermas).

[74] M.W. Wilson, 'Revelation 19:10 and Contemporary Interpretation', in M.W. Wilson (ed.), Spirit and Renewal: Essays in Honor of J. Rodman Williams, (Sheffield: Sheffield Academic Press, 1994), pp. 191–202.

[75] According to D.E. Aune, the form, content, and function of the Apocalypse of John solidly places the book in the apocalyptic genre. Aune suggests that no ancient revelatory literature was considered to be unequivocal. The intentional ambiguity necessitates an interpretation, therefore perpetuating further revelations. According to Aune, 'the hearers

opening phrase cannot be overstated. When reading the Apocalypse or any other passage of scripture, the Pentecostal reader expects to experience a revelation of Jesus Christ as Jesus unveils the meaning of the text for the reader. In a similar fashion, the Pentecostal reader also expects to experience the presence of the Spirit. Therefore, the reader is not surprised when the words of Christ are attributed to the Spirit in the closing endorsement of each letter to the seven churches (i.e. 'let anyone who has an ear, hear what the Spirit is saying to the churches').

Pentecostals accept the Bible by faith as the Word of God which will speak directly to their lives. The Bible is not merely an object to be studied, but the Bible is used by Jesus to reveal to the believer personal insight so that as a Pentecostal reader I am apt to find out as much about myself as I am about the text. To put it in theoretical terms, the binary opposites of subject and object are deconstructed in a Pentecostal reading so that, at times, the interpreter of the text will be interpreted by the text.[76]

As for the genitive construction of Ἰησοῦ Χριστοῦ, the Pentecostal interpreter need not decide between objective and subjective genitive but rather understand the construction to be both objective and subjective. Jesus is certainly the subject as the revealer of the mysteries of God, yet He is also the object in that He reveals himself to John and to those who believe. The initial vision that John receives in Rev. 1.10–16 is a vision in which Christ reveals himself to John. I am proposing that the only interpretation of the biblical texts that a Pentecostal community will endorse is an interpretation which is centered on Jesus Christ.[77] Thus, I suggest that ἀποκάλυψις should be translated instead of being transliterated so that the experiential nature of the word might be emphasized and thereby shared with the reader. Acknowledging the necessity of revelation within

---

must use their imaginations to understand [the visions]...[and] experience for themselves the revelatory experience narrated by John' (D.E. Aune, *The New Testament in its Literary Environment*, p. 231). Cf. C. Rowland, *The Open Heaven: A Study of Apocalyptic in Judaism and Early Christianity* (New York: Crossland, 1982), pp. 403–41. Against this, F.D. Mazzaferri argues that on the basis of generic definition Revelation fails to qualify as classical apocalyptic literature (F.D. Mazzafern, *The Genre of the Book of Revelation from a Source-Critical Perspective* [New York: de Gruyter, 1989], pp. 223–58).

[76] Moore, 'Pentecostal Approach to Scripture', p. 4.

[77] The Christocentric theology of Pentecostals baffles outsiders who would think that the movement is obsessed with the Spirit only. Ironically, one of the major divisions of the Pentecostal movement which is centered on the nature of the Godhead does not revolve around the role of the Spirit but rather the identity of Jesus Christ: Oneness Pentecostals (Jesus Only) baptize in the name of Jesus (the formula found in Acts), while Pentecostal Trinitarians baptize in the name of the Father and of the Son and of the Holy Ghost (the formula found in Matthew).

the interpretative process of reading the Bible raises additional questions concerning the objective and subjective nature of the text and of interpretation.[78]

5.2. *The Status of Scripture*

The status of scripture is addressed early in the first chapter of Revelation, where John declares in the first beatitude, 'Blessed is the one who reads and those who hear the words of the prophecy and keep what is written therein, for the time is near' (Rev. 1.3). In Rev. 1.11, John records Jesus' instruction for him to 'write in a book what you are seeing and send it to the seven churches'. These two statements concerning John's own written work raise three questions concerning my understanding of scripture. First, what is the relationship between the written dimension of the text and the oral/aural dimension of the text? Second, what is the relationship between properly interpreting the words of the prophecy and the admonition to keep the words of the prophecy? Third, what role do the seven churches play as the recipients of the prophecy in the task of interpretation?

Although Pentecostals are a 'people of the Book', they are foremost a 'people of the Spirit',[79] who expect the Spirit to speak an *inspired* message to the congregation which is relevant for the time.[80] S.J. Land describes the Spirit as 'the Spirit of Christ who speaks scripturally but also has more

---

[78] Bridges Johns, 'Meeting God in the Margins, Ministry among Modernity's Refugees', pp. 24–25.

[79] I am in agreement with J.K.A. Smith's proposal that Pentecostals (who are an oral community rather than a textual community) are primarily a 'people of the Spirit'. This understanding of Pentecostalism as an oral community does not preclude the use of scripture in the Pentecostal community, indeed it affirms the use of scripture; rather, it places scripture in a subservient relationship to the Spirit. Furthermore, Smith's emphasis on orality does not sanction all spoken word but he acknowledges the authority of the Spirit of Christ who 'resides and abides within the community of the faithful' (J.K.A. Smith, 'The Closing of the Book', p. 68, n. 68).

[80] Traditional doctrines of scripture include an understanding of *inspiration* which is regulated to the writing of scripture; conversely, the act of reading is described as an *illumination*, suggesting that there is a qualitative difference between the divine participation in the act of writing scripture and the divine participation in the act of reading scripture. I agree with Clark Pinnock that the word 'inspiration' serves well to describe both dynamic experiences of writing and reading (cf. Pinnock, 'The Work of the Holy Spirit in Hermeneutics', p. 3). See also the comment by J.C. Thomas, who writes, 'Scripture cannot be properly appreciated apart from divine inspiration' (J.C. Thomas, *Ministry & Theology: Studies for the Church and Its Leaders* [Cleveland: Pathway Press, 1996], p. 16). Cf. J. Goldingay, *Models for Scripture* (Carlisle: Paternoster, 1994), pp. 257–60.

to say than scripture'.[81] Pentecostals place in high regard the oral Word of God spoken in the worship services which comes in the form of tongues, interpretation of tongues, prophecies, preaching, and testimonies.[82] The community's role in discerning the interpretation of the oral Word mirrors the community's involvement in discerning the proper interpretation of the written Word.[83]

The blessing of the beatitude is not only for reading and hearing but for *keeping* the words of the prophecy. John seems to be proposing an integration of belief and practice (orthodoxy and orthopraxis). To this integration of belief and practice, Pentecostals would add passion (orthopathy).[84] The ethic derived from the beatitude prepares the believer for the eschatological return of Christ. Keeping the Word of God also has implications for catechesis. Pentecostal children (and students) learn not only to read and hear scripture, but to keep the words as well.[85]

Jesus' command to John to write (Rev. 1.11) was accompanied with the instruction to send his writing to the seven churches. These churches served as communities in which the words of the prophecy could be interpreted. The task of discerning the proper interpretation of the prophecy resides in the community of believers.[86] In Rev. 2.2b, the church at Ephesus is commended for its previous acts of discernment; 'you have tested those who claim to be apostles but are not, and have found them to be false'.

---

[81] Land, *Pentecostal Spirituality*, p. 100.

[82] The preference towards speech over writing is a characteristic which Pentecostals share with the early church. Cf. L. Alexander, 'The Living Voice: Scepticism towards the Written Word in Early Christianity and in Graeco-Roman Texts', in Clines *et al.* (eds.), *The Bible in Three Dimensions*, pp. 221–47.

[83] The Bible for Pentecostals is not a history book which is free of errors, but rather a testimony of believers who have experienced the provision of God. There is also a sacramental use of the Bible in Pentecostal services. Pentecostal preachers have used their Bibles sacramentally as a sign of the power which is represented within the pages by either raising the book over their heads as if they are wielding a literal sword or by placing their Bibles on the chest or forehead of someone in the altar who has come forward for a prayer of healing.

[84] Land has proposed that Pentecostal spirituality is an integration of these three elements, belief, passion, and praxis (Land, *Pentecostal Spirituality*, p. 44).

[85] The close connection between word and action is repeated in Rev. 12.17 where the children are identified as keeping the commandments of God and holding the testimony of Jesus. C. Bridges Johns has stressed the necessity of ethical praxis accompanying catechesis (Bridges Johns, 'Meeting God in the Margins, Ministry among Modernity's Refugees', pp. 22–23).

[86] Cf. J.C. Thomas's emphasis on the current and future need for community and accountability within Pentecostal theology (Thomas, 'Pentecostal Theology in the Twenty-First Century', pp. 3–19). See also Fish, *Is There a Text in This Class? The Authority of Interpretative Communities*, pp. 303–71.

It is at this point that the significance of my title comes into play, 'hearing what the Spirit says to the churches'. The title is an adaptation of a repeated endorsement which is recorded in every letter to the individual churches (Revelation 2–3). Although Christ is the speaker of the letters, the churches are admonished to hear the words of the Spirit.

5.3. *A Community in the Spirit*

In a postmodern world, Pentecostals no longer need to acquiesce to the evangelical doctrine *sola scriptura*, because the revelation of God is not transmitted to new generations by scripture alone but by the work of the Holy Spirit. The Protestant doctrine of *sola scriptura* in its original form contained a connotation that scripture was accompanied by the Spirit. However, American Evangelical theologians have often not maintained such a prominent place for the Spirit. R.D. Moore has proposed that it may be more beneficial for Pentecostals to adhere to *solus spiritus* (with the Scripture) as opposed to *sola scriptura* (with the Spirit). According to Moore, the former is far less susceptible to overstatement than the latter.[87] In response to Moore, F.D. Macchia writes:

> I would only want to qualify 'Spirit alone' with 'Word and Spirit alone' in order to make this fully trinitarian. But I would hasten to add that 'Word' here is primarily the *living Christ* who was anointed and directed by the Spirit and now bestows the same Spirit upon us to serve God in Christ-like ways. In this light, 'Word' is not simply *identifiable* with 'Scripture', but Scripture is *subordinate* to Word and participates in Word *only* through the Spirit (hence a place for (Moore's) 'Spirit alone').[88]

Interpretation of the scriptures continues for Pentecostals as it always has 'not by might nor by power' nor by educational level, social status, or economic success, but by the Spirit of the living God. This view will require a new emphasis on the doctrine of the priesthood (1 Pet. 2.5, 9) and prophethood[89] of all believers (Num. 11.27–29; Joel 2.28–32; Acts 2.16–20).

---

[87] R.D. Moore, 'A Letter to Frank Macchia', *JPT* 17 (2000), p. 13.

[88] F.D. Macchia, 'A Reply to Rickie Moore', *JPT* 17 (2000), p. 18.

[89] R. Stronstad, *The Charismatic Theology of St. Luke* (Peabody: Hendrickson, 1984), p. 77; *idem*, *The Prophethood of All Believers* (Sheffield: Sheffield Academic Press, 1999). See also Eduard Schweizer's proposal that according to Rev. 19.10 all members of the community (at least potentially) are prophets. E. Schweizer, 'Πνεῦμα', TDNT (1968), VI, p. 449. R.J. Bauckham is willing to agree that prophecy in the Apocalypse is equivalent with the testimony of Jesus and that the churches function prophetically in their witness to Jesus; however (*contra* Stronstad and Schweizer), he disagrees that every believer can therefore be identified as a prophet (R.J. Bauckham, 'The Role of the Spirit', p. 166).

John describes his own experience as being 'in the Spirit' (Rev. 1.10, ἐν πνεύματι). It is the Spirit that enables John to receive the revelation of Jesus Christ. Pentecostals easily identify with John's testimony of being in the Spirit.[90] The communal dimension of the Spirit enables the churches to share in John's experience. Within Pentecostalism, the Spirit is not limited to the leaders, but all who believe experience the presence and the power of the Spirit. In addition to enabling the revelation and inspiring the reading of scripture, the Spirit also plays a vital role in inspiring the testimonies of the believers. The central challenge placed before the seven churches in Revelation is to be faithful witnesses to Jesus Christ in spite of the power of the beast which would have them do otherwise.

In Rev. 1.5, Jesus is identified as *the* faithful witness, yet the followers of Jesus who were being assaulted by the dragon were able to 'conquer him by the blood of the Lamb and by the word of their testimony, for they loved not their lives even unto death' (Rev. 12.11). F.F. Bruce argues that 'no doubt their Lord was bearing *his* testimony in theirs, and suffering in them, but it is through their own testimony that they conquer, and their own testimony is that which they bear to Jesus and his redeeming power'.[91] The provision of God is paramount in the historical context of the Asian churches, as they face the possibility of martyrdom for their faithful witness of Jesus Christ. Pentecostal theology, which is often a theology from the bottom, also shares the need for reliance on the provision of God with the Asian churches in Revelation. Moreover, the definition of μάρτυς took on new meaning with the death of Antipas from the church in Pergamum. Although being a witness might not mean an immediate physical death, a type of death does occur when a believer becomes a faithful witness (μάρτυς). The faithful witness receives a new life in Christ, and therefore, has no reason to fear the beast.

5.4. *Fearing God in Worship and in Bible Reading*

John experiences fear when he sees the vision of Christ and falls at his feet as though dead. In this encounter with Christ, Jesus instructs John not to be afraid and offers him comfort saying, 'Do not fear, I am the First and

---

[90] Cf. R.L. Jeske, 'Spirit and Community in the Johannine Apocalypse', *NTS* 31 (1985), pp. 452–66.

[91] F.F. Bruce, 'The Spirit in the Apocalypse', in B. Lindars and S.S. Smalley (eds.), *Christ and Spirit in the New Testament: In Honour of Charles Francis Digby Maule* (Cambridge: Cambridge University Press, 1973), p. 338.

the Last, the living One. I was dead, and behold I am alive forever and ever. And I have the keys of death and Hades' (Rev. 1.17-18). John's act of falling is not only a result of fear but it is also identified as an act of worship. On two occasions he fell down and attempted to worship an angel (Rev. 19.10; 22.8).[92] In both cases, John is instructed to worship God and not the angel who is a fellow servant of God. The angel identifies John's fear as an act of worship. Jesus' instruction for him to stop being afraid is echoed in Rev. 2.10, where Jesus admonishes the church at Smyrna not to fear what they are about to suffer at the hands of the devil. The close relationship between fear and worship intensifies the necessity for the churches to avoid fearing the devil or the beast, which would thereby be an act of worship.

John's fearful reaction to the vision of Christ is a common reaction to theophanies found in scripture. Although Jesus subsequently tells John not to be afraid, I suggest that Jesus is not prohibiting the fear of the Lord but rather encouraging John not to fear his circumstances or 'what is now and what will take place later' (Rev. 1.19b).[93] The identification of Christ at the end of the vision affirms Him as the figure worthy of worship and fear. Furthermore, I want to propose that the fear of the Lord is at least an initial requirement in the interpretation of scripture for the Pentecostal. Pentecostals believe they will encounter God when they read the Bible, and I have proposed that a revelation of Jesus is necessary in order to interpret scripture properly. Therefore, a reading of the biblical text, not unlike the christophany experienced by John, should involve a certain amount of fear and worship.

---

[92] *Contra* R.W. Wall, who argues that John was worshiping God in the presence of the angel. Wall notes that John does not explicitly state an intention to worship the angel and he argues that angel worship would be uncharacteristic of an apostolic figure such as John. Wall suggests that John is using the angel as a mouthpiece to endorse worship of God, the only one deserving of worship (R.W. Wall, *Revelation* [Peabody: Hendrickson, 1991], pp. 223, 264).

[93] *Contra* Aune, who classifies Jesus' exhortation to 'fear not' as 'a comfort formula meant to allay the reaction of fear at the experience of a divine epiphany', rather than an 'oracle of assurance...spoken to allay the fears which motivated the recipient of the revelation to address a lament to God (as in the case of the OT oracles of assurance)' (D.E. Aune, *Prophecy in Early Christianity and the Ancient Mediterranean World* [Grand Rapids: Eerdmans, 1983], p. 281).

6. Conclusion: Intertextuality and Pentecostalism

In my reading of Revelation, I have juxtaposed the experiences of John as a seer, a prophet, and a witness to Jesus with the experiences of contemporary Pentecostalism. I suggest that Pentecostals (and perhaps others as well) should follow the example in the text and rely on Jesus to reveal, in the Spirit, the meaning of the Word of God which is both oral and written. Further, I have emphasized the necessity of a community in which discernment must take place. I am committed to the Pentecostal interpretation of scripture which endorses the prophethood of all believers. The entire world is called by the Spirit to engage in testimony to Jesus which is a participation in the prophecy of Revelation. The scripture truly becomes an intertext for the reader/believer. The text becomes the words which the churches use to define themselves. Their experience intersects and is integrated with the texts that they read as they continually testify to the presence of God in their midst. As Christ is revealed, the church adopts an identity that reflects the image of Christ that has been revealed.

In addition to being avowedly Pentecostal, I have also been heavily influenced by the academic context in the University of Sheffield, where biblical studies often partners with various other disciplines in the examination of literary texts. In this setting, I have been introduced to a particular literary theory which seems to fit quite nicely with Pentecostalism (i.e. intertextuality). The integration of orthodoxy, orthopraxis, and orthopathy within Pentecostalism finds resonance with the multiple intersections of literary and cultural (con)texts within the theory of intertextuality. The next chapter turns more directly toward the text of Revelation and analyses Rev. 11.1–13, which I argue is the intertextual center of the book. In keeping with the model of a non-modern hermeneutic which is multiple in method, the analysis will portray characteristics of a multilevel hermeneutic.

CHAPTER TWELVE

HEARING THE VOICE OF GOD:
PENTECOSTAL HERMENEUTICS AND THE BOOK OF JUDGES*

Lee Roy Martin**

Introduction

Although the methodological section in Chapter 1 together with the conclusions of Chapter 2 should serve as sufficient prerequisites for the commencement of my study proper, I have chosen to offer this chapter as further description of the goals of a Pentecostal hermeneutic. I propose in Chapter 1 an approach to Scripture that is theologically motivated, canonically based, and narratively oriented.[1] I conclude in Chapter 2 that a Pentecostal approach might pursue a theological study of Judges that appreciates the canonical authority, spiritual meaning, transformative power, and particularity of the text.

Furthermore, I embrace the thoroughness of critical methods and the appropriation of critical discoveries that include the historical (human) dimensions of the text. My approach claims the freedom to wrestle with difficult texts; to examine the narrative qualities of the text, and recognize the divergent voices within the text, utilizing an integration of multiple interpretive approaches. I take into account the three worlds of the text (behind, in, and in front of), but as a Pentecostal, I seek to enter the world of the living, dynamic, charismatic word of God, a world that is manifested through encounter with the God who is in, around, above, below, and in front of every text. In this charismatic encounter, the text is no longer the object of my critical critique, but I become the object of critique

---

* Chapter 3 of Lee Roy Martin, *The Unheard Voice of God: A Pentecostal Hearing of the Book of Judges* (JPTSup, 32; Blandford Forum: Deo Publishing, 2008), pp. 52–79.
** Lee Roy Martin (DTh, University of South Africa) is Professor of Old Testament and Biblical Languages at the Pentecostal Theological Seminary in Cleveland, TN USA.
[1] A combination of theological and narrative approaches is proposed and demonstrated by John Goldingay, *Old Testament Theology: Israel's Gospel* (Downers Grove, IL: InterVarsity Press, 2003), pp. 15–41.

to the voice of God that speaks from the midst of the fire (Deut. 5.24).[2] Furthermore, this encounter itself must be submitted to the discernment of the community of faith so that interpretation is not allowed to be an individualistic mystical affirmation that is disconnected from the text and the covenant people.[3]

In this chapter I explore further the goals of a Pentecostal approach to Judges based upon the biblical concept of 'hearing' (Heb. שמע), which I use in contrast to the commonly used term 'reading'. In some ways the terms 'hearing' and 'reading' are similar—they both refer to a synchronic, holistic, contextual hermeneutic. The term 'hearing', however, more closely approximates the goals of my Pentecostal hermeneutic because: (1) it is a thoroughly biblical term; (2) it accords with the orality of the biblical and Pentecostal contexts; (3) it is relational, implying the existence of a 'person' who is speaking the Word;[4] (4) it denotes a faithful adherence to the Word, since in Scripture to hear often means to obey;[5] (5) it implies transformation, since the hearing of the Word produces change; and (6) it demands humility because, unlike the process of 'reading' Scripture, 'hearing' entails submission to the authority of the word of God (as per [4] above).[6]

---

[2] Moore, 'Canon and Charisma', pp. 85–87. Moore's piece is not the most complete description of Pentecostal hermeneutics, but is the most pointed and powerful one.

[3] Thomas, 'Women, Pentecostalism and the Bible', pp. 41–56. Thomas observes a hermeneutical paradigm in Acts 15 that integrates the voices of the text, the Spirit, and the believing community. See also Paul D. Hanson, 'Scripture, Community and Spirit: Biblical Theology's Contribution to a Contextualized Christian Theology', *JPT* 6 (1995), pp. 3–12.

[4] Cf. Karl Barth, *Church Dogmatics* (5 vols.; Edinburgh: T. & T. Clark, 1936), I, pp. 132–43.

[5] Cf. Francis Brown et al., *The New Brown, Driver, Briggs, Gesenius Hebrew and English Lexicon: With an Appendix Containing the Biblical Aramaic* (trans. Edward Robinson; Peabody, MA: Hendrickson, 1979), p. 1034; and William L. Holladay, *A Concise Hebrew and Aramaic Lexicon of the Old Testament* (Grand Rapids, MI: Eerdmans, corrected 10th edn, 1988), p. 423.

[6] It might be argued that the terminology is unimportant, but I would insist otherwise. In many ways the use of language shapes the development of ideas within the community. Feminists have helped us rethink gender relationships through the introduction of inclusive language, and minorities have created more a more healthy understanding between racial and ethnic groups through their resistance to bigoted language. Likewise, the language of interpretation will help to shape the content of the interpretation.

Opportunity for a Pentecostal Approach to Judges

The diversity of scholarly approaches to Judges suggests that the book is capable of functioning in an assortment of legitimate modes, with each mode affording unique opportunities for study. Gale Yee's aforementioned volume is an example of the current diversity within biblical studies, setting forth six different types of criticism that have been applied recently to Judges: narrative, social scientific, feminist, structuralist, deconstructive, and ideological.[7] Surely, if this multiplicity of scholarly methods can be acknowledged, there should be room for a Pentecostal approach. According to Daniel Patte, the healthy practice of critical methods 'must allow us to affirm the legitimacy of a plurality of interpretations'.[8]

In the first issue of the *Journal of Pentecostal Theology*, Rickie D. Moore lamented the lack of models for the integrating of Pentecostalism and critical biblical scholarship, and the way ahead for him was 'far from clear'.[9] In that same issue, Jackie David Johns and Cheryl Bridges Johns added, 'Pentecostals are only now beginning to formulate a hermeneutic which takes seriously the dynamics of the Pentecostal faith'.[10] The situation is quite different today, and because of the creative and faithful work of Pentecostal scholars, who have wrestled with the issues of hermeneutics over the last few years, a newly constructed pathway leads forward.[11] To state the situation differently, the pathway is newly constructed only in some of its parts, while other parts of the path are actually ancient ways rediscovered, uncovered, and restored. After all, according to Rickie D. Moore, a charismatic hermeneutic was practiced as far back as the time of Moses and the book of Deuteronomy.[12] Furthermore, John Christopher Thomas argues for the presence of a Pentecostal hermeneutic in Acts 15,[13] and Kenneth Archer finds the charismatic approach in early Pentecostalism.[14]

---

[7] Gale A. Yee, *Judges and Method: New Approaches in Biblical Studies* (Minneapolis: Fortress Press, 1995).

[8] Daniel Patte, *Ethics of Biblical Interpretation: A Reevaluation* (Louisville, KY: Westminster John Knox Press, 1995), p. 27.

[9] Moore, 'Canon and Charisma', p. 76.

[10] Johns and Johns, 'Yielding to the Spirit', p. 110.

[11] Cf. the title of Kenneth J. Archer, 'Forging a New Path: A Contemporary Pentecostal Hermeneutical Strategy for the 21st Century', (PhD thesis, St. Andrews University, 2001).

[12] Moore, 'Canon and Charisma', p. 90. See also Randall J. Pannell, *Those Alive Here Today: The 'Day of Horeb' and Deuteronomy's Hermeneutical Locus of Revelation* (Longwood, FL: Xulon Press, 2004).

[13] Thomas, 'Women, Pentecostalism and the Bible', pp. 41–56.

[14] Kenneth J. Archer, 'Early Pentecostal Biblical Interpretation', *JPT* 18 (2001), pp. 79–117.

It seems more accurate to say that some Pentecostal scholars have escaped the byway of Enlightenment methodologies and have returned to the main pathway of Pentecostal epistemology, where approaches to the Bible embody more holistic, relational conceptions of truth.[15] Therefore, the recent advances in Pentecostal hermeneutics represent not so much a new *prescription* for biblical interpretation, but a critical *description* of the interpretive process that has been practiced in the past and is practiced currently by many Pentecostals.[16]

In addition, recent Pentecostal approaches enjoy the openness of post-critical methodologies as described by Patrick D. Miller:

> Contemporary theology and biblical studies have opened wide the door to a multivalent reading of Scripture. That is, in general, a good development. We have broken out of a modern concern for the meaning of a text—a concern that many of our interpretive forebears did not share—and have come to recognize that any text is rich and open toward a breadth of interpretive inferences as well as that readers and audiences have much to do with what is heard from the text.[17]

Many Pentecostals would agree with Daniel Patte, who writes: 'Different readers, because of their specific interests, concerns, or backgrounds, perceive different yet coherent meanings in a text (or better, produce these meanings with the text) by selecting one of these dimensions of the text'.[18] Allowing multiple interpretations, however, opens the door to improper, misinformed, and even dangerous interpretations, which means that the critical task is vital. All interpretations must be held accountable, and any legitimate interpretation must derive from the text itself. The Pentecostal approach is not tantamount to uncritical subjectivism, because, although Scripture can mean many things, it cannot mean anything and everything. In fact some interpretations are dangerous, even evil. Oppressors have used the Bible as an excuse to enslave peoples, persecute the Jews, and exterminate ethnic groups. Women and children have been subjugated

---

[15] Cf., e.g., the discussions of the Pentecostal worldview in Johns, 'Pentecostalism', pp. 73–96, and Ellington, 'Pentecostalism and the Authority of Scripture', pp. 16–38; and the exploration of the relationship between Pentecostal theology and the interpretation of Scripture in Land, *Pentecostal Spirituality*.

[16] The most complete description of the Pentecostal approach, both its history and current practice, is Archer, *Pentecostal Hermeneutic*; and the best short overview is Robby Waddell, *The Spirit of the Book of Revelation*, pp. 97–131.

[17] Patrick D. Miller, 'Popularizing the Bible', *ThT* 53 (1997), p. 437.

[18] Daniel Patte, Daniel, *Ethics of Biblical Interpretation: A Reevaluation* (Louisville, KY: Westminster John Knox Press, 1995), p. 28.

and abused because of erroneous interpretations of the Bible.[19] Robert P. Carroll pleads for the responsible and careful interpretation of the Bible as he alerts us to the 'desperate need for sustained critical readings of the Bible and that never again should a group of theologians be allowed to enslave a nation with their uncritical readings of the Bible'.[20]

During the time of first and second generation Pentecostal scholars, the academy did not have a place nor a language for Pentecostal hermeneutics, but since 1992 over forty articles and books on the topic have been published.[21] In light of the large number of recent works devoted to Pentecostal hermeneutics, including helpful summaries from Matthew Clark,[22] Veli-Matti Kärkkäinen,[23] Kenneth Archer,[24] Matthias Becker,[25] and Robby Waddell,[26] an extensive discussion of the field is not necessary. Nevertheless, I should say that I find considerable agreement between Pentecostal scholars that a postmodern hermeneutic 'accords well with the original Pentecostal ethos',[27] an ethos that regards the Scripture as the dynamic and living 'Spirit-Word'.[28]

Walter Brueggemann declares that 'a hermeneutic is not only necessary but inevitable. There are no uninterpreted events',[29] but one could question the need for a distinctive Pentecostal hermeneutic. I believe,

---

[19] For numerous examples of the immoral use of the Bible, see Jim Hill and Rand Cheadle, *The Bible Tells Me So: Uses and Abuses of Holy Scripture* (New York: Anchor Books/Doubleday, 1996).

[20] Robert P. Carroll, '(South) Africa, Bible, Criticism: Rhetorics of a Visit', in Gerald O. West and Musa W. Dube Shomanah (eds.), *The Bible in Africa: Transactions, Trajectories, and Trends* (Leiden: Brill, 2000), p. 197.

[21] The terminology of 'first generation' and 'second generation' Pentecostal scholars follows Rickie D. Moore, John Christopher Thomas, and Steven J. Land, 'Editorial', *JPT* 1 (1992), p. 3.

[22] Matthew S. Clark, 'An Investigation into the Nature of a Viable Pentecostal Hermeneutic', (DTh, University of South Africa, 1996), pp. 167–77.

[23] Veli-Matti Kärkkäinen, 'Pentecostal Hermeneutics in the Making: On the Way From Fundamentalism to Postmodernism', *JEPTA* 18 (1998), 76–115.

[24] Archer, *Pentecostal Hermeneutic*, pp. 127–55.

[25] Matthias Becker, 'A Tenet Under Examination: Reflections on the Pentecostal Hermeneutical Approach', *JEPTA* 24 (2004), pp. 31–34.

[26] Waddell, *The Spirit of the Book of Revelation*, pp. 108–18.

[27] Kärkkäinen, 'Pentecostal Hermeneutics in the Making', p. 89.

[28] Land, *Pentecostal Spirituality*, p. 100. For arguments against the 'uncritical adoption of theological methods and forms which contain epistemological and theological perspectives that undermine the Pentecostal spirituality which shaped its story', see Kenneth J. Archer, 'A Pentecostal Way of Doing Theology: Method and Manner', *IJST* (forthcoming).

[29] Walter Brueggemann, 'The Legitimacy of a Sectarian Hermeneutic: 2 Kings 18–19', *Interpretation and Obedience: From Faithful Reading to Faithful Living* (Minneapolis, MN: Fortress Press, 1989), p. 62.

however, that the inevitability of a hermeneutic requires Pentecostals to be intentional about their approach, otherwise they will be subjugated by the 'dominant rationality'.[30] Every faith community has a hermeneutic, whether they recognize it or not; and Pentecostals will have a hermeneutic, whether by default or by intention.[31] We can choose either to adopt the current dominant models without considering the subsequent effect upon our tradition,[32] or we can carefully and intentionally formulate contextual models of interpretation that integrate available contemporary methods with the ethos of our tradition. I propose that we follow the latter course, and construct a Pentecostal hermeneutic that employs the hermeneutical methods that are more conducive to our ethos, theology and view of Scripture.[33] We cannot be precritical; we must not be anticritical; but we should be postcritical, pursuing the path that Iain Provan calls 'believing criticism', an approach that 'marries probing, reflective interpretation of the text to loyal biblical devotion and warm Christian affection'.[34] Thus, the central Pentecostal concern is to hear and obey the word of God, what Dirkie J. Smit calls 'a hermeneutics of consent, of engagement, of trust, of transformation; in short, a theological hermeneutics'.[35] Consequently, the Pentecostal approach to Scripture prefers obedience over correctness, openness over exactness, humility over certitude, and faithfulness over objectivity. Scott Ellington writes:

> Doctrines may be challenged and even overturned without striking at the very heart of Pentecostal faith because the central emphasis of Pentecostalism is

---

[30] Brueggemann, 'Legitimacy of a Sectarian Hermeneutic', p. 62.

[31] Cf. Marius D. Herholdt, 'Pentecostal and Charismatic Hermeneutics', in Adrio König and S.S. Maimela (eds.), *Initiation into Theology: The Rich Variety of Theology and Hermeneutics* (Pretoria: Van Schaik, 1998), p. 417.

[32] Note the lamentation of a critical scholar: 'In my case, critical biblical studies demanded that I disregard the transforming religious power of the biblical text upon me, upon others and upon society!' Daniel Patte, 'The Guarded Personal Voice of a Male European-American Biblical Scholar', in *Personal Voice in Biblical Interpretation* (London: Routledge, 1999), p. 14.

[33] Herholdt, 'Pentecostal and Charismatic Hermeneutics', p. 428.

[34] Iain W. Provan, *1 and 2 Kings* (New International Biblical Commentary; Peabody, MA: Hendrickson Publishers, 1995), p. x. Not all Pentecostals are enthusiastic about a postcritical approach. Cf. Robert P. Menzies, 'Jumping Off the Postmodern Bandwagon', *PNEUMA* 16 (1994), pp. 115–20; Hannah K. Harrington and Rebecca Patten, 'Pentecostal Hermeneutics and Postmodern Literary Theory', *PNEUMA* 16 (1994), pp. 109–14; and John C. Poirier and B. Scott Lewis, 'Pentecostal and Postmodernist Hermeneutics: A Critique of Three Conceits', *JPT* 15, (2006), pp. 3–21.

[35] Dirkie J. Smit, 'Biblical Hermeneutics: The 20th Century', in Adrio König and S.S. Maimela (eds.), *Initiation into Theology: The Rich Variety of Theology and Hermeneutics* (Pretoria: Van Schaik, 1998), p. 314.

not a teaching which must be believed or a proof which can be deduced and defended against all challenges, but a God who must be reckoned with in direct encounter.[36]

The integration of rigorous study and faith commitment is possible partially because the heart of the Pentecostal pursuit of truth is different from the rationalist pursuit of truth. While religious rationalists (Evangelical fundamentalists) define truth in terms of their dogma that is undergirded by the historicity and inerrancy of Scripture, Pentecostals define truth in terms of the genuineness of their encounter and continuing relationship with God through his Word and his Spirit.[37]

Biblical interpretation certainly involves guidelines, rules, and principles but it is more than a step-by-step process. For a Pentecostal, every part of the process of interpretation is performed in the presence of God, who is Lord of past, present, and future. Prayer and worship fuse all the elements together into one pursuit, the pursuit of God himself. The mystery of this encounter is akin to what is described by Daniel Patte, who comes to the matter from a context that is other than Pentecostal:

> My personal voice is truly heard in interpretations of the Bible that are transformative encounters with an Other who transcends me, that is, in *pro me* (or *pro nobis*) biblical interpretations which reflect experiences of a mysterious Otherness that I cannot control and encompass in my interpretations.[38]

For the Pentecostal who sees God in all things, the study of history, backgrounds, archaeology, linguistics, and other areas normally assigned to the realm of science, become a spiritual pursuit when submitted to the ultimate authority of God, who created, sustains, and fills all things.

---

[36] Cf. Ellington, 'Pentecostalism and the Authority of Scripture', p. 17.

[37] For this reason early Pentecostals displayed little interest in the Fundamentalist-Modernist controversy. Cf. Althouse, 'Toward a Theological Understanding of the Pentecostal Appeal to Experience', pp. 399–411. For other differences between early Pentecostals and Fundamentalists, see Jacobsen, *Thinking in the Spirit: Theologies of the Early Pentecostal Movement*, pp. 356–58; and Kimberly Ervin Alexander, *Pentecostal Healing: Models in Theology and Practice* (JPTSup, 29; Blandford Forum, UK: Deo Publishing, 2006), pp. 65–66, 163–64, 218. Unfortunately, much of American Pentecostalism is now aligned with Fundamentalist concerns, and I am calling for a return to the distinctive heart of Pentecostalism. Cf. Timothy B. Cargal, 'Beyond the Fundamentalist-Modernist Controversy: Pentecostals and Hermeneutics in a Postmodern Age', *PNEUMA* 15 (1993), pp. 163–87. For the influence of Fundamentalism on the Assemblies of God, especially in the area of eschatology, see Vinson Synan, *The Holiness-Pentecostal Tradition: Charismatic Movements in the Twentieth Century* (Grand Rapids, MI: Eerdmans, 2nd edn, 1997), pp. 207–209; and William W. Menzies and Robert P. Menzies, *Spirit and Power: Foundation of Pentecostal Experience* (Grand Rapids, MI: Zondervan, 2000), pp. 19–22.

[38] Patte, 'The Guarded Personal Voice', p. 13.

History is God's history; sociology is the sociology of the community of faith, and the study of language is a means to hear the voice of God.

When I speak of a Pentecostal approach, I do not claim to speak for everyone in the Pentecostal-Charismatic movement, a movement that is worldwide and diverse. I do speak, however, as a practicing Pentecostal who for many years has struggled to integrate the critical interpretation of Scripture with the ongoing life of the Church.[39] Furthermore, I am not arguing that approaches other than mine are invalid, nor would I insist that Pentecostals will use only one method. As Willie Wessels writes, 'There is more than one correct method of interpretation and this is to the benefit of the believing community who should realize that interpretation is a dynamic, open-ended and ongoing process'.[40] I do not demand that every Pentecostal scholar utilize a Pentecostal approach. For example, a Pentecostal may be a historian who is using Judges as a resource for places, names, and events of history. A Pentecostal may be a sociologist who studies the customs and social structures of the pre-monarchic period. A Pentecostal may be an expert in literature who examines the narratives of Judges in light of their setting, plot, characterizations, and other rhetorical features. Different interpreters come to the text with different aims, and as W. Randolph Tate explains, 'Interpretive aims dictate interpretive methods'.[41] Although there is no distinctive Pentecostal methodology for biblical studies, several methodologies seem to commend themselves to the Pentecostal ethos. Rickie D. Moore, for example, claims

---

[39] My description of Pentecostal hermeneutics is based upon thirty years of daily participation in the Pentecostal church, education at a Pentecostal college and seminary, and teaching at a Pentecostal college and seminary. I have enjoyed close association with Pentecostals from many countries who came as students to the seminary, and I have taught courses in Korea and Puerto Rico. Furthermore, my hermeneutical model has been shaped by many years of pastoral praxis, where I have been forced to integrate scholarship with spirituality, and where I have attempted to merge sound exegesis and prophetic preaching.

[40] Willie J. Wessels, 'Biblical Hermeneutics', in Adrio König and S.S. Maimela (eds.), *Initiation into Theology: The Rich Variety of Theology and Hermeneutics* (Pretoria: Van Schaik, 1998), p. 272.

[41] W. Randolph Tate, *Biblical Interpretation: An Integrated Approach* (Peabody, MA: Hendrickson Publishers, 1991), p. 195. For a deeper discussion of academic aims versus religious aims, see Robert Morgan, and John Barton, *Biblical Interpretation* (Oxford Bible Series; New York: Oxford University Press, 1988), pp. 8–26. Not only are different methods required depending upon the specific academic discipline, but different methods and approaches are required for the different genres in the Bible. See John Goldingay, *Models for Interpretation of Scripture* (Grand Rapids, MI: Eerdmans, 1995).

a literary-theological method,[42] Kenneth Archer recommends a semiotic approach,[43] and Robby Waddell fuses the methods of intertextuality with goals of theological inquiry.[44]

Recent scholarly discussions have called attention to the possibility of different *readings*, and most biblical scholars have admitted that all readings are subjective and biased from their beginning. Pentecostals, like everyone else, have both conscious and unconscious presuppositions and agendas that affect their biblical interpretation. Pentecostals *read* the text, and they create *readings* of the text. The term 'reading', however, does not describe precisely enough the intent and goals of a Pentecostal approach to Scripture. In place of the word 'reading', I suggest that we utilize the word 'hearing', a term that is more prevalent in the Bible itself, and more consistent with Pentecostal practice. The use of the term 'hearing' is consistent with the critical aim of biblical exegesis, which is, according to Patrick D. Miller, 'to hear as much as one can and to avoid mishearing'.[45] The appropriateness of 'hearing' as a hermeneutical term is confirmed further by its frequent use within the titles of books and articles devoted to the subject of biblical interpretation.[46]

---

[42] Moore, 'Canon and Charisma', pp. 75–92. See also Moore, 'Deuteronomy and the Fire of God', pp. 11, 15, 16. Literary methods are approved also by Robert O. Baker, 'Pentecostal Bible Reading: Toward a Model of Reading for the Formation of the Affections', *JPT* 7 (1995), pp. 41–42, and Archer, *Pentecostal Hermeneutic*, pp. 4, 5, 166. See Appendix D for a more detailed description of literary method.

[43] Archer, *Pentecostal Hermeneutic*.

[44] Waddell, *The Spirit of the Book of Revelation*.

[45] Patrick D. Miller, 'Popularizing the Bible', *Theology Today* 53 (1997), p. 437.

[46] Cf. Richard Aczel, 'Hearing Voices in Narrative Texts', *NLH* 29, no. 3 (1998), pp. 467–500; Richard Aczel, 'Understanding as Over-hearing: Towards a Dialogics of Voice', *NLH* 32, no. 3 (2001), pp. 597–617; Frederick H. Borsch, 'Ears that Hear and Do not Hear: Fundamental Hearing of the Bible', *Scripture Today* (Wilton, CT: Morehouse-Barlow, 1980), pp. 23–49; Robert A. Coughenour, 'Hearing and Heeding: Tasks for Old Testament Interpretation', *RefR* 41 (1988), pp. 117–38; Joel B. Green, *Hearing the New Testament: Strategies for Interpretation* (Grand Rapids, MI: Eerdmans, 1995); John Alexander Hutchison, 'On Hearing the Word of God', *JBR* 19, no. 2 (1951), pp. 67–70; Jacqueline E. Lapsley, *Whispering the Word: Hearing Women's Stories in the Old Testament* (Louisville, KY: Westminster John Knox Press, 2005); Arie C. Leder and David A. Vroege, 'Reading and Hearing Leviticus', *CTJ* 34 (1999), pp. 431–42; Elizabeth Struthers Malbon, *Hearing Mark: A Listener's Guide* (Harrisburg, PA: Trinity Press International, 2002); James Muilenburg and Thomas F. Best, *Hearing and Speaking the Word: Selections From the Works of James Muilenburg* (Chico, CA: Scholars Press, 1984); James Nogalski and Marvin A. Sweeney, *Reading and Hearing the Book of the Twelve* (Atlanta: Society of Biblical Literature, 2000); Gerald T. Sheppard, 'Canonization: Hearing the Voice of the Same God Through Historically Dissimilar Traditions', *ExA* 1 (1985), pp. 106–14; Klyne Snodgrass, 'Reading to Hear: A Hermeneutics of Hearing', *HBT* 24, no. 1 (2002), pp. 1–32; Clarence Vos and Sierd Woudstra, *Hearing the Word of the Lord: The Prophets* (Revelation Series for Adults; 2 vols.; Grand Rapids, MI: CRC

Judges as a Prophetic Text to be Heard

Several important factors make 'hearing' a fitting paradigm for a Pentecostal approach to Judges. For most Pentecostals, Scripture is interpreted within the context of the believing, worshiping community. Consequently, Judges does not function as historiography to be examined or as ideology to be evaluated; rather, it functions as a prophetic voice to be heard. The function of Judges as a word of prophecy is in harmony with the Jewish tradition, which places the book within the category 'Former Prophets'.[47] Many Christian scholars also classify Judges within the category of Former Prophets;[48] this is true even of Christian writers whose interests are primarily historical critical.[49] Judges, therefore, is more than history; it is 'salvation history',[50] 'counter-history',[51] or prophetic history, whose purpose is not 'primarily to offer an explanation of the past, but to function as scripture for the new generation of Israel who are instructed from the past for the sake of the future'.[52] According to Walter Brueggemann, the narrative that we call the Former Prophets 'does not intend to be historical reportage in any modern sense of the term...the material is theological testimony, that is, a believing effort to give an account of

---

Publications, 1994). In most of these works, the concept of 'hearing' goes no further than the title. I could add another list of works that use the word 'listen/listening'.

[47] What the Jews call the Former Prophets (Josh., Judg., Sam., and Kgs) scholars call the Deuteronomic History, and while the allusion to Deuteronomy is a valid theological equation, the use of 'History' distracts from the theological purposes of the corpus and produces a multitude of misconceptions from the very inception of it use, since it misrepresents the genre of Josh.-Kgs.

[48] E.g., Brevard S. Childs, *Introduction to the Old Testament as Scripture* (Philadelphia: Fortress Press, 1st American edn, 1979); James L. Crenshaw, *Story and Faith: A Guide to the Old Testament* (New York: Macmillan, 1986); William Sanford La Sor et al., *Old Testament Survey: The Message, Form, and Background of the Old Testament* (Grand Rapids, MI: Eerdmans, Rev. edn, 1996).

[49] See Otto Eissfeldt, *The Old Testament; an Introduction, Including the Apocrypha and Pseudepigrapha, and Also the Works of Similar Type from Qumran: The History of the Formation of the Old Testament* (New York: Harper and Row, 1965); Georg Fohrer and Ernst Sellin, *Introduction to the Old Testament* (Nashville,: Abingdon Press, 1968); Pfeiffer, *Introduction to the Old Testament*; Claus Westermann and Robert Henry Boyd, *Handbook to the Old Testament* (Minneapolis: Augsburg Pub. House, 1967).

[50] Gerhard von Rad, *Old Testament Theology* (2 vols.; New York: Harper, 1962), I, p. 344.

[51] Walter Brueggemann, *Abiding Astonishment: Psalms, Modernity, and the Making of History* (Louisville, KY: Westminster/John Knox Press, 1991), p. 43.

[52] Childs, *Introduction to the Old Testament as Scripture*, pp. 236–38. Cf. Provan, *1 and 2 Kings*, pp. 6–15.

faith, an account of God'.[53] Terence Fretheim agrees, writing that the primary purpose of the Former Prophets is not historical, but 'religious... the biblical narrators used the materials at their disposal for theological (or kerygmatic-didactic) purposes. Their goal is to tell the story of the interaction between God and Israel in order to elicit a response from their audience'.[54] Consequently, as a part of the canonical Former Prophets, Judges is theologically intentional in its final, canonical form.[55] It is appropriate, then, for the interpreter to utilize 'the more confessional approach to Scripture, which, one could argue, is the context out of which the Bible arose and for which it was created'.[56]

As prophecy, Judges presents a theological message to its original readers; but a Pentecostal would assume that Judges presents a message for today's reader as well. As a prophetic word, the book of Judges challenges and informs the hearer from outside himself/herself.[57] My goal as a Pentecostal reader is to seek for the theological message of the text, to be confronted by it, and to then to be conformed to it. Thus, Judges is an authoritative word for today; and as part of the canon a Pentecostal would hear the canonical text in its final form.[58] The term 'hearing', therefore, is consistent with the nature of Judges as a prophetic word that challenges and informs the hearer from outside himself/herself. Hearing Judges as prophecy means: (1) The text is a divine word confronting the

---

[53] Walter Brueggemann, *An Introduction to the Old Testament: The Canon and Christian Imagination* (Louisville, KY: Westminster John Knox Press, 2003), p. 103. The New Historicism maintains that historiography itself is a fiction; cf. Joyce W. Warren and Margaret Dickie, *Challenging Boundaries: Gender and Periodization* (Athens, GA: University of Georgia Press, 2000), p. xii.

[54] Terence E. Fretheim, *Deuteronomic History* (Interpreting Biblical Texts; Nashville: Abingdon Press, 1983), p. 30.

[55] It should be noted that the term 'canon' is not commonly used by Pentecostals outside the academy. In the Pentecostal church, the Scriptures are most often referred to as the 'Word of God'.

[56] Miller, 'Popularizing the Bible', p. 436.

[57] Regarding the implications of the Old Testament as prophetic literature, see John W. McKay, 'When the Veil is Taken Away: The Impact of Prophetic Experience on Biblical Interpretation', *JPT* 5 (1994), p. 30.

[58] Childs, *Introduction to the Old Testament as Scripture*; Bruce D. Chilton, 'Biblical Authority, Canonical Criticism, and Generative Exegesis', *The Quest for Context and Meaning* (Leiden: E. J. Brill, 1997). For a Pentecostal understanding of canonical criticism, see Simon Chan, *Pentecostal Theology*, pp. 27–31. Other Pentecostals who call for hearing the final form of the text include Moore, 'Deuteronomy and the Fire of God', pp. 19–20; Baker, 'Pentecostal Bible Reading', pp. 35–36; and Archer, *Pentecostal Hermeneutic*, pp. 163, 167.

human community; (2) The text is authoritative (canonical) for the believing community; and (3) The text will criticize/transform its hearers.[59]

Not only is the text a prophetic word to the community of faith, but the Pentecostal community is a prophetic community,[60] and the Pentecostal interpretation is a prophetic interpretation. As mentioned above, prophetic interpretation begins in the canon as early as Deuteronomy, which is a reenactment of earlier events, making them present for a new generation.[61] After Deuteronomy, the traditions of the Torah are continually being activated prophetically for each new generation.[62] According to John McKay, the charismatic experience of Pentecostals means that they 'are prophets, or at least prophetically sympathetic, and so read the Bible with the eye and intellect of prophetical persons'.[63] Pentecostal interpretation is an attempt at Spirit empowered prophetic reappropriation of the Scriptures that flows out of the transformative experience of Pentecost. Regarding the prophetic nature of Pentecostal hermeneutics, Roger Stronstad writes:

> [C]harismatic experience in particular and spiritual experience in general give the interpreter of relevant biblical texts and experiential presupposition which transcends the rational and cognitive presuppositions of scientific exegesis. Furthermore, this charismatic experience results in an understanding, empathy, and sensitivity to the text, and priorities in relation to the text which other interpreters do not and cannot have.[64]

In other words, as a Pentecostal listens to the text he or she is made aware of textual features that are brought to the surface through the interaction of the text and the prophetic experience of the hearer.[65]

---

[59] For the transformative effect of Scripture, see Eugene H. Peterson, *Eat this Book: A Conversation in the Art of Spiritual Reading* (Grand Rapids, MI: Eerdmans, 2005). Cf. Land, *Pentecostal Spirituality*, who writes, 'Even as the Spirit formed Christ in Mary, so the Spirit uses Scripture to form Christ in believers' (p. 100).

[60] Roger Stronstad, *The Prophethood of All Believers: A Study in Luke's Charismatic Theology* (JPTSup, 16; Sheffield: Sheffield Academic Press, 1999); and McQueen, *Joel and the Spirit*.

[61] Moore, 'Canon and Charisma', pp. 75–92.

[62] Cf. Brueggemann, *The Creative Word*, pp. 40–66.

[63] McKay, 'When the Veil is Taken Away', p. 24.

[64] Roger Stronstad, 'Pentecostal Experience and Hermeneutics', *Paraclete* 26 (1992), p. 17. The unique experiences of every interpreter act as a set of interpretive lenses through which that interpreter sees the text, with the result that certain elements of the text that are overlooked by one reader appear quite obvious to another.

[65] I do not suggest, however, that Pentecostal scholars are free to ignore the work of other critical scholars. Critical findings must be evaluated and applied to interpretation on a case-by-case basis. Cf. my discussion in Chapter 2.

'Hearing', Orality and Literacy

'Hearing' and the Orality of Scripture

Not only does the term 'hearing' accord with the nature of Judges as a prophetic book, but it also corresponds to the orality of biblical society, and it fits into the tradition of Pentecostalism as an oral community. Until modern times, the Bible was mostly encountered aurally, through teaching and preaching, or through one person who read the text within the hearing of the congregation (whether Jewish or Christian).[66] Before the time of Plato written texts were constructed based upon their aural effect rather than their visual effect.[67] Even in medieval times written texts were normally read aloud, even when read privately, which is the reason for Augustine's amazement that Ambrose should read without uttering the words.[68] Conventions of oral culture continued to exercise significant impact on literature until the Reformation period, and Marshall McLuhan has demonstrated that it was the printing press that converted the Western world from orality to literacy, producing what McLuhan calls 'typographic man'.[69]

According to Walter J. Ong, the characteristics of communication within an oral culture include: simple sentence structures, frequent use of stock words and phrases, repetition of words, phrases, and ideas, importance of story over ideas, focus on situational particularity rather than conceptual abstraction, and episodic narrative instead of linear logic.[70]

---

[66] For biblical examples where one person acts as the reader, while others listen, cf. Exod. 24.7; Deut. 31.11; Josh. 8.34f; 2 Kgs 22.10; 23.2; 2 Chron. 34.18, 24, 30; Ezra 4.18, 23; Neh. 8.3, 8, 18; 9.3; 13.1; Est. 6.1; Jer. 29.29; 36.6, 10, 13, 21; Lk. 4.16; Acts 13.27; 15.21, 2 Cor. 3.14, 15; Col. 4.16; 1 Thess. 5.27; Rev. 1.3.

[67] Richard A. Jensen, *Thinking in Story: Preaching in a Post-literate Age* (Lima, Ohio: C.S.S. Pub., 1993), pp. 19–20.

[68] Jensen, *Thinking in Story*, pp. 32–33. *Confessions* 6.3.3. For the Latin text, see James J. O'Donnell, *The Confessions of St. Augustine: An Electronic Edition*; available from http://www.stoa.org/hippo. The central text reads: 'sed cum legebat, oculi ducebantur per paginas et cor intellectum rimabatur, vox autem et lingua quiescebant'.

[69] Marshall McLuhan, *The Gutenberg Galaxy: The Making of Typographic Man* (Toronto: University of Toronto Press, 1962).

[70] Walter J. Ong, *Orality and Literacy: The Technologizing of the Word* (New York: Routledge, 1988), pp. 31–49. For a limited but helpful approach to interpreting the Old Testament from an oral perspective, see Susan Niditch, *Oral World and Written Word: Ancient Israelite Literature* (Library of Ancient Israel; Louisville, KY: Westminster John Knox Press, 1996), who lists three characteristics of oral style: repetition, formulas, and epithets (pp. 13–24). Niditch includes a chapter in which she applies her methodology to specific texts. See also Lou H. Silberman, *Orality, Aurality and Biblical Narrative* (Decatur, GA: Scholars Press, 1987). Battle reports in Judges and Samuel are seen as oral patternings

Oral communication, because it requires the face-to-face confrontation between participants, suggests a relational model of knowledge, which is manifested in the Hebrew word for knowing (יָדַע).[71] All of these characteristics assume the existence of community, for without community there is no oral discourse.[72]

The Bible, because of its historical location, must be understood first as an oral performance text.[73] Just as in other preliterate communities, 'A strong tradition of oral transmission of stories existed in early Israelite society'.[74] John Goldingay proposes that the biblical narratives are 'speech-acts'; they are 'utterances'; and 'they issue a promise, a challenge, or an invitation that opens up a future or a possible world';[75] they are oral discourse in written form. It is likely that the first biblical writings were composed under the rules of orality,[76] and only later did literate discourse become the dominant model. Jaroslav Pelikan argues that 'the prophet writes the words in the book precisely for the purpose of their being spoken words again at some future time'.[77] Therefore, models of interpretation based on linear, philosophical, and rational methods cannot do justice to the oral dimensions of the biblical text.

Numbers of scholars have recognized the deep significance of the Bible as a witness to God's speech. James Barr, for example, argues that the emphasis on God's actions has overshadowed God's speech;[78] Karl Barth asserts that the Bible is the speech of God, that it is spiritual in nature,

---

by David M. Gunn, 'Battle Report: Oral or Scribal Convention?' *JBL* 93 (1974), pp. 513–18; but not by John Van Seters, 'Oral Patterns or Literary Conventions in Biblical Narrative', *Semeia* (1976), pp. 139–54.

[71] Cf. Johns and Johns, 'Yielding to the Spirit', pp. 109–34.

[72] McLuhan, *Gutenberg Galaxy*, p. 193; and Walter J. Ong, *The Presence of the Word: Some Prolegomena for Cultural and Religious History* (Terry Lectures, Yale University; New Haven, CT: Yale University Press, 1967), p. 54.

[73] A possibility entertained by Niditch, *Oral World and Written Word*, pp. 2–5.

[74] Wessels, 'Biblical Hermeneutics', p. 262. Cf. Hermann Gunkel, *Die Israelitische Literatur* (Darmstadt: Wissenschaftliche Buchgesellshaft, 1963), p. 3.

[75] John Goldingay, *Models for Scripture* (Grand Rapids, MI: Eerdmans, 1994), p. 65.

[76] Cf. David M. Gunn, 'Narrative Patterns and Oral Tradition in Judges and Samuel', *Vetus Testamentum* 24 (1974), pp. 286–317.

[77] Jaroslav Jan Pelikan, *Whose Bible Is It?: A History of the Scriptures Through the Ages* (New York: Viking, 2005), p. 21. Pelikan includes a helpful discussion of orality and literacy (pp. 13–25).

[78] James Barr, 'Revelation through History in the Old Testament and in Modern Theology', *Int* 17 (1963), pp. 193–205; cited in Brueggemann, *Theology of the Old Testament*, p. 46. See also Pelikan, *Whose Bible Is It?: A History of the Scriptures Through the Ages*, who discusses the speech of God in his first chapter, which is entitled 'The God Who Speaks' (pp. 7–26).

and that it is personal speech;[79] and Walter Brueggemann insists that the speech of God 'is a given of the text and thus the material for theological interpretation'.[80] What Brueggemann discovers in the book of Genesis, I find also in the book of Judges:

> [T]he God of the Bible is a God who speaks, one whose speaking is so sovereign and magisterial that it functions as decree, summons, invitation, order, command, assurance, and promise... The speech of Yahweh, the God of the Bible, is the source of the world that is called to be. The speech of Yahweh is the source of Israel, through Abraham and Sarah, who are called to be. Both the world and Israel are evoked by Yahweh's sovereign word.[81]

The God whose speech in Genesis creates Israel, speaks again in Exodus to join Israel to himself in covenant, and in Judges to challenge Israel to be faithful to that covenant. By using the term 'hearing', I seek to restore to my biblical interpretation a renewed awareness of and a reinvigorated attention to the speech of God, which has a prominence in Judges, as I intend to show, that has been scarcely noticed in modern scholarship.

'Hearing' and the Orality of Pentecostalism

Early Pentecostals were mostly uneducated and they functioned primarily as an oral culture. Walter Hollenweger argues that Pentecostalism emerged out of the African-American oral context and that Pentecostal theology is primarily oral in nature.[82] Like the early Christian community, early Pentecostalism was a 'charismatic community which placed emphasis on *hearing*, not reading'.[83] 'The major mode of Pentecostal theology has been from the beginning orality, a mode which still dominates in the Two Thirds World'.[84] Preaching and teaching are still a vital element in the Pentecostal experience, and Pentecostals tend to approach Scripture

---

[79] Barth, *Church Dogmatics*, I, pp. 132–43.
[80] Brueggemann, *Theology of the Old Testament*, p. 46.
[81] Walter Brueggemann, 'Genesis', in Bernhard W. Anderson (ed.), *The Books of the Bible* (2 vols.; New York: Charles Scribner's Sons, 1989), I, p. 22. See also Walter Brueggemann, *The Prophetic Imagination* (Philadelphia: Fortress Press, 1978), p. 67, where he writes, 'the real world is the one that has its beginning and dynamic in the promising speech of God'.
[82] Walter Hollenweger, 'The Critical Tradition of Pentecostalism', *JPT* 1 (1992), pp. 7–17; Cf. also Ellington, 'Pentecostalism and the Authority of Scripture', pp. 20–26; Archer, 'Pentecostal Hermeneutical Strategy', pp. 106, 118, 119.
[83] James K.A. Smith, 'The Closing of the Book: Pentecostals, Evangelicals, and the Sacred Writings', *JPT* 11 (1997), p. 50 (emphasis Smith).
[84] Kärkkäinen, 'Pentecostal Hermeneutics in the Making', p. 79.

as if it were a spoken word from God himself.[85] As an oral culture, argues Gordon Anderson, Pentecostalism is in a position to contribute to the understanding of Scripture as oral discourse, particularly when it comes to narrative, non-propositional texts.[86]

The Pentecostal theology of Scripture insists that the Holy Spirit communicates through the written Word, and that an encounter with the Scriptures is an encounter with the presence of God through the Holy Spirit. The tension that Rickie D. Moore finds between Deuteronomy's 'law so righteous' and 'God so near' may illustrate the tension between the written word and the oral word. Although modernity tempts us to eliminate the tension between Scripture and charisma, Moore claims that we should not do so, since the tension is present within the canon itself.[87] Many Pentecostal scholars who entered the academy were required to abandon their oral culture and to adopt the modes of literacy, logic, reason, and linear thought. Those who accepted the Western Enlightenment model either (1) forsook their Pentecostal tradition entirely; (2) remained in the Pentecostal church but aligned themselves with evangelical fundamentalism as a rationalistically framed reaction against 'liberalism'; (3) separated their scholarly life from their spiritual life; or (4) adopted an elitist mentality of 'enlightened' Pentecostalism, attempting to retain a connection to the Pentecostal church, but no longer embracing the ethos of the movement.[88]

The tension between orality and literacy exists not only between confessional interpreters (such as Pentecostals) and critical approaches, but also between critical approaches and postmodern culture. Postmodernism is entering a post-literate stage,[89] an age that is literate, but because of the prevalence of electronic media is secondarily oral.[90] Because of this

---

[85] For a discussion of the oral/aural element in Pentecostal hermeneutics see Michael B. Dowd, 'Contours of a Narrative Pentecostal Theology and Practice', 15th Annual Meeting of the SPS, Gaithersburg, MD (1985). The conflict between theological education and oral community in Africa is explored in Draper, '"Less Literate are Safer": The Politics of Orality and Literacy in Biblical Interpretation', pp. 303–18. The same challenge within the African-American community is highlighted in Reid, 'Endangered Reading', pp. 476–88.

[86] Gordon L. Anderson, 'Pentecost, Scholarship, and Learning in a Postmodern World', *PNEUMA* 27 (2005), pp. 120–22.

[87] Moore, 'Canon and Charisma', pp. 78–91.

[88] This tension between literacy and orality and its bearing on the education of Pentecostal ministers is explored by Jerry Camery-Hoggatt, 'The Word of God from Living Voices: Orality and Literacy in the Pentecostal Tradition', *PNEUMA* 27 (2005), pp. 225–55.

[89] Tony Schwarz, *Media: The Second God* (New York: Random House, 1981), p. 11.

[90] Ong, *Orality and Literacy*, p. 11.

secondary orality, the post-literate age is more appreciative of narrative discourse and relational modes of knowing. This contemporary openness to non-Enlightenment models means that Pentecostals no longer are forced to choose between the academy and their heritage. Instead, they can adopt integrative models of biblical studies that engage the academy, the Church, and the postmodern world. The approach that I call 'hearing' is a way to bring together in a holistic fashion, the Pentecostal tradition of orality, the postmodern culture of post-literacy, and the oral dimensions of biblical narrative.

'Hearing' in the Biblical Context

'Hearing' as a Biblical Term

Pentecostals hold the Bible in high esteem, and they prefer to utilize biblical terminology whenever possible. In the Bible, hearing is the most frequent method of encounter with the word of God.[91] The command to 'hear' (Qal imperative of שׁמע) is found two hundred one times in the Old Testament, and all forms of the verb together are found one thousand one hundred fifty-nine times.[92] Thirty-one times the prophet declares, 'Hear the word of the Lord'. Moses called the people together and said, 'Hear (שׁמע), O Israel, the statutes and the ordinances which I speak in your hearing this day, and you shall learn them and be careful to do them' (Deut. 5.1). Joshua used a similar formula when he gathered Israel and said, 'Come and hear (שׁמע) the words of Yahweh your God' (Josh. 3.9). This prophetic formula is used by Micaiah, who said to King Ahab, 'Therefore hear (שׁמע) the word of Yahweh' (1 Kgs 22.19). Jeremiah cried out, 'Hear the word of Yahweh, O house of Jacob' (Jer. 2.4). Later, Isaiah prophesied to Hezekiah saying, 'Hear (שׁמע) the word of Yahweh' (2 Ki. 20.16). Isaiah 55.3 expands the formula, saying, 'hear, that your soul may live'. This expansion of the formula shows that שׁמע calls for more than the act of listening, because the one who hears will have life. In biblical thought, to hear is to act upon that which is heard.[93] The root שׁמע is the most

---

[91] Parts of this chapter and most of this section are dependent upon Lee Roy Martin, 'Purity, Power, and the Passion of God: A Pentecostal Hearing of the Book of Judges', *Ekklesiastikos Pharos* 87 (2005), pp. 274–300.
[92] Avraham Even-Shoshan, *A New Concordance of the Old Testament* (Jerusalem: Kiryat Sefer, Baker/Ridgefield edn, 1983), pp. 1175–81.
[93] For the meaning 'obey', cf. Brown *et al.*, *BDB*, p. 1034; Holladay, *Lexicon*, p. 423; R. Laird Harris, Gleason L. Archer, and Bruce K. Waltke, *TWOT* (2 vols.; Chicago: Moody

common Hebrew term for 'obey', and when expanded to תשמעם, it means 'obedient band, body of subjects'.[94]

Conversely, a failure to hear is a failure to obey. Those who are unwilling to obey the word of God are described in the following passages by using the verb שמע with the negative particle: Moses said to Pharaoh, 'behold, you have not yet obeyed (לא תשמע)' (Exod. 7.16). Moses warned Israel, 'if your heart turns away, and you will not hear (לא תשמע), but are drawn away to worship other gods and serve them, I declare to you this day, that you shall perish' (Deut. 30.17–18). Jehoash the king of Israel 'sent word to Amaziah king of Judah... But Amaziah would not hear (לא תשמע)' (2 Ki. 14.11). Similarly, 'Yahweh warned Israel and Judah by every prophet... But they would not hear (ולא תשמע), but were stubborn, as their fathers had been, who did not believe in Yahweh their God' (2 Ki. 17.13–14).[95] In the Old Testament, a failure to hear the word of the Lord signifies the spiritual state of stubbornness or rebellion (Ezek. 12.2; Neh. 9.17). Zechariah goes so far as to claim that the cause of the Exile is Israel's unwilling stubbornness and hardness of heart that is expressed in their refusal to hear the voice of Yahweh as spoken through the 'law' and the 'former prophets':

> Thus says Yahweh of hosts, Dispense true justice, and practice kindness and compassion each other; and do not oppress the widow or the orphan, the stranger or the poor; and do not devise evil in your hearts against one another. But they refused to *pay attention*, and turned a stubborn shoulder and closed their ears from *hearing*. And they made their hearts like flint so that they could not *hear* the law and the words which Yahweh of hosts had sent by his Spirit through the former prophets; therefore great wrath came from Yahweh of hosts. And it came about that just as he called and they would not *hear*, so they called and I would not *hear*, says Yahweh of hosts;

Press, 1980), I, p. 938; Even-Shoshan, *Concordance*, p. 1175. There is no biblical Hebrew word that is equivalent to the English 'obey'. Some form of the word 'obey' is found 109 times in the RSV, and in 103 of those the Hebrew word is שמע. The other six cases use the words שמר, עשה, עבד, and יקהה. Cf. the New Testament word ἀκούω, which means 'hear', but also include 'a clear inference of subsequent obedience'. The compound ὑπακούω even more clearly means 'to obey'. J. P. Louw and Eugene Albert Nida, *Greek-English Lexicon of the New Testament: Based on Semantic Domains* (2 vols.; New York: United Bible Societies, 2nd edn, 1989), II, pp. 467–68.

[94] Brown *et al.*, *BDB*, p. 1036.

[95] Other clear examples include Isa. 30.9 and 65.12. Cf. the New Testament word παρακούω, which means 'to refuse to listen to and hence to disobey,' Louw and Nida, *Lexicon*, II, p. 469. There are many New Testament texts calling for the hearing of God's Word that could be added to the Old Testament examples found here.

but I scattered them with a storm wind among all the nations whom they have not known (Zech. 7.8–14, emphasis showing the verb שמע).[96]

'Hearing' as Obedience and Transformation

Since the Hebrew שמע can signify hearing and obeying, it is well-suited as a paradigmatic term for the Pentecostal community that embraces a holiness tradition. We might say that the most crucial element in the study of the Bible is not the need for better understanding of the text, rather it is the need for willing obedience to the text. Gordon Fee remarks that the problem with the biblical text 'is not with understanding it, but with obeying it'.[97] Mary W. Patrick states the point another way when she insists, 'to understand a text you must first stand under the text'.[98] Marius Herholdt adds that 'interpretation only follows obedience';[99] and Brueggemann writes, 'Interpretation that seeks to let the old word be the live, authoritative word, if it is faithful to the material interpreted, must be an act of obedience'.[100]

The hearing/obedience that is called for in Scripture is more than a legalistic response produced by a sense of duty or fear of punishment (even though both of these motivations are present to a degree). The hearing of the voice of God is the hearing of faith that produces a radical affective transformation of the hearer,[101] just as Isaiah is transformed by his encounter with the living God. Unlike Isaiah himself, however, his audience will not hear; therefore, they will not be healed (transformed):

---

[96] It seems unlikely that 'former prophets' is a description of Josh.-Kings, but rather the term probably refers to the pre-exilic prophets such as Isaiah and Micah.

[97] Gordon D. Fee and Douglas K. Stuart, *How to Read the Bible for All Its Worth: A Guide to Understanding the Bible* (Grand Rapids, MI: Zondervan, 2nd edn, 1993), p. 15.

[98] Mary W. Patrick, 'Understanding "The Understanding Distance" Today: The Love command of Jesus', in L. Dale Richesin and Larry D. Bouchard (eds.), *Interpreting Disciples: Practical Theology in the Disciples of Christ* (Fort Worth, TX: Texas Christian Univ Pr, 1987), p. 102; cf. Johnson Lim Teng Kok, *Grace in the Midst of Judgment: Grappling with Genesis 1–11* (New York: Walter de Gruyter, 2002), p. 64.

[99] Herholdt, 'Pentecostal and Charismatic Hermeneutics', p. 424.

[100] Walter Brueggemann, *Interpretation and Obedience: From Faithful Reading to Faithful Living* (Minneapolis: Fortress Press, 1991), p. 1. Brueggemann's chapter entitled 'The Legitimacy of a Sectarian Hermeneutic: 2 Kings 18–19' (pp. 41–69) should encourage Pentecostals to develop their own approach to Scripture. While Brueggemann sees imagination and obedience as necessarily inseparable, Paul Ricoeur argues that revelation appeals to the imagination alone; it does not appeal to obedience. Paul Ricoeur and Lewis Seymour Mudge, *Essays on Biblical Interpretation* (Philadelphia: Fortress Press, 1980), pp. 73–117.

[101] Cf. Herholdt, 'Pentecostal and Charismatic Hermeneutics', pp. 422–23.

And he said, go, and tell this people: keep on listening, but do not perceive; keep on looking, but do not understand. Render the hearts of this people insensitive, their ears dull, and their eyes dim, lest they see with their eyes, hear with their ears, understand with their hearts, and return and be healed (Isa 6.9–10).

The word of the Lord (דבר יהוה) is more than sound waves in the atmosphere or letters on a scroll, it is an apocalyptic event that produces transformation.[102] Moses, in his farewell sermon, admits that the hearing of God's voice is terrifying, but his juxtaposition of hearing with love suggests it is also attractive. He challenges the Israelites to choose life, 'by loving the LORD your God, by hearing his voice, and by holding fast to him' (Deut. 30.20). The kind of devoted relationship expressed in this text supports Robert O. Baker's argument that the hearing of God's Word is a means of transforming and forming the affections.[103] Affective transformation is explored fully by Steven J. Land, who deconstructs the often cited oppositions of being vs. doing, and of head vs. heart, when he argues that the center of Pentecostal spirituality is the integration of orthodoxy and orthopraxy within orthopathy. Orthopathy refers to the affections that constitute the motivations and character of the believer in their relation to God. Regarding the affections, Land writes,

> Affections are neither episodic, feeling states nor individualistic sentiments...Unlike 'feelings', these affections are distinctively shaped and determined by the biblical story and evidence the marks of particular communal and historical location.[104]

A hearer of the word of God, therefore, not only will obey but will obey joyfully. A hearer of the Word not only will attend to the Torah but will 'rejoice' in it (Ps. 119.62), 'love' it (Ps. 119.97), hide it in the heart (Isa. 51.7; Ps. 119.1), and 'delight' in it day and night (Ps. 1.2). To those who love God, his Word is treasured above their necessary food (Job 23.12) and is 'more to be desired' than fine gold (Ps. 19.10).

'Hearing' and Covenant Community

Throughout the Old Testament, the challenge to hear the voice of God occurs within the relational context of covenant. While hearing the voice

---

[102] Moore, 'Canon and Charisma', p. 90.
[103] Baker, 'Pentecostal Bible Reading', pp. 34–38.
[104] Land, *Pentecostal Spirituality*, p. 44. See pp. 141–72 for a full explication of the affections and how they are formed by the Spirit, the Word, the community, and the experience of Pentecost.

of God can and must be an individual act,[105] this faithful hearing of the word of God takes place within the community of faith.[106] After the Lord established his covenant with Israel at Mount Sinai, Moses said to them, 'Hear, O, Israel, Yahweh our God is one Yahweh' (Deut. 6.4). They were to hear God's Word in light of their covenant, a covenant that formed them into a community. Biblical interpretation has functioned too often as an enterprise of the individual scholar, and Daniel Patte argues that critical scholarship should be accountable not only to the academy but also to 'those who are affected by their interpretations', that is, to the believing communities outside the academy.[107] For Patte, interpretation in the context of Christian community is a way of minimizing the 'hierarchical structure of oppression and marginalization' that places the experts in a position of superiority when deciding the legitimacy of interpretations.[108]

The Bible itself seems to suggest that hearing the voice of the text is best accomplished when the community is involved. John Christopher Thomas has discovered a model of hermeneutics that includes the faith community as an integral part of the act of reading (or hearing) Scripture.[109] Thomas observes that in Acts 15 the community gathers together to consider the relationship between Jewish law and the reception of Gentile converts. The community offers testimony and hears testimony about their experiences, which they attribute to the acts of God. Furthermore, although James is clearly the leader of the meeting, the final decision is regarded as 'coming from the community under the leadership of the Holy Spirit'.[110] Thomas concludes that the faith community 'provides the forum for serious and sensitive discussions about the acts of God and the Scripture. The community can offer balance, accountability and support. It can guard against rampant individualism and uncontrolled subjectivism'.[111] Acts 15 demonstrates that contradictory claims about what God has revealed can

---

[105] The singular form of the imperative occurs 76 times in the Hebrew Bible, while the plural is found 110 times; Even-Shoshan, *Concordance*, pp. 1179–80.

[106] Cf. Herholdt, 'Pentecostal and Charismatic Hermeneutics', pp. 422–23.

[107] Patte, *Ethics of Biblical Interpretation*, p. 30.

[108] Daniel Patte, 'Reading with Gratitude: The Mysteries of "Reading Communities Reading Scripture"', *Reading Communities, Reading Scripture* (Harrisburg, PA: Trinity Press Intl, 2002), p. 378.

[109] Thomas, 'Women, Pentecostalism and the Bible', pp. 41–56.

[110] Thomas, 'Women, Pentecostalism and the Bible', p. 49.

[111] Thomas, 'Women, Pentecostalism and the Bible', p. 55. Cf. Archer, *Pentecostal Hermeneutic*, pp. 5, 99, 145, 152, 156–92, who agrees that interpretation must be performed through the integration of text, community, and the Spirit. Recent theories of learning emphasize the importance of community. Cf. Etienne Wenger, *Communities of Practice: Learning, Meaning, and Identity* (Learning in Doing; Cambridge: Cambridge University

and do arise within the faith community and that it is the role of the community to mediate these claims by submitting to the guidance of the Holy Spirit. It should be said, however, that unity does not require uniformity. That is, while the Spirit-filled community must make every effort to provide accountability and to reach a common witness, small remaining differences must not be allowed to create divisions in fellowship.

This accountability and support serves not only as a guardian for proper interpretation, but also as a witness to the aforementioned transformative effect of the hearing of Scripture. While a hearer may lay claim to this transformation, such a subjective experience is difficult to verify; but within the relationships of the community of faith these transformations can be witnessed and confirmed by fellow believers.[112]

The role of the community in biblical interpretation is shaped partially by its theology of mission, and since the Pentecostal community is very much a missionary fellowship, obedience to the voice of God implies faithfulness to the mission of God in the world. The missional emphasis of the Pentecostal interpretation of Scripture prefers practical application above philosophical speculation.[113] Consequently, most Pentecostals seek to understand Scripture not in order to refine abstract theological ideas but in order to seize on the command of God, which in turn effectuates God's kingdom in the world.[114] They read Scripture with the expectation of a personal and corporate revelation that will then be communicated to others through the oral/aural ministries of preaching and teaching.[115] Biblical interpretation, therefore, goes hand in hand with evangelism and Christian formation.[116]

Press, 1998), pp. 72–85, who concludes that 'learning is fundamentally experiential and fundamentally social' (p. 227).

[112] The question might be asked how it can be verified that the interpreter has truly 'heard' the Word of God and has not constructed simply a clever argument. In other words, does the goal of 'hearing' really make any difference in the resultant interpretation? I would argue that deception and self-deception are always an obstacle to faithful exegesis, no matter what approach or method may be employed, but that a perceptive readership and a discerning community can detect the genuineness of the interpreter's 'hearing'.

[113] Cf. Herholdt, 'Pentecostal and Charismatic Hermeneutics', p. 430.

[114] The Pentecostal church is an eschatological missionary fellowship according to Land, *Pentecostal Spirituality*, pp. 122–81.

[115] Although Pentecostals are writing more than ever before, the oral dimensions of mission take priority over written communication.

[116] Cf. Brueggemann, *The Creative Word*, Johns and Johns, 'Yielding to the Spirit', pp. 109–34, and Cheryl Bridges Johns, *Pentecostal Formation: A Pedagogy among the Oppressed* (JPTSup, 2; Sheffield: Sheffield Academic Press, 1993).

'Hearing' and the Holy Spirit

Pentecostal theology claims that the kind of hearing that produces transformation of the affections, divine manifestation within the community and mission to the world is the kind of hearing that is a gift of God through his Spirit. In addition to utilizing historical data and linguistic evidence in biblical interpretation, Pentecostals, in every stage of biblical study, will seek for the guidance of the Holy Spirit in an attempt to hear the word of the Lord.[117] A Pentecostal hermeneutic, as Larry McQueen observed, 'embraces the critical claim of the Holy Spirit'.[118] John Christopher Thomas discovers in his aforementioned study of Acts 15 that it is the Holy Spirit who brings into creative dialogue religious experience (originating in the acts of God), the biblical text, and the discernment of the faith community, in order to form meaning.[119] Thomas writes:

> Such explicit dependence upon the Spirit in the interpretive process clearly goes far beyond the rather tame claims regarding 'illumination' which many conservatives (and Pentecostals) have often made regarding the Spirit's role in interpretation.[120]

In the historical critical method, the interpreter (through human reason) controls the interpretation,[121] but a Pentecostal prophetic interpretation cannot be controlled by the interpreter, because the God who reveals himself will do so at his own will and choosing. Thus, when taking on the attitude of a hearer, the interpreter is not passive, but neither is s/he in complete control, because 'the concentration of hermeneutical effort is on God's side, and not on human endeavor...It is God who speaks and makes his message known'.[122] According to Steven J. Land, just such an approach characterizes the perspective of early Pentecostals: 'Reason could

---

[117] A recent and helpful discussion of the role of the Holy Spirit in interpretation is Clark H. Pinnock, 'The Work of the Holy Spirit in Hermeneutics', *JPT* 2 (1993), pp. 3–23. See also, Land, *Pentecostal Spirituality*, pp. 40, 41, 71–77, 98, 100, 106, 118; and G. C. Berkouwer, *Holy Scripture* (trans. Jack B Rogers; Grand Rapids, MI: W. B. Eerdmans Pub. Co., 1975), pp. 108–115.
[118] McQueen, *Joel and the Spirit*, p. 112.
[119] Thomas, 'Women, Pentecostalism and the Bible', pp. 41–56.
[120] Thomas, 'Women, Pentecostalism and the Bible', p. 49.
[121] Cf. Paul K. Feyerabend, *Farewell to Reason* (London: Verso, 1987), p. 301; who claims that the scientific appeal to 'reason' is destructive because it discourages diversity and claims unilateral superiority over other epistemologies.
[122] Herholdt, 'Pentecostal and Charismatic Hermeneutics', p. 429.

not produce revelation, and without revelation reason did not discover what was truly important'.[123]

'Hearing' as a Theme in the Book of Judges

Not only does 'hearing' serve as a fitting term for describing the goal of Pentecostal hermeneutics, it also emerges as a vital theme within the book of Judges. The underlying cause of Israel's problems in Judges is their lack of attention to the voice of God. The Angel of Yahweh appears to Israel with a stinging rebuke: 'I said... "you shall not make a covenant with the inhabitants of this land. You shall tear down their altars". But you have not heard (שמע) my voice' (Judg. 2.2). The Israelites had renewed their covenant with Yahweh in Joshua 24.23-25: 'The people said to Joshua, "Yahweh our God we will serve, and to his voice we will hearken (שמע)". So Joshua made a covenant with the people that day'. According to the Angel of Yahweh, the people have now abandoned their promise, and no longer are they hearing the voice of Yahweh. The Israelites had vowed to hear his voice, but now their vows are broken. In refusing to hear Yahweh, they are refusing the covenant of their liberator, and they are rejecting the care of their benefactor. The charge against Israel is repeated three more times in Judges: 'They would not hear/obey the judges' (2.17a); 'They have not heard/obeyed my voice' (2.20); 'You have not heard/obeyed my voice' (6.10). In addition to the four direct accusations, the question of Israel's obedience surfaces two other times. First, they are contrasted to their faithful ancestors when Yahweh laments that Israel 'turned aside from the way walked by the ancestors, who had obeyed (שמע) the commandments of Yahweh' (2.17b). Second, the narrator of Judges declares that the remaining Canaanites 'were for the testing of Israel, to know whether Israel would obey (שמע) the commandments of Yahweh' (3.4). Furthermore, the theme of hearing is found twice in the concluding chapters of the book: The Gibeonites would not listen to reason, but were intent on executing sexual molestation (19.25); and the Benjaminites would not 'hear' the other tribes, but insisted on pursuing civil war (20.13). Throughout Judges, the Israelites refuse to hear the voice of God, and they suffer because of their stubbornness. The demand for hearing the word of God, therefore,

---

[123] Land, *Pentecostal Spirituality*, p. 105.

emerges from the biblical text as a theological concern that informs the Pentecostal hermeneutical task.

In light of the Pentecostal interpreter's aim, which is to hear the prophetic voice of God speaking through the text, some critical methods immediately become more appealing; for example, linguistic, literary, narrative, theological, and canonical approaches.[124] Approaching Judges as a Pentecostal, but armed with these critical methods, the interpreter is able to hear the voice that cries out from the prophetic text.[125]

As a result of applying my approach to the book of Judges, I perceive that the role of God (and the speech of God) has received too little attention from critical scholars. According to John Goldingay, the role of God throughout the Old Testament narratives is not appreciated by interpreters as much as it should be. He maintains that the 'interpretation of biblical stories should focus more upon God and less upon the human participants'.[126] Concerning the book of Judges in particular, I would offer several reasons why there has been so little interest in the role that God plays as a character in the narratives. First, the greater part of the book of Judges is devoted to the lives of six major characters: Ehud, Deborah, Gideon, Abimelech, Jephthah, and Samson. Therefore, many studies of Judges focus on these characters and their electrifying exploits. Second, other studies of Judges have focused on history rather than theology, and, given the modern historiographical presuppositions in play, God is not a verifiable participant in historical events. Thus, these studies have routinely depreciated and disregarded the role of God as a central character in the book because of their governing perspectives on history and culture.[127]

---

[124] On Pentecostals utilizing narrative methods, see Archer, 'Pentecostal Hermeneutical Strategy'; and Dowd, 'Narrative Pentecostal Theology'. For a description of narrative methodology, see my summary in Chapter 1. Cf. also, Alter, *The Art of Biblical Narrative*; Bal, *Narratology: Introduction to the Theory of Narrative*; Shimeon Bar-Efrat, *Narrative Art in the Bible* (JSOTSup, 70; Sheffield: Almond Press, Pbk. edn, 1989); Johannes C. de Klerk, 'Situating Biblical Narrative Studies in Literary Theory and Literary Approaches', *RTh* 4/3 (1997); Hans W. Frei, George Hunsinger, and William C. Placher, *Theology and Narrative: Selected Essays* (New York: Oxford University Press, 1993); and Gunn and Fewell, *Narrative in the Hebrew Bible*.

[125] Cf. Patrick, 'Understanding "The Understanding Distance" Today', pp. 102–103, who suggests that literary methods are more likely to produce interpretations that exhibit 'humility'.

[126] Goldingay, *Models for Interpretation of Scripture*, pp. 56–57.

[127] Cf. Moore, 'Deuteronomy and the Fire of God', p. 33, who frames this point in terms of the mutual exclusivity of the precritical and critical worldviews. Moore writes that the speech of God is regarded by critical scholars as not particularly 'noteworthy' or 'central' because it belongs to the commonplace notions of the precritical worldview.

Third, the book's sheer quantity of violence, coupled with its concentrated involvement of women characters, has attracted and dominated the attention of ideological critics from all persuasions,[128] leaving few scholars who choose to devote their energies to the study of an ancient deity.

To the Pentecostal scholar, however, Yahweh is not merely an ancient deity; he is an ever present God whose words and actions are more important than the ideologies of either ancient Israel or contemporary culture.[129] Birch states aptly:

> To read the Old Testament theologically is to recognize that when we read as people of faith within a confessional community, we are interested in more than conveying information about an ancient community. [The Old Testament] is of interest because we read as a part of communities that still seek to stand in the presence of that same God.[130]

As an apocalyptic movement, Pentecostalism sees God as the beginning and the end of all things; and it views itself as a participant in the drama of the last days.[131] It is this God-centered worldview of the Pentecostal,[132] therefore, that opens up a perspective on the primacy of God's role in the narrative and the theological implications of that role. I would suggest further, that the Pentecostal goal of hearing the word of God brings to the fore the three speeches of God in Judges (2.1–5; 6.7–10; 10.10–16), and highlights, in a way that previous scholarship has not noticed, their importance to the overall message of the book.

Conclusion

I have argued that the goal of my Pentecostal hermeneutic, which is to hear the voice of Yahweh, is both justifiable and suitable as an approach to the study of Judges. I propose that 'hearing' is an attempt to appropriate

---

[128] In the last ten years, ideological approaches have dominated the study of Judges.

[129] Cf. Herholdt, 'Pentecostal and Charismatic Hermeneutics', p. 420.

[130] Bruce C. Birch *et al.*, *A Theological Introduction to the Old Testament* (Nashville: Abingdon Press, 1999), p. 2.

[131] Cf. Land, *Pentecostal Spirituality*, pp. 58–121, who asks 'How could one truly know the significance of the past and present... without an understanding of the purpose and goal of all existence?' (p. 105); and William Faupel, *The Everlasting Gospel: The Significance of Eschatology in the Development of Pentecostal Thought* (JPTSup, 10; Sheffield: Sheffield Academic Press, 1996).

[132] For an insightful introduction to the Pentecostal worldview as God-centered, see again Johns, 'Pentecostalism', pp. 73–96. See also Anderson, 'Pentecost, Scholarship, and Learning in a Postmodern World', pp. 116–17.

the theological message of the word of God through a careful and critical (discerning) attendance to the canonical biblical text. The goal of 'hearing', though parallel in some ways to 'reading', is more descriptive of Pentecostal intentions toward biblical study. The location of Judges within the Former Prophets combined with the Pentecostal view of Scripture as divine word suggest that Judges functions not as historiography to be examined or as ideology to be evaluated but as a prophetic voice that demands to be heard. Pentecostals, by virtue of their own prophetic experience, are well equipped to hear the voice of the prophetic text. I contend further that, by their recognition and use of the terms 'hearing' and 'listening', critical scholars have demonstrated their instinctual approval of 'hearing' as an attitude toward the text. Also, even though critical scholarship has not explored fully the implications of an oral dimension to biblical study, the importance of 'hearing' the text is acknowledged tacitly by the resurgence of emphasis on divine speech as a vital element of the Old Testament concept of God.

I have shown that 'hearing' is an approach that coincides with the orality of Old Testament times, the orality of the Pentecostal church, and the secondary orality of postmodernity. It is likely that the first biblical writings were composed under the rules of orality; therefore, models of interpretation based on linear, philosophical, and rational methods cannot do justice to the oral dimensions of the biblical text. Pentecostals, because of their oral culture, are attuned to the text in ways that are foreign to modern literacy; and postmodernity, because of the new post-literacy, is more appreciate of oral modes of discourse. The approach that I call 'hearing' is a way to bring together in a holistic fashion, the Pentecostal tradition of orality, the postmodern culture of post-literacy, and the oral dimensions of biblical narrative.

The Pentecostal preference for biblical concepts over philosophical categories grants inherent authority to the goal of 'hearing', since 'hearing' is the most fundamental and most common biblical mode of encountering the word of God. The covenant community is commanded to 'hear' the word of the Lord. Furthermore, the holiness stream of Pentecostal theology is appreciative of the biblical conjunction of hearing, transformation and obedience. The 'hearing' of Judges, therefore, is a conversation between the text and the hearer in a way that acknowledges the authority of the word of God over the life of the hearer. In spite of the fact that the hearer brings a worldview, a history and theological presuppositions to the interpretive task, all of these elements may be challenged and transformed through the hearing of the word of God.

I argue further that the faithful hearing of the word of God is best accomplished within the context of the believing community and under the guidance of the Holy Spirit. The community offers accountability and support that serves both as a guardian for proper interpretation and as a witness to the transformative effect of the Scripture. The obedience and transformation that result from the hearing of God's Word are witnessed and confirmed within the community of faith. Furthermore, the kind of hearing that produces transformation of the affections, divine manifestation within the community and mission to the world is a gift of God. To form meaning, the Holy Spirit brings into creative dialogue religious experience, the biblical text, and the discernment of the faith community.

Finally, my goal of hearing the word of God finds specific correspondence in the three speeches of God in Judges (2.1–5; 6.7–10; 10.10–16), in which the Israelites are reprimanded for failing to hear the voice of Yahweh. Like the Israelites, modern biblical scholarship has failed to hear the voice of Yahweh in the book of Judges. The challenge to hear God's voice is not forced upon the text by my presuppositions and my experience; rather, it emerges from the text itself and serves as a provocation to deepen my understanding and my experience. As a Pentecostal hearer of the voice of Yahweh, I echo the cry of the Psalmist: 'Let me hear what God the LORD will speak' (Psalm 85.8).[133]

---

[133] I recently discovered that a journal article offering 'hearing' as a paradigm for hermeneutics was published soon after I had presented the first draft of this chapter at the annual meeting of the Society for Pentecostal Studies. Snodgrass, 'Reading to Hear', pp. 1–32, makes several points that parallel my own: (1) 'hearing' is the primary mode of communication in the Bible (pp. 11, 12, 23–27); (2) 'hearing' requires willing, humble attention; (pp. 28–29) and (3) 'hearing' demands obedience (p. 31). Unlike my proposal, however, Snodgrass focuses his hearing upon the original intent of the author (p. 19). His hermeneutic is rooted firmly in modernity and may be described as confessional rationalism.

CHAPTER THIRTEEN

THE WORK OF THE SPIRIT IN THE INTERPRETATION OF HOLY SCRIPTURE FROM THE PERSPECTIVE OF A CHARISMATIC BIBLICAL THEOLOGIAN*

Clark H. Pinnock**

Introduction

One would expect that Pentecostals and charismatics, given their passion for all things pneumatological, would take a keen interest in Spirit-hermeneutics. It would be only natural. More than most believers, they would be familiar with the promise and perils of doing it. Keen to hear a contemporary word of the Lord, they should approach the possibility with great expectations, while (at the same time) being wary of another possibility, the possibility of drowning in a sea of subjectivity. Apparently (however) this did not dissuade the early Christians from entertaining the idea in more than a rudimentary way. They were after all, according to the apostle Paul, 'not lacking in spiritual gifts but were enriched in Christ with speech and knowledge of every kind', including prophecy (1 Cor. 1.4–7). It sounds as if they would be very interested in what I am calling 'Spirit-hermeneutics'. They would be keen to know, not just what God said to people long ago in the scriptures, but what the Spirit is saying to the churches now. It is important to remember that Pentecostal and charismatic believers, ancient and/or modern, are people of the Spirit and not yet people of the book only.[1]

---

* First published in the *Journal of Pentecostal Theology* 18.2 (2009), pp. 157–71.
** Before his death in 2010, Clark H. Pinnock (PhD, University of Manchester) was Professor Emeritus of Theology at McMaster Divinity College, Hamilton, Ontario, Canada.
[1] Clark H. Pinnock 'The Work of the Holy Spirit in Hermeneutics', *Journal of Pentecostal Theology* 2 (1993), pp. 2–23. James K.A. Smith, 'The Closing of the Book: Pentecostals, Evangelicals, and the Sacred Writings', *Journal of Pentecostal Theology* 11 (1997), pp. 49–71.

Part One: A Rational-propositional Model

Some believers, however, shy away from Spirit-hermeneutics. The very idea of it makes them nervous because they see the text in 'cut and dried' terms and because they emphasize the Bible's rational/propositional character. This makes it awkward for them to show interest in any 'fuller' meaning of texts or in their acquisition. Any dynamism in hermeneutics could prove to be irresponsible and lead the church into uncontrolled subjectivity. Therefore, they keep Spirit-hermeneutics at arm's length despite the rich plurality of meaning that is conveyed by language.

Earlier in my own life, I did not think much about Spirit-hermeneutics because I was myself committed to scholastic habits of thinking and did not welcome exegetical liberties. I was committed to a rational-propositional model of biblical authority and more than a little suspicious of human subjectivity. I wanted no part in any possible diminishing of the objective authority of the Bible as I understood it. I was working with a model which claimed that the meaning of texts is discovered by using reason and the best scholarly tools, linguistic and otherwise. I thought that the Spirit had fulfilled his obligations to his people millennia ago through inspiration, when he delivered the Bible to the church. What else was there for the Spirit to do now, I wondered.[2]

After a decade of struggling with rational-propositionalism, I came across something more promising. Why not, instead of attempting to derive a doctrine of biblical inspiration from the 'proof texts' which are not (one has to admit) really up to the task, why not take a different tack? Why not look to the hermeneutical practices of Jesus for insight into a doctrine of Scripture, evidence which has often glossed over and neglected for so long? The fact is, that the proof texts of inspiration do not rise to the challenge. There are four such proofs.[3] The favorite text, 1 Tim. 3.15–16 (for example) is content to say that Scripture is 'inspired and profitable' and leave it at that. It says nothing about inerrancy but places the focus on the practical benefits which the scriptures offer. 2 Peter 1.20–21 tells us that the Spirit inspires prophecies. Well and good but it does not say anything about what is the case when it comes to non-prophetic verses. Nor does

---

[2] On my pilgrimage in this area, see Roy C.W. Roennfeldt, *Clark H. Pinnock on Biblical Authority: An Evolving Position* (Berrien Springs, MI: Andrews University, 1993).

[3] See B.B. Warfield, *The Inspiration and Authority of the Bible* (Philadelphia: Presbyterian and Reformed, 1948), ch. 3.

it assure us that prophecies themselves are always error free. In Jn 10.35, Jesus says that 'scripture cannot be broken', but what that entails is not explained. It likely means that Scripture is never null and void and never empty of meaning. Matthew 5.17 says that 'not a jot or tittle will pass from the law until all is fulfilled'. Yet Jesus abandoned segments of the law such as food laws, circumcision, and holy days. Jesus himself did not seem to be much bothered by 'jots and tittles'. Such thinking does not take us very far. There is another more promising way to learn about the nature of Scripture.

Part Two: The Scripture Principle

There is something else in the biblical witness to help us. I refer to the dynamic ways in which scriptures are employed by other scriptures. One sees it in Jesus' exegetical practices. No one can doubt that Jesus regarded Scripture as inspired and authoritative. Less certain though would it be that he regarded every text as equally binding and/or relevant. Consider his appeal to Isa. 61.1–2: 'The Spirit of the Lord is upon me because he has anointed me to bring good news to the poor; he has sent me to heal the brokenhearted, to preach deliverance to the captives, and recovering of sight to the blind, to set at liberty them that are bruised, to preach the acceptable year of the Lord' (Lk 4.18–19). But he omits the portion of the text that mentions any divine wrath ('the day of vengeance of our God', Isa. 61.2b).

Jesus read the text on this occasion as good news even though he was taking liberties with the scriptures. What right did he have to do that? He did it because he knew the will of God in this matter and at this time. Jesus blended the original word of Scripture with its current significance for his hearers. It was his familiar practice. In Mt. 5.38, Jesus set aside the 'tooth for a tooth' maxim in order to say that his disciples are called by God to a higher level of ethical behavior. He did not deny the text or dismiss it. It had been the word of God in times past and it has meaning for today, a much more radical meaning. Jesus took liberties when it came to Scripture. He would distinguish between the original meaning and what texts mean now. At one time, the distinction between clean and unclean foods stood, but no more. At one time, you could divorce but no more. At one time, oaths were permissible, but no more. Jesus did not see all texts as being on the same level or as having the same authority. He recognized a degree of historical relativity. He knew that texts can open up.

His critique does not diminish Scripture—it sets texts free to function as the word of God in new ways.[4]

One could say that Jesus was a certain kind of 'liberal', who broke with the approaches of his contemporaries and placed God's word and promise above mere law.[5] He set the authority of his own Spirit baptism above Jewish traditions and interpretations. Jesus worked in a climate where there were different approaches to interpretation, as there are today. There were 'techniques' in which one could expand upon a biblical narrative to bring out a subtle insight. The Qumran community employed a *midrash pesher* which concentrated on discerning the significance of some text for the present time. Such practices lead one to meaning beyond the literal in the direction of significance. Jesus does not want us merely to know the text but also to know 'what time it is' (Lk. 12.54–56). For example, his followers did not regard the laws of sacrifice as binding.

At the first church council, the delegates said, 'It seemed good to the Spirit and to us to impose on you no further burden than these essentials' (Acts 15.28–29). In so doing, they put aside a good deal of the Old Testament. Peter could say that he had not eaten anything common or unclean, but this was about to change. Paul taught that respect for holy days was a question of freedom. As for circumcision, it is was mandated in the OT but not required of gentile believers. Obviously, a sacred text which would have been binding when first given may not be valid today. Jesus and the disciples were alive to the dynamic of their texts. A word which was good in its time could be rescinded later if when it did more harm than good. He wants us to remember—'that was then and this is now'. They were alive to the dynamic nature of texts in the Bible. We today may give the text too much respect when we exalt the letter above the Spirit. The truth is that a word that was good for people in one situation may become destructive for people at other times.

Certainly the scriptures are inspired but not in the sense of their being a static deposit of revealed propositions that we can systematize and make into an idol. Scripture is not something that we control. It has a dynamic authority and is a living guide. Its proclamation is not primarily intellectual in nature either but a life transforming interaction. The purpose of the Bible (according to the Bible) is to be the power of transformation.

---

[4] Very helpful was James D.G. Dunn, 'The Authority of Scripture According to Scripture', *Churchman* 96 (1982), pp. 104–125.

[5] See 'Was Jesus a Liberal?', ch. 1 of Ernst Käsemann, *Jesus Means Freedom* (London: SCM Press, 1979), pp. 16–41. Or was he a post-conservative evangelical in the new parlance?

It serves to enrich the community and keep it on track. Literalism is not the goal either—what is essential is whether we are listening to the living word and grasping what is most crucial for the church.[6]

Part Three: Spirit-hermeneutics

It seems to me that Jesus and his disciples practiced a Spirit-hermeneutic in which God's self-revelation is presented in a dynamic fashion. Great themes are discussed over centuries and dialectically in a process of conversation and refinement which generated a rich process of interpretation and re-interpretation. The resulting truth is not 'cut and dried' but balanced and nuanced. Beginning with the Hebrew scriptures, we find a text orientated to God's future salvation. The older testament is itself an ongoing hermeneutic of the fulfillment of God's promises to Abraham and the New Testament reveals the same approach.[7] We study the text historically, not just to recover past events, but also to anticipate promises contained in those events. The stories are told and re-told because the history of God's salvation is not finished but still open. We read it with an eye on the extension of the story. We ask of Scripture, not only what past it calls us to remember, but what promises it wants us to claim and what future it wants us to work for. We should not pretend that the full meaning of the Gospel has been completely actualized. We should not be nostalgic for biblical times so much as to be sensitive to the direction in which the Gospel is moving us.

In the synoptic gospels, Jesus experienced the Spirit and was conscious of being the beloved Son of God. His intimate relationship with the Father was revealed in his 'Abba' prayers which were unlike anything in Judaism. The Father knew the Son and the Son knew the Father in unique ways. Jesus was aware of the presence and power of the Spirit on him. As we see in the exorcisms and healings Jesus had the strong sense that he was the anointed of God and that the end-time prophecies were being fulfilled in him. James Dunn writes, 'Jesus thought of himself as God's son and as one anointed by the eschatological Spirit, because he experienced God as Father and in ministry he experienced the power to heal which he could only understand as the power of the end-time and an inspiration

---

[6] Clark H. Pinnock, *The Scripture Principle: Reclaiming the Full Authority of the Bible* (Grand Rapids: Baker Academic, 2nd edn, 2006).

[7] See Pinnock, *The Scripture Principle*, ch. 8, entitled 'Unfolding Revelation'.

to proclaim a message which he could only understand as the Gospel of the end-time'.[8]

As a charismatic theologian, Jesus experienced manifestations of the Spirit such as works of power, healing, and exorcisms. His Spirit-hermeneutical practices would have grown up amidst these manifestations. Open to the Spirit and the living word, Jesus enjoyed a prophetic awareness about God's openness to the ever changing human situations to the Spirit speaking here and now. Thus, 'beginning with Moses and all the prophets, he could interpret to them the things about himself in all the scriptures' (Lk 24.7). In this context their eyes were opened and they recognized him. They said, 'Were not our hearts burning within us while he was talking to us on the road, while he was opening the scriptures to us?' (Lk 24.32).

Thinking about and reflecting upon Spirit-hermeneutics is evident in John's gospel. When it came time for Jesus to depart from this world, he said that the Spirit would come and lead the disciples into all truth. The Paraclete (he said) will teach them things which he had not been able to teach them while on earth. I think this means that the Spirit will cause everything that Jesus said and did to be seen in 'a new light'. Not that they were to expect new revelations and innovations. What the Spirit has to reveal to the church was not new doctrine and new revelation which go beyond and add to what Jesus had said. It is not said that he will lead the church into 'new' truths but into 'all' truth. The Spirit will help us see things in a new light, while bound to the definitive word of God in Jesus. The Spirit leads the church forward in history. One sees it in the apostolic declaration of Acts 15: 'It seemed good to the Holy Spirit and us' (Acts 15.28). The Spirit leads the community along a pilgrim path and guides the interactions. The Spirit leads the community to think and rethink tradition in conversation with others in the unity of the church. The experience of the presence of Christ in the community brings to their mind things that were said beforehand, giving new insight. The anointing of the Spirit dwells in all of us, creating an enriched understanding of God's word (1 Jn 2.20). It is important to remember that the Spirit will bind himself to the saving action of God in Jesus Christ.

---

[8] James D.G. Dunn, *Jesus and the Spirit* (London: SCM, 1975), p. 27. Compare Richard N. Longenecker, 'Can We Reproduce the Exegesis of the New Testament?' *Tyndale Bulletin* 21 (1970), pp. 3–38.

The apostle Paul also sheds light on Spirit hermeneutics. It arises out of his teachings about the various gifts of the Spirit that are at work in all believers and therefore in their interpretive labors. Paul offers this text: 'God gives us a spirit of wisdom and revelation in the knowledge of him' and 'the Spirit enlightens the eyes of our hearts so that we may know what is the hope to which he has called us' (Eph 1.17). God also gives us guidance and firm convictions regarding the word of God. It is not, however, a liberty that is without 'checks and balances. The gifted community itself and its leadership does a lot to prevent the church going 'off the rails'. Spirit-hermeneutics, although it can be abused and misused, should be practiced nevertheless, because of the rich possibilities which it holds out for our mission.

Part Four: The Revelatory Text

Thus far, I have presented Spirit-hermeneutics as it may have been practiced in the beginnings of Christianity, as presented in the New Testament. Let us now consider how it can be practiced fruitfully today. The key point to remember is to recognize the richness of language which makes it such an excellent instrument for God to use when communicating with humans.[9]

Language has qualities which make it an ideal instrument at the Spirit's disposal. Texts have a way of opening up and they invite playful interaction. Even more so in dialogue, there is much to mull over. The Spirit loves to work with Scripture, which has qualities that make possible a ministry of the Spirit. The Pilgrim preacher John Robinson remarked that there is always 'more light to break forth from' God's word.[10] Classic texts in particular are well-nigh inexhaustible sources of insight. Texts create space and make room for Scripture which in turn make room for God to speak by the Spirit. Spirit-hermeneutics is a strategy of reading Scripture in such a way that the Spirit has liberty to speak. As a result we are grasped by the revelatory text which transforms.[11]

---

[9] On human communication, see Mortimer Adler, *The Difference of Man and the Difference it Makes* (New York: Holt, Rinehart, and Winston, 1967).
[10] Cited by Jack Bartlett Rogers, *Presbyterian Creeds: A Guide to the Book of Confessions* (Philadelphia: Westminster Press, 1st edn, 1985), p. 230.
[11] Joel B. Green, *Seized by Truth* (Nashville: Abingdon, 2007).

Language can move us and grip us profoundly. If you read a book like Elie Wiesel's *Night*, you will be hopelessly drawn in because such books deal with important issues.[12] One gets involved in them and wants to engage the material. One is not particularly interested in the historical details or the literary techniques of the writer. Rather, we are gripped by the big life issues. We may enjoy an existential encounter with the material and experience transformation. We are engaged by the experience. The text becomes an instrument of revelation. Texts change us through personal engagement. Texts have the power to free the interpreter for new life. The text can open up for all it was meant to be. Effective interpretation has an 'event character' that can shake us and move us. As Scripture says, 'The word of God is living and active, sharper than any two edged sword, piercing until it divides soul and spirit, joints from marrow. It is able to judge the thoughts and intentions of the heart' (Heb. 4.12).

There is some similarity between the way science works and the way theology works. Often the scientist begins with an intense engagement with some puzzle which needs resolving. Sometimes it just does not want to yield. So one puts it aside and goes to work on something else. Then 'the penny drops' and our eyes are opened. The solution resolves itself spontaneously and unbidden. Is it a gift from the unconscious mind, a God-given creative moment. The Spirit can ensure that interpretations are effective. A 'dead letter' is not what is needed. We need a revelatory text which can be a power in our lives. Exegesis is important, even indispensable, for working on the text-horizon but grasping the text's significance is another matter. We need to be *seized* by the text. We need to have eyes to see and ears to hear and open hearts. God wants us to recognize his word for today through the Spirit who searches the depths of God (1 Cor. 2.10–16). God wants us to know the gifts that are freely given to us by God. God wants us to have the mind of Christ in our work (1 Cor. 2.16). The Spirit takes the things of Christ and make them known to us. He plays the pivotal role in making the text God's revelatory word. The Spirit makes the knowledge of God a possibility in and through an 'I-Thou' encounter. Just as the human spirit enables us to have self knowledge, so the divine Spirit enables us to comprehend God's truth.[13]

---

[12] Elie Wiesel, *Night* (New York: Bantam, 1982).

[13] Graham A. Cole, *He Who Gives Life: The Doctrine of the Holy Spirit* (Wheaton, IL: Crossway Books, 2007), pp. 259–77.

In Spirit-hermeneutics, I believe that the breath of God which inspired the prophets and apostles binds himself to their words and opens up the significance. Anchored in the canon of Scripture, the Spirit opens up what is written in a kind of 'controlled liberty'. A liberty that honors both the original meaning and the text which needs to be opened up. The Spirit fuses the past and present horizons. One mark of the church is its apostolicity. The church is established on the testimony of the apostles and prophets and is bound to its unique testimony as valid for all time and not rendered invalid by later testimony. This is the norm by which the church ought to measure itself. When the Spirit opens up the text, one assumes that it will be coherent with the apostolic witness. This is an important check. One assumes that what Christ says today will not contradict what his witnesses have said beforehand in Scripture. Some matters need to be made more explicit and developed, and in this way go beyond the text. True orthodoxy is not content to live in the past and ignore a fresh word from God. When we invite the Spirit to help in the interpretive process, we surrender some of our own autonomy as readers and acknowledge our dependency on the Holy Spirit.

The scriptures lend themselves to dynamic interpretation because, unlike the Koran, the Bible is a record of a developing historical revelation. Thus it is very open to diverse readings and it creates a surplus of meaning. Out of it come treasures old and new. There is a dynamic in the text which promotes endless reflection.[14] Texts of the Bible do have definite meanings in the historical situation and that meaning is the anchor of our interpretation. But the 'total' meaning cannot be restricted to that. Texts can carry implied meanings too, but they cannot mean just anything we want. Some interpretations are more plausible than others. The field is not without boundaries. Because we respect the text, we permit it to establish the range of possible meanings, and we are open to richer and deeper interpretations.

Because of their form and structure, scriptures lend themselves to dynamic interpretation. They get caught up in a dynamic reading in which the truth can develop and deepen over time. The Bible is more like a wind tunnel than a pile of bricks and more like an orchestra than a

---

[14] Sandra M. Schneiders, *The Revelatory Text: Interpreting the New Testament as Sacred Scripture* (Collegeville, MN: Liturgical Press, 2nd edn, 1999), pp. 157–79. The diversity of Scripture creates space for a creative diversity of interpretation and fresh perspectives: e.g. the reconsideration of Paul in relation to the Roman Empire or the never ending quest for the historical Jesus.

solo instrument. Scripture is an inexhaustible resource for the community because of its development of themes and the fecundity of interpretations. Scripture is at the disposal of the Spirit for new and subtle uses. It creates room for the Spirit to open up the divine plan and place it in new situations as they arise. With good reason we read the Bible with the positive hope of finding 'treasures old and new' in it.

Part Five: Opening up the Scriptures

Texts are very remarkable, especially classic texts. They can transcend themselves and open up to richly textured and diverse interpretations. As a result, they can come to 'mean more' than was originally intended. They can achieve a fuller sense and a deeper meaning, intended by God, but not clearly expressed by a human author. Often the existence of a fuller sense is revealed when one studies a text in the light of other texts. Matthew, for example, could see a deeper purpose in the words which God spoke through Isa. 7.14 than the prophet realized himself. Similarly, later teaching may reveal a more precise conception of a matter.[15]

Consider the gradual expansion of meaning of the affirmation over centuries contained in the American Declaration of Independence that 'all men are created equal'. Originally, the doctrine applied to adult, white, property-owning males; whereas nowadays it is taken to include all people. The interaction between the surplus of meaning and its effective history was such that the text 'All men are created equal' generated a larger meaning. The historical experience of the new nation gradually 'revealed' to Americans the humanity of all people, including slaves and women. It illustrates how texts are not imprisoned in the past but can have direction and power. They may not only call us to remember past events but to anticipate future events. The Jesus story is not finished yet but is still open. The power of the story is still at work, even though it may still be incomplete now as to its full realization. The Spirit can help us be sensitive to the direction in which things are moving and we can be free from a nostalgia for 'New Testament times'. It can even happen that a text can be used as an instrument of oppression or instrument of liberation. Reading the Bible historically is more than just remembering past events. We also read it in order to anticipate the promises contain in the texts. No event

---

[15] Cf. 'The Fuller Sense', ch. 14 in Peter S. Williamson, *Catholic Principles for Interpreting Scripture* (Rome: Pontificio Instituto Biblico, 2004).

can be understood apart from the future which it may engender. Let us learn to read the Bible with an eye on the extension of the story of salvation into our time and beyond it. After all, truth was not was not fully realized in New Testament times.

The place of women's ministries in church, for example, had not yet been resolved but it is surely being resolved. On one level, God's people are aware of Jesus' openness to women and of Paul's magna charter of liberty in Jesus Christ (Gal. 3.28). On another level, we need to be sensitive to the direction in which God is moving us forward. What can be hoped for in this matter? Scriptures are not imprisoned in the past. We are not antiquarians. We need to tune our ears to hear God speak a word to us. As we keep our eyes open to the extension of the story of God's liberating activity, let us ask ourselves what past God is calling us to remember and what future God is calling us to work toward. We must remember that the total meaning of salvation in Jesus Christ was not fully actualized in the early church. Let us be sensitive to the directions in which redemptive history is moving. The meaning of texts is not limited to the meaning intended by the authors.

Texts have a surplus of meaning that interacts with the historical consciousness of contemporary persons. Most of us, partly because of our Christian formation, can see now the moral unacceptability of patriarchalism, slavery, anti-semitism, and such like. We create a dialogue between the textual horizon and the contemporary horizon from which meaning arises. The dialogue itself is never ending because of the text's surplus of meaning which enables it to generate an effective history in interaction with the historical consciousness of the community. Such dialogues should be pursued with relentless love by those who believe that this Bible text, thoroughly human as it is can mediate an encounter between God and humanity.

The Bible can be thought of as a series of love letters. Just think of it. A person, lost in love, is transformed by them and cannot begin to grasp all that is involved. Lovers need to get to know each other. Love unfolds over time. Love cannot be grasped all at once. What we need from the Spirit is to have light cast upon the journey. We all need the Spirit's leading of his people in their pilgrimage to help them to walk worthy of the Gospel. Their history is going to be a dynamic process. God help us if we cannot get any new light on the journey. It is not primarily an intellectual problem. We are really asking the Lord what to do next. In a post-9/11 world, is the Spirit sending us to war against global jihadism? Does he want us to honor the gifts of believing women more? How about homosexuality? How should we respond to that? I believe that insight is forthcoming on such issues, a consensus forming insight, we hope, and a *sensus fidelium*.[16]

Part Six: Criteria of Valid Interpretation

How do we know when we have interpreted the Bible well? How do we know that we have attained genuine meaning? I am not talking about attaining 'the' right meaning, because there is no one and only possible meaning. There are levels of meaning and not a single one. Multiple interpretations are not only possible, but inevitable, owing to the fluid nature of texts. There are many possible interpretations although not all of them are equally valid. Some are better than others. Interpretation involves testing and discerning.

The criterion of 'fruitfulness' helps with testing and discernment. Fruitful interpretation is something that lets the text speak and lights up the faith of the community. A good interpretation energizes disciples and launches them into self-sacrificing behavior. They tell us that something good is happening. They prove themselves. A reading should be able first to account for the text as it stands and ought to be able second to put the truth 'into play' in the form of transformed living. Good interpretation is very often a matter of being moved by love to act.

Are there any safeguards with Spirit-hermeneutics? There are some. The best safeguard is the authority of the charismatic community. We are all members of a Spirit-community and not merely individualists. Every one of us has responsibility for the common life. All are called to teach, admonish, and judge. Thus, the community as a whole is 'taught by God' (1 Thess. 4.9). All enjoy a spontaneous understanding of the word of the Lord. Some can discern and evaluate prophecies well and can interpret glossolalic speech. The main point is this—believers are not left to themselves. God's gifts include their own safeguards as when a teaching trumps a prophecy. Even when few 'lay' people are theologically trained, the *sensus fidelium* works rather well. Mature believers can often spot a false apostle miles away. Then there is apostolic authority in the community by which I mean people who may have founded the church and who can speak with authority and protect the community when it comes under

---

[16] Willard M. Swartley, *Slavery, Sabbath, War and Women: Core Issues in Biblical Interpretation* (Scottdale, PA: Herald Press, 1983).

threat. There are prophets and apostles and teachers in the churches and such leaders would have commanded respect. Leaders exercise godly control and can spare the congregation grief.[17]

In the year ad 1905 in Los Angeles, we experienced a huge interpretive event that has shaken the faith from top to bottom. It has moved across the world, ever growing in strength and maturity. In that year, a 'new hermeneutic' was born. Based upon the theology of St. Luke, it has unleashed the power of Pentecost for mission. It would not be an exaggeration to say that the Pentecostal movement is the most important event in church history until now, characterized by impulses of power, tongues of fire, fearless witnessing, extraordinary praise, and boldness of witness. What was it if it was not the witness of St. Luke igniting again? We read, 'You shall receive power when the Holy Spirit has come upon you, and you will be my witnesses in Jerusalem, in all Judea and Samaria, and to the ends of the earth' (Acts 1.8). More than a reformation, it was revolution within Christianity and a time of God's incredible visitation (Lk. 19.44). Did the scriptures not come alive in new ways on that occasion?

Final Thoughts

(1) The central message of Christianity is the epic story of redemption. This explains why much of our Scripture, if not the bulk of it, takes the form of narrative. The Bible is not a book of concepts but a grand meta-narrative. Narrative was needed if God is to be properly identified as a living and personal agent. God is the God of history not the God of philosophy. On the Feast of Pentecost, Peter recalled what God had promised his people by the prophet Joel and explained what was going on in front of the listening crowd. He could give meaning to the wonderful deeds which were happening among the people. Peter was opening up Israel's story and inviting everyone to make the story their own.

(2) It belongs to the nature of stories that they engage and change us. Stories, like life itself, have a beginning, a middle, and an end. We identify with the characters and are drawn in. Stories are important. They provide the meaning of our lives. Christians in particular have

---

[17] Catholics enjoy a huge safeguard in the office of the magisterium and the papal office. On the one hand, it meets the need to fend off error; on the other hand, it concentrates enormous power in hands of a few. Some times though, I feel a tinge of jealousy.

a story—how we lived apart from Christ and how we were saved and how we appropriated Israel's grand narrative. We have a story to tell to the nations, a story that sets sinners free. They need to hear our story because there are few hopeful and redemptive narratives out there in the world. Alas, there are many stories that confuse and destroy. Without telling our story, re-lived in our time, the survival of the churches will be placed in peril amidst the competing and corrosive forces of the contemporary world. The resources of Scripture help us recover and maintain our identity. Telling the story is not only important—it is absolutely essential for the life of the community and for the salvation of the world.[18]

(3) We cannot understand the bare words of scriptures unless we understand the realities that are behind them. The Spirit bears unique testimony to the living God as revealed in Jesus Christ. Readers get caught up and get lost in the text and are changed. Scripture is less the demand to submit to God than it is an invitation to indwell the narrative of God's grace. The task is not an attempt to adapt the words of Scripture to our reality but an invitation to make sense of our reality within its purview of new creation. The reader, by means of interpretation, enters into and appropriates the world of meaning that the text projects. The text creates a space into which the reader is being invited for transformation.

(4) The best readers of the Bible are those who let themselves be shaped by the text. As we grow in the Spirit, our capacity to understand deep realities will grow too. Scripture is given to 'form' us as much as it is to 'inform' us. It equips God's people to carry God's plans forward his purposes, which it does by drawing us into the grand story. The scriptures promote God's new creation in the world. They are a means of grace to that end. By means of them the community is challenged to be God's agents in the world. Scripture is primarily God's instrument of sanctification and discipleship. It is about following Jesus. The purpose of interpretation is the edification of believers and the discovery of God's word for humanity. The Spirit is the agent of sanctification using Scripture to that end and in the context of the community. Scripture is about 'performing' the word of God and putting it into

---

[18] Frank D. Macchia, *Baptised in the Spirit: A Global Pentecostal Theology* (Grand Rapids: Zondervan, 2006), pp. 244–47.

practice. To become familiar with the story means living in the world of the story and living it out in the world. We are becoming vessels of the living word in the world around us. Reading the Bible as narrative Scripture, we consent to be taken on a journey of Christian formation. We wish to be shaped and formed through the reading. On the one hand, we discern God's purposes better; and on the other hand, we learn more of God's character. Scripture is meant to shape us in the midst of the church.

(5) The Scriptures are inspired but not in the sense of their being a static deposit of revealed truth that we can systematize into idols of ink and paper. The fundamentalist tendency is to encourage people to believe that they have the final and last word on everything. In actual fact we are to interact with others and learn to grow and to change in dialogue and not to pontificate. Scripture is meant to be embraced as a living witness to Jesus Christ, granting us ongoing wisdom and power to serve one another and the world in Christ's name. As breathed by the Spirit, Scripture is a living guide and measure of our walk with God. Within the charismatic structure of the church, the Spirit functions through the scriptures as a living book of both freedom and order to guide our gracious interactions with one another and our mission in the world. Scriptures themselves are a universally relevant and binding gift of the Spirit to the church in order to direct the particular and diverse charismata in its own going life and mission.

(6) The divine witness to us is not at our disposal, a deposit to be mastered and placed at the behest of our systems. We do not control it. The text is living and active and we do not control it. God's wisdom is ever at work in the community. Without it, preaching becomes an intellectual exercise instead of a life transforming dialogue. The purpose of biblical interpretation is to discover God's purpose and will for humanity and the edification of God's people. Interpretation stands in the service of obedience and worship. It calls us to walk humbly with God and depends on the vision and power of the Spirit of God. Though methods of interpretation are important, no precise set of rules can be rigidly formulated or followed. This freedom arising from the Spirit should not be taken however as an excuse for self-justifying tendencies or laziness in study and exegesis. Biblical interpretation is not a private enterprise. It is not the domain of either the individual or scholar. It needs to be tested and validated by communities of faith and tested by other communities. The interpreter should look to the

community of faith not to the society as a whole as we seek to carry out the teachings and the ethical vision of the Bible.[19]

(7) Learning to interpret the Bible is like learning to paint or learning to drive. There are procedures and steps to follow. But the principles will need to become operative on a pre-conscious level and need to become second nature to us. That comes from reading the Bible in the community and from putting its truth into action.

---

[19] Donald W. Dayton, 'The Pietist Theological Critique of Biblical Inerrancy', in Vincent Bacote, Dennis L. Okholm, and Laura C. Miguélez (eds.), *Evangelicals and Scripture: Tradition, Authority and Hermeneutics* (Downers Grove, IL: InterVarsity Press, 2004), pp. 76–89.

CHAPTER FOURTEEN

WHAT DOES IT MEAN TO READ THE BIBLE AS A PENTECOSTAL?*

Andrew Davies**

I. *Introduction*

I have friends who have a plaque on their wall which I, being of Cambrian descent, have long admired. It reads: 'To be born Welsh is to be born privileged; not with a silver spoon in your mouth but with music in your heart and poetry in your soul'. Those inspirational words have for me always reflected not only my Celtic ancestry but also my Pentecostal heritage. Pentecostalism was born, if not quite in the gutter, then perhaps not too far above it. Historically it has been a religion of the people, a faith of the underclass, and to this day, certainly in the UK but also in many other corners of the globe, the classic Pentecostal groupings share little of the prestige and wealth of some of the historic denominations.[1] Yet the

---

* First published in the *Journal of Pentecostal Theology* 18.2 (2009), pp. 216–29.
** Andrew Davies (PhD, University of Sheffield) is Senior Lecturer in Intercultural Theology and Pentecostal Studies and Director of Undergraduate Studies in Theology and Religion at the University of Birmingham, UK.
[1] I should emphasise at the outset that the following observations arise from my reflection on the handling of Scripture in the British Pentecostal churches, and that increasing transatlantic experience is teaching me that, for all our similarities, there are significant and substantial differences between the cultures of Assemblies of God in the UK and the USA in this and many other regards. For instance, whilst I have heard American colleagues bemoan the lack of commitment to education that they sometimes feel handicaps their ministers, the US does now have an established and burgeoning academic tradition in the sphere of Pentecostalism, as the meeting of the Society for Pentecostal Studies demonstrates. Though the recent Research Assessment Exercise in the UK (published December 2008) highlighted Pentecostal and Charismatic Studies as an area of significant growth and development within British theological research over the last five years, still academic study of the Pentecostal movement in the UK is focussed essentially on the lifework of a few major scholars working out of really just two or three major centres, with a little support from the Bible and theological colleges. Standards of education and training in the ministry of AoG UK have been, for many years and by objective measure, the lowest required by any sizeable denomination or network in the British Isles (at least until a new training system was introduced during the last calendar year). It is important to note, therefore, that most of our ministers have had no professional training in exegetical methods and hermeneutics and essentially most frequently read the Bible without subjecting either the text or their reading of it to critical analysis. Also it is important to note that

movement more than compensates for any lack in that area in its 'music' and its 'poetry', the fire and passion that are evident in the way Pentecostals go about every aspect of their spiritual lives—be it mission and evangelism, music and worship, preaching and proclamation, or prayer and prophecy.

But Pentecostal fires never burn more fervently than when they encounter the kindling of the biblical text. When Walter Hollenweger famously dedicated his great study 'The Pentecostals' to the Pentecostals who taught him to love the Bible, and the Presbyterians who taught him to understand it, he was undoubtedly right to note the deep and passionate commitment to the scriptures which Pentecostals have always had (if perhaps a little unfair to us by insinuation in the second part of the inscription).[2] In fact I would suggest that we Pentecostals have always considered ourselves to have something of a special relationship with the sacred page, almost as if we have a unique affinity with the Bible and hold a significant position among the guardians of its truth.[3] Perhaps more than any other Christian tradition, we have sought to identify our own experiences with those of the earliest church, described in detail in what we recognise as the historical narrative of the Acts of the Apostles, and we have believed, prayed and worked in the Spirit's power that we might see our own worlds turned upside down just as first century Palestine was. 'This is that which was spoken by the prophet' has become our rallying cry as we have sought to see the biblical text reworked and re-enacted in our lives and churches today.[4]

---

there is no British tradition of academic use of the text from a distinctively Pentecostal perspective at all. That alone results in a major difference of opinion and culture between the UK and North America in the field of Pentecostal biblical interpretation.

[2] Dedication to Walter J. Hollenweger, *The Pentecostals* (London: SCM, 1972), p. xvi. Hollenweger's little apothegm might be taken as something of a slight upon the Pentecostal academic tradition. If that was his intention then perhaps it was always slightly unfair, and nearly forty years on it seems completely unreasonable. North American Pentecostal theologians in particular now carry considerable sway and influence in broader circles (take the recent cooperation between the SPS and the SBL, for instance) and have taken many helpful new insights to the bigger table, though the fact of our movement's historic aversion to the academy remains, and its effects are still felt in much of the world today. Even in the UK, there is evidence of an embryonic academic tradition developing among the Pentecostal colleges, which to my mind bodes well for our future as a movement.

[3] Hollenweger argued, for instance, 'The critics of the Pentecostal movement who accuse it of neglecting the written word in favour of individual illuminations by the Spirit are ignorant of the role which the Bible plays in the Pentecostal movement. Pentecostals live with the Bible. They read it every day and know many passages by heart...Many of them hardly read any books apart from the Bible' (*The Pentecostals*, pp. 321–22).

[4] An observation that is mirrored by that of Kenneth J. Archer, *A Pentecostal Hermeneutic for the Twenty-First Century: Spirit, Scripture & Community* (Cleveland, TN: CPT

Reading the Bible, then, whether it be in public or private worship, is and should be a priority for every Pentecostal believer. In the UK at least, the tradition of reading as a Pentecostal is almost exclusively a devotional one.[5] We do not yet have a formal Pentecostal academic tradition (and it might be argued that in Britain there are a number of sociocultural and educational factors which combine to make it highly unlikely that such a tradition could develop to anything like the same extent as it has done in North America). So it is not Pentecostal approaches to the academic discipline of hermeneutics which I wish to address in this discussion, but our everyday practice of reading Scripture—what Pentecostals feel, do, think and say when we have the Bible in our hands.[6] This is still a developing field of study, as any literature search will highlight, but it is not difficult for any Pentecostal to write in such a field out of experience, because I am talking about something that we do routinely, day in and day out. Perhaps, as Keith Warrington has highlighted,[7] there has been a decreasing emphasis on the function of the Bible in public worship for us in the UK, and if the Bible Society's research is to be trusted then it is clear that not as many Christians in general spend as much time reading the Bible as we like to think they would, but it is still true to say that both corporate and private Bible reading and study remain fundamental to our spirituality and are presented as priorities.[8]

Let me begin with some comments on how I believe we feel about the Bible before turning to the more practical concerns.

II. *Philosophical Issues*

What are we Pentecostals seeking to do when we read the Bible? What do we want or expect to happen? Fundamentally, I think, it is not about knowledge, nor should it ever be. Ordinarily Pentecostals read the Bible not to learn of the history of Israel, the development of the earliest Christian

---

Press, 2009), p. 87: 'Pentecostalism's lived experience was coloring their understanding of Scripture and Scripture was shaping their lived experiences' (in discussing the early Pentecostals).

[5] I include the use of the Bible in preaching as devotional here.

[6] I hesitate to label the devotional usage of Scripture as hermeneutical, lest it be seen to imply rather more coherency and strategy than really exists in the process.

[7] Keith Warrington, *Pentecostals and the Bible* (European Pentecostal Charismatic Research Conference, University of Uppsala [September 2007]), p. 29.

[8] See for instance the society's report 'Taking the Pulse: Is the Bible alive and well in the Church today?' of February 2008, available at http://www.biblesociety.org.uk/l3.php?id=209 [accessed January 2009].

theology or even of the life of Christ, but to meet God in the text, and to provide an opportunity for the Holy Spirit to speak to our spirits. This is generally true of our preaching too. Tim Cargal is right to observe that 'most pastors of Pentecostal churches continue to employ a pre-critical, and indeed in some senses a fundamentalist, hermeneutic within their sermons and the Bible instruction of their Christian education programs'.[9] I certainly observed this tendency when teaching homiletics to first year students at Mattersey![10] Within our tradition, the reading, interpretation and proclamation of Scripture have little to do with intellectual comprehension and all to do with divine self-revelation.

That means that we do not have to understand all we read for such an encounter with the deity to take place. In fact, I am not at all sure that Pentecostals should lay claim to anything that could be called a full understanding of the Bible, or even particularly think it desirable. Explain it, preach it, study it, sure. But hardly *understand* it, for that might mean grasping it, containing it, knowing it, and that might imply an attempt at grasping, containing and knowing the God it reveals, and thereby, in some measure at least, seeking to control and restrict him and his actions in the world and in our lives, to define him out of dangerousness. I do not think we could ever endure such a boxed and prepackaged deity; Pentecostalism requires a God on the loose, involving himself with the fine details of our earthly existence and actively transforming lives. I think Pentecostal theology, in both its systematic and more popular forms, requires a degree of uncertainty.

That might be thought a strange claim to make. Our proclamation, of course, can be incredibly confident and assured. Pentecostals are not

---

[9] T. Cargal, 'Beyond the Fundamentalist-Modernist Controversy: Pentecostals and Hermeneutics in a Postmodern Age', *Pneuma* 15.2 (Fall 1993), pp. 163–87 (170). Cargal also notes, however, that many Pentecostal academics have ongoing involvement in local church ministry—this is certainly true in the UK as well (cf. p. 171).

[10] It is, however, somewhat disconcerting that such a disjunction between church and academy in this area has been allowed to develop. Cf. Veli-Matti Kärkkäinen, 'Authority, Revelation, and Interpretation in the Roman Catholic-Pentecostal Dialogue' (*Pneuma* 21.1 [Spring 1999], pp. 89–114 [97–98]), who ascribes the 'growing divergence in the practice of biblical interpretation between Pentecostals in the parish and in the academy' largely to the adoption, for good or ill, of the historical-critical method by Pentecostal biblical scholars. Though this was perhaps inevitable and probably necessary for the wider acceptance of our community at the academic table, it was also of questionable desirability. Certainly I would argue that whilst the methods of traditional biblical scholarship still serve a useful purpose, it is time for the discipline to move away from questions of historical context and authorial intent, and a new distinctively Pentecostal hermeneutic could well contribute to this process.

known for being shrinking violets. Our fourfold gospel has never been that Jesus might be able to save us, would like us to consider receiving the baptism in the Spirit, will see what he can do to heal us and may consider returning at some stage. It announces who Jesus is, what he does, and that he does it every time (and that he will do it for you tonight before you leave this meeting if you will only permit him). When Pentecostals bring our shared experience to the text, we find the confidence we need support our faith from Scripture, and we have no doubts as to what we see there. If our experience has yet to match the model of biblical perfection, then on the whole we smile sweetly, consider ourselves a work of grace still in process, and believe to see that experience brought in line with the teaching of the Bible in God's good time.

But it is precisely our faith and certainty against all the odds which causes us problems. Why 'God's good time' is not now is in itself just one of the puzzles that we encounter daily. Our experience of that God and his indwelling Spirit has taught us something of the mystery of Godliness. We are confronted with practical theological challenges that do not afflict our sisters and brothers in other groups in quite the same way. We, arguably more than any other Christian tradition, struggle with how those we lay hands on are not always healed even though our Lord Jesus himself promised us they would be (Mk 16.18). We appreciate that praying with our understanding has its deficiencies and inadequacies and our most heartfelt intercessions arise in the 'sighs too deep for words' (Rom. 8.26, NRSV) of the Holy Spirit within us. The words we speak in other languages under divine inspiration need to be interpreted before even the speaker can understand them. And, most significantly, if sadly a little theoretically in many contexts, we operate our gatherings for worship on the assumption that God can, and will, do exactly what he wants exactly as he wants, and reject formal liturgical structure to provide him that opportunity. A meeting can never be truly Pentecostal unless he chooses to intervene; yet he does so on his own terms and not simply in response to any invocation or summoning ritual on our part. For all our apparent dogmatism, it seems to me that in reality, the unknowable and unfathomable are at the very heart of our religious experience. Indeed it might be argued that, in common with our heritage in the epic mystical traditions of Christianity, Pentecostals are hesitant to claim to encounter the Godhead in the comprehensible. It is almost as if we believe as a matter of course that our God is so far above and beyond our grasp that anything we can assimilate intellectually cannot be from him. As a result, we should and do seek to approach and read the text with an unremitting humility which confounds and yet inspires the profound certainty with which we expound it corporately.

Our common heritage, then, has taught us the miracle and the mystery of personal experience of God's presence, experienced and mediated through the biblical text among other ways, and, therefore, the value of knowing by perception over knowing by proof. As a result we prefer to interpret Scripture by encounter more than exegesis. So we read 1 Corinthians not to learn of some of the challenges Paul faced through his apostolic ministry and mission, or even particularly to better grasp the workings of the Holy Spirit through his gifts; but so that we might be inspired to fulfil our function in the Body of Christ; and, even more elementally, so that we might allow God the Spirit to say to us whatever he might want out of the words on the page. If he should choose to rearrange them into different concepts and reapply them into different contexts as he impresses them on to our spirits, then that is perfectly fine by us, and certainly not an infrequent occurrence in the experience of millions of Spirit-filled believers throughout the world as well as in my own. Pentecostals read the Bible as dialogue partners with it and with the inspiring Spirit; we bring our own questions, circumstances and needs to the text, and through it to the Lord, and allow him to bring his own agenda about as he speaks to us. There is therefore little interest for us as spiritualising readers in the surface meaning of the text, and scant attention paid to the original intention of the author. Rather we seek to push behind the plain sense of the text to experience what Aquinas would have labelled its *anagogic* power, its capacity to edify and inspire. Are Pentecostals alone in adopting such an approach as this? Probably not; but I do think that to default instinctively to the method in such a way and prioritise it to such an extent is typical of our tradition to the extent that it might be considered a distinctive.

Clearly such a model is open to criticism. It will be considered subjectivist, experiential, self centred even; but then is there really any other kind of reading? Anthony Thiselton, hardly the doyen of radical liberalism, critiques forcefully the mindset of those who 'seek to silence their own subjectivity, striving for the kind of objective neutrality which is...an illusion'.[11] Objections have been raised to this perspective from within the Pentecostal academic community itself, though I have to say I find the

---

[11] Anthony C. Thiselton, 'The New Hermeneutic', in I.H. Marshall (ed.), *New Testament Interpretation* (Grand Rapids, MI: Eerdmans, 1977), p. 316.

work I have read from this perspective both unnecessarily defensive and singularly unconvincing. We need to reassert our confidence in an ideological approach to reading the biblical text, and acknowledge without shame the plain fact that our distinctive preconceptions invite us to a distinctive appropriation of the text—and that our readings are worth hearing by others. Here, as well, we start to find ourselves in interesting territory, for if we relate these concepts to the academic context it becomes apparent that we have rather more in common methodologically with the liberal progressive wing of biblical scholarship than the traditional evangelicals.[12] To me this can only be a good thing, for I consider that far and away the most interesting work being done in contemporary biblical scholarship is in non-traditional fields. It seems to me Pentecostal biblical scholarship should be at the forefront of innovation in the broader discipline. I might even go so far as to suggest that now that progressive scholars have embedded their many diverse methodological pebbles firmly and squarely in the forehead of the giant of grammatico-historical criticism, we should be the ones to lift the sword (of the Spirit?) to cut its head from its shoulders and finally do to death this monstrous alien construct from a generation gone by (though I would be doing so with my tongue at least heading in the general direction of my cheek).

So, in terms of their interpretative philosophy, Pentecostals stand alone in our suspicion of ever treating the Bible as a book just to learn from. Instead we want engage with it and utilise it as a resource for divine encounter. We read the Bible not, as I have emphasised, to grasp it; but so that God might grasp us through it. And once his Word has taken hold in our hearts by that means, it becomes fire in our bones. It seems to me this is the very heart of the Pentecostal philosophy of Bible reading. Let us then consider how that philosophy appears to be outworked among individual believers.

III. *Practical Issues*

When we read the Bible, we are reading it out of precise and particular contexts and for a specific and distinct purpose. And we do not read it

---

[12] It is interesting to note an increasing tendency over the last 25 years or so for Pentecostals to be less comfortable with associating ourselves with evangelicals methodologically; this issue has been addressed by Gordon Anderson, Kenneth Archer and Veli-Matti Kärkkäinen among others.

purely for entertainment and leisure, but because of what encountering the divine in the text does in, through, for and to us. Our philosophical engagement with and commitment to the text is expressed practically for most Pentecostals in what I might call 'agendad reading'—reading with an intended result and a goal in mind. That purpose is demonstrated and outworked in the questions that we bring to the text as we read it. And whilst what I will now seek to identify as the typical Pentecostal questions may well be asked out of other groups and traditions as well, their combination, prioritisation and emphasis all contribute to the designation of a distinctively Pentecostal approach.

To call it a methodology would certainly be exaggeration and oversystematisation. I am not that sure it is even always conscious. But I think there is a Pentecostal culture of Bible reading. It is creative, positive, but also in a sense adversarial, in that it approaches the text not as a construct which might be understood and appreciated in its own right, but as a resource to be mined for specific treasures. I remember being taught at Bible college as a first year student that the best way of writing notes on my daily devotional Scripture readings was to ask myself three questions:

- What did this mean to its original readers?[13]
- What does this mean to me?
- What should I do about it?

With the benefit of hindsight, this was an extremely useful induction into the Pentecostal way of reading. Though this was, I assume, entirely unintentional, it is striking to note how similar the model these questions suggest is to the analysis of hermeneutics that J. Severino Croatto offers. Having initially considered the original context of a text, Croatto argues, 'all interpreters condition their reading of a text by a kind of *preunderstanding* arising from their own life context... [and then] the interpreter *enlarges* the *meaning* of the text being interpreted'.[14] I believe that Pentecostals are infinitely less interested in the first of those three areas, that

---

[13] Perhaps this question was something of a concession to the more academic context in which we were reading, but even then, note that the emphasis was on the reception of the text rather than its authorship. We were never asked to consider what Paul meant, for instance, but what his readers heard him say (which could be quite different, as any communicator will know).

[14] J. Severino Croatto, *Biblical Hermeneutics* (New York: Orbis, 1987), p. 1.

of original context, but the contextual preunderstanding (what does this mean to me?) and the enlarged meaning phases (what do I go and do about it?) are both of fundamental importance to us. Let me expand on them briefly.

A. *What does this mean to me?*

It seems to me that this straightforward query is indeed the starting point of most private Bible study, particularly among Pentecostals. The experiential (expressionist?) nature of our tradition certainly invites, and to a large extent expects it. After all, if Pentecostalism is truly an expression of 'primal spirituality', is not a measure of primal exegesis appropriate?[15] The truth is, of course, that the significance of a passage to its readers is inherently of more interest to them than any meaning it might have had for others. Allan Anderson has highlighted that in an African Pentecostal context, 'it is meaningless to discuss the interpretation of the text by itself'.[16] It only has value as it becomes personalised and directly related to the specific location of the reader. That does not mean that Pentecostal readers have adopted a neo-orthodox approach to the nature of the text as the Word of God. It does, however, suggest a more phenomenological approach. The Bible on the shelf is still God's word; it is just not God's word to me at that time. I would like to suggest this is a strength of our model. The Bible unread is the Bible powerless, devoid of transformative influence. If we do not encounter God within it then it is little more than a cultural artefact of principally antiquarian significance—interesting but ultimately (and in every sense) meaningless. (I also like the Kierkegaardian aspect of this principal, for what it is worth; the need for passionate appropriation of the text's meaning for myself if it is to have any meaning at all.)

Clearly such a model can result in selective reading. If my primary concern is with what a passage means to me, then quite naturally it will be the passages that I find most meaningful with which I will want to spend most of my time. The result, potentially, is increased dependence on a few key texts for my spiritual growth and development and increasing isolation

---

[15] The famous phrase of Harvey Cox in *Fire from Heaven: The Rise of Pentecostal Spirituality and the Reshaping of Religion in the Twenty-First Century* (Reading, MA: Addison-Wesley, 1995).

[16] Allan Anderson, 'The Hermeneutical Processes of Pentecostal-type African Initiated Churches in South Africa', *Missionalia* 24.2 (1996), p. 1.

from the message of Scripture as a whole—and, in the worst case scenario, the production of a customised, individually-specified canon within the canon, of the texts that are most inspirational to me and thereby 'most inspired' in my thinking. Systematic expository preaching which shows the relevance of the whole body of Scripture might be a powerful vaccination against such thinking, and can also introduce listeners to new texts which can evolve into favourite texts.[17]

Additionally it is important to note one further significant implication of this individualised approach. If the focus of my interpretation is what God wants to say to me through a passage, then I have to accept that he might not be saying quite the same to you. There is no such thing as a universal interpretation.[18] This is the inevitable result of moving the locus for the production of meaning out of the conceptualisation of authorial intent and into the private sphere of the reader's encounter with the text. What makes the difference for individual readers? Our extratextual experience and our context in life.[19] The text has meaning to us in different ways because we approach it from different perspectives. Yet that is precisely what makes it worth reading, and rereading. Our growing and diversifying experience means that even at a cultural level, without taking the spiritual into account, there is more to be drawn from the text each new time we encounter it.

In this regard we need to realise that we read both out of our context in the world, and into our context as Pentecostals. This is essentially what Archer is addressing when he talks of Pentecostals as 're-experiencing' the text.[20] He argues that the early Pentecostals 'believed Scripture inherently possessed the ability to speak meaningfully in different social settings than the one from which it originated' and therefore removed it from its original context in their thinking to read it in their own.[21] In a new location, many biblical texts find new significance and meaning. In this way, as Gail O'Day has identified, we see that 'Scripture is not a repository of authority once fixed in the past, but authority and life are generated in the present

---

[17] I am indebted to Lee Roy Martin for the observation that the Church of God for quite a few years now has encouraged its adherents to read the Bible through each year as part of a corporate Bible reading programme.

[18] Mark E. Roberts, 'A Hermeneutic of Charity: Response to Heather Landrus', *JPT* 11.1 (2002), pp. 89–97 (96).

[19] I offer a rather more detailed explanation of the significance and value of reader-response approaches to the Bible in the introductory chapter of Andrew Davies, *Double Standards in Isaiah* (Leiden: Brill, 2000).

[20] Archer, *A Pentecostal Hermeneutic*, p. 168.

[21] Archer, *A Pentecostal Hermeneutic*, p. 96.

as Scripture is proclaimed and heard'.[22] For many years, the Statement of Fundamental Truths of British Assemblies of God pointed to Isa. 28.11 (KJV 'For with stammering lips and another tongue will he speak to this people') as scriptural support for the doctrine of speaking in tongues as the initial evidence of the baptism in the Holy Spirit. Clearly it is nothing of the sort in its context in Isaiah; it is not talking of glossolalia, let alone of any evidence of the Spirit's outpouring. However, for Pentecostals, this is a perfectly legitimate recontexualisation of a divine promise. As Archer highlights, 'Pentecostals found biblical parallels with their life experiences and would incorporate these into their testimonies'. He continues:

> Early Pentecostals did not place a lot of emphasis on explaining the historical context of Scripture, nor were they concerned with the author's original intention. They used Scripture in such a way as to allow for slippage between what it meant and what it means. They read the Bible as the Word of God and attempted to understand it presently. The horizons of past and present were fused, or from a critical perspective, confused.[23]

That is precisely what happened here. Admittedly with some support of the reapplication of this text by Paul in 1 Corinthians 14, the formulators of our fundamental truths read Isaiah's words anew in their own context and saw them as evidence of the key Pentecostal distinctive. Essentially they knew a real-world situation for which they sought a biblical explanation. That they found one confirms our assessment of the nature of Pentecostal biblical interpretation; that they sought it in the first case re-emphasises neatly for us just how dependent our tradition has sought to be on the scriptures. O'Day highlights for us, however, that the capacity for such recontextualising interpretations is actually a feature of the biblical text itself and not exclusively a Pentecostal formulation. She talks of the 'generativity' of the Bible, its capability for producing new meaning in new contexts, observing, 'In the reading and rereading of Scripture, something new is created. Scripture does not remain static while the contexts around it change. Scripture generates new life and meanings for itself in a community's appropriation of it.'[24]

So we read as individuals addressing specific individual circumstances and contexts. But the isolationist nature of individual focussed readings emphasises forthrightly their incompleteness and their dependence upon

---

[22] Gail R. O'Day, ' "Today this word is fulfilled in your hearing": A Scriptural Hermeneutic of Biblical Authority', *Word and World* 26.4 (2006), pp. 357–64 (357).

[23] Archer, *A Pentecostal Hermeneutic*, p. 181.

[24] O'Day, 'Today this Word is Fulfilled', p. 359.

other readings of the tradition. The more we read from our own perspective, the more we realise how much we need the insights of others. Pentecostalism is by no means an isolationist or solitary faith. We have a sense of being in our great task together. The missionary task that began when the believers were 'all together in one place' (Acts 2.1) continues today in the expression of the abiding presence of Jesus whenever even two or three are gathered in his name (Mt. 18.20). Pentecostals across the world recognise their shared experience and commission. When Pentecostals read the Bible, we do it with a sense of commonality, cohesion and togetherness. Our reading and readings arise from and within a community, and a community of faith, in every sense of the latter word, at that.

It is precisely this community of faith—which I consider has its similarities with the Fishian and Clinesian 'interpretative community' models but also some differences—which facilitates the uniting of a myriad of contrasting individualised, contextualised applications of meaning in an arena of mutual coherence and significance.[25] Because we are in the task of understanding and applying the Bible together, we can accept diversity of interpretation and rejoice in the way the Spirit reapplies to transformative effect the words he initially inspired into the lives of our brothers and sisters. Reading, for all I want to argue for its inherently individual nature, must become reading *together*, and as it does so its community-forming nature emerges, and we sense that we belong together because of our shared reading experience. As Robby Waddell has highlighted, we have learned that belief, but *our* belief, belief arising in and out of community, is the key to comprehension.[26]

Acceptance of a reading by the community as valid does not on its own mean that it has in any sense broader value or truth, however. The traditional Pentecostal explanation as to how we might discern the meaning of the text is that it is the task of the Holy Spirit himself to 'lead us into all truth'. Archer highlights that, in our thinking, it is 'The Holy Spirit [who] enables the interpreter to bridge the historical and cultural gulf between the ancient authors of the Scriptures and the present interpreter'.[27] This is

---

[25] Clines outlines his approach to this issue most clearly in D.J.A. Clines, 'A World Established on Water (Psalm 24): Reader-Response, Deconstruction and Bespoke Interpretation', republished in Clines, *Interested Parties: The Ideology of Writers and Readers of the Hebrew Bible* (JSOT Sup, 205; Gender, Culture, Theory, 1; Sheffield: Sheffield Academic Press, 1995), pp. 172–86.

[26] Robby Waddell, *The Spirit of the Book of Revelation* (JPT Sup, 30; Blandford Forum: Deo, 2006), p. 118.

[27] Archer, *A Pentecostal Hermeneutic*, p. 196.

true at both an individual and a communitarian level. When we see ourselves in the text we credit the Spirit for placing the mirror in front of our eyes; when we arrive at a consensus on a valid reading, or accept and are inspired, blessed or encouraged by the experience of an individual who shares their story with the congregation, we put that down to his working among us. The Spirit is the ultimate arbiter of meaning and significance, 'the self authenticating key in the hermeneutical process'.[28] Whilst Pentecostals in general subscribe to the Rabbinic 'seamless robe' model of Scripture which allows any two texts to speak to each other with no real understanding of the critical and contextual issues involved, we do not accept the Bible on its own as entirely internally explicable.[29] We need, and actively invoke, the empowering and inspiration of the Spirit in making those connections. When that truly happens, as Catholic charismatic Andrew Minto notes,

> The collaboration between the Holy Spirit and believer-interpreter results in a living faith-knowledge of the very spiritual, paschal realities of which the text speaks. As such, this collaboration makes the act of divine revelation a completed act of communication. What God communicates through Christ in the Holy Spirit is now obtained as knowledge on the part of the believer.[30]

Here it seems to me that we need help from the work of systematicians. Whilst Pentecostals almost universally assume the role of the Spirit in guiding our interpretation, there is a notable weakness in the literature in terms of how this process is understood and defined. How does the Spirit truly guide us in interpretation? How do we listen? Truly critical engagement with biblical scholarship from other perspectives by Pentecostal interpreters, which is clearly increasing, will require us to define this process and put our answers into the broader public sphere for scrutiny, so I suggest there is much work to be done in describing the process of what is sometimes labelled 'pneumatic interpretation' instead of merely advocating it as a model.[31]

---

[28] Anderson, 'The Hermeneutical Processes', p. 3.
[29] Cf. Waddell, *The Spirit of the Book of Revelation*, p. 127: 'In a postmodern world, Pentecostals no longer need to acquiesce to the evangelical doctrine *sola scriptura*, because the revelation of God is not transmitted to new generations by Scripture alone but by the work of the Holy Spirit'.
[30] Andrew L. Minto, 'The Charismatic Renewal and the Spiritual Sense of Scripture', *Pneuma* 27.2 (2005), pp. 256–72 (262).
[31] Cf. Howard M. Ervin, 'Hermeneutics: A Pentecostal Option', *Pneuma* (Fall 1981), pp. 11–25 (17).

B. *What should I do about it?*

Finally, some brief comments on what Pentecostals would call the need to be 'doers as well as hearers' of the Word (Jas 1.22). If meaning starts with me, then it is only correct that the responsibility for implementing that meaning as practical application should also end there. Truly Pentecostal interpretation always requires reading with an end in mind. There is no abstract exegesis; what ever treasures that, together, we uncover are there to be shaped into agendas for action. From the Day of Pentecost onward, our preaching has sought to draw a response from our listeners and motivate action as much as it invites acceptance. For us, the application is vital in that it connects the text to 'real world' issues and affords us the opportunity to read and appropriate it for transformative ends. As Gordon Anderson has observed, 'Pentecost links rational discourse with powerful demonstrations and emotional responses. It moves preaching from the sterile pulpit and lecture hall of rationality and transforms it into prophetic witness in the very untidy arena and marketplace of street level experience'.[32] Pentecostal biblical interpretation is at its best when formulated 'on the hoof' and most meaningful when it confronts real-world situations with the Word of God. Generally, therefore, it offers a practical rather than a theological response. And perhaps, in conclusion, this is why our tradition has become one of action more than reflection. Confronted with the power of the Word of God we love so dearly in such a way, no one with any sort of Pentecostal blood in their veins could hold back from offering the Lord our Spirit-inspired service. Ultimately, as Andrew Minto has noted, 'It is not method, nor scholarship, nor cutting-edge, creative interpretation that will renew biblical studies, but God's own work'.[33] Pentecostal readers of the Bible learned this in terms of their personal reading and study many generations back, and, still today, seek to take what they have received from God in their interaction with his Word and reinterpret it for, and reapply it into, the new contexts they encounter day after day, living biblical truth out as it lives in them. And long may they continue to do so.

---

[32] Gordon Anderson, 'Pentecost, Scholarship, and Learning in a Postmodern World', *Pneuma* 27.1 (Spring 2005), p. 122.

[33] Minto, 'Charismatic Renewal', p. 272.

CHAPTER FIFTEEN

PSALM 63 AND PENTECOSTAL SPIRITUALITY:
AN EXERCISE IN AFFECTIVE HERMENEUTICS*

Lee Roy Martin**

I. *Introduction*

In my first semester at Bible college, I began reading through the entire Bible. As might be expected, a number of Scripture passages made a deep impression upon me, and one of those was Psalm 63, particularly the first two verses: 'my soul is thirsty for you; my flesh longs for you ... thus I have seen you in the sanctuary, beholding your power and your glory'. I heard in Psalm 63 a passionate prayer, an articulation of deep spiritual inclinations. I heard an expression of the psalmist's intense desire to encounter God and to experience God's presence. I also recognized the psalmist's commitment to seek after God and to respond to God's gracious acts with praise and with constant loyalty. Because of the content of the psalm and its passionate tone of expression, I memorized the psalm and began to recite it regularly as a part of my own prayers.

The longing for God expressed in Psalm 63 gave voice to the passion for God that was generated by my own Pentecostal spirituality, a spirituality that Steven Jack Land has characterized as 'a passion for the kingdom', which is 'ultimately a passion for God'.[1] I suggest in this study that Psalm 63 can function as an individual and/or communal prayer that voices the passionate aspects of Pentecostal spirituality. Furthermore, in its function as Holy Scripture, this psalm can guide Pentecostals in their pursuit of an encounter with God and in their longing for God's presence.

---

* First published as 'Longing for God: Psalm 63 and Pentecostal Spirituality', *Journal of Pentecostal Theology* 22.1 (2013), pp. 54–76.
** Lee Roy Martin (DTh, University of South Africa) is Professor of Old Testament and Biblical Languages at the Pentecostal Theological Seminary in Cleveland, TN, USA.
[1] Steven Jack Land, *Pentecostal Spirituality: A Passion for the Kingdom* (Cleveland, TN: CPT Press, 2010), pp. 2, 97, 120, 73–80, 212, 219. Cf. Mark J. Cartledge, 'Affective Theological Praxis: Understanding the Direct Object of Practical Theology', *International Journal of Practical Theology* 8.1 (2004), pp. 34–52 (36).

In this constructive and integrative study, I examine Psalm 63 through the lens of Pentecostal spirituality; however, before examining Psalm 63, I will describe what I am calling an 'affective approach' to the biblical text. The affective approach calls for the hearer to attend to the affective tones that are present in the text and to allow the affections of the hearer to be shaped by the text. Once I have described the affective approach, I will present an affective Pentecostal hearing of Psalm 63 that emerges from my location within the Pentecostal community.[2] Then I will suggest ways in which Psalm 63 can contribute to the affective formation of the Pentecostal church of today. On the one hand, therefore, my hearing of Psalm 63 is informed by and shaped by my own Pentecostal experience. On the other hand, my Pentecostal spirituality and experience is influenced by my engagement with Psalm 63.

Before proceeding to the study, I would offer four explanatory comments: 1) Although my work is generated by my Pentecostal spirituality and is aimed at the Pentecostal tradition, I recognize that affective engagement is common to all humans.[3] Therefore, all readers of Scripture are invited to 'listen in' to the conversation in hope that they too may find this study beneficial. 2) The Pentecostal movement is a global, diverse, and multifaceted tradition; therefore, I do not claim to speak for all Pentecostals. 3) Biblical exegesis and hermeneutics demand the utilization of a variety of methods and approaches. Therefore, within a holistic biblical hermeneutic, the affective dimension of Scripture is only one of the many dimensions of the text that should be investigated as a part of sound exegesis. I would argue, however, that the affective dimension has been overlooked and underutilized in the academic study of Scripture. 4) This article is a provisional proposal that I submit to the community of scholars for a discerning response. I hope that it will generate further conversation about creative engagement with the biblical text.

---

[2] Instead of the commonly used term 'reading', I prefer the term 'hearing' because (1) it is a biblical term; (2) it reflects the orality of biblical and Pentecostal contexts; (3) it is relational, presupposing an external voice who is speaking; (4) it suggests faithful obedience since 'hearing' often means 'obeying'; (5) it implies transformation, since faithful hearing transforms; (6) unlike the process of 'reading' Scripture, 'hearing' implies submission to the authority of the text. See Lee Roy Martin, *The Unheard Voice of God: A Pentecostal Hearing of the Book of Judges* (JPTSup, 32; Blandford Forum, UK: Deo Publishing, 2008), p. 53.

[3] James K.A. Smith, *Desiring the Kingdom: Worship, Worldview, and Cultural Formation* (Cultural Liturgies, 1; Grand Rapids, MI: Baker Academic, 2009), argues convincingly that human life is shaped largely by the affections.

II. *An Affective Approach to Interpretation*

The development of my affective approach to the Psalter takes into consideration Walter Brueggemann's insightful critique of both the pre-critical and critical approaches to the study of the Psalms. He argues on the one hand that the 'devotional tradition of piety is surely weakened by disregarding the perspectives and insights of scholarship' and on the other hand that the critical tradition 'is frequently arid, because it lingers excessively on formal questions, with inability or reluctance to bring its insights and methods to substantive matters of exposition'.[4] Brueggemann's proposal for a postcritical 'functional' approach,[5] in which the critical and pietistic traditions inform and correct each other, places the psalms within the journey of faith and recognizes their value as prayers for the ancient Hebrews and for subsequent faith communities.[6]

Brueggemann's functional approach in its broad parameters makes room for scholarly consideration of the emotive quality of the Psalms. It might be argued that the affective dimension is too 'subjective' to be included in academic study. Expecting objections to the affective approach, Daniel C. Mcguire remarks, 'It is not for nothing that the rationalist is upset by the inclusion of affectivity...Affectivity imports mystery and depth. We can feel more than we can see or say.'[7] For this reason, biblical scholarship has given little attention to this affective dimension of biblical poetry in general and of the Psalms in particular. Yet I would argue that the function of poetry is to evoke (and provoke) the passions and to form the affections. The study of the Psalms, therefore, can benefit from a hermeneutic that appreciates the affective dimensions of the text and that takes full advantage of the passions that are brought to the text by the interpreter.

---

[4] Walter Brueggemann, *The Message of the Psalms: A Theological Commentary* (Augsburg Old Testament Studies; Minneapolis: Augsburg Pub. House, 1984), p. 16.

[5] Walter Brueggemann, *The Psalms and the Life of Faith* (Minneapolis, MN: Fortress Press, 1995), pp. 3–32.

[6] Brueggemann, *The Psalms and the Life of Faith*, pp. 33–66. My approach should not be confused with the resurgent mystical, spiritual, or allegorical approach presented by David C. Steinmetz, 'The Superiority of Pre-Critical Exegesis', *Theology Today* 37 (1980), pp. 27–38, or Celia Kourie, 'Reading Scripture through a Mystical Lens', *Acta Theologica* 15/Suppl. (2011), pp. 132–53. I have argued that returning to allegory or the medieval mystics is not an option. See Lee Roy Martin, 'Pre-Critical Exegesis of the Book of Judges and the Construction of a Post-Critical Hermeneutic', *Ekklesiastikos Pharos* 88 (2006), pp. 338–53.

[7] Daniel C. Maguire, '*Ratio Practica* and the Intellectualistic Fallacy', *Journal of Religious Ethics* 10.1 (1982), pp. 22–39 (23).

It is well known that the affections played a significant role in the spirituality of Jonathan Edwards[8] and John Wesley.[9] Deep affective currents have been observed also in the Eastern Orthodox tradition,[10] a tradition that influenced both Edwards and Wesley.[11] Recently, B.I. McGroarty has argued that it was the view of the 14th-Century English mystic Hilton that human wholeness ('health') cannot be attained outside of an affective engagement with God.[12] Dale Coulter has expounded upon the affective dimension in Catherine of Siena,[13] Bernard of Clairvaux, Richard of

---

[8] See, for example, Jonathan Edwards, *Religious Affections* (Works of Jonathan Edwards; New Haven: Yale Univ Pr, 1959); Timothy Hessel-Robinson, 'Jonathan Edwards (1703–1758): A Treatise Concerning Religious Affections', in *Christian Spirituality* (London: Routledge, 2010), pp. 269–80; John E. Smith, 'Testing the Spirits: Jonathan Edwards and the Religious Affections', *Union Seminary Quarterly Review* 37.1–2 (1982), pp. 27–37; Roger Ward, 'The Philosophical Structure of Jonathan Edward's Religious Affections', *Christian Scholar's Review* 29.4 (2000), pp. 745–68; Wayne L. Proudfoot, 'From Theology to a Science of Religions: Jonathan Edwards and William James on Religious Affections', *Harvard Theological Review* 82.2 (1989), pp. 149–68, and Iain D. Campbell, 'Jonathan Edwards' Religious Affections as a Paradigm for Evangelical Spirituality', *Scottish Bulletin of Evangelical Theology* 21.2 (2003), pp. 166–86.

[9] See Gregory S. Clapper, 'John Wesley's Abridgement of Isaac Watts' the Doctrine of the Passions Explained and Improved', *Wesleyan Theological Journal* 43.2 (2008), pp. 28–32; idem, *John Wesley on Religious Affections: His Views on Experience and Emotion and Their Role in the Christian Life and Theology* (Pietist and Wesleyan Studies; Metuchen, NJ: Scarecrow Pr, 1989); Kenneth J. Collins, 'John Wesley's Topography of the Heart: Dispositions, Tempers, and Affections', *Methodist History* 36.3 (1998), pp. 162–75; and Randy L. Maddox, 'A Change of Affections: The Development, Dynamics, and Dethronement of John Wesley's Heart Religion', in *'Heart Religion' in the Methodist Tradition and Related Movements* (Lanham, MD: Scarecrow Press, 2001), pp. 3–31.

[10] Cf. Edmund J. Rybarczyk, 'Spiritualities Old and New: Similarities between Eastern Orthodoxy & Classical Pentecostalism', *Pneuma* 24.1 (2002), pp. 7–25, who argues that the Orthodox, like Pentecostals, insist firmly that 'knowledge of God is not limited to the intellectual domain of human existence, but that the believer can sense and hear God in visceral and profound ways' (p. 10). See also Edmund J. Rybarczyk, *Beyond Salvation: Eastern Orthodoxy and Classical Pentecostalism on Becoming Like Christ* (Paternoster Theological Monographs; Carlisle, UK: Paternoster Press, 2004). In the Orthodox writers, the affective dimension of spirituality is usually couched in the language of encountering the presence and mystery of God. See Ecumenical Patriarch Bartholomew, *Encountering the Mystery: Understanding Orthodox Christianity Today* (New York: Doubleday, 1st edn, 2008); Vladimir Lossky, *The Mystical Theology of the Eastern Church* (London: J. Clarke, 1st edn, 1957), and Alexander Schmemann, *The Historical Road of Eastern Orthodoxy* (Chicago: H. Regnery, 1966).

[11] See, for example, Michael James McClymond and Gerald R. McDermott, *The Theology of Jonathan Edwards* (New York: Oxford University Press, 2012), and S.T. Kimbrough, *Orthodox and Wesleyan Spirituality* (Crestwood, NY: St. Vladimir's Seminary Press, 2002).

[12] Brendan Ignatius McGroarty, 'Humility, Contemplation and Affect Theory', *Journal of Religion and Health* 45.1 (2006), pp. 57–72.

[13] Catherine of Siena, *The Dialogue* 13 (trans. and intro. Suzanne Noffke, OP; New York, NY: Paulist Press, 1980), p. 48; cited in Dale Coulter, 'Pentecostals and Monasticism: A Common Spirituality?', *Assemblies of God Heritage* 30 (2010), pp. 43–49 (45).

St. Victor, Catherine of Genoa, and Martin Luther, concluding that their common theology of 'encounter centers upon affectivity as the point of contact between the divine and human.'[14] And Jeffrey Gros points out the importance of the Franciscan movement's 'concern for direct human experience of Christ'.[15] These studies, among many others, have shown that the concern for the formation of the affections is present in a wide variety of traditions.

Steven Land observes that while Pentecostals accept the necessity of orthodoxy (right doctrine) and orthopraxy (right practice), they see orthopathy (right affections) as the integrating center for both orthodoxy and orthopraxy.[16] Consequently, a Pentecostal approach would recognize the Psalms not only as a witness to right theology and practice, but also as an aide in the formation of the affections. The affections, not to be confused with transitory feelings or emotions, are the abiding dispositions and passions of the heart that characterize a person's deepest desires.[17] The psalms, therefore, teach us not only what to think (orthodoxy) and what to do (orthopraxy) but also what to desire (orthopathy). To say it another way, the psalms contribute to both intellectual and affective learning: 'Intellectual learning aims at learning facts and their relation and at rational analysis... In affective learning, on the other hand, feelings and emotions are predominant. With affective learning one aims to develop emotional and moral sensitivities and to achieve a deep commitment to certain values.'[18] Mark Cartledge adds, 'Indeed, one could argue that the affections inform not only believing and action but also the imagination as well, without which significant advances in understanding would be impossible'.[19]

The process of affective interpretation requires at least four cooperative moves on the part of the hearer. First, the hearer of the psalm must identify and acknowledge the affective dimensions of the text, an

---

[14] Dale M. Coulter, 'The Spirit and the Bride Revisited: Pentecostalism, Renewal, and the Sense of History', *Journal of Pentecostal Theology* 21.2 (2012), pp. 298–319 (318).

[15] Jeffrey Gros, 'Ecumenical Connections across Time: Medieval Franciscans as a Proto-Pentecostal Movement?', *Pneuma* 34.1 (2012), pp. 75–93 (75). Gros calls for 'a robust appreciation of spiritual experience' (p. 91).

[16] Land, *Pentecostal Spirituality*, pp. 21, 34, 127–59. See also Cartledge, 'Affective Theological Praxis', pp. 34–52 (36).

[17] Land, *Pentecostal Spirituality*, p. 34. Cf. Thomas Ryan, 'Revisiting Affective Knowledge and Connaturality in Aquinas', *Theological Studies* 66.1 (2005), pp. 49–68 (55–58, 63). The affections, of course, play a key role in the creation of feelings and emotions.

[18] Richard Ognibene and Richard Penaskovic, 'Teaching Theology: Some Affective Strategies', *Horizons* 8.1 (1981), pp. 97–108 (98).

[19] Cartledge, 'Affective Theological Praxis', p. 38. Cf. Smith, *Desiring the Kingdom*, pp. 135, 52.

acknowledgement that is by no means automatic or common for scholars, who tend to concentrate their attention upon historical critical concerns. Every psalm includes an affective dimension, which may involve hope or despair, love or hate, trust or fear, admiration or scorn, pride or shame, joy or despondency, to mention but a few examples. The poetic genre demands that the hearer give attention to its emotive content.

Second, the hearer of the psalm must acknowledge his or her own passions that are brought to the interpretive process. It is important that the hearer of the text recognize when his or her affections correspond to the affections of the psalmist and when they do not correspond, because the passions of the hearer can dramatically impact the resulting interpretation.

Third, the hearer of the psalm must be open to the emotive impact of the text. Before the hearer can experience the affective dimension of the text, he or she may be required to enter the world of the psalmist and to enter the emotive flow of the textual stream. Robert O. Baker argues that the reading of the biblical text involves both the mind and the affections of the reader. He insists that 'reading the Bible is not just a cognitive experience, but an affective one as well'.[20] He argues further that seeking

> to understand the ideational/rational content of a text without also seeking to experience and reflect upon its emotive effect is to skew the text's message... By committing to read the text objectively from a critical distance, the professional reader subverts the text's evocative power or is at least unable to express the feeling that the text evokes in him or her.[21]

Fourth, the hearer must allow himself or herself to be transformed by the affective experiencing of the psalm. As the hearer engages the biblical text, his or her affections are shaped by that engagement. 'The affective capacity of the person can be modified and hence grow in sensitivity, intensity, and scope.'[22] In its canonical role as Scripture, the book of Psalms makes a significant contribution toward a theology of worship, and part of the

---

[20] Robert O. Baker, 'Pentecostal Bible Reading: Toward a Model of Reading for the Formation of the Affections', *Journal of Pentecostal Theology* 7 (1995), pp. 34–48 (46). Cf. Martin, *The Unheard Voice of God*, pp. 70–71. See also W. Dow Edgerton, *The Passion of Interpretation* (Literary Currents in Biblical Interpretation; Louisville, KY: Westminster/John Knox Press, 1992), who agrees that every interpretation involves the passions of the interpreter. See also Cartledge, 'Affective Theological Praxis', pp. 42, 51, and Kenneth J. Archer, *A Pentecostal Hermeneutic: Spirit, Scripture and Community* (Cleveland, TN: CPT Press, 2009), p. 234.
[21] Baker, 'Pentecostal Bible Reading', pp. 34–35.
[22] Ryan, 'Revisiting Affective Knowledge', p. 57.

message of the Psalms is that right worship begins with rightly oriented affections. Thus, through the hearing of the Psalms the desires of the heart are transformed and redirected toward God so that the affections of gratitude, trust, and love (affections that foster worship) are generated and nourished.

Although I would insist that the third and fourth moves are essential to an affective engagement with the text, I would admit that they are difficult (if not impossible) to accomplish within a written document. They are experiences that may be validated by testimony and description (as in my own testimony that began this article), but the transformative experience itself is outside the bounds of written discourse. Consequently, the bulk of my study will give attention to the first two movements of the affective hermeneutical process.

In what follows, I will offer an affective hearing of Psalm 63. My interpretive location within the Pentecostal community has caused me to appreciate the affective dimension of the Psalms,[23] and I find Psalm 63 to be particularly suited to an affective Pentecostal interpretation. The Psalmist's yearning to encounter God's power and glory is consistent with Pentecostal aspirations, and the passionate prayers and exuberant praises that we find in Psalm 63 are consistent with the ethos of Pentecostal worship.

As stated above, appreciation for the affective dimension of the text is only one aspect of a holistic hermeneutic. The affective elements become clearer and more precise when they emerge from sound exegesis. Therefore, as a foundation for the study, we will overview the text of Psalm 63 and examine its structure and genre.

III. *A Translation of Psalm 63*

¹מִזְמוֹר לְדָוִד בִּהְיוֹתוֹ בְּמִדְבַּר יְהוּדָה	A psalm of David when he was in the wilderness of Judah
²אֱלֹהִים אֵלִי אַתָּה אֲשַׁחֲרֶךָּ	¹ God, you are my God; I will seek you earnestly;
צָמְאָה לְךָ נַפְשִׁי	My soul is thirsty for you
כָּמַהּ לְךָ בְשָׂרִי	My flesh longs for you
בְּאֶרֶץ־צִיָּה וְעָיֵף בְּלִי־מָיִם	In a dry and weary land without water.

---

[23] Lee Roy Martin, 'Delight in the Torah: The Affective Dimension of Psalm 1', *Old Testament Essays* 23.3 (2010), pp. 708–27 (18).

³כֵּן בַּקֹּדֶשׁ חֲזִיתִיךָ לִרְאוֹת עֻזְּךָ וּכְבוֹדֶךָ	² Thus in the sanctuary I have seen you, Beholding your power and your glory.
⁴כִּי־טוֹב חַסְדְּךָ מֵחַיִּים שְׂפָתַי יְשַׁבְּחוּנְךָ ⁵כֵּן אֲבָרֶכְךָ בְחַיָּי בְּשִׁמְךָ אֶשָּׂא כַפָּי	³ Because your kindness is better than life, My lips will praise you. ⁴ Thus I shall bless you during my life; In your name I shall lift up my hands.
⁶כְּמוֹ חֵלֶב וָדֶשֶׁן תִּשְׂבַּע נַפְשִׁי וְשִׂפְתֵי רְנָנוֹת יְהַלֶּל־פִּי	⁵ Like marrow and fatness my soul will be satisfied, And my mouth will offer praise with joyful lips.
⁷אִם־זְכַרְתִּיךָ עַל־יְצוּעָי בְּאַשְׁמֻרוֹת אֶהְגֶּה־בָּךְ	⁶ Whenever I remembered you on my bed, In the night watches I would meditate on you,
⁸כִּי־הָיִיתָ עֶזְרָתָה לִּי וּבְצֵל כְּנָפֶיךָ אֲרַנֵּן	⁷ Because you were my help, In the shadow of your wings I would shout for joy.
⁹דָּבְקָה נַפְשִׁי אַחֲרֶיךָ בִּי תָּמְכָה יְמִינֶךָ	⁸ My soul has stuck close behind you; Your right hand has upheld me.
¹⁰וְהֵמָּה לְשׁוֹאָה יְבַקְשׁוּ נַפְשִׁי יָבֹאוּ בְּתַחְתִּיּוֹת הָאָרֶץ ¹¹יַגִּירֻהוּ עַל־יְדֵי־חָרֶב מְנָת שֻׁעָלִים יִהְיוּ	⁹ As for them who will seek to ruin my life, They will go into the depths of the earth. ¹⁰ They will be delivered over to the power of the sword; They will be a prey for foxes.
¹²וְהַמֶּלֶךְ יִשְׂמַח בֵּאלֹהִים יִתְהַלֵּל כָּל־הַנִּשְׁבָּע בּוֹ כִּי יִסָּכֵר פִּי דוֹבְרֵי־שָׁקֶר	¹¹ But as for the king, he will rejoice in God; Everyone who swears by him will glory, Because the mouth of those speaking deception will be stopped.

IV. *Structure and Genre of Psalm 63*

The structure of Psalm 63 is unclear,[24] and scholars have divided the psalm in a variety of ways.[25] I suggest a four part structure, beginning after the superscription (v. 1):[26]

---

[24] Cf. Michael Wilcock, *The Message of Psalms 1–72: Songs for the People of God* (Bible Speaks Today; Downers Grove, IL: InterVarsity Press, 2001), I, p. 222, and Marvin E. Tate, *Psalms 51–100* (Word Biblical Commentary, 20; Dallas, TX: Word Books, 1990), p. 125.

[25] James Limburg, *Psalms* (Westminster Bible Companion; Louisville, KY: Westminister John Knox Press, 1st edn, 2000), pp. 208–10, divides the psalm into three parts: vv. 1–4, body and soul; vv. 5–8, remembering; and vv. 9–11, rejoicing. J.P. Fokkelman, *The Psalms in Form: The Hebrew Psalter in Its Poetic Shape* (Tools for Biblical Study, 4; Leiden: Deo Publishing, 2002), p. 71, finds six divisions made up of the following verses: 2–3, 4–5, 6–7, 8–9, 10–11, 12.

[26] I will follow the Hebrew versification. Each of the four sections consists of three bicola except for the final verse, which concludes emphatically with a tricola. Cf. Samuel L.

1. *Longing for God's Presence (vv. 2–3)*

Verses 2–3 hold together as an introduction that establishes the overall topic of the psalm as the psalmist's intention to passionately and habitually pursue the presence of God.

2. *Praise for God's Kindness (vv. 4–6)*

The second section, like the first, includes an affirmation that is expressed syntactically with a verbless clause ('you *are* my God' and 'your kindness *is* better than life'). The verbless clauses are followed by statements of future intent ('I will seek you' and 'my lips will praise you'). The first two sections each include verses held together by the conjunction 'thus' (כִּי). The first section begins with seeking God and ends with seeing God. The second section both begins and ends with the mention of praise, and each of its verses (4–6) mentions praise either literally or figuratively. Each verb in this section is a *yiqtol* and should be translated as future tense.

3. *Remembrance of God's Faithfulness (vv. 7–9)*

The third section (7–9) his held together by a focus upon remembrance of God's actions in the past.[27] Verses 7–8 consist of two compound sentences, each of which begins with a *qatal* verb and is followed by a habitual *yiqtol*.[28] Verse 9 is made up of two sentences that utilize *qatal* verbs.

4. *Rejoicing in God's Covenant Protection (vv. 10–12)*[29]

The fourth section turns to the eventual downfall of the psalmist's enemies, and all of the verbs are *yiqtols* that should be translated as future tense.

Terrien, *The Psalms: Strophic Structure and Theological Commentary* (Eerdmans Critical Commentary; Grand Rapids, MI: Eerdmans, 2003), pp. 460–61, and Hans-Joachim Kraus, *Psalms 60–150: A Commentary* (trans. Hilton C. Oswald; Minneapolis, MN: Augsburg, 1989), p. 18. See also J.W. Rogerson and John W. McKay, *Psalms* (3 vols.; Cambridge: Cambridge University Press, 1977), II, pp. 64–65, who find the same structure, except that they separate the final verse as a separate section.

[27] Cf. Susanne Gillmayr-Bucher, 'David, Ich Und Der König: Fortschreibung Und Relecture in Psalm 63', in Josef M. Oesch, Andreas Vonach, and Georg Fischer (eds.), *Horizonte Biblischer Texte: Festschrift Für Josef M. Oesch Zum 60. Geburtstag* (Göttingen: Vandenhoeck & Ruprecht, 2003), pp. 71–89 (76), and Charles Augustus Briggs and Emilie Grace Briggs, *A Critical and Exegetical Commentary on the Book of Psalms* (International Critical Commentary; 2 vols.; Edinburgh: T. & T. Clark, 1969), II, p. 74, and in ref. to v. 8 as past tense, see Kraus, *Psalms 60–150*, p. 17.

[28] Cf. Gillmayr-Bucher, 'David, Ich Und Der König', p. 74.

[29] Gillmayr-Bucher, 'David, Ich Und Der König', p. 76, agrees that verses 10–12 hold together as a unit.

The four sections of Psalm 63 are held together by two parallel threads that span the entire psalm. The first thread is the psalmist's affirmations about God that are either stated directly or are implied by the passive voice: God is his God (v. 2); God's covenant kindness is greater than life (v. 3); God will satisfy the psalmist's desires (v. 5); God has been the psalmist's help (v. 7) and support (v. 8); God will destroy the psalmist's enemies (vv. 9, 10, 11). The second thread consists of statements that describe the psalmist's response to God. These responses can be summarized in two categories: seeking God (v. 2) and praising God (vv. 3, 4, 5, 7, 11). We may also infer that the psalmist's past actions are appropriate for the present and future. These past responses are remembering God (v. 6), meditating upon God (v. 6), and sticking close to God (v. 8).

Like the laments, Psalm 63 begins with a direct address to God (v. 2), and it includes other elements that are common to the laments: a mention of enemies (v. 9), a promise to praise God (v. 11), and a statement of trust (v. 7). Consequently, a number of scholars have classified Psalm 63 as an individual lament.[30] However, the direct address to God, though common to the laments, is not confined to them (e.g. Pss. 8.1; 9.1; 18.1; 21.1; 30.1; 65.1; 84.1; 101.1; 104.1; 115.1; 138.1; 145.1), and therefore is not a defining feature of the lament. Moreover, the laments function as a voice of protest and complaint to God, and Psalm 63 does not contain a protest or complaint,[31] neither does it contain any of the usual indicators of complaint, such as the questions 'Why...?' and 'How long...?'. Enemies are mentioned, but they are not presented as a direct and immediate threat. Instead, they exist as a constant political reality, an everyday obstacle to the king. Furthermore, the lament psalms function as petitions to God for his immediate intervention, but Psalm 63 contains no such plea. Some commentators would translate the verbs in verses 10–11 as petitions, but I suspect that they do so because they are predisposed to classifying the psalm as a lament.[32]

---

[30] Nancy L. DeClaissé-Walford, *Introduction to the Psalms: A Song from Ancient Israel* (St. Louis, MO: Chalice Press, 2004), p. 147; C. Hassell Bullock, *Encountering the Book of Psalms: A Literary and Theological Introduction* (Encountering Biblical Studies; Grand Rapids, MI: Baker Academic, 2001), p. 144.

[31] Bullock classifies the psalm as a lament even though he admits that it contains no complaint or petition (p. 44).

[32] On the difficulties involved in interpreting Hebrew verb tense in poetry, see Alviero Niccacci, 'Analysing Biblical Hebrew Poetry', *Journal for the Study of the Old Testament* 74 (1997), pp. 77–93, especially p. 91.

The laments normally emerge from the perception that God is absent, distant, and unresponsive. The absence of God is perceived through the presence of troubles, such as enemies or sickness, that plague the psalmist. In the lament psalm, the plea for God's return and for God's presence is associated with a petition for deliverance. When God returns to the psalmist, he will intervene to answer the psalmist's petitions. Psalm 63, however, is different from the lament in that it expresses a plea for God's presence quite apart from a specific petition for deliverance. The plea for God's presence is not associated with any other petition. The presence of God is an end in itself. Enemies may be present and will soon be vanquished, but still the petition is focused more directly upon a yearning for God himself.

In light of the above considerations, John Goldingay, along with other scholars, has identified Psalm 63 as a song of trust.[33] The songs of trust or 'songs of confidence', as Brueggemann describes them, may have developed as an expansion of the statement of trust that is commonly found in the laments. Within Brueggemann's typology, these songs function to express a 'new orientation' similar to the perspective conveyed by the songs of thanksgiving. The songs of confidence, however, are more 'generalized' and 'more distanced from the crisis and more reflective' than the songs of thanksgiving.[34] Offering a new orientation to living in covenant with God, Psalm 63 reflects upon God's past faithfulness, expresses the psalmist's deep longing for God's presence, and affirms the psalmist's lifelong commitment to seek God and to praise God.

V. *A Pentecostal Hearing of Psalm 63*

Our overview of the text, structure, and genre of Psalm 63 reveals a number of affective components that intersect with Pentecostal spirituality. In the first section of the psalm (vv. 2–3), the suppliant expresses an unquenchable longing for God's presence. A mood of joy and thankfulness permeates the second section (vv. 4–6). The third section (vv. 7–9)

---

[33] John Goldingay, *Psalms* (Baker Commentary on the Old Testament Wisdom and Psalms; 3 vols.; Grand Rapids, MI: Baker Academic, 2006), II, p. 255. Claus Westermann, *The Living Psalms* (Grand Rapids, MI: Eerdmans, 1989), classifies it as a song of trust (p. 57), but for him the song of trust is a subcategory of the lament (p. 58). Tate, *Psalms 51–100*, p. 125, insists that 'the affirmative, testimony-like statements in vv 4–5, 6–8, 9 indicate clearly that this is a psalm of confidence'.

[34] Brueggemann, *Message of the Psalms*, p. 152.

expresses thankfulness, but it is a thankfulness that leads to expressions of deep trust and commitment to God. The final section (vv. 10–12) of the psalm registers a mood of confident hope for the future.

A. *Longing for God's Presence (vv. 2–3)*

A passion for God is evident in the first words of the psalmist: 'God, you are my God'.[35] The entire psalm, therefore, is grounded upon the certainty of the divine human relationship;[36] 'the emphatic "my God" expresses the covenantal bond with all its assurances'.[37] God had said to Israel, 'I will be your God and you will be my people' (Lev. 26.12). The relationship is one of covenant.

Because God is his God, the psalmist determines that he will seek God 'earnestly' (שחר). Rather than use the more formal בקש[38] the psalmist chooses a denominative verb from the word that means 'dawn' and that 'connotes to seek with one's whole heart',[39] to 'seek longingly, wholeheartedly, desperately'.[40] Thus, the psalmist 'expresses a powerful, longing desire for the near presence of God.'[41]

The longing for God is made more concrete through the metaphorical, yearning cry, 'My soul is thirsty for you, my flesh longs for you'.[42] The language of hunger and thirst 'voices the intensity of emotional intimacy between the psalmist and God'.[43] Combination of 'soul' and 'flesh' signifies

---

[35] Kraus, *Psalms 60–150*, p. 17, argues that אֱלֹהִים אֵלִי אַתָּה אֲשַׁחֲרֶךָּ should be rendered, 'God, my God, you—I seek you', so that אַתָּה functions to add emphasis (Cf. Gen. 49.8). However, it is clear that in its four other occurrences (Pss. 22.11; 118.28; 140.7; cf. also Ps. 31.15), the phrase אֵלִי אַתָּה should be translated 'you are my God', and I would argue that it carries the same meaning here. Cf. Franz Delitzsch, *Biblical Commentary on the Psalms* (trans. Francis Bolton; 3 vols.; Grand Rapids, MI: Eerdmans, 1867). In any case, the personal claim ('my God') is clear and striking.

[36] Briggs and Briggs, *The Book of Psalms*, II, p. 72.

[37] John Eaton, *The Psalms: A Historical and Spiritual Commentary with an Introduction and New Translation* (London: T & T Clark International, 2003), p. 235.

[38] A.A. Anderson, *The Book of Psalms: Based on the Revised Standard Version* (New Century Bible Commentary; 2 vols.; Grand Rapids, MI: Eerdmans, 1981), I, p. 456.

[39] Mitchell J. Dahood, *Psalms* (Anchor Bible; 3 vols.; Garden City, NY: Doubleday, 1966), p. 96.

[40] David J.A. Clines (ed.), *The Concise Dictionary of Classical Hebrew* (Sheffield, UK: Sheffield Phoenix Press, 2009), p. 456.

[41] Tate, *Psalms 51–100*, p. 127.

[42] The verb כמה is a *hapax legomenon* whose meaning, 'long, yearn for', is deduced from Semitic cognates and from the context. See Clines (ed.), *The Concise Dictionary of Classical Hebrew*, p. 178.

[43] James L. Crenshaw, *The Psalms: An Introduction* (Grand Rapids, MI: Eerdmans, 2001), p. 15. It is likely that צמא in the perfect signifies a state of thirst that began in the past and continues into the present (cf. Judg. 4.19).

that the whole person is involved in the longing.[44] The longing of body and soul speaks of 'a religion that is satisfied with nothing less than God himself and is prepared to wait and wait for him.'[45]

The psalmist's level of yearning is equal to that of 'a dry and weary land without water'. Although the reference to the 'dry and weary land' is probably metaphorical,[46] it nevertheless provides a vivid image that would be readily identifiable to the original Palestinian hearers of the psalm. It recalls a similar statement found earlier in the Psalter: 'As the deer pants for the water brooks, so my soul pants for you, O God. My soul thirsts for God, for the living God' (Ps. 42.1–2).

The psalmist longs, body and soul, for his God. He longs deeply and passionately for God's presence, a presence that he has experienced in the past. The absence of God is even more painful given the memory of previous joyful times in the 'sanctuary', among the people of God.[47] In God's holy place, recounts the psalmist, 'I have seen you, beholding your power and your glory'. 'Thus' (כֵּן), 'as his soul thus thirsted for God and longed for him, he was allowed to behold him'.[48] The psalmist's longing to encounter God in the sanctuary finds echoes in other psalmic texts: 'My soul longed and even yearned for the courts of the Lord' (Ps. 84.2); 'I will dwell in the house of the Lord forever' (Ps. 23.6); and 'that I may dwell in the house of the Lord all the days of my life, to behold the beauty of the Lord (Ps. 27.4).

---

[44] Briggs and Briggs, *The Book of Psalms*, II, p. 73.
[45] John W. McKay, 'The Experiences of Dereliction and of God's Presence in the Psalms: An Exercise in Old Testament Exegesis in the Light of Renewal Theology', in Paul Elbert (ed.) *Faces of Renewal: Studies in Honor of Stanley M. Horton Presented on His 70th Birthday* (Peabody, MA: Hendrickson Publishers, 1988), pp. 3–19 (10). In his study of the Psalms, McKay proposes to 'look for a moment beneath the skin of (reconstructed) rituals in an attempt to tap the heartbeat of religious experience in many psalms of lamentation that speak of dereliction and longing for the presence of God.'
[46] Artur Weiser, *The Psalms: A Commentary* (Philadelphia: Westminster, 1962), p. 454. Cf. Tate, *Psalms 51–100*, p. 127, and Crenshaw, *Psalms*, p. 16.
[47] Weiser, *The Psalms: A Commentary*, p. 454, claims that the setting for the whole psalm is the sanctuary. Cf. E.W. Hengstenberg, *Commentary on the Psalms* (3 vols.; Cherry Hill, NJ: Mack Publishing, 4th edn, 1972), II, p. 303. I would argue, however, that nothing in the psalm suggests that the psalmist is in the sanctuary. Instead, he is away from the sanctuary, and he 'describes his former times of worship in the sanctuary' (Stephen J. Lennox, *Psalms: A Bible Commentary in the Wesleyan Tradition* [Indianapolis, IN: Wesleyan Pub. House, 1999], p. 197).
[48] Weiser, *The Psalms: A Commentary*, pp. 454–55.

The psalmist testifies to having 'seen' (חזה) God.[49] Kraus suggests that the verb probably refers to a theophany,[50] but Anderson counters that although חזה is 'used as a technical term for receiving prophetic visions... the allusion in verse 2 need not be to a theophany or vision'.[51] Attempting to describe the Psalmist's encounter, Tate writes, 'The visionary experience of the verb חזה ("to see/have a vision") is not described in detail, and doubtless differed in form and degree among worshipers.' The psalmists vision of God may have involved physical rituals and it may included the 'verbal and mental, combined with the rich symbolism of the temple'.[52]

Whatever form the vision took, it is described here as a manifestation of God's 'power and glory'. The two lines of v. 3 stand in parallel to each other with the second line refining the first. The phrase, 'I have seen you', is restated as 'beholding your power and your glory'.[53] God's 'power' is his sovereign capacity to choose, to act, and to intervene in the world (for both judgment and salvation). His 'glory' is the display of his weightiness, his awesomeness, his majesty, and his holiness. The seeing of God and the beholding of God's power and glory refer to an encounter with God, an experience of God's presence which he had enjoyed on earlier occasions and 'for which the psalmist's heart thirsts'.[54] Kraus concludes, 'This profound high esteem of the communion with God forms the actual center of the profound psalm'.[55]

B. *Gratitude (vv. 4–6)*

Following upon the moving articulation of his unquenchable longing for God's presence, the psalmist breaks forth in joyous praise. 'I will praise you', he declares to God, 'because your kindness (חסד) is better than life'. Before Psalm 63, human life in its fulness, enjoyed in covenant with

---

[49] Clines (ed.), *The Concise Dictionary of Classical Hebrew*, p. 111, indicates that the word means 'see, perceive'.
[50] Kraus, *Psalms 60–150*, p. 19.
[51] Anderson, *The Book of Psalms*, I, p. 456.
[52] Tate, *Psalms 51–100*, p. 127.
[53] The infinitive construct here is epexegetical or circumstantial. See Wilhelm Gesenius, E. Kautzsch, and A.E. Cowley, *Gesenius' Hebrew Grammar* (Oxford: The Clarendon Press, 2d English edn, 1910), §1140; Bruce K. Waltke and Michael Patrick O'Connor, *An Introduction to Biblical Hebrew Syntax* (Winona Lake, IN: Eisenbrauns, 1990), §36.2.3e; Paul Joüon and T. Muraoka, *A Grammar of Biblical Hebrew* (Subsidia Biblica, 14; Rome: Pontifical Biblical Institute, 1991), §1240. Cf. the RSV.
[54] Rogerson and McKay, *Psalms*, II, p. 65.
[55] Kraus, *Psalms 60–150*, p. 21.

God, was understood as the ultimate benefit of God's חסד, his covenant loyalty.[56] Now, however, the psalmist suggests that God's kindness and human life might be envisioned as two separate spheres. Kraus insists that this 'discrimination between lovingkindness and life was something wholly new'.[57] Eaton surmises that the psalmist is striving 'to express the inexpressible wonder of one who experiences' God's covenant love.[58] In agreement with Eaton, Terrien asserts, 'No other psalmist expresses with such ambiguous and yet convincing overtones his apprehension of the divine embrace'.[59]

In celebration of God's faithful love, the psalmist pledges to 'praise' God, to 'bless' God, and to 'lift up' his hands to God in worship. Lifting up the hands is the 'customary attitude of the worshipper in prayer... a sign of an expectant trust that one's empty hands will be "filled" with divine blessings.'[60] This elaborate praise will not be offered briefly or intermittently; it will continue throughout the psalmist's 'life'. He promises to bless the Lord 'in perpetual worship'.[61]

The mood of exuberant jubilation is reinforced with the statement, 'Like marrow and fatness my soul will be satisfied'. 'Marrow and fatness' may 'form a hendiadys meaning "very rich food"',[62] or the expression may refer to 'the sacrificial feasts which characterised seasons of rejoicing before God in the worship of the temple'.[63] Either way, the psalmist anticipates a great feast, but not literally; he is instead contemplating a kind of satisfaction that will be 'like' the satisfaction of a great feast. Thus, the psalmist again imagines the blessings of God to be distinct from the material world. The lovingkindness of God is like a sumptuous feast that quenches the thirst and satisfies the hunger. Because of God's kindness, the psalmist can look forward to a full and joyous life; and because he is blessed, his 'mouth will offer praise with joyful lips'.

---

[56] Clines (ed.), *The Concise Dictionary of Classical Hebrew*, p. 126, defines חסד as 'loyalty, faithfulness, kindness, love, mercy', a quite broad definition.
[57] Kraus, *Psalms 60–150*, p. 20.
[58] Eaton, *The Psalms*, p. 235.
[59] Terrien, *The Psalms*, p. 462.
[60] Anderson, *The Book of Psalms*, I, p. 457.
[61] Briggs and Briggs, *The Book of Psalms*, II, p. 73.
[62] Tate, *Psalms 51–100*, p. 124. Cf. Anderson, *The Book of Psalms*, I, p. 458.
[63] Briggs and Briggs, *The Book of Psalms*, II, p. 73.

C. Trust and Commitment (vv. 7-9)

The third section of Psalm 63 continues to express thankfulness, but the tone transitions to a mood of deep trust and commitment to God. While vv. 4-6 declare the present and future value of God's immeasurable kindness, vv. 7-9 recall the past benefit's of the psalmist's relationship to God. The psalmist asserts that just as God has been faithful to him, he has been faithful to God by remembering (זכר) God and meditating (הגה) upon God, two activities that signal deep devotion and commitment.

The psalmist remembers that, with God as his 'help', he shouted for joy underneath the covering of God's 'wings', which represent God's 'protection'.[64] He remembers further that he 'stuck close' to God and that God supported him. The phrase 'stuck close' is difficult to translate into English. The verb דבק means 'to cling, cleave, stick to' (cf. Gen. 2.24), but in combination with אחרי, it apparently means to 'pursue or follow very closely behind'.[65] Metaphorically, it signifies 'loyalty, affection, etc.'.[66] Israel is commanded to 'cling' to Yahweh (Deut. 10.20; 13.5; Josh. 23.8; Ps. 119.31). While the psalmist 'stuck close' to God, God 'upheld' him with his powerful 'right hand'. 'With all the strength of his will he clings to God, to whom he owes his outward and inward support'.[67] This reciprocal relationship 'is almost a definition in personalized language of the *hesed* relationship between God and his people in the covenant'.[68] Calvin comments that the psalmist would 'follow with unwearied constancy, long as the way might be, and full of hardships, and beset with obstacles.'[69]

D. Confident Hope (vv. 10-12)

This final section of the psalm registers a mood of confident hope for the future. The section unfolds through a contrast between the psalmist's ene-

---

[64] Anderson, *The Book of Psalms*, I, p. 458.

[65] Ludwig Koehler and Walter Baumgartner, *The Hebrew and Aramaic Lexicon of the Old Testament* (2 vols.; Leiden: Brill, Study edn, 2001), I, p. 209.

[66] Francis Brown et al., *The New Brown, Driver, Briggs, Gesenius Hebrew and English Lexicon: With an Appendix Containing the Biblical Aramaic* (trans. Edward Robinson; Peabody, MA: Hendrickson, 1979), p. 179. Cf. Tate, *Psalms 51-100*, p. 128.

[67] Weiser, *The Psalms: A Commentary*, p. 455.

[68] Rogerson and McKay, *Psalms*, p. 67. Cf. Stephen J. Lennox, *Psalms: A Bible Commentary in the Wesleyan Tradition* (Indianapolis, IN: Wesleyan Pub. House, 1999), p. 198.

[69] John Calvin, *Commentary on the Book of Psalms* (trans. James Anderson; Grand Rapids, MI: Eerdmans, 1949), p. 383.

mies and 'the king'. The enemies, who seek 'to ruin'[70] the psalmist, will 'go into the depths of the earth', and they will become the 'prey of foxes'.[71] The king, however, will rejoice in God, along with all those who swear allegiance to God, because the mouths of the deceivers 'will be stopped'.

The psalmist is confident that justice will prevail, that evil will be punished, and that God's people 'will glory' in their covenant relationship with God. Wicked enemies, struck down by 'the sword', 'will most certainly receive their due punishment... their dead bodies will be desecrated' by wild animals.[72] Deprived of a proper burial,[73] they will cast down to the 'underworld' of the dead.[74] In the end, those who seek to ruin God's people will themselves be ruined.

The king,[75] however, will 'rejoice in God', and those who swear allegiance to 'him' will glory. In the phrase 'swear by him', the antecedent of the pronoun 'him' is God.[76] All who swear by him is the psalmist's way of connecting the psalm to the community of faith.[77] It 'is a poetic description of the Israelites',[78] and the combined reference to the king and all who 'swear' by God's name is 'probably a comprehensive phrase denoting the whole community of the faithful with the king as its head'.[79] Thus, the king is 'representative or exemplary of the person who seeks God'.[80]

The last section of Psalm 63 is a fitting conclusion to this psalm of reorientation. The psalmist has admitted his sense of separation from God's presence (v. 2) and his need to be satisfied by God's kindness (v. 6). He has remembered (v. 7) times when he needed God's help (v. 8) and God came to his aid. In this final strophe, he acknowledges the ongoing presence of

---

[70] The Hebrew for 'ruin' is actually a noun, prefixed with a preposition that suggests purpose: 'They seek my life for the purpose of ruin'. See Clines (ed.), *The Concise Dictionary of Classical Hebrew*, p. 450, and Koehler and Baumgartner, *HALOT*, II, p. 1427.

[71] Koehler and Baumgartner, *HALOT*, II, 1445, define שׁוּעָל as 'fox'. So do Brown *et al.*, *BDB*, but they add, 'perhaps also jackal' (p. 1048).

[72] Anderson, *The Book of Psalms*, I, p. 459.

[73] Lennox, *Psalms: A Bible Commentary in the Wesleyan Tradition*, p. 198.

[74] Kraus, *Psalms 60–150*, p. 20.

[75] Anderson, *The Book of Psalms*, I, p. 459. Contra Eaton, *The Psalms*, p. 235, and Hengstenberg, *Commentary on the Psalms*, II, p. 301, who argues that the reference to the king does not necessarily mean that the psalmist must be the king or that this is a royal psalm.

[76] Tate, *Psalms 51–100*, p. 128; cf. Terrien, *The Psalms*, p. 464; contra Anderson, *The Book of Psalms*, I, p. 459.

[77] Tate, *Psalms 51–100*, p. 128.

[78] Weiser, *The Psalms: A Commentary*, p. 456.

[79] Rogerson and McKay, *Psalms*, p. 67.

[80] J. Clinton McCann, Jr., 'Psalms', in *The New Interpreter's Bible* (Nashville, TN: Abingdon Press, 1996), IV, pp. 639–1280 (928).

dangerous enemies who threaten his safety. Nevertheless, his past experiences of God's presence (v. 3), God's covenant loyalty (v. 4), and God's tender care (v. 9) have generated a renewed confidence in God's faithfulness. The Psalmist is convinced that God's people will prevail in the end.

VI. Acknowledging Pentecostal Passions

Psalm 63 is a passionate expression of the psalmist's spiritual longings after God. These longings are suggestive of the affective component of Pentecostal spirituality. I find that the Psalmist's 'hunger' and 'thirst' for God is consistent with Pentecostal spirituality and that the desire to encounter God in the sanctuary is consistent with the goals of Pentecostal worship. Chris Green insists that 'Pentecostal spirituality is nothing if not a *personal* engagement' with God.[81] Although I am most familiar with North American Pentecostalism and do not claim to speak for all Pentecostals, my associations with Pentecostals in Latin America, Africa, Australia, Asia, Europe, and the UK lead me to conclude that a passionate affective spirituality is common to all Pentecostals.[82] Like the Psalmist, the Pentecostal community is hungry and thirsty for God and seeks to behold God's power and glory, to lift up their hands in adoration, to testify of past blessings, to praise God with joyful lips, to shout for joy, to stick close to God, to rejoice in God, and to live in hope of the coming reign of God.

The psalmist's longing for the manifestation of God's 'power and glory' can be compared to Pentecostalism's 'holy desire for God Himself'.[83] This longing for God is described repeatedly in early Pentecostal literature. For example, Alice Flower writes, 'All I seemed to sense was a deep craving for the overflowing of His love in my heart. At that moment it

---

[81] Chris E.W. Green, *Toward a Pentecostal Theology of the Lord's Supper: Foretasting the Kingdom* (Cleveland, TN: CPT Press, 2012), p. 289 (emphasis in the original).

[82] Regarding Korean spirituality, see Julie C. Ma, 'Korean Pentecostal Spirituality: A Case Study of Jashil Choi', *Asian Journal of Pentecostal Studies* 5.2 (2002), pp. 235–54, and Myung Soo Park, 'Korean Pentecostal Spirituality as Manifested in the Testimonies of Believers of the Yoido Full Gospel Church', *Asian Journal of Pentecostal Studies* 7.1 (2004), pp. 35–56 (40–41, 44–48, 55). For African spirituality, see David J. Maxwell, 'The Durawall of Faith: Pentecostal Spirituality in Neo-Liberal Zimbabwe', *Journal of Religion in Africa* 35.1 (2005), pp. 4–32 (5–6, 21).

[83] Daniel Castelo, 'Tarrying on the Lord: Affections, Virtues and Theological Ethics in Pentecostal Perspective', *Journal of Pentecostal Theology* 13.1 (2004), pp. 31–56 (53).

seemed I wanted Jesus more than anything in all the world.'[84] Reflecting on her passion for God, Zelma E. Argue recalls, 'my whole heart seemed to just one big vacuum craving and crying for God'.[85] Echoing the words of Ps. 63.6, Alice E. Luce affirms, 'the Lord is our portion. We have had a real taste of the Lord and found out that he is a satisfying portion.'[86]

The Pentecostal longing for God can be described partly as the desire for a personal encounter with God. Albrecht argues that for 'Pentecostals, the entire ritual field and the drama that emerges within the ritual matrix is aimed toward an *encounter*'.[87] Jaichandran and Madhav agree:

> It cannot be denied that the most important value that governs Pentecostal spirituality is the locus of individual experience. Viewed positively, this means that the Pentecostal is not satisfied until he or she has had an experience with God... A person is not satisfied by hearing about someone else's experience with God; they must experience God themselves.[88]

Of course, as with any revivalist movement, Pentecostalism has generated unwelcomed excesses and unbiblical experiences.[89] The psalmist's longing for God, however, is not a longing for an experience for experience's sake, but it is a longing for God in relation, in covenant; and it is a longing that Pentecostals seek to imitate.[90]

The psalmist's experience of 'seeing' God and 'beholding' the power and glory of God are signs to the Pentecostal that God is open to human encounter. Keith Warrington writes, 'Two pertinent words when referring to Pentecostal spirituality are "expectancy" and "encounter". Pentecostals expect to encounter God. It undergirds much of their worship and

---

[84] Alice Reynolds Flower, 'My Pentecost', *Assemblies of God Heritage* 20 (Winter 1997–98), pp. 17–20 (18); excerpted from her *Grace for Grace: Some Highlights of God's Grace in the Daily Life of the Flower Family* (Springfield, MO: privately published, 1961).

[85] Cited by Edith Waldvogel Blumhofer, *'Pentecost in My Soul': Explorations in the Meaning of Pentecostal Experience in the Assemblies of God* (Springfield, MO: Gospel Pub. House, 1989), p. 159.

[86] Cited by Blumhofer, *Pentecost in My Soul*, p. 136.

[87] Daniel E. Albrecht, 'Pentecostal Spirituality: Looking through the Lens of Ritual', *Pneuma* 14.2 (1992), pp. 107–25 (110) (emphasis in the original).

[88] Rebecca Jaichandran and B.D. Madhav, 'Pentecostal Spirituality in a Postmodern World', *Asian Journal of Pentecostal Studies* 6.1 (2003), pp. 39–61 (55).

[89] Jaichandran and Madhav, 'Pentecostal Spirituality in a Postmodern World', pp. 57, 59.

[90] Cf. Cecil M. Robeck, Jr., 'The Nature of Pentecostal Spirituality', *Pneuma* 14.2 (1992), pp. 103–106 (105), and Veli-Matti Kärkkäinen, '"Encountering Christ in the Full Gospel Way": An Incarnational Pentecostal Spirituality', *Journal of the European Pentecostal Theological Association* 27.1 (2007), pp. 9–23 (11–12). Kärkkäinen explicates Pentecostal worship as the 'longing for meeting with the Lord' (pp. 17–20).

theology and may even be identified as another way of defining worship.'[91] From Azusa Street until now, Pentecostals everywhere have insisted upon the present reality of God's presence to save, sanctify, fill with the Holy Spirit, heal, and reign as coming king.[92]

VII. Conclusions and Implications for Pentecostal Spirituality

In his article on 'Community and Worship', Jerome Boone argues that the 'single most important goal of any Pentecostal worship service is a personal encounter with the Spirit of God'.[93] This encounter will often include the manifestation of spiritual gifts and the worshipers will experience 'the Spirit as transformational power'.[94] He points to the importance of prayer as a 'divine-human encounter in which burdens are relinquished' to God, who cares and who has the power to eliminate those burdens.[95] Furthermore, Boone observes the value of personal testimony as a means of honoring God and of forming the faith of the listeners. Boone warns, however, that the Pentecostal movement is in danger of losing its distinctive Pentecostal spirituality. Perhaps we should ask, 'Has Pentecostalism left its "first love" (Rev. 2.4)?'

If the Pentecostal movement is to maintain its vitality from generation to generation, it must periodically reclaim the spiritual passion that we find demonstrated in Psalm 63. The biblical text functions as a vehicle of spiritual formation that can inform Pentecostal spirituality and practice. I would suggest the following ways in which Psalm 63 can help to shape the spirituality of the Pentecostal movement both now and in the future. These implications are only suggestive, and they (along with the article in its entirety) are meant to promote dialogue and creative engagement with the biblical text.

---

[91] Keith Warrington, *Pentecostal Theology: A Theology of Encounter* (New York: T & T Clark, 2008), p. 219. Cf. Daniel E. Albrecht, *Rites in the Spirit: A Ritual Approach to Pentecostal/Charismatic Spirituality* (JPTSup, 17; Sheffield, UK: Sheffield Academic Press, 1999), pp. 226, 38–39.

[92] *The Apostolic Faith* 1.1 (Sept. 1906), p. 1 and *passim*. Writing in the first issue of *Pneuma*, William MacDonald, 'Temple Theology', *Pneuma* 1.1 (Spring 1979), insists, 'Unless we dare claim that Christianity was fossilized in the first century, we must contend that the Spirit is still speaking to the churches' (p. 48). Cf. Cecil M. Robeck, *The Azusa Street Mission and Revival: The Birth of the Global Pentecostal Movement* (Nashville, TN: Nelson Reference & Electronic, 2006), p. 132.

[93] R. Jerome Boone, 'Community and Worship: The Key Components of Pentecostal Christian Formation', *Journal of Pentecostal Theology* 8 (1996), pp. 129–42 (137).

[94] Boone, 'Community and Worship', p. 138.

[95] Boone, 'Community and Worship', p. 130.

1. The Pentecostal approach to spiritual formation should include the nurture and development of the affect. Opportunities for affective engagement and expression should be offered. These opportunities include affective expressions through worship, prayer, testimony, and waiting upon God.

In a recent article, Johnathan Alvarado elaborates on the distinctive characteristics of Pentecostal worship. He writes, 'Spirit-filled worship is marked and characterized by a vivid awareness of the presence of God and the activity of the Holy Spirit within the lives of the saints and within the context of the worship experience'.[96] Alvarado argues that Spirit-filled leadership in worship requires three things: 1) the 'skillful handling of the biblical text' as the Word of God, 2) 'an understanding of the Spirit's presence' and influence, and 3) 'the intentional involvement of the congregation'.[97] After looking at Psalm 63, I would suggest a fourth requirement (perhaps as an expansion of number 2): the worship leader must possess a deep longing to encounter God through the Holy Spirit and to lead others into that encounter. Worship leaders must conceive of their ministry as formative, for 'in worshipping God we come to behold the object that orients and disposes us properly. One learns to love God by beholding Him and communing with Him.'[98]

2. The Pentecostal church must provide frequent and open-ended opportunities for prayer. Psalm 63.2–9 is a sustained direct address to God, in which the psalmist uses the second person address, 'you', 18 times. The spiritual life cannot be nurtured without times of deep communion with God in prayer. Pentecostal spirituality is formed and expressed through regular and intensive times of prayer and fasting.[99] Christian formation can not be accomplished quickly and without struggle. Discipleship consists of more than just right thinking, right teaching, and right doctrine; it must include right 'feeling', that is, rightly oriented affections.

When we read Psalm 63, we are overhearing the prayers of the psalmist, and in so doing we are being shaped to follow the psalmist's example. Similarly, our prayers should be overheard by others,[100] who will learn from us that honest expressions of pain and struggle are acceptable to God and that a passion for God's presence is commendable.

---

[96] Johnathan E. Alvarado, 'Worship in the Spirit: Pentecostal Perspectives on Liturgical Theology and Praxis', *Journal of Pentecostal Theology* 21.1 (2012), pp. 135–51 (143).
[97] Alvarado, 'Worship in the Spirit', pp. 146–47.
[98] Castelo, 'Tarrying on the Lord', p. 38.
[99] Ma, 'Korean Pentecostal Spirituality', p. 238 and *passim*.
[100] Gerald T. Sheppard, 'Theology and the Book of Psalms', *Interpretation* 46 (1992), pp. 143–55 (143).

3. In our practice of the Pentecostal life and ministry, we must become hungry and thirsty for God, desperate for God's presence. The psalmist expresses dependence upon God as a 'help' and as a 'support'. The psalmist feels that he will die of hunger and thirst unless God appears with his refreshing presence. In many cases, however, our desperation for God's presence and help has been supplanted by structures of our own invention, substitutes for the power and glory of God. We can do 'church' without God. Consequently, prayers of desperation are rarely heard because we have back up plans, safety nets, and formal structures that can exist without God's help.

4. Pentecostalism must reaffirm its eschatological hope. I observe that verses 10–12 point to the future and could even be considered eschatological in focus: The wicked will be punished; those who are faithful to God will rejoice in God's protection; and the kingdom of God will manifest itself as a kingdom of justice and righteousness.

5. Pentecostals face the danger of seeking out experiences rather than seeking God for God's sake. In the past, Pentecostals called this kind of shallow emotionalism 'wild fire'. On the one hand, it is all to easy for worship to become no more than entertainment or self-gratification. On the other hand, genuine encounter with God results in a dramatic experience. It is an experience that cannot be manipulated by ministers and worship leaders who prompt and prod the congregation until they are worked up into a frenzy. The disciples' encounter with God through the Holy Spirit in Acts 2 was powerful and moving, but it did not occur as a result of their own artificial efforts. In response to their prayer, their worship, and their waiting, the Holy Spirit came upon them as an external force sent from heaven. Similarly, the focus of Psalm 63 is upon the relational quality of the encounter between the psalmist and God.

6. Pentecostalism must recover the practice of testimony. Psalm 63 is directed to God, but it is a song that is meant to be heard by the congregation, and as such, it functions as testimony. The psalmist testifies to the experience of seeing God's glory in the sanctuary, and to the many times when God has been a help and a support. This testimony includes aspects of the psalmist's spiritual journey, such as times of praise, meditation, and sticking close to God. The recounting of the psalmist's own longing for God is an implicit challenge to the hearer to pursue God with the same fervent intensity and with the same unreserved yearning.

BIBLIOGRAPHY OF WORKS ON PENTECOSTAL HERMENEUTICS

Abraham, Joseph, 'Feminist Hermeneutics and Pentecostal Spirituality: The Creation Narrative of Genesis as a Paradigm', *Asian Journal of Pentecostal Studies* 6.1 (2003), pp. 3–21.
Althouse, Peter, 'Toward a Theological Understanding of the Pentecostal Appeal to Experience', *Journal of Ecumenical Studies* 38.4 (2001), pp. 399–411.
Miguel Álvarez, *La Palabra, el Espíritu y la Comunidad de Fe: Endendiendo a la Hermenéutica Pentecostal* (Cleveland, TN: Editorial Evangélica, 2007).
Anderson, Gordon L., 'Pentecostal Hermeneutics: Part I', *Paraclete* 28.1 (Winter 1994), pp. 1–11.
—— 'Pentecostal Hermeneutics: Part II', *Paraclete* 28.2 (Spring 1994), pp. 13–22.
Archer, Kenneth J., 'Pentecostal Hermeneutics: Retrospect and Prospect', *Journal of Pentecostal Theology* 8 (1996), pp. 63–81.
—— 'Early Pentecostal Biblical Interpretation', *Journal of Pentecostal Theology* 18.1 (2001), pp. 79–117.
—— 'Pentecostal Story: The Hermeneutical Filter for the Making of Meaning', *PNEUMA: The Journal of the Society for Pentecostal Studies* 26 (2004), pp. 36–59.
—— *A Pentecostal Hermeneutic for the Twenty-First Century: Spirit, Scripture and Community* (JPTSup, 28; London: T. & T. Clark, 2004).
—— *A Pentecostal Hermeneutic: Spirit, Scripture and Community* (Cleveland, TN: CPT Press, 2009).
Archer, Kenneth J., and Richard E. Waldrop, 'Liberating Hermeneutics: Toward a Holistic Pentecostal Mission of Peace and Justice', *JEPTA: Journal of the European Pentecostal Theological Association* 31.1 (2011), pp. 65–80.
Arrington, French L., 'Hermeneutics', in Stanley M. Burgess and Gary B. McGee (eds.), *Dictionary of Pentecostal and Charismatic Movements* (Grand Rapids, MI: Eerdmans, 1988).
—— 'The Use of the Bible by Pentecostals', *PNEUMA: The Journal of the Society for Pentecostal Studies* 16.1 (1994), pp. 101–107.
Asamoah-Gyadu, J. Kwabena, ' "God's Laws of Productivity": Creation in African Pentecostal Hermeneutics', in *Spirit Renews the Face of the Earth* (Eugene, OR: Pickwick, 2009), pp. 175–90.
—— 'Learning to Prosper by Wrestling and by Negotiation: Jacob and Esau in Contemporary African Pentecostal Hermeneutics', *Journal of Pentecostal Theology* 21.1 (2012), pp. 64–86.
Atkinson, William, 'Worth a Second Look?: Pentecostal Hermeneutics', *Evangel* 21.2 (2003), pp. 49–54.
Autry, Arden C., 'Dimensions of Hermeneutics in Pentecostal Focus', *Journal of Pentecostal Theology* 3 (1993), pp. 29–50.
Baker, Robert O., 'Pentecostal Bible Reading: Toward a Model of Reading for the Formation of the Affections', *Journal of Pentecostal Theology* 7 (1995), pp. 34–38.
Becker, Matthias, 'A Tenet under Examination: Reflections on the Pentecostal Hermeneutical Approach', *Journal of the European Pentecostal Theological Association* 24 (2004), pp. 30–48.
Brathwaite, Renea, 'Seymour on Scripture' (38th Annual Meeting of the Society for Pentecostal Studies, Eugene, OR, March 2009).
—— 'Seymour the "New" Theologian: An Investigation into the Theology of an Early Pentecostal Pioneer' (PhD, Regent University School of Divinity, 2013).
Brubaker, Malcolm R., 'Postmodernism and Pentecostals: A Case Study of Evangelical Hermeneutics', *Evangelical Journal* 15 (1997), pp. 33–45.

Byrd, Joseph, 'Paul Ricoeur's Hermeneutical Theory and Pentecostal Proclamation', *PNEUMA: The Journal of the Society for Pentecostal Studies* 15.2 (1993), pp. 203–14.

Camery-Hoggatt, Jerry, 'The Word of God from Living Voices: Orality and Literacy in the Pentecostal Tradition', *PNEUMA: The Journal of the Society for Pentecostal Studies* 27 (2005), pp. 225–55.

Cargal, Timothy B., 'Beyond the Fundamentalist-Modernist Controversy: Pentecostals and Hermeneutics in a Postmodern Age', *PNEUMA: The Journal of the Society for Pentecostal Studies* 15 (1993), pp. 163–87.

Cartledge, Mark J., 'Empirical Theology: Towards an Evangelical-Charismatic Hermeneutic', *Journal of Pentecostal Theology* 9 (1996), pp. 115–26.

Cheung, Luke L., 'A Preliminary Study on Pentecostal Hermeneutics', *CGST Journal* 33 (2002), pp. 97–118.

Clark, Mathew S., 'An Investigation into the Nature of a Viable Pentecostal Hermeneutic', DTh, University of South Africa, 1996.

—— 'Pentecostal Hermeneutics: The Challenge of Relating to (Post)-Modern Literary Theory', *Acta Patristica et Byzantina* 12 (2001), pp. 41–67.

Coombs, Clayton, 'Reading in Tongues: The Case for a Pneumatalogical Hermeneutic in Conversation with James K. Smith', *PNEUMA: The Journal of the Society for Pentecostal Studies* 32.2 (2010), pp. 261–68.

Davies, Andrew, 'Reading in the Spirit: Some Brief Observations on Pentecostal Interpretation and the Ethical Difficulties of the Old Testament', *Journal of Beliefs & Values: Studies in Religion & Education* 30.3 (2009), pp. 303–11.

—— 'What Does It Mean to Read the Bible as a Pentecostal?', *Journal of Pentecostal Theology* 18.2 (2009), pp. 216–29.

—— 'The Spirit of Freedom: Pentecostals, the Bible and Social Justice', *JEPTA: Journal of the European Pentecostal Theological Association* 31.1 (2011), pp. 53–64.

Debelak, Robert Paul, *Hidden in Plain Sight: Esther and a Marginalized Hermeneutic* (Eugene, OR: Wipf & Stock, 2008).

Dempster, Murray W., 'Paradigm Shifts and Hermeneutics: Confronting Issues Old and New', *PNEUMA: The Journal of the Society for Pentecostal Studies* 15 (1993), pp. 129–35.

—— 'Pentecostal Hermenuetics', *PNEUMA: The Journal of the Society for Pentecostal Studies* 16.1 (1994), pp. 101–41.

Dowd, Michael B., 'Contours of a Narrative Pentecostal Theology and Practice' (15th Annual Meeting of the Society for Pentecostal Studies, Gaithersburg, MD, 1985).

Ellington, Scott A., 'Pentecostalism and the Authority of Scripture', *Journal of Pentecostal Theology* 9 (1996), pp. 16–38.

—— 'History, Story, and Testimony: Locating Truth in a Pentecostal Hermeneutic', *PNEUMA: The Journal of the Society for Pentecostal Studies* 23.2 (2001), pp. 245–63.

—— 'Locating Pentecostals at the Hermeneutical Round Table', *Journal of Pentecostal Theology* 22.2 (2013), forthcoming.

Enyinnaya, John O., 'Pentecostal Hermeneutics and Preaching: An Appraisal', *Ogbomoso Journal of Theology* 13.1 (2008), pp. 144–53.

Ervin, Howard M., 'Hermeneutics: A Pentecostal Option', *PNEUMA: The Journal of the Society for Pentecostal Studies* 3 (1981), pp. 11–25.

Fee, Gordon, *Gospel and Spirit: Issues in New Testament Hermeneutics* (Peabody, MA: Hendrickson Publishers, 1991).

—— 'Hermeneutics and the Historical Precedent: A Major Problem in Pentecostal Hermeneutics', in R.P. Spittler (ed.), *Perspectives on the New Pentecostalism* (Grand Rapids, MI: Baker, 1976), pp. 118–32.

Graham, Stephen R., ' "Thus Saith the Lord": Biblical Hermeneutics in the Early Pentecostal Movement', *Ex Auditu* 12 (1996), pp. 121–35.

Green, Chris E.W., ' "Treasures Old and New": Reading the Old Testament with Early Pentecostal Mothers and Fathers' (41st Annual Meeting of the Society for Pentecostal Studies, Virginia Beach, VA, 2012).

―― *Toward a Pentecostal Theology of the Lord's Supper: Foretasting the Kingdom* (Cleveland, TN: CPT Press, 2012).
Grey, Jacqueline, *Them, Us and Me: How the Old Testament Speaks to People Today* (APSS; Macquarie Centre, NSW: APSS & SCD Press, 2008).
―― *Three's a Crowd: Pentecostalism, Hermeneutics, and the Old Testament* (Eugene, OR: Pickwick, 2011).
Harrington, Hannah K., and Rebecca Patten, 'Pentecostal Hermeneutics and Postmodern Literary Theory', *PNEUMA: The Journal of the Society for Pentecostal Studies* 16 (1994), pp. 109–14.
Herholdt, Marius D., 'Pentecostal and Charismatic Hermeneutics', in Adrio König and S.S. Maimela (eds.), *Initiation into Theology: The Rich Variety of Theology and Hermeneutics* (Pretoria: Van Schaik, 1998), pp. 417–31.
Hey, Sam, 'Changing Roles of Pentecostal Hermeneutics', *Evangelical Review of Theology* 25.3 (2001), pp. 210–18.
Holmes, Paula Elizabeth, 'Charismatic Fundamentalism and Orality' (MA, University of Calgary, 1995).
Holmes, Pamela M.S., 'Acts 29 and Authority: Towards a Pentecostal Feminist Hermeneutic of Liberation', in *Liberating Spirit* (Eugene, OR: Pickwick, 2010), pp. 185–210.
Hoover, Jesse A., '"Thy Daughters Shall Prophesy": The Assemblies of God, Inerrancy, and the Question of Clergywomen', *Journal of Pentecostal Theology* 21.2 (2012), pp. 221–39.
Israel, Richard D., Daniel E. Albrecht, and Randal G. McNally, 'Pentecostals and Hermeneutics: Texts, Rituals and Community', *PNEUMA: The Journal of the Society for Pentecostal Studies* 15.2 (1993), pp. 137–61.
Jacobsen, Douglas, 'Pentecostal Hermeneutics in Comparative Perspective' (Annual Meeting of the Society for Pentecostal Studies, Oakland, CA, March 13–15, 1997).
Johns, Cheryl Bridges, *Pentecostal Formation: A Pedagogy among the Oppressed* (JPTSup, 2; Sheffield: Sheffield Academic Press, 1993).
―― 'The Adolescence of Pentecostalism: In Search of a Legitimate Sectarian Identity', *Pneuma* 17.1 (Spring 1995), pp. 3–17.
―― 'Partners in Scandal: Wesleyan and Pentecostal Scholarship', *Wesleyan Theological Journal* 34.1 (1999), pp. 7–23.
―― 'Meeting God in the Margins, Ministry among Modernity's Refugees', in M. Zyniewicz (ed.), The Papers of the Henry Luce III Fellows in Theology (3 vols.; Atlanta: Scholars Press, 1999), III, pp. 7–31.
Johns, Jackie David, 'Pentecostalism and the Postmodern Worldview', *Journal of Pentecostal Theology* 7 (1995), pp. 73–96.
Johns, Jackie David, and Cheryl Bridges Johns, 'Yielding to the Spirit: A Pentecostal Approach to Group Bible Study', *Journal of Pentecostal Theology* 1 (1992), pp. 109–34.
Kärkkäinen, Veli-Matti, 'Pentecostal Hermeneutics in the Making: On the Way from Fundamentalism to Postmodernism', *Journal of the European Pentecostal Theological Association* 18 (1998), pp. 76–115.
Martin, Francis, 'Spirit and Flesh in Doing of Theology', *Journal of Pentecostal Theology* 18 (2001), pp. 5–31.
Martin, Lee Roy, 'Introduction to Biblical Hermeneutics', in Homer G. Rhea (ed.) *Rightly Dividing the Word* (Cleveland, TN: Church of God School of Ministry, 2003), pp. 25–52.
―― 'Pre-Critical Exegesis of the Book of Judges and the Construction of a Post-Critical Hermeneutic', *Ekklesiastikos Pharos* 88 (2006), pp. 338–53.
―― *The Unheard Voice of God: A Pentecostal Hearing of the Book of Judges* (JPTSup, 32; Blandford Forum, UK: Deo Publishing, 2008).
―― 'Hearing the Book of Judges: A Dialogue with Reviewers'; *Journal of Pentecostal Theology* 18.1 (2009), pp. 30–50.
―― '"Where Are the Wonders?": The Exodus Motif in the Book of Judges', *Journal of Biblical and Pneumatological Research* 2 (2010), pp. 87–109.

—— 'Delight in the Torah: The Affective Dimension of Psalm 1', *Old Testament Essays* 23.3 (2010), pp. 708-27.
—— *Biblical Hermeneutics: Essential Keys for Interpreting the Bible* (Miami, FL: Gospel Press, 2011).
—— 'Longing for God: Psalm 63 and Pentecostal Spirituality', *Journal of Pentecostal Theology* 22.1 (2013), pp. 54-76.
—— 'Interpreting the Affective Dimensions of the Biblical Text: A Holistic Hermeneutical Strategy', *Journal for Semitics* 23 (2014), forthcoming.
McCall, Bradford, 'The Pentecostal Reappropriation of Common Sense Realism', *Journal of Pentecostal Theology* 19.1 (2010), pp. 59-75.
McKay, John W., 'When the Veil Is Taken Away: The Impact of Prophetic Experience on Biblical Interpretation', *Journal of Pentecostal Theology* 5 (1994), pp. 17-40.
McLean, Mark D., 'Toward a Pentecostal Hermeneutic', *PNEUMA: The Journal of the Society for Pentecostal Studies* 6 (1984), pp. 35-56.
McQueen, Larry R., *Joel and the Spirit: The Cry of a Prophetic Hermeneutic* (Cleveland, TN: CPT Press, 2009).
Menzies, Robert P., 'Jumping Off the Postmodern Bandwagon', *PNEUMA: The Journal of the Society for Pentecostal Studies* 16 (1994), pp. 115-20.
Menzies, William W., 'Biblical Hermeneutics', in *Conference on the Holy Spirit Digest, Vol 1* (Springfield, Mo: Gospel Pub House, 1983), pp. 62-69.
Moore, Rickie D., 'A Pentecostal Approach to Scripture', *Seminary Viewpoint* 8.1 (1987), pp. 4-5, 11.
—— 'Approaching God's Word Biblically: A Pentecostal Perspective' (Paper presented to the Annual Meeting of the Society for Pentecostal Studies, Fresno, CA, 1989).
—— 'Canon and Charisma in the Book of Deuteronomy', *Journal of Pentecostal Theology* 1 (1992), pp. 75-92.
—— 'Deuteronomy and the Fire of God: A Critical Charismatic Interpretation', *Journal of Pentecostal Theology* 7 (1995), pp. 11-33.
—— '"And Also Much Cattle": Prophetic Passions and the End of Jonah', *Journal of Pentecostal Theology*.11 (1997), pp. 35-48.
—— 'Raw Prayer and Refined Theology: "You Have Not Spoken Straight to Me, as My Servant Job Has"', in Terry Cross and Emerson Powery (eds.), *The Spirit and the Mind: Essays in Informed Pentecostalism* (Lanham, MD: University Press of America, 2000), pp. 35-48.
Moore, Rickie D., John Christopher Thomas, and Steven J. Land, 'Editorial', *Journal of Pentecostal Theology* 1.1 (1992), pp. 3-5.
Nadar, Sarojini, '"The Bible Says!" Feminism, Hermeneutics and Neo-Pentecostal Challenges', *Journal of Theology for Southern Africa* 134 (2009), pp. 131-46.
Nel, M., 'Pentecostals' Reading of the Old Testament', *Verbum et Ecclesia* 28.2 (2007), pp. 524-41.
Newman, Larry Vern, 'Pentecostal Hermeneutics: Suggesting a Model, Exploring the Problems' (21st Annual Meeting of the SPS, Lakeland, FL, 1991).
Noel, Bradley Truman, 'Gordon Fee and the Challenge to Pentecostal Hermeneutics: Thirty Years Later', *PNEUMA: The Journal of the Society for Pentecostal Studies* 26.1 (2004), pp. 60-80.
—— *Pentecostal and Postmodern Hermeneutics: Comparisons and Contemporary Impact* (Eugene, Ore: Wipf and Stock, 2010).
Norris, David S., 'Creation Revealed: An Early Pentecostal Hermeneutic', in *Spirit Renews the Face of the Earth* (Eugene, OR: Pickwick, 2009), pp. 74-92.
Oliverio, L. William, *Theological Hermeneutics in the Classical Pentecostal Tradition: A Typological Account* (Leiden: Brill, 2012).
Omenyo, Cephas N., 'The Bible Says! Neo-Prophetic Hermeneutics in Africa', *Studies in World Christianity* 19.1 (2013), pp. 50-70.

Pinnock, Clark H., 'The Work of the Holy Spirit in Hermeneutics', *Journal of Pentecostal Theology* 2 (1993), pp. 3-23.
—— 'The Work of the Spirit in the Interpretation of Holy Scripture from the Perspective of a Charismatic Biblical Theologian', *Journal of Pentecostal Theology* 18.2 (2009), pp. 157-71.
Plüss, Jean-Daniel, 'Azusa and Other Myths: The Long and Winding Road from Experience to Stated Belief and Back Again', *Pneuma* 15.2 (1983), pp. 189-201.
—— 'The Saviour, Healer and Coming King I Know, but Who in the World Is Jesus? Pentecostal Hermeneutics Reconsidered', *Transformation* 14 (1997), pp. 14-20.
Poirier, John C., 'Narrative Theology and Pentecostal Commitments', *Journal of Pentecostal Theology* 16.2 (2008), pp. 69-85.
Poirier, John C., and B. Scott Lewis, 'Pentecostal and Postmodernist Hermeneutics: A Critique of Three Conceits', *Journal of Pentecostal Theology* 15.1 (2006), pp. 3-21.
Powery, Emerson B., 'Ulrich Luz's *Matthew in History*: A Contribution to Pentecostal Hermeneutics?', *Journal of Pentecostal Theology* 14 (1999), pp. 3-17.
Rhea, Homer G. (ed.), *Rightly Dividing the Word* (Cleveland, TN: Church of God School of Ministry, 2003).
Sheppard, Gerald T., 'Biblical Interpretation after Gadamer', *PNEUMA: The Journal of the Society for Pentecostal Studies* 16 (1984), pp. 121-41.
—— 'Pentecostals and the Hermeneutics of Dispensationalism: The Anatomy of an Uneasy Relationship', *PNEUMA: The Journal of the Society for Pentecostal Studies* 6.2 (1984), pp. 5-33.
—— 'Word and Spirit: Scripture in the Pentecostal Tradition—Part One', *Agora* 1.4 (Spring 1978), pp. 4-5, 17-22.
—— 'Word and Spirit: Scripture in the Pentecostal Tradition—Part Two', *Agora* 2.1 (Summer 1978), pp. 14-19.
Smith, James K.A., 'The Closing of the Book: Pentecostals, Evangelicals, and the Sacred Writings', *Journal of Pentecostal Theology* 11 (1997), pp. 49-71.
Solivan, Samuel, *The Spirit, Pathos and Liberation: Toward an Hispanic Pentecostal Theology* (JPTSup, 14; Sheffield: Sheffield Academic Press, 1998).
Spawn, Kevin L., and Archie T. Wright, *Spirit and Scripture: Exploring a Pneumatic Hermeneutic* (New York: T & T Clark, 2012).
Spittler, Russell P., 'Are Pentecostals and Charismatics Fundamentalists? A Review of American Uses of These Categories', in Karla Poewe (ed.) *Charismatic Christianity as a Global Culture* (Columbia, SC: University of South Carolina Press, 1994), pp. 103-16.
—— 'Scripture and the Theological Enterprise: View from a Big Canoe', in Robert K. Johnston (ed.), *The Use of the Bible in Theology: Evangelical Options* (Atlanta, GA: John Knox Press, 1985), pp. 56-77.
Stronstad, Roger, 'Trends in Pentecostal Hermeneutics', *Paraclete* 22.3 (1988), pp. 1-12.
—— 'Pentecostal Experience and Hermeneutics', *Paraclete* 26.1 (1992), pp. 14-30.
—— 'Pentecostal Hermeneutics: A Review of Gordon D. Fee', *PNEUMA: The Journal of the Society for Pentecostal Studies* 15.2 (1993), pp. 215-22.
Thomas, John Christopher, 'Women, Pentecostalism and the Bible: An Experiment in Pentecostal Hermeneutics', *Journal of Pentecostal Theology* 5 (1994), pp. 41-56.
—— 'Pentecostal Theology in the Twenty-First Century', *PNEUMA: The Journal of the Society for Pentecostal Studies* 20.1 (1998), pp. 3-19.
—— 'Reading the Bible from within Our Traditions: A Pentecostal Hermeneutic as Test Case', in Joel Green and Max Turner (eds.), *Between Two Horizons: Spanning New Testament Studies and Systematic Theology* (Grand Rapids, MI: Eerdmans, 2000), pp. 108-122.
—— 'Pentecostal Explorations of the New Testament: Teaching New Testament Introduction in a Pentecostal Seminary', *Journal of Pentecostal Theology* 11.1 (2002), pp. 120-29.
—— 'Healing in the Atonement: A Johannine Perspective', *Journal of Pentecostal Theology* 14.1 (2005), pp. 23-39.

—— *The Spirit of the New Testament* (Blandford Forum: Deo, 2005).
—— 'The Holy Spirit and Interpretation', in S.E. Porter (ed.), *Dictionary of Biblical Criticism and Interpretation* (London: Routledge, 2007), pp. 165–66.
—— '"Where the Spirit Leads": The Development of Pentecostal Hermeneutics', *Journal of Beliefs & Values: Studies in Religion & Education* 30.3 (2009), pp. 289–302.
—— '"What the Spirit Is Saying to the Church"—The Testimony of a Pentecostal in New Testament Studies', in Kevin L. Spawn and Archie T. Wright (eds.), *Spirit and Scripture: Exploring a Pneumatic Hermeneutic* (New York: T & T Clark, 2012), pp. 115–29.
—— 'Pentecostal Biblical Interpretation', in *Oxford Encyclopedia of Biblical Interpretation* (Oxford: Oxford University Press, forthcoming).
Thomas, John Christopher, and Kimberly Ervin Alexander, '"And the Signs Are Following": Mark 16.9–20—A Journey into Pentecostal Hermeneutics', *Journal of Pentecostal Theology* 11.2 (2003), pp. 147–70.
Wacker, Grant, 'Functions of Faith in Primitive Pentecostalism', *Harvard Theological Review* 77 (1984), pp. 353–75.
Waddell, Robby, *The Spirit of the Book of Revelation* (JPTSup, 30; Blandford Forum: Deo Publishing, 2006).
Wall, Robert W., 'Waiting on the Holy Spirit (Acts 1.4): Extending a Metaphor to Biblical Interpretation', *Journal of Pentecostal Theology* 22.1 (2013), pp. 37–53.
Wessels, Willie J., 'Biblical Hermeneutics', in Adrio König and S.S. Maimela (eds.), *Initiation into Theology: The Rich Variety of Theology and Hermeneutics* (Pretoria: Van Schaik, 1998), pp. 261–73.
Wyckoff, John W., 'The Relationship of the Holy Spirit to Biblical Hermeneutics' (PhD, Baylor University, 1990).
Yong, Amos, *Spirit-Word-Community: Theological Hermeneutics in Trinitarian Perspective* (Aldershot, England: Ashgate, 2002).
—— 'Reading Scripture and Nature: Pentecostal Hermeneutics and Their Implications for the Contemporary Evangelical Theology and Science Conversation', *Perspectives on Science & Christian Faith* 63.1 (2011), pp. 3–15.

INDEX OF BIBLICAL REFERENCES

Genesis
1 — 68
2.24 — 278
4.1 — 12
49.8 — 274n35

Exodus
7.16 — 222
19.5 — 86
24.7 — 217n66

Leviticus
26.12 — 274

Numbers
11.25 — 20
11.27–29 — 12, 200
11.29 — 20

Deuteronomy
1 — 119
1–4 — 123
1.1 — 122, 123
1.2–3 — 126
1.6 — 114, 126, 129
1.19–2.25 — 123
1.28–35 — 118
1.29–33 — 126
1.30 — 126
1.33 — 126
1.37 — 123
2.3 — 126
2.16 — 126
3.22–23 — 123
4 — 16, 21, 22, 23, 24, 28, 29
4–5 — 28
4.1 — 24n20
4.5–8 — 22
4.7 — 22, 22n, 23, 25, 127n41
4.7–8 — 23, 26, 29, 127n41
4.8 — 22, 127n41
4.9–40 — 23
4.10 — 119
4.10a — 22
4.10–12 — 126
4.10–15 — 114
4.11 — 22
4.12 — 22, 24, 25, 25n
4.13 — 22, 23, 27n
4.15 — 30
4.15–16 — 24, 126
4.15–24 — 24
4.17–19 — 26
4.21–22 — 123
4.23–24 — 24
4.24 — 25, 126
4.24–27 — 123
4.25 — 25, 123
4.25–31 — 25
4.26–27 — 25
4.29–30 — 25
4.31 — 25
4.32–40 — 25
4.33 — 25
4.34–35 — 26n24
4.35 — 26, 29
4.36 — 25, 26n23, 24
4.38 — 26n24, 26
4.39 — 26, 27
4.40 — 27
4.44 — 122, 123, 125
5 — 16, 21, 22, 24, 27, 28, 29, 123, 127
5.1 — 24n20, 221
5.1–3 — 27
5.1–5 — 27
5.2–4 — 115, 127
5.2–33 — 114
5.4–5 — 125
5.5 — 28
5.15 — 118
5.22 — 27
5.22–29 — 125
5.22–33 — 27
5.23–26 — 27
5.24 — 206
5.24–27 — 126
5.24–31 — 127
5.25 — 27
5.26 — 128
5.27 — 23, 27
5.29 — 28, 119, 125
5.30 — 129n46
5.31 — 27, 127, 127n40
6–28 — 123, 124, 127
6.1 — 122, 123

INDEX OF BIBLICAL REFERENCES

6.4	225	31.18	129
6.4–5	122	31.21	129n46
7.6	86	31.23	129
7.17–18	118	31.29	125, 129n46
8.2–16	118	32	122, 124, 129
8.3	26n24, 118	32.26–43	125
8.16	118	33	123, 125
9.7	118	33–34	123, 125, 129
9.8–10.11	124, 128	33.1	123
9.13	118	33.2	129
9.19	128	33.8	19n10
9.25	118, 128	34	123, 128
10.20	278	34.10	18, 114, 128, 129
12–28	122, 124, 127n40, 128	34.10–11	26n24
12.1	122, 127n40		
13.5	278	Joshua	
14.2	86	3.9	221
15.15	118	8.34f	217n66
17.18–19	18	23.8	278
17.19	19	24.23–25	228
18	23n18		
18.9–22	17	Judges	
18.15	19, 124	2.1–5	230, 232
18.15–18	27	2.2	228
18.15–22	124	2.16	19
18.16	124	2.17a	228
18.16–17	23	2.17b	228
18.16–18	21, 127	2.18	19
18.16–20	114	2.20	228
18.18	124, 127, 129	3.4	228
18.19	19	3.9	19
18.22	19, 19n10	3.15	19 23n18
26.18–19	86	4.19	274n43
29–30	122, 124, 129	6.7–8	23n18
29–32	122, 123, 124, 128	6.7–10	230, 232
29.1	122, 123, 128	6.10	228
29.16–30.7	125	10.10–16	230, 232
30.11	22n	19.25	228
30.11–14	22n, 30n32	20.13	228
30.17–18	222		
30.20	224	1 Samuel	
31	18, 122, 125, 129	10.10–13	20
31.2	125	19.20–24	20
31.9–11	18		
31.10	19	1 Kings	
31.10–13	122	13	69
31.11	217n66	18.3–4	20
31.11–13	18	22	69
31.13	19	22.19	221
31.14	125, 128		
31.14–23	128	2 Kings	
31.16	125	2.3	21n15
31.16–18	129n46	4.1	21n15
31.17	129	5.22	21n15

INDEX OF BIBLICAL REFERENCES

6.1	21n15	63.1–2	263
9.1	21n15	63.1–4	270n25
10	30, 174n11	63.2	272, 276, 279
14.11	222	63.2–3	270n25, 271, 273, 274–76
17.13–14	222		
20.16	221	63.2–9	283
22–23	21	63.2–11	270
22.10	217n66	63.3	272, 276, 280
22.14–20	21	63.4	272, 280
22.15–17	30n32	63.4–5	270n25, 273n33
23.2	217n66	63.4–6	271, 273, 276–77, 278

2 Chronicles
		63.5	272
34.18	217n66	63.5–8	270n25
34.24	217n66	63.6	272, 279, 281
34.30	217n66	63.6–7	270n25
		63.6–8	273n33

Ezra
		63.7	272, 279
4.18	217n66	63.7–8	271
4.23	217n66	63.7–9	271, 273, 278
		63.8	271n27, 272, 279

Nehemiah
		63.8–9	270n25
8.3	217n66	63.9	271, 272, 273n33, 280
8.8	217n66		
8.18	217n66	63.9–11	270n25
9.3	217n66	63.10	272
9.17	222	63.10–11	270n25
13.1	217n66	63.10–12	271, 271n29, 274, 278–80, 284

Esther
		63.11	272
6.1	217n66	63.12	270n25
		65.1	272

Job
		84.1	272
23.12	224	84.2	275
42.5	66	85.8	232
		101.1	272

Psalms
		104.1	272
1.2	224	115.1	272
8.1	272	118.28	274n35
9.1	272	119.1	224
18.1	272	119.31	278
19.10	224	119.62	224
21.1	272	119.97	224
22.11	274n35	138.1	272
23.6	275	140.7	274n35
27.4	275	145.1	272
30.1	272		
31.15	274n35	Isaiah	
42.1–2	275	6.9–10	224
63	263, 264, 269, 270, 272, 273, 276, 278, 279, 280, 282, 283, 284	7.14	22n, 242
		11	192
		28.11	259
		30.9	222n95
63.1	269, 270	51.7	224

INDEX OF BIBLICAL REFERENCES

55.3	221	Luke	
61.1–2	235	1.27	87
61.2b	235	1.32–33	87
65.12	222n95	1.69	87
		2.4	87
Jeremiah		2.11	87
1.5	12	3–7	71
2.4	221	3.31	87
20.8	24n21	4.1–30	71
20.9	128n42	4.16	217n66
22.16	12	4.18–19	235
23.23	22n	6.3	87
23.29	24n21, 128n42	6.12	71
29.29	217n66	10.17	71
31.31–34	52	10.21	71
31.34	12	11.1–13	71
36.6	217n66	12.54–56	236
36.10	217n66	13.27	217n66
36.13	217n66	14–16	71
36.21	217n66	15.21	217n66
		18.38–39	87
Ezekiel		19.44	245
12.2	222	20.41–44	87
		24.7	238
Hosea		24.32	238
11.9	22n	24.49	71
Joel		John	
2.23	5	1–5	105
2.28–29	71–72	1.1–14	104
2.28–32	12, 200	1.29	73
		1.33	73
Amos		2.4	105
5.14	22n	2.19–21	105
5.25–27	87	3.3–10	105
9.11–12	84, 85, 86	4.10–15	105
		4.31–33	105
Zechariah		4.48	105
7.8–14	222–23	5.1–10.42	105
14.6–7	8	6.50–51	106
		9.4	8
Matthew		9.38	101, 104
5.14	12	10.11–18	106
5.17	235	10.17–18	105
5.38	235	10.35	235
7.22	69	12.14	7
11.4	77	12.23	105
18.20	13, 260	13–17	48, 105
		13.31–14.4	48
Mark		13.34	39
12.28–31	122n30	13.35	39
13	196n73	14	97
16	133	14.1–2	97
16.18	253	14.4	48

INDEX OF BIBLICAL REFERENCES

14.5	48	2.29–36	87
14.6	79	2.33	77
14.7	38	2.38–39	66
14.15	39, 107	2.42–47	13
14.16–17	37	3	17
14.20	38	3.22	17
14.21	39, 107	4.20	77
14.23	39, 107	4.25	87
14.25	51	5.9	85
14.25–26	37, 38	7.42–44	87
14.25–27	51	7.45	87
14.26	51	13	87
14.27	39n21, 48	13.22–23	87
14.28	104	13.34	87
14.31	39	13.36	87
15.9	39, 107	15	7, 13, 51, 85, 87, 88, 89, 90, 91, 93, 145, 146, 206n3, 207, 225, 227, 238
15.10	39		
15.11	39n21		
15.12	48		
15.12–13	101	15.1–29	84
15.13	39, 107	15.17	86
15.17	39, 48	15.24	88
15.18–25	48	15.28	85, 238
15.18–27	48	15.28–29	236
15.26–27	37, 54	18.26	93
16.4–11	54	21.9	93
16.7–11	37, 48		
16.12–15	37, 38, 54	Romans	
16.14–15	56	4.17	167
16.15	193	8.1–27	11
16.20–22	39n21	8.26	253
16.22	39n21	12	13
16.27	39, 107	12.1	56n54
16.33	39n21, 101	12.6–8	66n
17.3	56	16.1	93
17.4–5	56	16.3	93
17.6–18	48	16.7	93
17.21	38		
18–19	105	1 Corinthians	
19.30	104	1.4–7	233
20.28	101, 104	2.1–10	76
		2.9–10a	145
Acts		2.10–16	240
1.6	1	2.12–13	62
1.8	12, 74, 77, 138, 245	2.13	65
1.16	87	2.14–15	65
2	24n21, 115	2.16	240
2.1	260	8.1–13	88
2.1–4	13	10.11	7
2.4	33	11.3–16	93
2.16–20	12, 200	11.5	92
2.17	2, 12	12	13
2.25	87	12.7–11	66n

INDEX OF BIBLICAL REFERENCES

12.14	11	**Hebrews**	
13.9	69	1.1–2	70
14	13, 67, 259	4.12	240
14.32	69	7–10	64
14.33b–35	92, 92n	10.25	13
15.20–28	196n73	12.22–25	196n73
16.19	93		
		James	
2 Corinthians		1.22	262
3.14	217n66		
3.14–18	60	**1 Peter**	
3.15	217n66	1–2	56n54
3.16–17	58	2.5	12, 200
5.1–5	196n73	2.9	12, 200
10	77	2.21	7
		3.20–21	64
Galatians			
1.6–9	139	**2 Peter**	
3.2	139	1.20–21	234
3.5	139	1.21	6
4.21–31	64		
3.28	243	**1 John**	
5.2–12	139	1.3	26n27
		1.7	12
Ephesians		2.3	37
1.17	239	2.3–5	37
4	13	2.20	238
4.1–16	56n54	2.27	12, 26n27
4.7–17	12	4.1	69
		4.1–3	67
Philippians		4.3	37
2.1–13	56n54	4.8	12
4.3	93	4.13–17	12
		4.16	37
Colossians		4.20	37
4.15	93	5.1–5	37
4.16	217n66	5.6–12	37
1 Thessalonians		**Jude**	
4.9	244	19	65
4.15–17	196n73		
5.19	13	**Revelation**	
5.19–21	67	1.3	71, 196, 198, 217n66
5.27	217n66	1.5	201
		1.10	71, 201
2 Thessalonians		1.10–16	197
2.1–12	196	1.11	198, 199
		1.17–18	202
1 Timothy		1.19b	202
2.11–12	92	2–3	200
3.15–16	234	2.2b	199
5.9–10	93n14	2.4	282
		2.7	191
Titus		5.6	193
2.4	92	11.1–13	203

INDEX OF BIBLICAL REFERENCES

11.11	193	22.10	71, 196, 202
12.11	201	22.17	193
14.13	193	22.18	71
19.10	193, 196, 202	22.18–19	196
22.7	71, 196	22.20	73
22.8	202		

INDEX OF AUTHORS

Abbott, N.A.   179
Aczel, Richard   213
Adler, Mortimer   239
Albom, M.   113
Albrecht, Daniel E.   34, 176, 281, 282
Alexander, Kimberly Ervin   211
Alexander, L.   196, 199
Alter, R.   227
Althouse, Peter   211
Alverado, Johnathan E.   283
Anderson, A.A.   274, 276, 277, 278, 279
Anderson, Allen   257, 261
Anderson, Gordon L.   220, 230, 262
Anderson, R.M.   176, 177
Anselm   191
Archer, Gleason L.   221
Archer, Kenneth J.   3, 4, 5, 7, 9, 83, 182, 191, 207, 208, 209, 213, 215, 219, 225, 229, 250, 258, 259, 260, 268
Arrington, French L.   6, 15, 83, 84, 132, 133, 134, 135, 140, 143, 144, 145, 146, 182
Aune, D.E.   196, 197, 202
Autry, Arden C.   83

Baker, Robert O.   83, 182, 213, 224, 268
Bar-Efrat, S.   229
Barr, David   173
Barr, James   35, 218
Barrett, C.K.   54
Barrett, D.B.   177
Barth, Karl   206, 219
Barthes, R.   98, 99, 100
Bartholomew   266
Barton, J.   175, 212
Bauckham, R.J.   86, 173, 200
Baumgartner, Walter   278, 279
Becker, Matthias   209
Beckwith, I.T.   172
Berkouwer, G.C.   227
Best, Thomas F.   213
Birch, Bruce C.   230
Birkey, D.   93
Blair, E.   114
Blenkinsopp, Joseph   115
Bloesch, D.G.   40, 139
Blumhofer, Edith Waldvogel   281
Boadt, L.   22
Boff, C.   46
Boone, Jerome R.   282

Borsch, Frederick H.   213
Botterweck, G.J.   36
Bowring, J.   106
Boyd, Robert Henry   214
Branick, V.   93
Brathwaite, Renea   4, 7
Brett, M.G.   183
Braun, M.A.   86
Briggs, Charles Augustus   271, 274, 275, 277
Briggs, Emilie Grace   271, 274, 275, 277
Brown, Francis   206, 221, 222, 278, 279
Brown, R.E.   37, 38, 51, 54
Bruce, F.F.   201
Brueggemann, W.   23, 29, 109, 114, 120, 166, 167, 181, 209, 210, 214, 215, 216, 218, 219, 223, 226, 265, 273
Bruner, F.D.   138, 139
Buber, Martin   120
Bullock, C. Hassell   272
Bultmann, R.   36, 37
Byrd, Joseph   34, 134, 143, 176

Calvin, John   278
Camery-Hoggatt, Jerry   220
Campbell, Iain D.   266
Cargal, Timothy B.   3, 6, 7, 83, 135, 142, 147, 176, 211, 252
Carroll, Robert P.   209
Carson, D.A.   54
Cartledge, Mark J.   187, 263, 267, 268
Castelo, Daniel   280, 283
Chan, Simon   215
Catherine of Siena   266
Cheadle, Rand   209
Childs, Brevard S.   184, 214, 215
Chilton, Bruce D.   215
Cimpean, F.   172
Clapper, Gregory S.   100, 101, 104, 266
Clark, Mathew S.   182, 209
Clements, R.E.   111
Clines, David J.A.   163, 173, 260, 274, 276, 277, 279
Cole, Graham   240
Collins, J.J.   196
Collins, Kenneth J.   266
Conn, Charles   151
Corner, M.   187
Coughenour, Robert A.   213

INDEX OF AUTHORS

Coulter, Dale   266, 267
Cowley, A.E.   276
Cox, H.   176, 188, 257
Crenshaw, James L.   214, 274, 275
Crite, S.   112
Croatto, J. Severino   256
Culler, J.   96
Culpepper, R.A.   104

Dahood, Mitchell J.   274
Davies, Andrew   258
Davies, P.   183
Dayton, Donald W.   132, 138, 139, 176, 180, 248
DeClaissé-Walford, Nancy L.   272
Deere, Jack   191
Delitzsch, Franz   274
Dempster, Murray W.   132, 176
Derrida, J.   174
Dickie, Margaret   215
Dowd, Michael B.   24, 34, 112, 220, 229
Draper   220
Dunn, James D.G.   138, 140, 141, 236, 238
Dupont, J.   87
Dykstra, Craig   56

Eaton, John   274, 277, 279
Edge, F.B.   41
Edgerton, W. Dow   268
Edwards, Johnathan   266
Eissfeldt, Otto   214
Ellington, Scott A.   9, 171, 190, 208, 211, 219
Ellis, E.E.   83
d'Epinay, Christian Lalive   136
Ervin, Howard M.   5, 6, 7, 83, 140, 145, 261
Evans, C.A.   83
Even-Shoshan, Avraham   221, 222, 225

Faupel, D.W.   176, 180, 230
Fee, Gordon   93, 143, 223
Fewell, Danna N.   26, 229
Feyerabend, Paul K.   227
Fiorenza, E. Schüssler   172
Fish, S.   172, 199
Flower, Alice Reynolds   281
Fohrer, Georg   214
Fokkelman, J.P.   270
Fowl, S.E.   172, 175, 185, 191
Franck, E.   37, 54
Frei, H.W.   175, 229
Freire, P.   44
Fretheim, Terence   215

Gadamer, Hans-Georg   158
Gause, R. Hollis   192, 193

Genette, G.   173
Gerkin, C.V.   113
Gesenius, Wilhelm   276
Gillmayr-Bucher, Susanne   271
Goldingay, John   155, 198, 205, 212, 218, 229, 273
Graham, Stephen R.   3, 5, 7
Green, Chris E.W.   5, 8, 9, 280
Green, Joel B.   213, 239
Groome, T.   36, 43, 44, 47, 157
Gros, Jeffrey   267
Gunkel, Hermann   140, 218
Gunn, David M.   218, 229

Handelman, S.   157
Hanson, Paul D.   181, 206
Harrelson, W.   28
Harrington, Hannah K.   210
Harris, R. Laird   221
Haverwas, Stanley   161
Haya-Prats, G.   140
Hays, R.B.   83
Hengstenberg, E.W.   275
Herholdt, Marius D.   4, 5, 7, 8, 210, 223, 225, 226, 227, 230
Hessel-Robinson, Timothy   266
Hill, D.   140
Hill Jim   209
Hocken, P.D.   178
Holladay, William L.   206, 221
Hollenweger, W.J.   34, 137, 141, 175, 176, 188, 195, 219, 250
Holub, R.C.   103
Horton, S.M.   192
Hubbard, D.A.   86
Hunter, H.D.   140
Huntsinger, George   229
Hutchison, John Alexander   213

Irenaeus   65
Iser, W.   102, 103, 104
Irvin, D.T.   181
Israel, Richard D.   34, 176

Jaichandran, Rebecca   281
Jefferson, A.   176
Jensen, Richard A.   217
Jeske, R.L.   201
Johns, Cheryl Bridges   26, 29, 44, 45, 83, 157, 158, 181, 184, 187, 189, 190, 194, 198, 199, 207, 218, 226
Johns, Jackie David   4, 26, 29, 38, 83, 133, 164, 184, 185, 207, 218, 226
Johnson, L.T.   85
Johnston, R.   142

INDEX OF AUTHORS

Jones, L.G. 172
Joüon, Paul 276
Joy, Donald 47

Kaiser, W.C. 86
Kärkkäinen, Veli-Matti 209, 219, 252, 281
Käsemann, Ernst 236
Kaufman, S. 122
Kautzsch, E. 276
Keil, C.F. 86
Kelsey, David 165
Kermode, F. 108
Kimbrough, S.T. 266
Kitchen, K.A. 112
Kleinart, P. 121
de Klerk, Johannes C. 229
Kline, M.G. 18, 112
Koehler, Ludwig 278, 279
Kok, Johnson Lim Teng 223
Kourie, Celia 265
Kraft, Charles 166
Kraus, Hans Joachim 271, 274, 276, 277, 279

Land, Steven J. 3, 4, 9, 96, 100, 101, 132, 136, 137, 138, 156, 172, 176, 180, 181, 187, 188, 190, 194, 199, 208, 209, 216, 224, 226, 227, 228, 230, 263, 267
Lake, K. 88
Lapsley, Jacqueline E. 213
LaSor, William Sanford 214
LeBar, Lois E. 47
Leder, Arie, C. 213
Lederle, H. 139
Lennox, Stephan J. 275, 278, 279
Levison, J. 187
Lewis, B. Scott 210
Lewis, J.P. 35
Lewis, W.H. 186
Limburg, James 270
Loder, James 42
Longenecker, Richard N. 238
Lossky, Vladimir 266
Louw, J.P. 222

Ma, Julie C. 280, 283
Macchia, F.D. 179, 200, 246
MacDonald, W.G. 34, 143, 282
Maddox, Randy L. 266
Madhav, B.D. 281
Maguire, Daniel C. 265
Malbon, Elizabeth Struthers 213
March, W.E. 20
Marshall, I. Howard 141

Martin, Francis 34, 50, 51, 52, 192
Martin, J.P. 147
Martin, Lee Roy 264, 265, 268, 269
Martin, R. 179
Maxwell, David J. 280
Mazzaferri, F.D. 197
McCann Jr., J. Clinton 279
McClymond, Michael James 266
McConville, J.G. 115, 119, 121
McDermott, Gerald R. 266
McDonnell, K. 179
McGroarty, Brendan Ignatius 266
McKay, John W. 2, 5, 16, 70, 83, 144, 170, 182, 215, 216, 271, 275, 276, 278, 279
McKnight, E.V. 147
McLean, Mark D. 83, 136, 142, 144
McLuhan, Marshall 217, 218
McNally, Randal G. 34, 83, 176
McQueen, Larry R. 2, 182, 216, 227
Millar, J.G. 115
Miller, Patrick D. 18, 22, 109, 129, 208, 213, 215
Minto, Andrew L. 261, 262
Menzies, Robert P. 83, 140, 141, 142, 176, 210, 211
Menzies, William W. 136, 142, 143, 211
Moody, D. 51
Moore, Rickie D. 2, 9, 52, 83, 84, 126, 174, 182, 184, 188, 189, 194, 197, 200, 206, 207, 209, 213, 215, 216, 220, 224, 229
Moore, S.D. 96, 173, 174
Morgan, R. 175, 212
Mowinckel, S. 20
Mudge, Lewis Seymour 223
Muilenburg, James 213
Muraoka, T. 276

Nave 3
Nel, M. 4, 7, 8
Niccacci, Alviero 272
Nida, Eugene Albert 222
Niditch, Susan 217, 218
Nogalski, James 213

O'Conner, Michael Patrick 276
O'Connor, E.D. 179
O'Day, Gail R. 259
O'Donnell, James J. 217
Ognibene, Richard 267
Olson, Dennis T. 109, 114, 121, 122, 123, 124, 127, 128, 129
Ong, Walter J. 217, 218, 220
Osborne, Grant R. 173

INDEX OF AUTHORS

Palmer, P.   39, 53, 165, 166
Pannell, Randall J.   207
Park, Myung Soo   280
Patrick, Mary W.   223, 229
Patte, Daniel   207, 208, 210, 211, 225
Patten, Rebecca   210
Paul, I.   183
Pelikan, Jaroslav Jan   218
Penaskovic, Richard   267
Peterson, Eugene H.   216
Peterson, N.R.   176
Peulo, P.-A.   87
Pietersen, L.   179
Pinnock, Clark H.   82, 148, 156, 160, 184, 185, 198, 227, 233, 237
Piper, A.   36, 37
Placher, William C.   229
Plüss, Jean-Daniel   3, 113, 176
Proudfoot, Wayne L.   266
Poirier, John C.   210
Poloma, Margaret M.   117, 133, 179
Polzin, Robert   109
Pope, L.   177
Pope-Levison, P.   187
Porter, J.R.   21
Powell, M.A.   173
Provan, Iain W.   210

Quebedeaux, R.   178

von Rad, Gerhard   214
Ranaghan, D.   179
Ranaghan, K.   179
Reid   220
Richards, Larry   47
Ricoeur, Paul   223
Robeck Jr., Charles M.   151, 281, 282
Roberts, Mark, E.   258
Rogerson, J.W.   271, 276, 278, 279
Roennfeldt, C.W.   234
Rofé, A.   17
Rogers, Jack Bartlett   239
Rowland, C.   187, 197
Runyon, Theodore   45
Ryan, Thomas   267, 268
Rybarczyk, Edmund J.   266

Sanders, J.A.   83
Schipani, Daniel   42, 46
Schmemann, Alexander   266
Schneiders, Sandra M.   241
Schwarz, Tony   220
Schweizer, E.   140, 200

Segovia, F.F.   187
Sellin, Ernst   214
Seymour, William J.   178
Shelton, J.B.   140
Sheppard, Gerald T.   1, 2, 3, 6, 83, 133, 135, 138, 147, 213, 283
Silberman, Lou H.   217
Smit, Dirkie J.   210
Smith, James K.A.   191, 198, 219, 233, 264
Smith, John E.   266
Snodgrass, Klyne   213, 232
Sobrino, J.   46
Spittler, Russell P.   3, 7, 135, 136
Stanton, G.   148
Steinmetz, David C.   186, 265
Stephanou, B.A.   179
Stibbe, M.   105
Stronstad, Roger   2, 6, 30, 83, 115, 140, 143, 144, 182, 200, 216
Stroup, G.W.   112
Stuart, Douglas K.   223
Sugirtharajah, R.S.   187
Sullivan, F.A.   116, 179
Swartley, Willard M.   244
Sweeney, Marvin A.   213
Synan, V.   136, 176, 211

Talmon, S.   16, 21
Tate, Marvin E.   270, 273, 274, 275, 276, 277, 278, 279
Tate, W.R.   173, 212
Terrien, Samuel   24, 270–71, 277, 279
Tertullian   65, 182
Thiselton, Anthony C.   175, 254
Thomas, John Christopher   6, 7, 9, 143, 145, 146, 147, 151, 171, 175, 182, 194, 198, 199, 206, 207, 209, 225, 227
Todorov, T.   173
Tolbert, M.A.   187
Tompkins, J.P.   174
van der Tourn, K.   20
Turner, B.   147
Turner, M.   88, 140

Valdes, M.J.   103
Van Seters, John   218
Vos, Clarence   213
Vroege, David A.   213

Wacker, Grant   3, 6, 132, 133, 134, 176
Waddell, Robby   209, 213, 260, 261
Wagner, C.P.   179
Walker, G.   135

Wall, Robert W.   202
Walsh, M.E.   95
Waltke, Bruce K.   221, 276
Ward, Roger   266
Warfield, B.B.   234
Warren, Joyce W.   215
Warrington, Keith   251
Watson, F.   148, 175, 183, 184, 185, 189
Watts, I.   107
Weber, Max   115
Weiser, Artur   275, 278, 279
Wenger, Etienne   225
Wesley, John   41

Wessels, Willie J.   212, 218
West, G.   187
Westermann, Claus   20, 273
Wiesel, Elie   240
Wilcock, Michael   270
Williamson, Peter S.   242
Wilson, M.W.   196
Wink, Walter   164
Woudstra, Sierd   213
Wyckoff, John W.   82, 182

Yee, Gale A.   207